CAESAR'S LEGION

THE EPIC SAGA OF JULIUS CAESAR'S ELITE TENTH LEGION AND THE ARMIES OF ROME

STEPHEN DANDO-COLLINS

John Wiley & Sons, Inc.

48466775

Published by John Wiley & Sons, Inc., New York
Published simultaneously in Canada

ISBN 0-471-09570-2

Printed in the United States of America

10 9 8 7 6 5 4 3 2 1

CONTENTS

ATLAS

"The West," First Century B.C.

©2001 by D. L. McElhannon

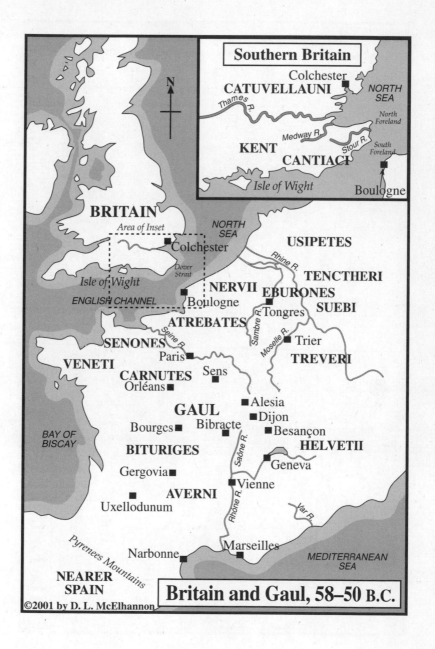

Southern Britain

Colchester

CATUVELLAUNI

NORTH SEA

Thames R.

North Foreland

Medway R.

Stour R.

South Foreland

KENT

CANTIACI

Isle of Wight

Boulogne

BRITAIN

Area of Inset

NORTH SEA

Colchester

USIPETES

Rhine R.

TENCTHERI

Dover Strait

Isle of Wight

ENGLISH CHANNEL

Boulogne

NERVII

EBURONES

Tongres

SUEBI

Sambre R.

Moselle R.

ATREBATES

Seine R.

Trier

SENONES

Paris

TREVERI

VENETI

CARNUTES

Sens

Orléans

Alesia

GAUL

Dijon

Bourges

Bibracte

Besançon

BITURIGES

Saône R.

HELVETII

Geneva

Gergovia

Vienne

BAY OF BISCAY

AVERNI

Uxellodunum

Rhône R.

Var R.

Pyrenees Mountains

Narbonne

Marseilles

MEDITERRANEAN SEA

NEARER SPAIN

Britain and Gaul, 58–50 B.C.

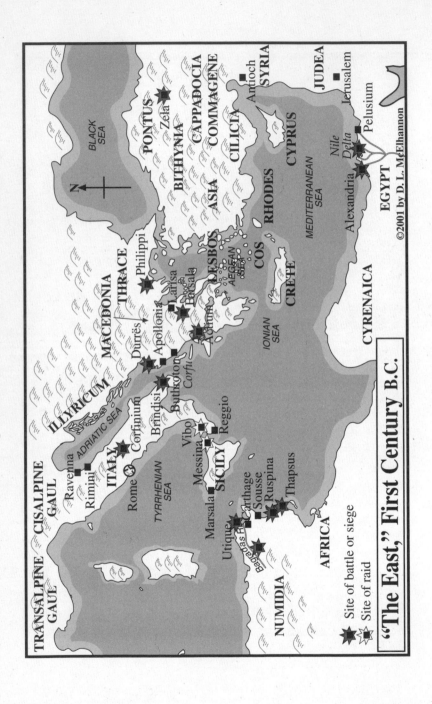

TRANSALPINE GAUL

CISALPINE GAUL

ITALY

Ravenna

Rimini

Rome

ADRIATIC SEA

Corfinium

Brindisi

Butkroton

Corfu

Vibo

Reggio

Messina

Marsala

SICILY

Utique

Carthage

Sousse

Ruspina

Thapsus

Bagradas R.

NUMIDIA

AFRICA

TYRRHENIAN SEA

ILLYRICUM

MACEDONIA

THRACE

Durrës

Apollonia

Actium

Larisa

Pharsala

Philippi

BLACK SEA

N

PONTUS

Zela

BITHYNIA

CAPPADOCIA

COMMAGENE

ASIA

CILICIA

LESBOS

COS

RHODES

AEGEAN SEA

IONIAN SEA

CRETE

CYPRUS

Antioch

SYRIA

JUDEA

Jerusalem

Pelusium

Nile Delta

Alexandria

EGYPT

MEDITERRANEAN SEA

CYRENAICA

©2001 by D. L. McElhannon

★ Site of battle or siege

☆ Site of raid

"The East," First Century B.C.

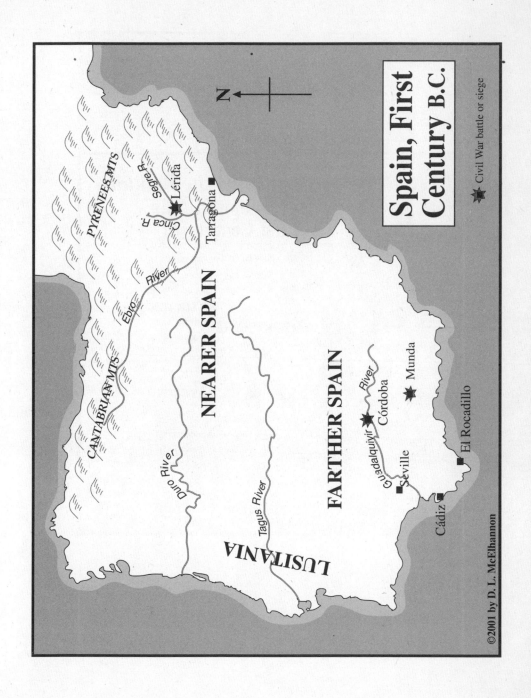

Spain, First Century B.C.

★ Civil War battle or siege

N

PYRENEES MTS

CANTABRIAN MTS

Segre R.
Lérida
Cinca R.
Tarragona
Ebro River

NEARER SPAIN

Duro River
Tagus River

LUSITANIA

FARTHER SPAIN

Guadalquivir River
Córdoba
Munda
Seville
El Rocadillo
Cádiz

©2001 by D. L. McElhannon

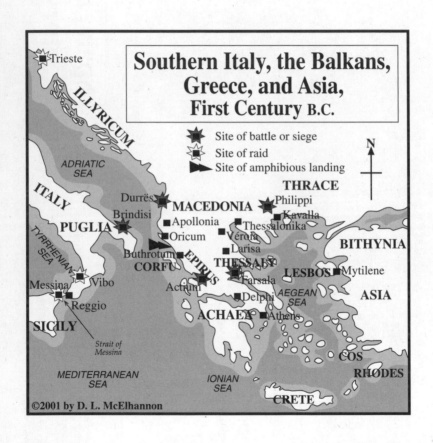

Southern Italy, the Balkans, Greece, and Asia, First Century B.C.

★ Site of battle or siege
☆ Site of raid
▶ Site of amphibious landing

N

Trieste

ILLYRICUM

ADRIATIC
SEA

ITALY

PUGLIA

Brindisi

Durrës

MACEDONIA

Apollonia

Oricum

Buthrotum

CORFU

EPIRUS

TYRRHENIAN
SEA

Messina

Vibo

Reggio

SICILY

Strait of
Messina

MEDITERRANEAN
SEA

Actium

THESSALY

Vérora

Larisa

Farsala

Delphi

ACHAEA

Athens

IONIAN
SEA

THRACE

Philippi

Kavalla

Thessalonika

BITHYNIA

LESBOS

Mytilene

AEGEAN
SEA

ASIA

COS

RHODES

CRETE

©2001 by D. L. McElhannon

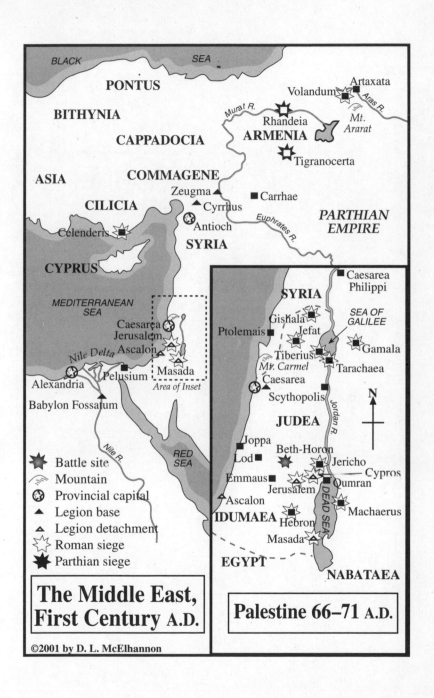

The Middle East, First Century A.D.

Palestine 66–71 A.D.

©2001 by D. L. McElhannon

ACKNOWLEDGMENTS

This book would not have been possible without the immense help provided over many years by countless staff at libraries, museums, and historic sites throughout the world. To them all, my heartfelt thanks. Neither they nor I knew at the time what my labor of love would develop into. My thanks, too, to those who read my research material as it blossomed into manuscript form and made invaluable suggestions.

Most particularly, I wish to record my appreciation for the role played by three people in bringing this work to fruition. First, I want to thank Stephen S. Power, senior editor at John Wiley & Sons, for his enthusiasm, encouragement, vision, and guidance.

Then there is Richard Curtis, my wonderful New York literary agent, who over a period of several years supported my aspirations, provided direction, and finally married me with an excellent publishing house. It was Richard who suggested I break down one massive tome on all the legions into histories of individual legions. Without him, there would have been no *Caesar's Legion*. In this increasingly impersonal new-fashioned electronic age, I can certify without reservation that in a brownstone on the Upper East Side there sits a man who embodies all the old-fashioned qualities that a writer dreams of finding in a literary agent. For a man who embraces technology and is at the forefront of the electronic publishing revolution, you really are a gentleman of the old school, Richard.

And then there is Louise, my wife of almost twenty years. What a roller-coaster ride she has taken with me all these years, never with a word of complaint, always with words of encouragement. How can I describe the role she has played in making this book, in making this writer? Roman historian Tacitus put it best, I think, in his *Agricola*. He was describing the relationship between his mother-in-law, Domitia, and Agricola, his father-in-law, but his words equally express the way I feel about the relationship my beloved wife and I have shared these past two decades: "They lived in rare accord, maintained by mutual affection and unselfishness; in such a partnership, however, a good wife deserves more than half the praise, just as a bad one deserves more than half the blame."

AUTHOR'S NOTE

Never before has a comprehensive history of an individual Roman legion been written. This book comes out of thirty years' research on the Roman military, in the process of which it was possible to identify the fifty Augustan and post-Augustan legions raised between 84 B.C. and A.D. 231 and to compile detailed histories of most of them.

The works of numerous classical writers who documented the wars, campaigns, battles, skirmishes, and most importantly the men of the legions of Rome have come down to us. Authors such as Julius Caesar, Appian, Plutarch, Tacitus, Suetonius, Polybius, Cassius Dio, Josephus, Pliny the Younger, Seneca, Livy, Arrian. Without their labors this book would not have been possible.

Enough material exists, from sources classical and modern—detailed in the appendices of this work—to write whole books on the 14th Gemina Martia Victrix, the legion that beat Boadicea (or Boudicca, as she was actually called); on the 3rd Augusta, the legion that saved the life of St. Paul the Apostle; on the 6th Victrix, the legion that kidnapped Cleopatra and gave rise to Julius Caesar's most famous message, "I came, I saw, I conquered"; and on the 12th Fulminata, the legion that gained its fame and its name in Marcus Aurelius's battles against the Germans so colorfully depicted in the movie *Gladiator*. To mention just a few.

But unquestionably the most renowned legion in its day was the 10th— *Legio* X. In fact, it was described as "world famous" when it arrived to join the Judean offensive of A.D. 67. Personally raised by Julius Caesar, the 10th Legion is on record as taking the leading role in all his battles, from a bloody initiation in Spain to the conquest of Gaul, the invasion of Britain, and the battles of the civil war against Pompey the Great that eventually made Caesar Dictator of Rome. The 10th Legion marched for Mark Antony and for Augustus. It whipped the Parthians under Corbulo, it squashed the Jewish Revolt for Vespasian, and it took the Temple at Jerusalem for Titus. It conquered Masada.

During the research for this work, light was shed on a number of issues relating to the legions, such as the uniqueness of legion commands in

Egypt and Judea. But the most enlightening aspect of all was the reenlistment factor. The legions of Rome were recruited *en masse*, and the survivors discharged *en masse* at the end of their enlistment—originally after sixteen years, later, after twenty. Replacements were not supplied in the interim. The reenlistment factor explains why particular units were crushed in this battle or that—in some they were made up of raw recruits; in others, they were comprised of men of thirty-nine and fifty-nine about to go into retirement. A later appendix elaborates on the reenlistment factor.

Now to the matter of dates and names. For the sake of continuity, the Roman calendar—which varied by up to two months from our own—is used throughout this work. Place names are generally first referred to in their original form and thereafter by modern name, where known, to permit readers to readily identify locations involved. Personal names familiar to modern readers have been used instead of those technically correct—Antony instead of Antonius, Julius Caesar for Gaius Caesar, Octavian for Caesar, Pilate for Pilatus, Vespasian instead of Vespasianus, etc.

In the nineteenth and twentieth centuries it became fashionable for some authors to refer to legions as regiments, cohorts as battalions, maniples as companies, centurions as captains, tribunes as colonels, and legates as generals. In this work, Roman military terms such as legion, cohort, maniple, and centurion have been retained, as it's felt they will be familiar to most readers and better convey the flavor of the time.

However, because of a lack of popular familiarity with the term "legate," "general" and/or "brigadier general" are used here. "Colonel" and "tribune" are both used, to give a sense of relative status. Likewise, so that readers can relate to their ranks in comparison to today's military, when referred to in the military sense "praetors" are given as "major generals" and "consuls" as "lieutenant generals." In this way, reference to a lieutenant general, for example, will immediately tell the reader that the figure concerned has been a consul.

I am aware that this approach to ranks is akin to having a foot in two camps and may not please purists, but my aim has been to make this book broadly accessible.

This is the story of the men of the 10th Legion. Men who made Rome great—one or two extraordinary men, and many more ordinary men who often did extraordinary things. In many ways they were not unlike us. But one wonders if we today could even begin to do what they did, to endure what they endured, to achieve what they achieved.

I

STARING DEFEAT
IN THE FACE

I t was a great day to die. And before the sun had set, thirty-four thousand men would lose their lives in this valley. The men of the 10th Legion would have had no illusions. They knew that some of them would probably perish in the battle that lay ahead. Yet, to Romans, nothing was more glorious than a noble death. And if the men of this legion had to die, there was probably not a better place nor a finer day for it, on home soil, beneath a perfect blue sky.

There was not a breath of wind as the legionaries of the 10th stood in their ranks, looking across the river valley toward the Pompeian army. It was lined up five miles away on the slope below Munda, a Spanish hill town near modern Osuna in Andalusia, southeast of Córdoba. The sun was rising in a clear sky on the mild morning of March 17, 45 B.C. After sixteen years of battles in Spain, France, Belgium, Holland, Germany, Albania, Greece, and North Africa, and having invaded Britain twice, Julius Caesar's 10th Legion had come full circle, back to its home territory, to fight the battle that would terminate either Rome's bloodiest civil war or Caesar's career, and possibly his life.

There were fewer than two thousand soldiers in the 10th now, a far cry from the six thousand men Caesar had personally recruited into the legion back in 61 B.C. Two-thirds of the legion's strength had fallen over the years. Aged between thirty-three and thirty-six, these surviving legionaries of the famous 10th were due for their discharge this very month. One more battle, Caesar had promised the tough Spaniards of the 10th, and then he would gladly send them home, weighed down by bonus pay and heading for land he would give them as a gift.

The 10th, recognized by friend and foe alike as Caesar's best legion, occupied the key right wing of his silent, stationary army, as it had in many a past battle. The 5th Legion, another Spanish unit, had formed up in its allocated position on the left. In between stood the men of the 3rd, 6th, 7th, 21st, and 30th Legions. Like the 10th, they were all under strength—the 6th Legion could field only several hundred men. About thirty thousand legionaries and auxiliaries in total, in eighty cohorts, or battalions. Split between the two flanks were eight thousand cavalry, the largest mounted force Caesar had ever put into the field, the horses restless as they sensed fear and apprehension on the early morning air.

In the midst of the 10th Legion's formation, on horseback and surrounded by his staff, helmeted, and clad in armor, fifty-four-year-old Julius Caesar wore his *paludamentum*, the eye-catching scarlet cloak of a Roman general. While his troops waited, he spoke briefly with his cavalry commander, General Nonius Asprenas, finalizing tactics. Then Asprenas galloped away to take up his position—almost certainly joining his cavalry on the right wing, while his deputy, Colonel Arguetius, commanded the mounted troops on the left.

Caesar gave an order. An orderly mounted close by and who held his red ensign inclined the general's flag toward the front. An unarmed trumpeter sounded "Advance at the March." Throughout the army, the trumpets of individual units repeated the call. The eagles of the legions and the standards of the smaller units all inclined forward. As one, the men of Caesar's army moved off, in perfect step, advancing to the attack at the march, in three lines of ten thousand men each.

Caesar had hoped to lure his opponents down onto the flat. But ahead, the men of the opposing army didn't budge, didn't advance to meet his troops. Instead, they stood stonily in their lines on the hillside, and waited for Caesar's army to come to them.

The general commanding the opposition army was Gnaeus Pompey. Eldest son of a famous general, Pompey the Great, and grandson of another, he was only in his late twenties and had no military reputation to speak of. He had captained a successful naval strike for his father on the Adriatic a few years back, followed by an unsuccessful land operation in Libya shortly after. More recently he'd led his forces in a gradual, fighting withdrawal through southwestern Spain ahead of Caesar's advance. That was the sum total of his experience of command. But he was Pompey's heir, and here in Spain, where his late father was revered, that counted for a lot. Besides, as his deputy commanders he had two of Pompey's best generals. What was more, one of them had been Caesar's second-in-command for nine years and knew how Caesar thought and fought.

While his younger brother Sextus held the regional capital of Córdoba, Gnaeus had assembled and equipped a large field army of between fifty thousand and eighty thousand men. But few of his units were of quality. Nine of his thirteen legions were brand-new, made up of raw, inexperienced teenagers drafted from throughout western Spain and Portugal. The weight of responsibility for success in this battle would lay with his four veteran legions.

There was his father's elite 1st Legion, the Pompeian equivalent of Caesar's 10th. The loyal, tough 1st had taken part in all the major battles of the civil war, but unlike the undefeated 10th Legion, it had been forced to fight its way out of one disaster after another. There were the 2nd and Indigena Legions, both originally Pompeian units that had gone over to Caesar, only to defect back to the Pompeys when Gnaeus and Sextus arrived in Spain the previous year. Then there was the 8th Legion, a brother unit of the 10th and one of three Caesarian legions to recently desert to the Pompeys. Young Gnaeus's suspicions had been raised by these mass defections and he'd only retained the 8th, sending the other two turncoat legions, the 9th and the 13th, to his brother at Córdoba.

The previous day, young Pompey had set up camp on the plain near Munda. Caesar had arrived with his legions after nightfall and set up his own camp five miles away. Then, in the early hours of the morning, Pompey had formed up his army in battle order on the slope below the town, determined to bring Caesar to battle. Pompey had decided to venture all and capitalize on his numerical superiority before his supporters tired of retreating and deserted the cause. As Pompey's advisers had no doubt suggested, Caesar had been quick to accept the invitation to fight. "To Arms" had sounded throughout his camp shortly after scouts woke him with news of young Pompey's preparations for action outside Munda.

Standards held high, Caesar's legions marched in step across the plain with a rhythmical tramp of sixty thousand feet and the rattle of equipment. Discipline was rigid. Not a word was spoken. On the flanks, the cavalry moved forward at the walk. Caesar and his staff officers rode immediately behind the 10th Legion's front line.

As they advanced, the men of the 10th would have warily scanned the landscape ahead. All around them were rolling hills, but here on the valley floor the terrain was flat, good for both infantry and cavalry maneuvers. But first they had a five-mile hike to reach the enemy. In their path lay a shallow stream that dissected the plain. They would have to cross that then traverse another stretch of dry plain to reach the hill where the other side waited. Because he'd chosen the battlefield, young Pompey had taken the high ground. For added support, the town of Munda was on the hill behind him, surrounded by high walls dotted with defensive towers manned by local troops.

As they narrowed the distance between the two armies, the legionaries of the 10th could see that Pompey's wings were covered by waiting cavalry supported by light infantry and auxiliaries—six thousand of each. The men of the 10th would have been anxious to make out the identity of the legion on the flank directly facing them, hoping it wouldn't be their brother Spaniards of the 8th. The 10th and the 8th had been through thick and thin together over the past sixteen years. It would not be easy to fight and kill old friends. But they would do it. For Caesar. The men of the 10th understood why their hard-done-by comrades of the 8th had defected, and as they had in the past, they sympathized with them. But when it came down to it, the legion's loyalty to Caesar would prevail.

As Caesar's men broke step and splashed across the stream, then reformed on the far side and continued to advance at marching pace, their commander realized that Pompey expected him to come up the hill to come to grips with his troops. There was nothing else to do. It was either that or back off. When his front line reached the base of the hill, Caesar unexpectedly called for a halt. As Caesar's men stood, waiting impatiently to go forward to the attack, Caesar ordered his formations to tighten up, to concentrate his forces, and limit the area of operation. The order was relayed and obeyed.

Just as his troops were beginning to grumble that they were being prevented from taking the fight to the opposition, Caesar gave the order for "Charge" to be sounded. The call was still being trumpeted when the standards of his eighty cohorts inclined forward. With a deafening roar, Caesar's lines charged up the hillside.

With an equally deafening roar, Pompey's men let fly with their javelins. The shields of the attackers came up to protect their owners. The missiles, flung from above, scythed through the air in unavoidable masses and cut swathes through Caesar's front-line ranks, often passing through shields. The charge wavered momentarily, then regained momentum. Another volley of javelins blackened the blue sky. And another, and another. The attackers in Caesar's leading ranks, out of breath, with their dead comrades lying in heaps around them, and still not within striking distance of the enemy, came to a stop. Behind them, the men of the next lines pulled up, too. The entire attack ground to a halt.

Caesar could see defeat staring him in the face for the first time in his career. Real defeat, not a bloody nose like Gergovia, Dyrrhachium, or the Ruspina Plain, or the skirmishes among the Spanish hills over the past few weeks. He'd broken all the rules—only an amateur would make his men march five miles, make them ford a river, then send them charging up a hill like this. An amateur, or a man who had become accustomed to victory, who had underestimated his opponents, who was impatient to bring the war to an end. If the Pompeians charged down the hill now, there was every possibility that Caesar's men would break—even the vaunted legionaries of the mighty 10th. And, veterans or not, they would run for their lives.

Swiftly dismounting, Caesar grabbed a shield from a startled legionary of the 10th in a rear rank, then barged through his troops, up the slope, all the way to the shattered front rank, with his staff officers, hearts in mouths, jumping to the ground and hurrying after him. Dragging off his helmet with his right hand and casting it aside so that no one could mistake who he was, he stepped out in advance of the front line.

According to the classical historian Plutarch, Caesar called to his troops, nodding toward the tens of thousands of teenage recruits on the Pompeian side: "Aren't you ashamed to let your general be beaten by mere boys?"

Greeted by silence, he cajoled his men, he berated them, he encouraged them, while his opponents smiled down from above. But none of his panting, sweating, bleeding legionaries took a forward step. Then he turned to the staff officers who'd followed him.

"If we fail here, this will be the end of my life, and of your careers," Caesar said, according to Appian, another classical reporter of the battle. Caesar then drew his sword and strode up the slope, proceeding many yards ahead of his men toward the Pompeian line.

A junior officer on Pompey's side yelled an order, and his men, those within range of Caesar, loosed off a volley of missiles in his direction. According to Appian, two hundred javelins flew toward the lone, exposed figure of Caesar. The watching men of the 10th held their breath. No one could live through a volley like that. Not even the famously lucky Julius Caesar. . . .

IMPATIENT FOR GLORY

I n the spring of 61 B.C., the staff at the governor's palace at Córdoba would have stood anxiously awaiting the arrival of the new governor of the province of Baetica, so-called Farther Spain. Several of them had probably served under him eight years before, in 69 B.C., when he'd been the province's quaestor, its chief financial administrator, under the then governor, Major General Vetus. They would have known him as a man with a phenomenal memory and an extraordinary grasp of detail. His name was Gaius Julius Caesar, and at the age of thirty-eight he was about to embark on a career that would make him one of the most famous men of all time.

That day, a small, lean, narrow-faced general alighted from a litter and strode purposefully up the steps into the palace. Almost certainly he would have remembered men he hadn't seen in eight years and greeted them by name. His hair had thinned over those years. According to Suetonius, conscious of his growing baldness, Caesar brushed his hair forward to disguise it, not altogether successfully, and donned headwear whenever appropriate. Later, on official occasions, he would habitually wear the crown of laurel leaves that went with the honors granted him by the Senate. His skin was pale and soft, and it appears that despite all the time he would spend in the field in the coming years he would never acquire a deep tan.

Appian says Caesar's overland journey from Rome took twenty-four days. Some might have wanted to rest after more than three weeks on the road, but impatience would be a recurring feature of the career of Julius Caesar, and he was in a hurry to begin making his mark on the world. Only the previous year, at age thirty-seven, he'd been appointed a praetor, which brought with it the equivalent modern-day military rank of major general. Most of his contemporaries had achieved a praetorship as much as eight years earlier in their careers. As for his great rival, Gnaeus Pompeius Magnus—Pompey the Great—he had been a famous general at age twenty-three. And always in the back of Caesar's mind was the example of Alexander the Great, the Macedonian king who had conquered large parts of the known world when still in his twenties. Suetonius says that during his first posting to Spain, while gazing at a statue of Alexander the Great in Cádiz, Caesar was to lament to his associates that at his age Alexander had already conquered the entire world.

Caesar, determined to make up for lost time, promptly instructed his chief of staff, Lucius Cornelius Balbus, to raise a new legion in Farther Spain. Balbus, a local from Cádiz, would have reminded him that there were already two legions based in the province—the 8th and the 9th—quartered together just outside Córdoba. The always well-informed Caesar would have been aware of that fact, would have known that both units had been raised in Spain four years earlier by Pompey, the last of seven new legions he created with Senate approval in 65 B.C. But Caesar's plans called for three legions. He issued orders for a new legion to be levied in his province without delay.

Recruiting officers were soon bustling around the province, drafting thousands of young men from throughout Baetica, which roughly corresponded with the modern-day region of Andalusia. Within days, the recruits assembled at Córdoba. Following the pattern set by Pompey, Caesar gave the new legion the number ten. And *Legio X* was born.

For its emblem, the 10th took the bull, a symbol popular in Spain then as it is now. The bull emblem would appear on the shield of every man of the legion, and on the standards of the legion. Romans were firm believers in the power of the zodiac and were greatly influenced by horoscopes, and the unit's birth sign, the sign of the zodiac corresponding with the time the legion was officially formed, also would appear on every legionary standard. In the case of the 10th Legion, which apparently was formed in March, the sign would have been the fish of Pisces or the ram of Aries.

Caesar took a personal interest in the appointment of the legion's six tribunes, all young colonels in their late teens and twenties, and of the middle-ranking officers, the sixty centurions of the legion. Within thirty years the role of the tribune would change, but for now the tribunes appointed by Caesar would share the command of the legion among them. On rotation, one would lead the legion, while the other five each commanded two of the ten cohorts or battalions of the 10th. All were members of the Equestrian Order, an order of knighthood and second only in status to membership of the Roman Senate, and as such were well-educated young men from respectable, wealthy Roman families.

But as far as Caesar was concerned, the centurion was the backbone of the army, and he was to rely heavily on his centurions throughout his career. During the heat of battle in Gaul a decade later, he would call to all his centurions by name to urge them on. He came to know not only the names but also the strengths and weaknesses of his junior officers. His centurions, he knew, were his future. If they performed well, the legion would perform well. And if the legion performed well, their general's reputation was made.

The centurions appointed to the 10th by Caesar would have come from the 8th and 9th Legions. The most senior, the so-called first-rank centurions, already held centurion rank. The junior centurions, and there were eleven grades of centurion, came out of the ranks of the ordinary enlisted men. It was not uncommon for legionaries to be promoted to centurion after four years as a private, in these and later times. Centurions controlled the lives of their men, enforcing tight discipline with the business end of a vine stick. Tacitus tells of a centurion serving in the Balkans in the first century who was nicknamed "Bring Another" by his troops, because when he broke a vine stick across the back of a legionary he was disciplining, as he regularly did, he would bellow, "Bring another!"

So now Caesar had his 10th Legion. Six tribunes, all young gentlemen. Sixty centurions, all originally from the ranks. And 5,940 enlisted men and noncommissioned officers—in Caesar's time, the ten cohorts of the legion each contained six hundred men. In Caesar's time, too, the legionary was a conscript aged between seventeen and twenty, who was enrolled for sixteen years' military service. Roman legionaries averaged just five feet four in height, primarily because of their diet—which was based around bread. Meat and vegetables were considered mere supplements. And potatoes, tomatoes, bananas, and coffee were unknown to Romans.

But despite their diminutive stature, Roman legionaries were fighting fit. After tough training and daily arms and formation drill, they were capable of marching twenty-five miles a day with a pack weighing up to a hundred pounds on their back. Part of the legion training implemented by the consul Gaius Marius forty years earlier involved running long distances with full equipment. These men joining the 10th had to be fit—not only would they have to tramp thousands of miles over the coming years, but also some of their hand-to-hand battles would last not just hours, but days.

Right from the start, skills the young men of the 10th brought with them to the legion were exploited. Blacksmiths became armorers, carpenters built artillery and siege equipment, cobblers made military footwear, literate men became clerks. And if you didn't have a skill, you were given one. You worked on the surveying officer's team, or the road-clearing team, or became an artilleryman. But when the trumpets sounded "Prepare for Battle," you formed up in your cohort like everyone else, fully armed and ready to go into action.

Once they had been equipped, allocated their special duties, and received their basic training, and once Caesar was satisfied that the men of the 10th were prepared for action, he put them in a column with the experienced 8th and 9th Legions, and marched out of Córdoba, crossing the Guadalquivir River, and headed north, into present-day Portugal. This part of the Iberian Peninsula—Lusitania, as the Romans called it—had yet to yield to Roman rule. Its hill towns closed their gates to Roman advances, its tribes actively and ferociously resisted Roman expeditions. Poorly led, poorly equipped, and poorly organized, the tribes of Lusitania provided the ideal opportunity for an able and ambitious commander like Julius Caesar to make his name.

Caesar had planned his campaign in advance and in detail. Over the next few months he led his force of eighteen thousand legionaries plus several hundred cavalry, supported by a baggage train involving thousands of pack animals and carts for his supplies, artillery, and heavy siege equipment, all managed by noncombatant muleteers, through the valleys of Portugal. Methodically, brutally, the men of the expeditionary force stormed one fortified hill town after another and destroyed all opposition. Rising before dawn, the legionaries would either go back to work besieging the walls of a Lusitanian town that had failed to yield, or, leaving a community in smoking ruins, they would march on to the next resistance point, tramping for an average of six hours until midday, then building a marching camp for the night.

While auxiliaries foraged for food, fodder, and firewood, the legionaries took entrenching tools from their backpacks and threw up a fortified camp—a new camp every day while they were on the march. Protected by advance infantry elements and cavalry patrols, surveying and road clearing parties commanded by a tribune proceeded ahead of the main body of the army and selected an elevated site, cleared it, and set out markers for the streets and tents of the new camp on a set grid pattern unaltered for centuries. After a few months of this, when the bulk of the legion arrived at the camp site the legionaries could construct the camp with their eyes closed.

With one cohort from each legion on guard, other legionaries dug a trench around the site, using the earth excavated to build a wall beside the trench. Polybius, who describes the construction of legion camps in fine detail, says the wall was normally twelve feet high, the trench twelve feet deep and three feet across. Caesar liked his trenches fifteen feet across.

Trees were felled, and four sets of wooden gates and guard towers were constructed on the spot and set up in the four walls—all would be burned when the legion resumed its march next day. The legion's artillery was sited along the parapet. A space of two hundred feet left between walls and the tent line, calculated to prevent burning arrows from reaching the tents, was occupied by cattle, plunder, and prisoners.

The *praetorium*, Caesar's headquarters tent, was erected first, followed by the quarters of his deputies, including General Balbus, the chief of staff, then those of the tribunes and centurions, each with a tent to himself. Next, legion workshops, the quartermaster's department, and a camp market were set up. Finally the troops could erect their own ten-man tents, leather originally, but universally made of canvas by the first century, in streets designated for each individual cohort.

While engaged in construction work, a legionary could stack his shield and javelin and remove his backpack and helmet, but otherwise he had to wear full armored jacket, sword, and dagger, on pain of death if caught improperly attired, to enable him to go into action immediately in the event of an enemy attack. Once the camp was complete, and Josephus was to say a new legion camp blossomed like a small town in no time, a set number of sentries occupied specific posts, for watches of three hours' duration, with four troopers from the legion's cavalry unit assigned to patrol the posts at night and report any sentry asleep or absent—both being crimes punishable by execution.

This campaign was the ideal baptism of fire for the young men of the 10th. The exertions of building a new camp day in day out after marching twenty-five miles, the strict regulations and severe punishments, all added to the swift military education of the youngsters of the 10th Legion even before they came to grips with the Portuguese tribesmen, toughening them up, preparing them for the bloody hill town assaults when they arrived. In Lusitania many legionaries killed their first man, and saw how the tight, often brutal discipline their centurions enforced paid dividends when Caesar's orders came and they obeyed without thinking. In those months of the spring and summer of 61 B.C., marching, digging, charging, breaking down gates with battering rams, going over walls on scaling ladders, storming through towns and villages, cutting down anyone who stood in their way, raw recruits became soldiers, and the 10th Legion became a killing machine.

In those few short, hot months, the 10th Legion helped Caesar subdue the tribes of the western Iberian Peninsula between the Tagus and Douro Rivers, tribes such as the Calaeci, and the Lusitani, who gave their name to the region, driving all the way to the Atlantic on the northwest coast—"the Ocean," as Romans called it. One after the other the towns fell, and thousands of tribespeople were killed or taken prisoner. Captives were sold at auctions to the slave traders who trailed the legions along with other scavenging camp followers. These included merchants and prostitutes who made their living from the legions, as well as the *de facto* wives and illegitimate children of the legionaries and the personal servants of the officers—hordes who at times were known to outnumber the men of the army they trailed.

Under the Roman army's rules of plunder, if a town was stormed, the spoils were divided among the legionaries. But if a town surrendered, the fate of the spoils was decided by the generals, who disposed of them as they saw fit. Generals also decided whether prisoners were executed or sold into slavery. As for the proceeds of the sale of slaves, Tacitus indicates that money from the sale of captured fighting men went to the legionaries, while that from the sale of nonmilitary prisoners did not. Smart COs such as Caesar would have made sure the rank and file always received a share of the spoils no matter what.

Most prisoners sold into slavery would die as slaves. A few would eventually be set free by generous masters, and it was the custom for some slaves to be granted freedom in their owners' wills. With wealthier Romans each owning up to twenty thousand slaves at their numerous estates, it was no sacrifice to free a hundred or two. There are one or two instances on record of captives being enslaved for set periods, such as thirty years, on the orders of their Roman captors. As for the slave traders, theirs could be a perilous existence, camping in unprotected tents outside the fortified camps of the legions. There are several first-century examples of unarmed camp followers being massacred in large number during enemy attacks on legion bases.

As the 8th, 9th, and 10th Legions returned victoriously to their winter quarters outside Córdoba in the fall of 61 B.C. with minimal casualties and a hefty share of the booty from the campaign, Caesar was already being hailed by his troops as a great general and back at Rome as a new Roman hero.

His appointment in Farther Spain had been for just one year, and in the new year he parted company with the 10th, no doubt going around to all the centurions to bid them farewell individually. Then he would have called for a parade, and stood on the camp tribunal, the reviewing stand always set up in front of the quarters of the legion's tribunes, and thanked his assembled legionaries for their brave and loyal service. He would have particularly thanked the 10th Legion, which he had quickly come to consider his own. From later events, it's likely he even promised the men of the 10th that if ever again he had the opportunity to lead troops in the service of Rome, he would send for the 10th Legion. And not just to march in his vanguard, but also to act as his personal bodyguard. Caesar would have left the legion camp for the last time and embarked on the road journey back to Rome with the cheers of his troops ringing in his ears.

As he returned to the capital, he was faced with a dilemma. To his mind, his highly successful military operations in Spain qualified him for a Triumph. The Triumph was one of the highest accolades a Roman general could receive, entitling him to a parade through the streets of Rome in a golden chariot followed by troops from his army and his spoils of war, receiving the cheers of the crowds lining the route of the procession. So he sent aides on ahead to demand that the Senate grant him a Triumph. Word came back to Caesar that he was being considered for a consulship. But he couldn't have both.

To be awarded a Triumph, a candidate had to wait outside Rome for the Senate vote to be taken. To be elected a consul, the candidate had to be in the city. When forced to choose between pursuing the consulship or the Triumph, Caesar went for the former. The two consuls appointed each year were the highest Roman officials in the land in these late days of the Republic. Power before glory, that was Caesar's tenet. He duly achieved a consulship in what turned out to be a hard-fought election in 59 B.C., his promotion elevating him to the equivalent rank of lieutenant general.

But Caesar wasn't finished with the 10th Legion. Their partnership had only just begun.

III

SAVAGING THE SWISS, OVERRUNNING THE GERMANS

C aesar was thoughtful for a moment, looking at the dust-covered faces of the cavalry scouts. He himself would write of what took place this eventful day, in his memoirs.

Turning to his quartermaster, he asked: "How many days' rations do the men have left?"

"Two days' rations, Caesar," the quartermaster replied.

Caesar nodded. One scout had told him that he was seventeen miles from Bibracte, capital of the Aedui tribe. Another told him the massive column of the Helvetii tribe from Switzerland that he'd been following across eastern France for weeks was still in the camp they'd established three miles from his the previous day. "We march for Bibracte," Caesar announced.

He would have looked over at Major General Titus Labienus, his second-in-command, a man in his midthirties, and informed him of his intention to secure the army's food supply from the Aedui before he concerned himself any further with the Helvetii. And then he issued the order for the trumpets to sound "Prepare to March."

It was the summer of 58 B.C., and Julius Caesar had kept his word to the men of the 10th Legion. As soon as he'd taken up his new appointment as governor of Cisalpine Gaul and Illyricum at the beginning of the year, a command soon extended by the Senate to also cover Transalpine Gaul on the death of its governor, he sent for the 10th Legion, and it marched from Spain to new quarters in the south of France.

At the same time, with the authority of the Senate—at the instigation of Pompey—to command four legions for five years, Caesar had sent for

13

the other two legions he'd led three years before, the 8th and 9th, plus the 7th, another Spanish legion raised by Pompey, and posted them all to the city of Aquileia in the northeast of Italy, near present-day Venice, so they were midway between his provinces. But before the winter was over he received reports that the huge Helvetii tribe of Switzerland had decided to migrate to the south of Gaul, modern France, where Rome had a large and prosperous province. The Helvetii had sent out messages to all their clans and four other tribes who intended joining their march, to mass at the Rhône River on March 28, then cross the bridge at Geneva and pass down into France. Caesar was determined to stop them.

He had quickly marched the 10th Legion to Geneva, destroyed the Rhône bridge, then had his legionaries build a sixteen-foot earth wall for eighteen miles along the bank of the Rhône from Lake Geneva to the Jura Mountains. For weeks the Helvetii had tried to cross the river using boats and rafts, even wading and swimming, usually at night, but the legion and the walls between them turned the tribesmen away, and the Helvetii had diverted to another route, marching between the Rhône and the Jura Mountains, and swarming down into the territory of the Aedui people of eastern France—present-day Burgundy, between the Saône and the Loire Rivers. The Aedui had sought Caesar's help in repelling the invaders, and he hadn't been slow to respond. Quickly recruiting two new legions in northern Italy, the 11th and 12th, he'd combined them with his existing legions and marched into southern France to do battle with the Helvetii.

His first battle plan had been ruined a few days back by a soldier who'd let him down. For weeks Caesar had hung on the tail of the ponderous Helvetii column, always staying just five or six miles behind it, waiting for an opportunity to attack to present itself. And then the Helvetii had camped at the base of a large hill. A cavalry patrol that reconnoitered the reverse side of the hill reported back to Caesar that it would not be difficult to climb, so, a little after midnight, Caesar had sent General Labienus with two legions to make the ascent, while he marched on the hill from the opposite direction with the remaining four legions. He sent his cavalry on ahead, and in advance of that again a patrol led by an officer by the name of Publius Considius.

A little after daybreak, Caesar was only a mile and a half from the hill when Considius came galloping up to him. "Turn back, Caesar," Caesar reports he'd breathlessly advised. "The enemy are in possession of the hilltop. I recognized their Gallic arms and their helmet crests."

One of Caesar's closest aides, Colonel (later General) Gaius Asinius Pollio, would write that Caesar had a habit of accepting the reports of his subordinates without corroborating them. So Caesar took Considius at his word and pulled back to another hill. Only late in the day did he learn that it was General Labienus's legions who'd occupied the hilltop at dawn, not the enemy.

Caesar says Labienus waited all day on the hilltop for him to appear before he himself was forced to withdraw. Plutarch says that Labienus in fact engaged the Germans, but Caesar's account of a botched operation is more credible. Labienus would have wanted answers when he reunited with his chief. An excellent commander, energetic, with a quick mind and a fine tactical sense, Labienus also became renowned for a sarcastic turn of phrase, which he tended for reserve for the lower ranks.

"Considius lost his head," Caesar sourly informed his deputy, in words he was to consign to his memoirs. "He was recommended to me as a first-class soldier who had served under Sulla and Crassus. But today he reported that he had seen what was not there to be seen."

The legions had turned away from the Helvetii column and were marching toward Bibracte to secure grain from the Aedui when Colonel Lucius Aemilius, commander of Caesar's Gallic cavalry, came galloping to his commander in chief from the rear.

"The Helvetii are following us, Caesar," Aemilius reported. "Their cavalry is harrying my rear guard, and the entire column is moving down the road to Bibracte behind us."

Caesar rode to the rear of the legion column and saw for himself the dust to the east raised by the feet and hooves and wagons and carts of the Helvetii trailing him in their tens of thousands. Now he ordered Colonel Aemilius to take all the cavalry and head off the Helvetii to give him enough time to prepare the legions for battle. As his four thousand mounted troops from southern and central France thundered away with Aemilius, Caesar chose a grassy hill close by as the place where he would form his battle lines, and in a hasty conference on horseback agreed unit dispositions with his generals. Soon the trumpets were sounding, standards were inclining to one side, and the legions were wheeling off the road and toward the hill.

The 10th and the three other Spanish legions, the 7th, 8th, and 9th, were formed up in three lines halfway up the hill. The two new legions, the 11th and 12th, took up their position on the top of the hill along with the auxiliaries—Caesar didn't have a great deal of faith in either the new legions or the auxiliaries. Veterans of the older legions occupied the third line, and they quickly dug entrenchments around the wagons of the baggage train, and the backpacks of all the legionaries of the army were brought and piled in the same enclosure. All this time, as lines were formed and trenches dug, the legionaries could see the Helvetii slowly flood across the plain toward them.

Standing with his men of the 10th Legion in the first line was Centurion Gaius Crastinus. His rank evidenced by the transverse crest of eagle feathers on his helmet, the metal greaves on his shins, and the fact that he wore his sword on his left hip rather than on the right like enlisted men, Centurion Crastinus had joined the 8th or 9th Legion in 65 B.C. when Pompey the Great raised the new legions in Spain. He had transferred over to the 10th when it was formed four years later as a junior grade centurion, being personally chosen by Caesar. Now, not more than twenty-seven, he would have commanded a cohort of six hundred men. Later events would suggest that Crastinus was a good centurion. He was a fearless fighter, but it took more than that to command the respect and attention of his men. He showed an interest in their welfare, on and off the battlefield. And he never tired of encouraging them. A few weeks back, the legion had turned back a mass of Helvetii tribesmen when they'd tried to make another river crossing, this time at the Saône, and if Crastinus remained true to form he would have dived from maniple to maniple of his cohort, exhorting his men.

Crastinus, standing on the extreme left of his cohort's front line, probably pondered the same question that would have been exercising the minds of his men as they watched the Helvetii roll up to their elevated position. Later, documents would be found in the Helvetii baggage, written in Greek, that turned out to be a register of the names of 368,000 men, women, and children who were taking part in the migration from Switzerland. And the vast majority of them were here, now.

Mounted Helvetii had dispersed Colonel Aemilius and his cavalry and were chasing them all over the plain as the main Helvetian body came up to the hill with all their wheeled transport. Their women, children, and elderly parked the vast train in a mass below the hill as their men-at-arms joined their traditional clans and formed into solid phalanxes of spearmen many men deep, each wearing a Gallic-style helmet with a plume like a horse's tail, a small breastplate, and carrying a spear up to twelve feet long. The Helvetii were Celts, larger men than the Romans, brave, and well versed in the arts of war. They had defeated Roman armies in the past and were confident of doing it again.

As Centurion Crastinus looked down the slope, he would have seen Caesar dismount and have his horse led away. At the commander in chief's instruction, all the other officers did the same. Crastinus was to become devoted to Julius Caesar, and it's probable that ever since he'd served under Caesar in Spain he'd been of the firm opinion that the general was a great man, a man destined for great things. And Crastinus would have recognized that in sending the horses away Caesar was cleverly sending a message to his troops that they all, officers and enlisted men alike, now stood in equal danger.

If Crastinus was as astute as he was brave, he wouldn't have had as high a regard for some of Caesar's generals as he did for Caesar himself, men sent by the Senate so that Caesar had to take the good with the bad. They were easy enough to pick out in their scarlet cloaks, one pacing nervously back and forth, another talking with aides, one or two resolutely arming themselves with shields. Even though the campaign was only months old, the centurion may have already summed up Caesar's mixed bag of commanders, with their strengths and weaknesses revealed by their actions. Labienus, the second-in-command—a damn fine general, despite his savage tongue, cool under pressure, and quick to see both dangers and opportunities. Galba—overconfident, petty, ambitious. Pedius, a relative of Caesar's—young, but competent and reliable. Sabinus—a fool, gullible, unadventurous, and too inclined toward the safe course, a man who shouldn't be leading troops. Cotta—stubborn, argumentative, but a good man to have at your head just the same. Crassus, youngest son of Consul Crassus who conquered Spartacus and his slave army—a well-liked young man with a good head and great promise. And Balbus, the chief of staff, a Spaniard from Farther Spain, which would have pleased the men of the 10th, from a very wealthy family, loyal, dependable, a skillful mediator, and an excellent organizer. Later serving as Caesar's private secretary and publishing his writings after his death, he would be made a consul by the Senate in 40 B.C., the first provincial ever to receive a consular appointment.

As Crastinus took a quick glance to his right, he would have seen the faces of his men as they stood stock-still in their rows with their expressions set, their eyes to the front, some betraying their tension with pale, bloodless faces. The breeze rustled the yellow horsehair crests on their helmets, the sun glinted on the bravery decorations they'd put on for the battle on Caesar's orders to awe the Celts. On their left arm, each legionary held his shield. Polybius tells us the legionary's rectangular, curved shield was as thick as a man's palm, curved, but with straight sides, four feet high and two and a half feet wide, made from two layers of wood covered with canvas and calfskin, the metal boss in the center fixed to the handle on the reverse. In these ranks, the shields were painted with the bull emblem of the 10th Legion. In his right hand each man held two javelins, straight up and down for now. On his right hip hung his sword. When the javelins had all been released, Crastinus would give the order for his men to draw their swords, in preparation for close combat.

If Crastinus had looked to the sky, he would have seen that the sun was directly overhead.

Walking along the front line, Caesar addressed his troops. Above him, the hill was covered with forty thousand men. Caesar had done plenty of public speaking, would even write a book on the subject. He chose his words with care, and he expertly elevated his voice so that even those in the rear ranks could hear him. He praised his men, and he urged them to victory. It had to be a short speech—the Helvetii had combined smaller phalanxes into one dense mass of spearmen, who were now advancing toward the hill.

The phalanx, a formation developed into an art form by earlier Greek armies, had two strengths. The Greek phalanx had been sixteen men deep, so that a graduated wall of spear points protruded for some eight feet from the front of the formation like the spines of a porcupine. The men of the tightly packed formation also overlapped their shields, so that there were sixteen solid lines of shield from front to rear. We don't know how deep the Helvetian phalanx was, but with no shortage of warriors it would have been as deep as was practicable.

Caesar withdrew behind his second line and waited as the phalanx began to move up the lower slope of the hill toward the Roman front line at walking pace. Then Caesar gave an order. With a roar from thousands of legionary throats, his front line launched a volley of javelins. On command, another volley flew through the air.

Coming up the slope, with the hill above them thick with Roman legionaries and the air full of missiles, the Helvetian warriors instinctively raised their shields to protect themselves from the Roman javelins. This, they quickly discovered, wasn't as easy as just blocking them. Forty years before, Consul Marius had introduced a revolutionary change to the design of Roman javelins; since his time, they had been manufactured with soft metal behind the point. Once the javelin struck anything, the weight of the shaft caused it to bend like a hockey stick where shaft and head joined. With its aerodynamic qualities destroyed, it couldn't be effectively thrown back. And if it lodged in a shield, it became extremely difficult to remove, as the Helvetii now found. What was worse, in their case, with their shields overlapping, javelins were going though several at a time, pinning them together. With some members of the phalanx downed and others struggling with tangled shields, their formation was broken by these initial volleys.

Caesar gave another order. His flag dropped, and the trumpets of the first line sounded the "Charge." With a roar, the front-line legionaries charged down the hill with drawn swords. After repeated attempts to free their shields, many Helvetii threw them away, leaving themselves virtually defenseless. Getting in past the massive but unwieldy spears, the legionaries cut the Celts to pieces, inflicting terrible wounds to necks, shoulders, arms, and torsos.

The bloodied Helvetii bravely stood their ground, despite their losses and despite their wounds, but after a while they were forced to begin to yield ground, and steadily withdrew to a hill a mile away, fighting all the way. Leaving the 11th and 12th Legions on the hill to guard his baggage, Caesar ordered all three lines in advance of them to pursue the Helvetii, at marching pace and maintaining formation. But as the Roman troops came up, a force of fifteen thousand members of the Boii and Tulungi clans, who had been acting as the Helvetii rear guard, unexpectedly swung around from the rear and attacked the Romans' right flank. Encouraged by this, the Helvetii on the hill regrouped and advanced to attack once more.

Caesar acted swiftly and decisively to this threat. He ordered his first and second lines to take on the Helvetii main force, while the third line wheeled to the right and engaged the Boii and Tulungi. With a blare of trumpets, the legions charged on two fronts. Time and again the Romans charged, re-formed, then charged again. The fighting lasted all afternoon. Not a single warrior of the Helvetii turned to run. But gradually their shattered formations were divided and pushed back. The men from the hill were forced to retreat up the slope, with Centurion Crastinus and his 10th Legion troops in the thick of the fighting. The enemy on the right were pushed all the way back to the parked wagons by men of other legions.

On the hill, the fighting for the 10th Legion and its companion units ended at sunset. But at the wagons, the battle continued well into the night, with defiant tribesmen raining spears from the vehicles and poking pikes out beneath them and through the wheels. Finally, the wagon laager was overrun by the legions. All the Helvetian worldly goods and all the tribe's supplies were captured, along with numerous noncombatants, including the children of nobility. The booty would be shared among the legions. It was later said that 130,000 Helvetii fled from the scene of the battle that night. How many were killed in the fighting no one could calculate; there were too many to count.

Caesar spent three days burying the dead of both sides and patching up his wounded before marching after the surviving Helvetii. Centurion Crastinus was leading his men of the 10th Legion down the road when envoys from the Helvetii approached the Roman column. When they were conveyed to Caesar, the Helvetians prostrated themselves in front of him, and, in tears, begged him to grant peace to their people. Caesar commanded them to cease their flight and wait for him.

The Helvetii obeyed, and the Roman army found them waiting apprehensively several miles ahead, their people on foot now—the fighting men and the women, children and old people, looking tired, hungry, bedraggled, and defeated. The legions formed up and watched in silence as the tribesmen lay down their arms, handed over escaped Roman slaves, and provided hostages. Apart from six thousand fighting men who slipped away at night and were rounded up by friendly tribes and put to death, the Helvetii received no punishment other than being sent back to Switzerland, repairing the damage they'd done to towns, villages, and farms *en route*. The tribe tramped back to where they'd come from and never ventured from Switzerland again. The official name of Switzerland today is the Helvetian Confederation.

The 10th Legion wasn't done with fighting for the year. It was barely the midsummer of 58 B.C., and on the heels of Caesar's defeat of the Helvetii the tribes of the region came to him and asked him to free them from the threat of a German king, Ariovistus, and his fierce German warriors, who had invaded northern Gaul. Caesar gave his legions the familiar order "Prepare to March." The trumpets of the legions sounded the call three times, as was customary. The camp was struck. Legionaries loaded the baggage train and formed up in marching order. On the third trumpet call, the lead elements moved out.

As the Germans advanced south toward the territory of the Sequani tribe in the modern Alsace region of eastern France, Caesar reached the Sequani capital of Besançon in three days of forced marches and occupied the town, which sat on a horseshoe bend of the Doubs River east of Dijon. Here Caesar's troops mixed with the locals, who spoke of the immense stature and terrifying military skills of the Germans who were marching toward the town. The newer tribunes and commanders of auxiliary units, pampered young men recently arrived from Rome, many with not a day's active service among them, were unnerved by the talk. Their growing dread of the Germans spread to the troops. Soon the campfire talk was all doom and gloom, and everywhere men were making and sealing their wills. Seasoned centurions such as Gaius Crastinus went to Caesar and warned him that when he gave the order to march, the men might refuse to obey.

Caesar now summoned all his centurions. He told them he intended moving camp that same night. If necessary, he said, he would advance against Ariovistus and his Germans with just the men of the 10th Legion, a unit he had every confidence would never let him down. And he repeated his old promise to make the 10th his personal bodyguard. When they heard this, the men of the 10th asked their tribunes to thank their general for his high opinion of them and to assure him they were ready to take the field with him at a moment's notice, no matter what the rest of the army did. But the rest of the army had no intention of letting the 10th enjoy all the glory, and the spoils, and was stirred into action. In the early hours of the morning, all six legions of the task force marched out of Besançon with Caesar and headed for the approaching German army. After six days of solid marching, scouts reported that Ariovistus was just twenty-three miles away.

No one doubted Julius Caesar's courage. According to Suetonius, Caesar was presented with the Civic Crown, one of Rome's highest bravery awards, in 81 B.C. when he was just a young staff officer of nineteen or twenty, after saving the life of a fellow citizen during the storming of Mytilene, modern Mitilini, capital of the island of Lesbos. And during his operations in Spain and now in Switzerland and France, Caesar always led from the front. But neither could he be called incautious. And now he was being particularly cautious.

Ariovistus, king of the Suebi Germans, had sent Caesar a message, accepting an offer of a peace conference. But he had attached an unusual condition to the meeting—both leaders were only to be accompanied by a bodyguard of mounted troops. This started Caesar thinking that perhaps the German had bribed members of the Roman general's Gallic cavalry to assassinate him on the way to or at the conference. To be on the safe side, Caesar ordered his cavalry to temporarily give up their horses, and mounted infantrymen of the 10th Legion in their place. He was to later write that by this stage he considered the legionaries of the 10th to be men in whose devotion he could rely absolutely.

As the legionaries were mounting up, a soldier of the 10th was heard to remark, "Caesar's being better than his word. He promised to make the 10th his bodyguard, and now he's knighting us." Caesar himself would have smiled when the comment was repeated to him, for he was to later include it in his memoirs.

The meeting took place on a rise halfway between the Roman and the German camps, with the mounted men of the 10th Legion formed up three hundred yards behind their general and King Ariovistus's big-framed cavalrymen a similar distance behind him. Accompanied by a personal escort of ten men each, and on horseback, Caesar and Ariovistus conducted a tense face-to-face conference. As the two leaders spoke at length, with each trying to convince the other to withdraw from Gaul, German cavalrymen tried to provoke the mounted legionaries of the 10th, and Caesar temporarily broke off discussions to order his men not to retaliate.

The day's conference ended in a stalemate, and next day Caesar sent two envoys to continue discussions on his behalf. When Ariovistus made prisoners of the envoys, his intent was clear enough. For days, the two armies jostled for position, with the Germans moving camp in an attempt to cut Caesar off from supplies coming up from Besançon, and with Caesar dividing his troops between two camps. The Germans attacked the camps, but whenever Caesar formed up his troops in battle lines, the Germans avoided a full-scale battle. Then, from prisoners, Caesar learned that the Germans believed they would not win if they fought a major encounter before the new moon. Ariovistus was stalling for time. So Caesar marched on the German camp, just fifteen miles from the Rhine River, determined to force Ariovistus to do battle before he wanted to. Even though his forty thousand men would be outnumbered, Caesar was counting on having a psychological advantage. As it turned out, pressing for a battle now had another advantage, which Caesar only later discovered: Suebi reinforcements were at that moment approaching the Rhine from the east, planning to link up with Ariovistus.

Forced to defend their camp, the Germans tumbled into the fields outside it and formed up in their clans: the Harudes; the Tribboci; the Vangiones; the Nemetes; the Eudusii; the numerous Suebi, who gave their name to the tribe as a whole; and a clan then based in the Main valley, the Marcomanni, which would grow in size and influence and within half a century settle in Bohemia, and, another 175 years later, during the reign of Marcus Aurelius, would prove to be one of Rome's fiercest foes. The

German warriors were on average several inches taller than the Romans, broad-shouldered, with long hair and beards. Their nobles, better dressed and armed than the rank and file, who often wore nothing but a fur cloak and went barefoot, wore their hair tied up in the characteristic Suebian knot. The principal weapon of the Germans was the long spear.

Caesar's four thousand cavalry and the six thousand German cavalry held back as the legions advanced in their customary three battle lines, with the 10th Legion occupying what was now its regular position on the right wing. Caesar personally took command on the right when he saw the enemy line at its weakest on that side, and when he ordered his first two lines to charge, the men of the 10th dashed forward enthusiastically.

Even though they had been unprepared to fight, the Germans opposite ran so quickly to the attack that the legionaries didn't even have time to throw their javelins. Dropping them, they drew their swords as the two armies came together. The Germans adopted the phalanx formation used by the Helvetii, with their line bristling with long spears, which, in theory, would keep them out of range of the short Roman swords.

Undaunted, men of the 10th brushed aside the spears and literally threw themselves on the front line of German shields. Some wrenched shields out of the hands of their owners. Others reached over the top of the shields and stabbed the points of their swords into German faces. Using these aggressive tactics, the 10th soon routed the German left.

Meanwhile, the German right was pushing back the Roman left. Seeing this, young Publius Crassus, whom Caesar had left behind in charge of the cavalry, ordered the stationary third line to advance to the relief of the Roman left. Their arrival turned the battle, and soon the entire German army was on the run. The legions pursued them all the way to the Rhine. A few Germans managed to swim the river. King Ariovistus and one or two others escaped in boats. But all the rest, including the king's wives and daughters, were hunted down and killed or captured by the Roman cavalry. East of the Rhine, when the Suebi reinforcements heard of the disastrous battle, they turned and fled for home. The 10th Legion could add another victory to its growing roll of honor.

IV

CONQUERING GAUL

I t had been a short but profitable campaign for the men of the 10th. They had stripped thousands of dead Swiss and German troops. They had looted their camps and baggage trains. All with only minimal casualties in their own ranks. By the fall they had settled into a massive camp in Alsace not far from Besançon, to spend a leisurely six months waiting out the winter before Caesar led them on new adventures in Gaul the following spring. Caesar himself had gone to northern Italy to carry out his duties as chief judge of his provinces, leaving the legions under the command of General Labienus. But as winter arrived, Labienus began sending Caesar intelligence reports that the tribes of northern Gaul, the Belgae, were planning to attack the Roman forces to prevent them from advancing farther into Gaul. Caesar had his own spies among the tribes, and when these insiders added credence to Labienus's reports, he acted quickly.

Raising two new legions in northern Italy, the 13th and the 14th, Caesar returned to Gaul to confront the rebellious tribes. Collecting his six existing legions then wintering in Alsace, he marched his bolstered army up into the present-day region of Champagne-Ardenne, northeast of Paris, the home territory of the Remi people, allies of Rome, who had their capital at Rheims. Against him it was estimated that the tribes of the Belgae could muster 260,000 men, although the actual number who met him at the Aisne River north of Rheims was perhaps a third of that.

After each army tried to outmaneuver the other, Caesar dealt the Belgae a defeat using just his cavalry and auxiliaries, and the tribes split up and retreated in disorder to their home territories. This allowed Caesar to march on individual tribes and defeat them piecemeal over the coming weeks, often accepting their surrender after laying siege to their chief towns. In this way he bloodlessly conquered the Suessiones, the Bellovaci—the largest of the Belgic tribes—and the Ambiani, then marched into the ter-

24

ritory of the Nervii, who occupied an area in central Belgium east of the Scheldt River.

The Nervii were a proud people, famous fighters originally from Germany who even barred traders from selling wine in their territory because they believed it made men soft, and they had no intention of submitting to the Romans. From spies they learned the Roman order of march—Caesar was advancing with each legion separated by its baggage train from the next—and saw an opportunity to attack part of the column before more legions could come up in support. The Nervii had few mounted troops of their own, and to hamper enemy cavalry they had long before planted hedgerows across their fields; this gave them the confidence to take on the Roman army without fear of Caesar's cavalry, and the king of the Nervii, Boduognatus, convinced his Belgian neighbors of the Atrebate and Viromandui tribes to join his people as they carefully prepared an ambush beside the Sambre River.

But Caesar's scouts had forewarned him that enemy troops were active near the Sambre, so he changed the order of march as he approached the river, putting the 10th and his five other experienced legions in battle order in the vanguard of his advance, with the baggage of all the legions coming up next and the two new legions forming a rear guard. Seeing Nervian cavalry pickets on the far bank, Caesar sent his cavalry across where the river was only three feet deep and ordered his legions to begin work building a fortified camp on the slope of a hill that ran down to the Sambre. The 10th and 9th Legions were assigned the left end of the encampment, under General Labienus. The 7th and the 12th took the right, while the 8th and the 11th set to work in the middle.

The Nervian cavalry retreated into a wood on the sloping far bank, but kept reappearing to harry the Roman cavalry. In the meantime, the legionaries stacked their backpacks, shields, and javelins, and set to work with entrenching tools building their camp. After a time the Roman baggage train came lumbering onto the scene. This was the moment the tribesmen had been waiting for—they had agreed to hold off their attack until the first Roman baggage train arrived. Not realizing the Romans now had just one large train, and that six legions, not one, were now on the far bank, the Belgae poured from the wood in their tens of thousands. Caesar was to estimate he faced sixty thousand warriors at the Sambre. In the face of this wall of screaming men, the surprised Roman cavalry fled in all directions, and the hollering tribesmen dashed to the river.

The Belgae were already splashing across the Sambre by the time Caesar was able to comprehend the scope of what was happening. He issued a minimum of orders; his flag went up, and the trumpets sounded "To Arms." Men were running everywhere as he galloped to the 10th Legion on his left. The legionaries of the 10th had dropped their tools, grabbed their arms, and hurried down the slope to form up in their cohorts below the camp works, with the leather weather covers still on their shields. Many were so pushed for time they didn't even have the chance to don their helmets, let alone add plumes or decorations.

"My soldiers of the 10th," Caesar yelled, "live up to your tradition of bravery, keep your nerve, meet the enemy's attack with boldness, and we shall win the day!"

The men of the 10th roared a hurrah, shaking their javelins in the air. Confident his favorite legion would hold their wing, and with a nod of assurance from General Labienus, Caesar galloped off to organize defenses elsewhere.

The slope, the hedgerows, and the suddenness of the attack combined to split up the Roman army. The 10th and the 9th found themselves separated from the other legions as warriors of the Atrebates tribe emerged from the river and came surging up the slope toward them. General Labienus coolly waited for the tribesmen to come within range, then gave the order for the front line to let fly with their javelins. A volley of missiles sliced down into the Atrebates. Out of breath, many of them wounded, with comrades falling dead all around them, the Atrebates stopped in their tracks.

Now the Roman commander gave the order to charge. With swords drawn, and with General Labienus leading the way, the men of the 10th and 9th Legions swept down the hill and overwhelmed the Belgian warriors. Tribesmen in the rear turned and ran to the river, and the legionaries chased them all the way across, cutting down many from behind as they fled in panic. The river was soon filled with bloody, dismembered bodies. The men of the 10th and the 9th pursued other Atrebates up the slope on the far bank, all the way to the woods at the top of the slope from which they had emerged a little time before.

On the Roman right wing, the 7th and 12th Legions had been all but surrounded by Boduognatus and his Nervii. Here, the Roman disorder, particularly among the men of the less experienced 12th Legion, most of whose centurions were already dead or wounded, threatened to give way to defeat. The legion's 4th Cohort, which had taken the brunt of the Nervian attack, had lost every centurion and a standard bearer. Caesar arrived on the scene to find men assembled behind any standard and packed tightly together in their fear. Caesar dismounted and grabbed a shield from a man in the rear, then made his way to the forefront of the battle, yelling orders. "Push forward! Spread out! Give yourselves room to fight!"

He addressed the surviving centurions by name, urging them and their men on. Given new heart by the arrival of their general, the men of the 12th rallied. Seeing the 7th Legion close by similarly hard pressed, Caesar shouted to their tribunes, ordering them to link up with the 12th and form one large square. As this formation was created, Boduognatus and his Nervii were held back, but Caesar and the two legions were still being pressed by compact phalanxes on three sides.

On the far bank of the river, General Labienus and his two legions had chased the Atrebates into the woods and discovered the tribes' camp, where the Belgians had lain in wait for the Roman column for days prior to Caesar's arrival. Quickly dealing with the few sentries, Labienus occupied the camp, then pushed on up to the top of the hill. Looking back across the river, he saw the predicament of Caesar and the 7th and the 12th, and quickly ordered the 10th Legion to go to Caesar's aid before the Nervii broke through.

As the men of the 10th came wading back across the river, the two legions of the rear guard, the 13th and the 14th, topped the hill above the Roman earthworks. From there, the recently recruited new arrivals from northern Italy could see Belgae tribesmen in the partly built Roman camp. The enemy were looting the baggage train as noncombatants, cavalry, and auxiliaries ran for their lives. They also saw that Caesar and his legions at the bottom of the hill were in big trouble. There was German auxiliary cavalry from the Treveri tribe with the rear guard—Caesar was to say Trever cavalry was the best and most numerous in all of Gaul. These German troopers were convinced all was lost and turned around and galloped away. Days later, when they reached their own capital, Trier, on the Moselle, they reported that Caesar and his army had been wiped out by the Nervii.

On the right, Boduognatus and his closely packed ranks only had eyes for Caesar and his trapped legions. They didn't know anything about the return of the 10th Legion until its leading cohorts plowed into their flank at the charge. The 10th was heavily outnumbered, but despite this, the legion's arrival turned the battle. The men of the 10th fought so fiercely to save Caesar that Plutarch was to say later that they displayed more than human courage this day. Stunned by their savage onslaught, the Nervii were pushed back to the river bank by the 10th, enabling Caesar to regroup the 7th and 12th Legions and lead them to join the 10th.

In the center, the 8th and 11th Legions succeeded in withstanding the attack of the Viromandui, then also pushed them back to the river's edge.

Once the Viromandui broke off and fled, the 8th and the 11th were able to swing over and join the other three legions throwing themselves at the Nervii, who made a brave stand on the bank, fighting from behind mounds of their own dead and refusing to flee. Thousands were felled. A handful escaped and others were made prisoners as the Roman cavalry regrouped and searched the countryside for enemy on the run.

Caesar was to estimate that just five hundred fighting men of the Nervii remained capable of carrying arms following this battle. Later events were to prove this an exaggeration, but there is no doubt that on this day the flower of the Nervii were cut down beside the Sambre. We never hear of Boduognatus again, so presumably he died with many of his men. Three surviving Nervian elders of an original six hundred on the Nervii governing counsel sent envoys to Caesar begging peace, which he agreed to, with lenient conditions.

Meanwhile, the Atuatuci, Belgian neighbors of the Nervii, were marching to their aid when news of their defeat at the Sambre reached them. As the Atuatuci turned around and retreated to a stronghold, probably at Mount Falhize, Caesar sent young General Publius Crassus with the 7th Legion to prevent the tribes on France's Atlantic seaboard from entering the conflict, while he himself marched on the Atuatuci with the 10th and his other legions. After a brief siege the Atuatuci surrendered. Caesar sold fifty-three thousand of them into slavery. Roman settlers from the south would soon spread into captured territory and acquire the homes and farms of defeated tribespeople.

At the same time, on the coast, Crassus and the 7th forced seven Gallic tribes into submission. On receipt of Caesar's dispatches describing his crushing victories in France and Belgium, the Senate at Rome, convinced he had conquered all of Gaul, voted him fifteen straight days of public thanksgiving. As Caesar himself would later point out, no one in Roman history had previously been granted such an honor. But the war in Gaul was not yet at an end.

Over the next three years Caesar would send Crassus and the 7th to conquer Aquitania and would himself destroy the tribes of Brittany, primarily in a naval battle off the coast in which men from his legions acted as marines and successfully boarded and destroyed the ships of the coastal tribes. Over the winter of 56–55 B.C., two German tribes, the Usipetes and the Tenctheri, crossed the Rhine near its mouth in Holland and occupied part of northern Gaul. Caesar, who had been wintering in northern Italy, as was his habit, hurried back into Gaul and marched his legions against the Germans.

After an initial cavalry skirmish, the German leaders came to the Roman camp to discuss a peace, but Caesar broke all the international rules of neutrality by making them his prisoners, an act that brought him much criticism. Plutarch says that Cato the Younger, speaking in the Senate, described the tactic as "madness and folly," and advocated handing Caesar over to the Germans for this breach. Caesar himself never offered a plausible excuse in his own writings. It was an act of expediency, pure and simple, one that enabled him to march his legions to the German camp, eight miles away, and to overrun the leaderless invaders.

Many Germans were killed by Caesar's troops; others were drowned trying to swim back across the Rhine. Plutarch says three hundred thousand died in total. To further awe the Germans, Caesar then had his legions put a wooden bridge across the Rhine, near modern Koblenz. Forty feet wide, according to Caesar it took just ten days to build. He then crossed the Rhine and destroyed German towns and farms east of the river for the next eighteen days, before withdrawing and destroying much of his bridge.

Now, at last, Gaul was quiet. Yet it was still summer. To the west, beyond the Channel ports Caesar had seized along the French coast, lay the largest island then known to the Romans, Britain. Caesar had the troops, he had the time, and he had ships, some provided by new Gallic allies, others captured from the tribes of Brittany the previous year. Now Caesar set plans in motion for a daring amphibious operation.

V

INVADING BRITAIN

There was an eerie silence as the dawn broke over the fleet of ships sailing in close company across the English Channel. With tense expressions, all on board the eighty transports and the dozen warships of their escort strained their eyes to study the foreign land ahead as the white cliffs of Dover began to shine luminously in the new day's light.

They had sailed from France at midnight, putting out with the tide, after a day of good late summer weather. With a southerly wind behind them they'd made excellent progress in the night, passing Cape Gris-Nez, then turning northwest. They were following a course planned in advance for them by young Colonel Gaius Volusenus, who had earlier reconnoitered potential landing sites along the southern coast of England in the frigate that would have now been leading the invasion convoy.

Julius Caesar and his senior officers were spread among the warships of the escort, frigates and cruisers with banks of oars that flashed and dipped in the early morning light to the beat pounded out by the warships' *keleustes*, their timekeepers, with wooden mallets on wooden blocks. On board the transports, locally built craft with relatively flat bottoms, high prows, and sterns and powered by just a single square sail each, were the Spanish legionaries of the 10th and 7th Legions, with an average of 150 men to each troopship.

With just enough vessels at his disposal to carry two legions and several hundred cavalry, it had been a given that one of the legions Caesar would take with him was the 10th. The 7th, four years older than the 10th, with its men aged between twenty-seven and thirty, had won a place in the invasion force after its dominating performances against the Gallic tribes of Brittany and Aquitania over the past few years. The two legions had built an embarkation camp at Boulogne in the Pas de Calais area, and there the preparations for the operation had been made, the equipment

30

readied, the fleet assembled, and the ammunition and supplies brought in for a brief exploratory visit across the Channel. Caesar himself admitted that little could be achieved in the short amount of campaigning time left to him that year, but, as Plutarch was to say, Caesar had a love of honor and a passion for distinction. He was on a high after his latest successes against the Gauls and the Germans, and, driven by a determination to exceed the reputations of rivals living and dead, he was determined to set foot on Britain, to go where no Roman general had gone before.

While Caesar was engaged on his British expedition, the rest of the army wasn't to be idle. He had divided the remainder of the legions into two forces. One, under General Publius Sulpicius Rufus, was guarding the embarkation area around Boulogne. The other, under General Quintus Titurius Sabinus, was marching up the coast to subdue a tribe in Belgium and another in Holland that had yet to send ambassadors and negotiate peace treaties with the Romans.

There was movement along the top of the chalk cliffs to their left as the invasion fleet slid up the coast of Kent, or Cantium, as the Romans dubbed it. Observing the ships from the heights were British tribesmen, cavalry and infantry, fully armed and waiting in their war paint—their exposed upper bodies and grim faces daubed in wild, tattoolike patterns with blue-green woad, a plant dye. The Britons' friends in Gaul had warned them of Roman preparations to cross the Channel, and they had initially sent envoys to Caesar to discuss an alliance with Rome, to forestall an invasion. But when Caesar sent his new ally King Commius of the Atrebates tribe—a man he'd installed as leader of the Atrebates after the Battle of the Sambre—as his ambassador, to continue discussions on his behalf, the Britons had made Commius and the thirty mounted Atrebatian warriors of his escort prisoners. Just as Caesar was really more interested in conquering British tribes on their doorstep than signing treaties with them from afar, the tribes were determined to repel invaders.

At about 9:00 A.M. the Roman fleet dropped anchor off a beach just past the South Foreland, which had been selected for the landing during Colonel Volusenus's earlier reconnaissance mission. But Caesar was far from happy with the site chosen by Volusenus, a narrow beach with high cliffs on either side from which the gathering Britons could send down a hail of missiles against a force trying to land from the sea. Caesar held off giving the order to go ashore, allowing time for all the ships of the convoy to arrive.

In particular he was waiting for his cavalry. The Roman mounted troops assigned to the operation had been sent to the little port of Amble-

teuse, six miles up the coast from Boulogne, where a smaller fleet of eighteen transports had been prepared for them. This second convoy, carrying
the cavalry units, was supposed to leave Ambleteuse at the same time the
infantry set sail. What Caesar didn't know was that the smaller convoy's
departure had been delayed by the late overland arrival of the cavalry
from Boulogne. By the time they'd been loaded with horses, riders, equipment, and feed, these ships missed the tide and were driven back to the
French coast in the darkness. There they remained still, at anchor and
waiting for a fresh tide and a favorable wind.

By the early afternoon, running out of patience with the missing cavalry, Caesar convened a conference of senior officers on board his flagship
to discuss the situation. They were all rowed to his cruiser in their warships' dinghies. There, on the deck, and in sight of the Britons on the
bluffs, Caesar briefed his generals and colonels on the alternative landing
sites previously identified by Colonel Volusenus. Caesar then passed on
his intention to land farther up the coast before nightfall. He tells us that
prior to dismissing them, he gave his commanders a warning: "For this
landing to succeed, my orders—and there are likely to be a number of
them, in rapid succession—will have to be obeyed instantly."

Wind and tide were running with them, and Caesar gave the order to
weigh anchor as soon as the officers had been rowed back to their ships.
It was 3:00 P.M. when the fleet began to move up the coast.

On land, the surprised Britons followed their progress. Then, realizing
the Roman intentions, their war chiefs sent cavalry galloping ahead. And
chariots. With each vehicle containing a seated driver and a standing warrior, a noble of his tribe, and drawn by a pair of horses, these two-wheeled
war machines were nothing like the idealized and historically inaccurate
statue of Boudicca and her Roman-style chariot on London's Thames
Embankment today. The British chariot was an open-ended platform with
low wicker sides. And, contrary to folklore, there were no blades attached
to the wheels. War chariots had ceased to be used in mainland Europe at
least a hundred years earlier, but they were still deployed by armies in
some parts of the East, as Caesar would find at the Battle of Zela in eight
years' time.

The new landing site was a long, flat beach between present-day
Walmer Castle and Deal. The Britons reached it first. As the leading ships
of the fleet came up, cavalry and chariots were galloping along the sands,
the warriors waving their javelins and challenging the invaders. Others
dismounted and came a little way into the water, shaking their javelins
and large rectangular shields and yelling insults. The nobles were better

clothed and equipped. The rank and file were generally lithe little men with mustaches but not beards, and stripped to the waist with their faces and torsos decorated with blue woad designs.

Caesar gave the order for the landing to go ahead, and the transports slid into the shallows and grounded. But because of their draft and heavy loads, the craft were still in relatively deep water. Spanish legionaries going over the sides fully armed with shields and javelins would find themselves up to their chests in water, even up to their necks in some cases, and they didn't like the idea at all. One stumble and they would be fish feed. There were a lot of heads shaking along the low rails of the transports.

Seeing this, Caesar signaled the warships of the escort to also run aground, farther down the beach on the Britons' right flank, from where they could cover the landing with their artillery and the auxiliary archers carried by several cruisers. Without hesitation, the masters of the warships obeyed—the cruisers and frigates slid into shore with their oars raking the surf, and ejecting volleys of arrows.

On the sand, the Britons, who had never seen ships powered by banks of oars before, lost their initial bravado and drew back out of range. This was the moment Caesar had been waiting for, and he gave the order for the legionaries of the 7th and the 10th to go over the side. But still the troops hesitated, looking at the deep water beside them and the rolling surf that could knock them off their feet.

It was now that the *aquilifer* of the 10th Legion, the bearer of its eagle standard, took the step that was to immortalize him, although his name has not come down to us. No more than twenty-seven years of age, he probably first uttered the Legionary's Prayer: "Jupiter Greatest and Best, protect this legion, soldiers all," adding, according to Caesar, "May my act bring good luck to us all." Then he went over the side with the eagle of the 10th.

"Jump in, boys!" he called to his comrades, holding the standard high, "unless you want to surrender our eagle to the enemy. I, for one, intend doing my duty by my homeland and by my general."

The men of the 10th on ships all around him gaped in horror as the *aquilifer* bore their eagle toward the beach. The eagle of the legion, silver at this time, gold by imperial times, was venerated by its legionaries. Kept at an altar in camp with lamps burning throughout the night, it and the ground it stood on were considered sacred. Conveyance and protection of the eagle were the tasks of the men of the 1st Cohort, but it was the obligation of every soldier in the legion to defend it with his life. Roman generals were feted as national heroes for retrieving eagles wrested from legions by the enemy. But the loss itself was never forgotten. It was the greatest dishonor a legion could suffer to have its eagle taken in battle, a stain to the reputation of legion and legionary alike that never went away.

Well did the men of the 10th know there were many instances in Roman history of eagle-bearers and legionaries and centurions giving their lives to save their eagle. And here was this idiot about to make a gift of the eagle of the 10th to the barbarian British! With a roar, affronted men of the 10th went over the side and then splashed through the water, following their crazy-brave eagle-bearer and their hallowed eagle through the surf toward the waiting Britons. Not to be outdone, on seeing the 10th proceeding to land, the men of the 7th Legion went over the side as well.

Legionaries managed to reach the beach without any great difficulty, but because only small groups were coming off the boats in long, thin lines, each group was quickly attacked by the British cavalry on the sands, with the Britons astutely aiming their missiles at the Romans' unprotected right sides. Many legionaries soon lost contact with their individual standards as they tried to keep the Britons at bay. The legionary was taught early in his training that if he couldn't find his own unit's standard in battle, any standard would do in an emergency. But in obeying this ethic now the men of the landing force found confusion, not clarity, bunching here, leaving gaps there.

Realizing that many of the men straggling ashore from each transport stood the risk of being isolated and wiped out, Caesar ordered the small boats of each larger vessel lowered. These were loaded with men who were then landed as ready-action squads wherever legionaries were in trouble. This tactic paid dividends as the reinforced maniples and cohorts were able to regroup in numbers behind their own standards, then drive the Britons back. As the natives began to turn and flee, Caesar cursed his missing cavalry. It was at this point in a battle that the cavalry arm usually followed up the infantry success and chased the enemy for miles. As it was, his legionaries were called back after half a mile or so rather than lose contact with their commanders on the beach.

Just the same, the success of the Roman landing had a humbling effect on the tribesmen. As the landing force began digging in just inland of the beachhead, British envoys came to Caesar, bringing the captive Atrebates king Commius, Caesar's ambassador, and his thirty-man cavalry escort, complete with their horses. The prisoners were all handed over unharmed, with Caesar warmly greeting the young king of the Atrebates. The British envoys now asked for peace. In return, Caesar demanded hostages. Some were handed over immediately, and others from tribes far and wide began to make their way to him.

Four days after Caesar's landing in Kent, the south wind picked up sufficiently for the cavalry to again set sail from Ambleteuse to join their commander in chief. But as the eighteen transports carrying the troopers and their horses slowly approached the Deal area and hove in sight of the Roman troops at the beachhead, a savage storm swept down from the north. Some of the transports were driven back to France, others were pushed down the English coast and forced to stand well out to sea during the night before making their way back to their starting point at Ambleteuse next day. None was sunk, but none reached Caesar either.

The ships of the first convoy fared even worse in the storm. The warships were still drawn up on the sand where they had beached themselves on day one, while the transports lay at anchor off the beach. There was a full moon that night, accompanied by a king tide. Romans had never previously taken note of the fact that particularly high tides accompanied full moons on the Atlantic shore, and no precautions had been taken, with the result that the high tide swamped the warships. Meanwhile, the storm drove the ships at anchor ashore. Some were wrecked on the coast, and all the others sustained often serious damage. Come the morning not a single ship was usable.

Now, all of a sudden, Caesar was cut off, without any long-term supplies or means of getting them from France, let alone transport for a speedy return to France for the winter as planned. Inspired by this, the British chieftains who'd been all for peace and fraternity a few days before put their heads together and decided to renew hostilities against the relatively small Roman force. As Caesar was to later learn, their plan was to starve the legionaries into submission, in the hope that their fate would discourage any future Roman forays onto British shores.

While the men of the 10th Legion concentrated on salvaging the wrecked ships, Caesar sent the 7th Legion out into the fields, which were ripe with British wheat. The 7th Legion's bold and successful commander of the past two years, young General Publius Crassus, had gone back to Rome over the winter of 56–55 B.C. to take up a civil appointment in his father's administration—he was consul for the year, along with Pompey the Great, in 55 B.C. The senior Crassus would travel to the Middle East the following year to take charge in Syria, and young Publius would go with him, becoming deputy commander of the force of seven legions that the elder Crassus was to take into Parthia in 53 B.C., when both father and son were killed at the infamous Battle of Carrhae, one of Rome's most costly defeats, in present-day Turkey. The younger Crassus would die first, leading the advance guard. The Parthians put his severed head on the point of a spear and taunted his father and the rest of the Roman troops with it. Ironically, perhaps, young Crassus's widow, Cornelia, soon married Pompey the Great, becoming his fifth wife. Pompey had been married to Caesar's daughter Julia, but she was to die in childbirth in 54 B.C.

So it was without the guiding hand and brave leadership of popular young General Crassus that the 7th went to Britain, and went in search of wheat this day. The first day of wheat-gathering had gone well, with the legionaries toting numerous sacks full of it back to the beachhead camp. After dawn, the men of the 7th marched back out into the fields. It was a pleasant, sunny late summer's morning as the legionaries marched along, passing small groups of Britons on their way to the camp to do business with the Roman supply officers at the beach. Away in the distance, men, women, and children were working in the fields, tilling the soil, tending their cattle. To the Spanish legionaries this would have been a rural scene reminiscent of home.

A few miles from the camp, and out of sight of it, they came to where they'd been working the previous day, a wheat field spreading to distant woods. Two-thirds of the wheat field had previously been leveled by the 7th, and just one section near the woods remained to be harvested. The men of the legion planted their standards in the ground, did the same with their javelins, leaned their shields against them, and removed their helmets. Then, taking scythes, wicker baskets, and empty sacks with them, they spread out in the rows of wheat stalks, cutting and collecting, chattering and laughing among themselves as they worked, closely supervised by their *optios*—sergeant majors—and centurions, who soon told them to shut up if they became too rowdy.

The legion hadn't been at work many minutes when, out of the blue, javelins began slicing into the ground around the feet of bent and toiling soldiers nearest the woods. Moments later, with terrifying war cries, thousands of Britons came streaming from the trees, brandishing their weapons, and after Roman blood. Legionaries closest to the woods were cut down before they knew what hit them. With centurions bawling orders, the men of the 7th dashed for their weapons. There wasn't time for trumpet calls, no time to form up by squad, century, maniple, or cohort. The Roman troops could only form a rough, disorganized battle line, with stranger beside stranger and each man realizing how much he'd become accustomed to the habits and company of the comrades of his own unit.

The Britons had hidden in the woods all night, knowing the legionaries would return in the morning for the last of the wheat. Now, while their infantry streamed along the perimeter of the wheat field and closed around the men of the 7th like the jaws of a vice, surrounding them, the tribal chieftains signaled to their cavalry and chariots, which had been waiting some distance away. The chariots sped up. Running back and forth along the Roman line, the vehicles were hard-to-hit weapon platforms, with the nobles standing beside the drivers and hurling javelins on each pass. The noise of pounding hooves and drumming wheels would have been deafening, with the legionaries losing count of how many chariots there were—hundreds, maybe thousands. The following year, according to Caesar, the Britons would put four thousand chariots into the field against him.

Sometimes the drivers would run out onto the chariot pole as far as the yoke as the chariots careered along at full speed, then ran back to their driving positions, as quick as lightning, just to awe the men of the 7th, who'd never seen anything like it in their ten years in the Roman army.

The British cavalry charged forward in bands, threw their javelins, then parted to allow the chariots to return in a rehearsed move, sliding through the gaps between the cavalry squadrons. To the legionaries, it would have been almost pretty to watch, had they not been fighting for their lives. Then a new tactic emerged: the chariots wheeled around and halted, the nobles jumped down, ran at the Roman line, and began hacking at the legionary shields with their swords. If the legionaries advanced against them, the nobles ran back to the waiting chariots, which then took off with them, leaving the Roman line disjointed so that the legionaries had to quickly retreat before they were caught out in the open by other chariots waiting close by for just such an opportunity.

There was an air of confidence about the Britons. They had the Romans surrounded in foreign territory and cut off from help. None had been allowed to escape to bring reinforcements. And these much-vaunted legionaries were looking disorganized and afraid. Probably as far as the tribesmen were concerned, the annihilation of the 7th Legion was just a matter of time.

Back at the Roman camp by the beach, Caesar was working in his headquarters tent, the *praetorium*, dictating to his Greek secretaries. Julius Caesar, man of destiny, man in a hurry, never wasted a minute. When traveling to and from Gaul, while carried in a litter he always had one of his secretaries riding with him, taking down his dictation. Sometimes he made part of the journey driving his own chariot, and on these occasions a secretary sat on the floor taking notes as his commander drove and composed at the same time, while a soldier of his bodyguard stood at the back of the chariot with a drawn sword in one hand and holding on for dear life with the other. On the march with his legions, Caesar often rode with a secretary mounted on either side of him, dictating a different piece to each. Occasionally Caesar would dictate to three or four different secretaries at a time. The material might be chapters of his numerous books—he wrote about subjects as varied as astronomy and public speaking, and his famous military memoirs. He even wrote poetry when the mood struck him—on the overland trip to Córdoba from Rome in 61 B.C. he'd passed the three and a half weeks writing a poem titled "The Journey." Then there were his official dispatches, orders to his subordinates, reports to the Senate. And a torrent of private letters to his friends and allies back home. Politics, like soldiering, was in his blood. And because intrigue is the currency of politics, Caesar had invented a secret cipher, known only to his most intimate friends, involving the transposition of letters on the written page. Using this, he was able to safely pass on instructions and advice, to seek favors and to promise them, and so to manipulate affairs at home in his absence without fear of the letters falling into the wrong hands and his plans being uncovered.

One of the nonmilitary projects Caesar was working on in Britain was a scientific study of the length of the days on the island. As a matter of course, his legions were equipped with water clocks to time the three-hour watches in camp, and Caesar had several servants meticulously time the hours of sunlight between dawn and dusk each day using dedicated water clocks. It's likely he was now pacing his tent, dictating a preliminary analysis, comparing the length of the days here to those in various parts of Gaul, when a colonel of the 10th Legion burst in. Stopping in midflow, Caesar would have looked up with an impatient frown, then recognized the colonel as the tribune of the watch, and noted a concerned look on his face.

The colonel would have advised that there was a worrying sight to be seen from the guard towers by the praetorian gate. Caesar would have followed the young colonel out into the main street of the camp, then hurried with him toward the nearby rear gate of the camp, passing off-duty men of the 10th lounging around in front of their tents who would have followed the general's urgent passage with turning heads. At the gate, the ten men of the sentry detail—ten was the standard number of sentries assigned to each camp gate, according to Polybius—can be sure to have stood with their hands on the hilts of their sheathed swords, looking anxious. Caesar and the colonel can be expected to have clambered up a ladder into one of the wooden guard towers on either side of the praetorian gate, the gate that traditionally faced the enemy.

There, legionaries on tower duty would have pointed to the west. As Caesar followed their gaze, he saw, rising above the trees on the still morning air, a massive dust cloud, obviously man-made. The legionaries would have remarked that the boys from the 7th Legion were over there. Caesar didn't have to be told that. He knew well enough which direction the men of the 7th Legion had taken when they set off on their foraging expedition that morning and would have already worked out that the dust cloud must have been raised by the pounding hooves of horses and the churning wheels of chariots.

Turning to the tribune of the watch, Caesar issued a stream of orders. The two guard cohorts were to march with him at once. Two off-duty cohorts were to relieve them, and all the remaining cohorts of the 10th Legion were to be called to arms and sent on his heels.

By the time his servants had strapped on Caesar's armor and equipment, the two guard cohorts would have formed up in their ranks behind their standards in the main street, facing the tribunal, while the rest of the camp was in a commotion of preparation, with men running to answer the call of "To Arms" being trumpeted all around them. Caesar is likely to have addressed them briefly from the tribunal. Looking out over the faces of the twelve hundred waiting men, he would have told them that their comrades of the 7th Legion were in trouble and that they were going to their aid.

The men of the new sentry detail drew back the gate. Orders issued forth from centurions, and the two guard cohorts swung about and marched out the open gateway, like all camp gateways built just wide enough so that ten legionaries could pass through side by side. Caesar led the way. With him marched his personal standard-bearer and his deputies and staff officers. All were on foot because even Caesar's own steed had been sent to Ambleteuse to make the crossing on the ships that had been modified with stalls for equine transport. There was not a single horse in the Roman camp—even the thirty horsemen of King Commius's escort were off searching for fodder.

At Caesar's order, the trumpets of the two guard cohorts would have sounded "Double Time," and the men of the 10th hurried in the direction of the ominous dust cloud in the distance. As they drew closer, they heard the thunder of horses' hooves, the rumble of chariot wheels, and the hollering and yelling of the attacking tribesmen. The distant fields were now empty of the tribespeople who had been innocently going about their business earlier in the day.

When Caesar and the men of the 10th came into view, the 7th Legion was holding its ground, but the ranks were tightly packed and suffering from the rain of missiles coming from the Britons surrounding them. When the tribesmen became aware of the approach of Roman reinforcements, their attack faltered. The tribesmen to the east, fearing an attack in their rear, pulled back, opening the way for Caesar to link up with the 7th. The men of the 7th were now able to regroup behind their correct standards and open up their ranks. Standing in their units with comrades of their own squads once more, they can be expected to have poked fun at each other in their relief to be back among friends, and waited for the next order from their own mean but familiar centurions.

Soon six more cohorts of the 10th came pounding over the horizon. As the two legions formed an extended battle line in their cohorts, Caesar held his position, and the Britons withdrew. When the danger had passed, Caesar marched the legions back to the beachhead. The men of the 7th gratefully regained the safety of their camp, refreshed themselves, and had their wounds seen to. But Caesar was not pleased with them. The 7th had not displayed the fighting qualities he'd come to expect of his best troops.

Several days of torrential rain followed, confining the legionaries to their tents. They kept their arms within reach, expecting to see more of the Britons. They weren't to be disappointed. In this interim, the tribes of southeastern England sent messengers far and wide, telling other tribes how paltry the Roman force was, how easy it would be to destroy the invaders, and how much Roman plunder was the Britons' for the taking—with the result that as soon as the weather cleared, a vast force of British infantry and cavalry converged on Caesar's camp. Roman lookouts gave plenty of warning, time enough for the legions to put on their decorations and helmet crests before they marched out and formed battle lines in front of the camp.

The British infantry immediately charged the Roman front line and were promptly repulsed. Steadily, the legions advanced, driving the Britons back the way they had come. Caesar now had a small cavalry force at his disposal—the squadron of thirty Atrebate troopers who had accompanied King Commius—and he sent them after the fleeing tribesmen. Not only did these mounted men harry the Britons for miles, they also set fire to every one of the numerous Gallic-style timber and thatch farmhouses they found dotted around a wide area of eastern Kent, before returning to camp.

Again the British sent envoys begging for peace. This time Caesar demanded twice as many hostages as before, to be sent to him on the Continent. His naval officers informed him that they had been able to repair all but twelve of the transports damaged in the storm, and every one of the warships had been baled dry. At a squeeze, Caesar could take all his men back to France. With the equinox about to bring infamously stormy weather down from the north, he was ready to go.

Within days the army reembarked and sailed away. The crossing back to Boulogne was uneventful except for the closing stages. A strong wind blew down from the north and separated two of the transports from the rest of the convoy, pushing them farther along the French coast. The three hundred legionaries on board—men from either the 10th Legion or 7th Legion—were able to land without difficulty, but once they were ashore, they were attacked by French warriors of the renegade Morini tribe, who saw them as easy pickings.

Although they were surrounded, the legionaries held their ground and slipped a messenger away to Caesar up the coast. He immediately sent his idle cavalry from Ambleteuse and followed with the remainder of the 7th and 10th Legions. The surrounded legionaries held out for four hours until relief arrived, suffering a few wounded but no fatalities. As soon as the Roman cavalry appeared, the Morini scattered.

So drew to an end the first invasion of Britain. The men of the 10th went into winter camp at Boulogne, suspecting that unfinished business lay across the water for them. And when they heard that just two of the dozens of British tribes who had promised to send Caesar hostages had kept their word, the men of the 10th knew where they would be heading once the next campaigning season arrived.

While Caesar spent the winter on business in northern Italy and the Balkans, the legions back in Gaul weren't idle. They worked industriously through the cold and wet, fulfilling Caesar's instructions to repair his existing ships and to have the maritime tribes build a large number of new ones, many to Caesar's own design. Some of the new craft were flat-bottomed, and all were equipped with oars as well as sails for added maneuverability.

When Caesar arrived back in Brittany in the spring of 54 B.C., he found he now had twenty-eight warships and more than six hundred new transports at his disposal, built from local timber, their sails and tackle brought up from Spain. Combining these with the surviving ships from the previous year's expedition, he had enough vessels to take five fully equipped legions and two thousand cavalry with him on his next jaunt across the Channel. The tribes that had failed to keep their word to him and withheld their hostages were soon to be in for a rude surprise.

The units allocated to the latest amphibious operation were the veteran Spanish legions—the 10th, of course, plus the 7th, 8th, and 9th—as well as the northern Italians of the 12th Legion. Even though it had been raised at the same time and in the same region as the 12th, Caesar didn't have much time for the 11th Legion. According to his staff officer Aulus Hirtius, even several years later he felt the 11th had yet to prove itself. Throughout its career, the 11th Legion would be like a new pair of shoes that you never really take to—they looked the part but were never a comfortable fit. Everything points to the 11th being left behind in France with the newer 13th and 14th Legions during the British operation, under the command of Caesar's deputy General Labienus, to guard the French ports and gather wheat.

From camps along the French coast, a force of some fifty thousand legionaries and auxiliaries headed for the embarkation point that spring. But first Caesar marched his four Spanish legions to Trier in Germany, capital of the Treveri Germans, on the Moselle River. The Treveri were proving troublesome to Caesar, the problem stemming from an internal power struggle. After awing the Germans with the pomp and steel of four veteran legions, he sorted out Trever political matters, then turned around and marched back to the Atlantic coast.

The embarkation point for the latest amphibious operation had been moved several miles up the coast from Boulogne to a place Caesar called Portus Itius, which modern historians believe was probably Wissant. This shortened the Channel crossing for the invasion force, which Caesar reckoned would now be a distance of just thirty miles.

Caesar had to delay the departure for almost four weeks because the prevailing wind from the northwest was against him. When the weather improved and the wind changed, he gave orders for the legions and the cavalry to embark. But while the troops were boarding their ships, one of the Gallic auxiliary leaders, Dumnorix, a noble of the Aedui tribe, deserted with some followers and rode off toward his home in central France, between the Loire and Saône Rivers. Putting the invasion on hold, Caesar sent a large cavalry force after the deserters, determined to make an example of them to keep his other auxiliary troops in line, and the cavalry soon overtook them. When Dumnorix refused to come back and drew his sword, he was cut down. Only once his followers returned to camp did Caesar give the green light for the new British operation to go forward.

It was well into spring by the time the invasion convoy sailed. The first ships of the massive fleet upped anchor at sunset, and with a light southerly breeze behind them made steady progress up the French coast and out into the Channel as the night closed around them. By midnight the wind had dropped away, and come the dawn the current had pushed the leading divisions well up the coast of Kent, past the North Foreland and beyond the previous year's landing zone.

Caesar was determined to land in familiar territory, and his decision to equip all the transports with oars now paid dividends. The legionaries on board the transports willingly manned the oars and pulled the heavily laden craft back down the coast toward present-day Deal, enjoying the fact that they were able to keep pace with the sleek warships of the escort with their trained oarsmen.

At midday, the fleet was off the coast from which Caesar had departed the previous fall. The shore was ominously deserted. Not a soul could be seen from the ships. But the tribesmen were there, skulking up on the hill-tops. Since daybreak they'd been watching the horizon fill with hundreds and hundreds of sails, and been dazzled by the thousands of flashing oars. The previous year the Britons had seen little more than 80 Roman vessels off their shores. Now they were staggered to see 800. As the hours passed, the Dover Strait darkened with brown hulls. Never again would an invasion fleet as large as this come to Britain's shores. The Spanish Armada of 1588 would comprise only a paltry 130 vessels, carrying little more than 19,000 troops. The British tribal leaders were so terrified by the sight of the Roman vessels that they decided to withdraw to higher ground.

Unopposed, the landing went ahead, on a long, sandy stretch of coastline between Deal and Sandwich a little north of the previous year's landing site. Today the greens of a golf course roll along this picturesque stretch of Kent coastline. Even as long lines of legionaries were still wading onto the sands from vessels in the shallows, work began on construction of a camp where fairways now run. At the same time, cavalry patrols fanned out inland. Soon the patrols returned with unwary tribespeople who'd been too slow to run when the troopers unexpectedly appeared in their fields. From the prisoners, Caesar learned that British warriors were massing, and where.

Throughout his career, Julius Caesar made a habit of marching in the early hours of the morning to catch his adversaries off guard, and a little after midnight, leaving his least experienced legion, the 12th, together with three hundred cavalry, to guard the new camp under the command of General Quintus Atrius, Caesar marched into the night with his four Spanish legions and seventeen hundred cavalry. The column covered twelve miles in the darkness, and with the dawn they saw that the Britons had advanced their chariots and cavalry to a river in their path, the Stour, not far from present-day Canterbury.

The surprised Britons quickly withdrew a short distance to higher ground, their chariot drivers showing impressive skill controlling their horses on the slopes at full gallop. As the legions came up, the chariots swept down from the hill. But Caesar had been expecting this, and his cavalry easily intercepted the chariots and drove them off.

The Britons pulled back to a woods, where they took refuge in an old stockade, previously used during intertribal warfare. They rolled massive logs in front of the gateways. Some small bands came out to skirmish with the Roman column as it marched to the woods but soon withdrew. Caesar now chose one of his legions to go against the stockade. He'd been disappointed with the 7th Legion the previous year. To his mind, it had allowed itself to be surrounded in the wheat field, and had to be rescued by him. He now gave the unit an opportunity to redeem itself.

While the 10th, 8th, and 9th Legions stood in battle formation and watched like spectators at a football game, the 7th went to work. Locking their shields over their heads in the *testudo,* or "tortoise" formation, the 7th went forward against British stones and javelins, and under cover of the *testudos* heaped earth against the walls of the stockade to form ramps, an activity that took several hours. They then surged up the ramps in formation and dropped into the stockade. The Britons fled in every direction, with the men of the 7th giving chase through the trees and cutting down all who tried to stand and fight, before Caesar sounded the "Recall." It was now late in the day, and he wanted to build a marching camp for the night. The 7th, which had suffered only a few wounded in the action, was once more the apple of Julius Caesar's eye.

Next morning, he kept one legion at the marching camp—probably the 7th after their exertions of the previous day—and led the other three as he went looking for the enemy. They had been marching for several hours and had caught sight of bands of British warriors in the distance when dispatch riders overtook the column. Caesar called a halt and read a hastily written dispatch from General Atrius back at the beachhead camp. Atrius reported that a severe storm had swept along the coast in the night and many ships of the invasion fleet had broken their cables and been driven into each other or onto the shore. The losses were significant, said Atrius's message. Always careful to secure his rear, Caesar promptly turned his column around and marched back to the coast, picking up the 7th Legion on the way.

On the beach next day, Caesar and his staff officers surveyed the damage. Forty transports were total wrecks. The rest could be repaired, but it would take time, valuable campaigning time. But Julius Caesar was a man who usually got his priorities right, and this occasion was no exception. He gave orders for all the skilled workmen of the legions to dedicate themselves to salvage and repair work. He also sent an undamaged frigate skimming back to France with orders for General Labienus to hastily build new ships to replace those that had been lost.

Toiling around the clock, with oil lamps burning through the night at the repair sites and work teams rostered in shifts, the damaged vessels were all repaired within ten days. The ships were then hauled up onto the beach, all 760 of them, and enclosed on three sides by fortifications extending down to the water's edge from the camp. Satisfied that the fleet would be safe, Caesar again allocated the 12th Legion to guard duty and marched off with the 10th and the three other Spanish legions to take up where he'd left off with the Britons.

During this pause in the offensive, the tribes had spread their alliance north of the River Thames. The Catuvellauni tribe, centered in Hertfordshire and Middlesex just to the north of modern London, was at that time the most powerful tribe in southern England. It had regularly waged war against the tribes south of the Thames in the past, but now it shelved old enmities and joined the British confederation, with the tribe's king, Cassivellaunus, elected as commander in chief of all the tribal forces for the war against the Romans. The wily king formulated a plan to harass the Romans with mixed forces of infantry, cavalry, and chariots, to keep them south of the Thames for as long as possible while he assembled a massive chariot force north of the Thames. If and when the Romans succeeded in crossing the river, the king was determined that they would be in for a shock.

When Caesar marched back to the Stour River with four legions, his scouts reported that the forest stronghold that had been overrun by the 7th Legion two weeks earlier was once more occupied by tribesmen, but in larger numbers than before. British cavalry and chariots attempted to get to the Roman column as it marched up, but yet again they were intercepted by Caesar's cavalry and driven back to the hills and woods.

Reaching the old marching camp used the last time they had come this way, Caesar halted for the day and set the legions to work strengthening the camp's defenses. As they worked, and while the legionaries' guard was down, British cavalry and chariots charged from the nearest woods and swooped on the men on picket duty in front of the camp. Knowing they faced the death penalty if they left their post, the men of the picket stood their ground and put up a furious fight, even though heavily outnumbered.

To support the pickets, Caesar sent out the two guard cohorts on duty—the 1st cohorts of two legions, as it happened—under the tribune of the watch, Colonel Quintus Durus, and sounded "To Arms" throughout the camp. The relief cohorts were soon in deep trouble, as the Britons drove between them and divided them. The tribesmen employed well-organized tactics, probably under the influence of King Cassivellaunus—squadrons of cavalry were held back at the tree line in reserve, and when those in the fray tired or ran out of ammunition, they were replaced by men from the reserve.

It was only when more Roman reinforcements arrived from the camp that the attackers were driven off. Both sides suffered only a few casualties in the skirmish, but one of the Roman fatalities was Colonel Durus, the young watch commander.

The next day, at noon, after their normal lunch of a piece of bread, the men of three legions were led out on a foraging expedition by General Gaius Trebonius, who had come up to Gaul to join Caesar's staff for this campaign after serving as a civil tribune at Rome the previous year. Once the column was well away from the camp, the British chariots and cavalry reappeared, driving into the column and almost reaching the legions' eagles. Trebonius was able to regroup the legionaries, then charged at the run, to the surprise of the charioteers. The Roman cavalry joined in. A number of chariots were overwhelmed, and the rest of the British forces ran for the hills.

The Britons were demoralized after this, seeing the Roman heavy infantry charge and overrun the chariots that many had thought invincible. Men went home to their farms in droves, and organized British resistance faltered.

Caesar now marched four legions to the Thames and followed its southern bank inland until he found a place where he could ford the waterway. The cavalry splashed across, and the infantry waded across, up to their necks in water at times. On the other side, they combined and easily dispersed warriors from Cassivellaunus's tribe who were supposed to be guarding the riverbank.

Appian tells the story that at one point in these operations beside the Thames, where the changing tides both revealed and covered treacherous pathways with frightening speed, Caesar and a group of senior Roman officers became trapped by a small group of Britons in the marshes. A lone legionary, almost certainly a man of Caesar's bodyguard from the 10th Legion, threw himself at the tribesmen and fought them off, allowing the officers to make their way to solid ground. The legionary then took to the water and, partly by swimming and partly by wading, joined the officers. But in the process he had to let go of his shield. As Caesar and his companions came up to him to congratulate him on his deed, the soldier dropped to his knees in front of the general.

"Forgive me, Caesar," said the soldier, close to tears.

"Forgive you?" Caesar responded with surprise. "But why?"

"For losing my shield," the legionary replied with genuine concern. Under legion regulations, he could be severely punished.

Appian doesn't tell us any more, but no such punishment is mentioned. And, if Caesar remained true to form, far from receiving a punishment, the legionary would have been the recipient of substantial rewards at the end of the campaign.

The legions crossed the Thames without further incident, and as Caesar continued north, guided by prisoners who knew where the British king's stronghold was located, Cassivellaunus shadowed the advancing column with a force of four thousand chariots he'd been assembling north of the river—two chariots for every one of Caesar's cavalrymen. Caesar was accustomed to sending his cavalry out on search-and-destroy missions while the infantry marched, but now, whenever the Roman cavalry strayed too far from the column, chariots appeared from the trees in vast numbers and swept in on the outnumbered troopers like hordes of locusts. In the end, Caesar had to keep the cavalry with the infantry.

On the march, envoys arrived from the Trinovantes tribe, old enemies of King Cassivellaunus, who asked for protection against the king. When Caesar granted the tribe the protection they asked for, five other tribes also came to him and surrendered. The Roman force then reached Cassivellaunus's stronghold. This was a densely wooded spot, heavily fortified with an earth wall and trench, thought to have been at Wheathampstead, five miles north of where Cassivellaunus's son and successor would build the settlement the Romans called Verulamium and that would grow into the modern city of St. Albans.

The stronghold was full of warriors and cattle, and Caesar wasted no time sending the legions against it. They attacked from two sides, the ferocity of their assault sending the defenders fleeing over a third wall in terror.

While the main body of the Roman army was capturing Cassivellaunus's stronghold, four tribes in Kent decided to launch an assault on the Roman supply base back on the coast. General Atrius, the rear-echelon commander, quickly sent cohorts of the 12th Legion out to meet the British infantry, and they charged the poorly led locals, who were routed without loss to the 12th Legion. A number of tribesmen were killed, and many, including a chieftain, taken prisoner.

When he heard of this defeat on the coast, and, now deprived of his stronghold, King Cassivellaunus bowed to the inevitable and sent envoys to Caesar for surrender terms. Caesar agreed to peace in return for hostages, an annual payment to Rome, and a guarantee from the king that he wouldn't molest the Trinovantes people.

As soon as the hostages were handed over, Caesar withdrew to the coast. It seems he never intended leaving a permanent Roman presence in Britain. As in Gaul, his intention was to make allies of the locals, if not subjects, without tying his troops down in garrisons. Caesar knew better than anyone that the secret of his legions' success was their mobility.

The damaged ships had all been repaired, but with a large number of prisoners who would be sold into slavery once ferried across the Channel, and because sixty new transports built in France by General Labienus were forced back by adverse winds every time they tried to sail, Caesar sent the troops back to Europe in two waves. He was in the second wave, which sailed as the autumnal equinox approached. After several calm days, he packed his last troops into the ships that had returned for him, and in the late evening they pulled away from the Kent shore with the tide. In their usual fashion, the legions would have left their camp of the past few months afire, so it was of no use to the Britons.

The flames would have offered an eerie farewell to the men of the 10th Legion sailing with Caesar. Looking back to the orange glow on the Kent coast, many of them would have guessed that they would never set foot in Britain again. Caesar had achieved all he'd set out to achieve among the barbarous Britons. Plutarch was to say that prior to this many Greek and Roman historians had even doubted that Britain existed. Caesar had proven otherwise, and in the process had rewritten history. But in his own eyes it was no major achievement. Britain, he felt, had nothing to offer Rome.

The return journey went smoothly and swiftly, with the convoy reaching France with the dawn. Both waves returned to the Pas de Calais without the loss of a single ship. Once they had landed, the 10th Legion and its brother legions marched to various camps in France and Belgium, hoping for a quiet winter.

To let the natives know that the Roman army was back, Caesar dispersed his troops, sending single legions to a variety of locations throughout the region. He was later to excuse his action by saying the wheat harvest that year had been poor and it was necessary to spread the legions far and wide to secure more grain for the winter. But breaking up the army like this was to prove a fatal mistake.

VI

REVOLT AND REVENGE

O n Caesar's orders, Generals Sabinus and Cotta led the 14th Legion and five unidentified cohorts from one or more of the other legions—also from the newer units, it seems—into eastern Belgium. They made camp for the winter of 54–53 B.C. at Atuatuca on the Geer River, northwest of modern Liège. The city of Tongres, oldest in Belgium, would grow on this site. Named Atuatuca Tongrorum, it would be the capital of the Tungri tribe, immigrants from Germany, but at this time the riverside camp built by the fifteen legionary cohorts under General Sabinus was on a virgin site in the territory of the Eburones, a native Belgic tribe.

Within weeks of the legionaries building their fortified camp at Atuatuca, the Eburones rose up under their chief, Ambiorix, determined to rid their homeland of the Romans. Ambiorix allied himself with Germans from across the Rhine, then surrounded and laid siege to the Roman fort with tens of thousands of fighting men. During a truce, Ambiorix offered General Sabinus and his men amnesty if they vacated their position and his territory. Sabinus's deputy, General Cotta, and most of the other Roman officers at Atuatuca argued that they would be going against Caesar's orders if they pulled out. Besides, they didn't trust Ambiorix. But Sabinus, worried that his troops would be starved into submission, decided to accept the Belgian offer. Many of Sabinus's own men had a low opinion of their general, but as the force's commanding general his word was law, and next morning the legionaries marched out of their camp behind him.

Passing through a forest two miles from Atuatuca, the 14th Legion and their accompanying five cohorts walked straight into an ambush. A few hundred men managed to fight their way back to the camp, but most of the others, including Generals Sabinus and Cotta, were surrounded and killed in the ambush, fighting to the last man in an *orbis*, the Roman army's circular formation of last resort. That night, the survivors holding

50

the camp, out of ammunition, out of food, and out of hope, entered into a pact, and every man took his own life. In the forest and in the camp, more than eight thousand legionaries died that day.

This success inspired other tribes throughout the region to rise up and attack the Roman forces stationed in their areas. The legion of General Quintus Cicero, younger brother of the famous orator Cicero, was besieged at its camp near the Sambre River by a force that grew to number sixty thousand men. We don't know which legion it was, but from its stout resistance it sounds like one of the veteran Spanish legions, possibly the 7th. Unlike Sabinus, General Cicero kept his troops behind the walls of their fortified camp.

For more than seven days Cicero and his surrounded legion held out without being able to send a messenger for help, but finally a loyal native of the area managed to get through enemy lines to Caesar, eighty miles away. Caesar immediately sent orders for the three nearest legions to march to Cicero's aid, and set off himself with a cavalry force. The 10th Legion would have been one of the three. General Labienus sent word that tribesmen were massing three miles from his camp and he and his legions didn't dare leave the protection of its walls, so the relief force was reduced to just one legion, possibly the 10th, plus cavalry, a total of seven thousand men.

A messenger galloped back to Cicero with a dispatch from Caesar, written in Greek so the tribesmen couldn't understand it if it fell into the wrong hands. But the courier couldn't get through the enemy. So, pretending to be one of the attackers, he joined their next raid against the Roman camp, and threw a javelin with the message tied to it. The javelin lodged in the woodwork of a Roman guard tower and went unnoticed for another two days before a sentry spotted the message, unfurled it, and took it to General Cicero.

Caesar was to write that the general read the message aloud to his exhausted legionaries: "Caesar is coming with the legions!" he announced. "He tells us to hold on and put on a bold front!"

As Cicero's legionaries cheered with relief, lookouts yelled that they could at that very moment see smoke on the horizon—farm buildings put to the torch by advancing Roman troops.

When they realized that Caesar was approaching, the Belgians gave up the siege and advanced to meet him. With only some five thousand infantrymen and two thousand cavalry, Caesar was significantly outnumbered, so he chose a camp site at the most favorable location he could find and set his men to work furiously constructing trenches and walls of earth

as the enemy advanced on him. Caesar was always thinking, always inno-
vative, and at the camp gates he had his men build walls made of a single
brick's thickness of earth. From the outside, it looked as if the gates were
as solid as the walls, and the tribesmen didn't even bother to attack there,
gates normally being the most heavily defended part of any Roman camp.
Instead, they tried to storm the walls at various places.

With sixty thousand Belgians and their German allies congregated
around the walls, Caesar gave an order. His flag dropped, trumpets sounded.
The apparently solid walls at the gateways suddenly tumbled outward, and
the Roman cavalry charged out into the massed ranks of the enemy. The
results were panic and slaughter. Tribesmen were still running at sundown.

Caesar and the 10th were then able to link up with General Cicero
and his legion. When the besieged legion paraded for their commander
in chief, Caesar saw that nine out of ten legionaries were wounded. He
praised the men, and he praised the centurions and tribunes, for holding
off a much superior force for so long. This was the stuff that legion legends
were made of. Unfortunately, we don't know which legion deserves the
credit for such stout resistance.

Caesar and his generals spent the rest of the winter putting out the fires of
revolt along the Rhine and nearby regions. During the winter, which Caesar spent in Gaul with the legions for the first time because of the volatile
situation, three legions were raised in northern Italy and Switzerland—a
whole new enlistment for the 14th Legion, to replace the cohorts wiped
out in Belgium with General Sabinus, and two brand-new legions, the 15th
and the 16th. Caesar now commanded ten legions, the largest Roman
army in the field at the time.

The campaigning season of 53 B.C. saw Caesar use the large number of
troops at his disposal in a single dominating force that crushed resistance
throughout northern France, Belgium, southern Holland, and those parts
of Germany west of the Rhine, a campaign that culminated in his second
crossing of the Rhine, a brief incursion to frighten off the Seubi tribe,
which had been massing in the region of the Ubii, a tribe allied to Rome.
But his first act was to march to the Geer River to punish the Eburones
for the Sabinus massacre. While he employed a scorched-earth policy
throughout Eburone territory, the new recruits of the 14th and the army's
recovering wounded were left by Caesar with General Cicero in his rear at
the old Atuatuca camp where the predecessors of the new men of the

14th had perished the previous winter. Every living thing was tracked down and either killed or captured by Caesar's army, while the timber buildings of the region attracted flaming Roman torches—every village, every farmhouse in Eburone territory was burned to the ground.

The Atuatuca fort seems to have been ill starred, for, in Caesar's absence, cohorts of new 14th Legion recruits were allowed to go foraging by General Cicero, and they were caught in the open by German cavalry on a raid across the Rhine. Another thousand young legionaries of the 14th died before the detachment made it back to the safety of the camp, and the Germans withdrew back across the Rhine with the legion's baggage animals for spoils.

At the end of the summer, Caesar, potentate of all he surveyed, convened a council of all the Gallic tribes who now submitted to Rome's authority. The tribal leaders gathered at Rheims, capital of the Remi. The culmination of the Gallic Council meeting was the trial of a leader of the Senones tribe accused of instigating the first uprising of the year. Found guilty by his peers, he was whipped, then publicly beheaded.

The legions went into camp for the next winter. But Caesar had learned his lesson after dispersing his units too broadly the previous year. This time two legions went into camp near Trier in Germany, and two in the region of Dijon in central France. The remaining six legions built a massive military camp at Sens, sixty-five miles south of the village of Lutetia on an island in the Seine that would grow into the city of Paris. From there they could strike in any direction, *en masse*, if further trouble were to break out. Inevitably, it did.

Vercingetorix was a young noble of the Arverni tribe in south-central France. In the winter of 53–52 B.C., he was living at the Arverni capital of Gergovia, some four miles south of present day Clermont-Ferrand on a plateau twelve hundred feet above sea level at the northern end of the Auvergne Mountains. A coin issued in 52 B.C. shows Vercingetorix as a handsome man probably in his twenties, with curly hair falling over his ears, and large eyes. He was the son of the late chief of the Arverni who had once tried to rule all the Belgic people of Gaul but who had been put to death by the tribes for his autocratic ways; the tribes of Gaul had a natural dislike of any man who tried to impose his rule on them.

Vercingetorix was unhappy about the Roman occupation of his homeland, and in January of 52 B.C. he was excited by news from the north that the Carnute tribe had risen up and massacred newly arrived Roman settlers at their capital of Orléans. He began talking openly about rebelling against the Romans, but this terrified his uncle and other Arvernian elders, and the young man was ejected from Gergovia.

Over the next few weeks, Vercingetorix went around the villages of the Arverni preaching rebellion and gathering supporters everywhere he went, until he was able to return to Gergovia like a messiah, eject his uncle and the other elders, and claim the leadership of his people. He then sent emissaries to neighboring tribes, urging them to join the Arverni to force the Romans from Gaul. From Paris to the Bay of Biscay, French tribes recently humbled by the legions had been waiting for just such an opportunity to combine against the invading Romans, and they threw their support behind the young man, unanimously electing him the commanding general of their renewed war effort.

Gathering a large force in the mountains, Vercingetorix and his lieutenant Lucterius marched into the territory of neighboring tribes who had previously been for Rome, and soon threatened the Roman province in the south of France, the later Gallia Narbonensis.

Caesar now hurried from his winter quarters in northern Italy and raised a defense force locally in the south of France that he left with Decimus Brutus, one of his future assassins. Then, saying that he would return shortly, so that spies wouldn't guess where he was going, he slipped north along snow-covered roads with just a small cavalry escort and joined the two legions based at Dijon. From there he summoned his eight remaining legions, and once they marched in he left two newest legions, the 15th and 16th, to guard the heavy baggage, then hurried to intercept Vercingetorix's growing army.

To secure his supply lines he laid siege to the Senone town of Montargis, or Vellaunodunum, as the Romans called it. Within two days, the quaking Senones sent out envoys to organize the town's surrender. Leaving General Labienus in charge of the arrangements, Caesar pushed on to Orléans, reaching it after a two-day march. The gates were closed, the walls lined with armed Carnutes. Arriving too late in the day to commence an assault, Caesar made camp, leaving two legions under arms all night. After midnight, the townspeople began to evacuate Orléans, flooding over the bridge that crossed the Loire. With the town gates open, Caesar sent in the two legions on standby. Orléans was quickly taken and ruthlessly plundered.

The legions crossed the Loire and advanced toward Vercingetorix, taking the town of Noviodunum. Vercingetorix's cavalry now approached.

But when Caesar's cavalry engaged it, the Roman troopers were soon in trouble, so Caesar sent in four hundred German mercenary troopers of his bodyguard, whose charge set the French horsemen to flight.

Farther south, Vercingetorix and the other tribal leaders held a council of war, voting to employ a scorched-earth policy, burning the towns and villages in Caesar's path to deny them to the Romans, and to make a stand at Avaricum, modern Bourges, sixty miles southeast of Orléans. Vercingetorix, who'd been against holding the town at first, sent ten thousand of his men to help the forty thousand people of Bourges defend their city. As the gates of Bourges creaked shut and the defenders began to prepare ammunition stockpiles around the town's solid walls, Vercingetorix encamped with his main army eighteen miles away.

Caesar was not long in accepting the invitation to attack Bourges. For three weeks his legions laid siege to the town in incessant winter rain, using their usual siege techniques. Two legions remained on standby during the night and slept during the day, with the remaining legions working in daylight shifts at undermining the town walls and battering the gates, using the shelter of mantlets and siege towers. The defenders weren't idle either. There were a number of copper miners in the town, and they dug tunnels out under the town walls to undermine the siege works.

But ultimately, inevitably, the legions came over the walls one wet night. Just eight hundred people in the town managed to escape to Vercingetorix's camp in the darkness. Tens of thousands more were cut down in the narrow streets of the town.

Delaying his next move to solve a constitutional problem of the loyal Aeduans, Caesar then divided his legions between General Labienus and himself. Of his two best legions, he kept the 10th with him and gave the 7th to Labienus. Then he sent Labienus with the 7th, 12th, 15th, and 16th Legions to sort out the rebellious tribes in the Paris area while he swung south with six legions and marched on Vercingetorix's mountain capital, Gergovia, following the Allier River, the Roman Elaver, south. Seeing this, Vercingetorix set off at forced-march pace down the opposite bank, determined to reach Gergovia first.

Both sides climbed up onto the plateau and reached Gergovia at much the same time after a march of five days, but Vercingetorix arrived just ahead of the Romans. With the town on a mountaintop and difficult to besiege, Caesar tried to cut off its access and water supply, lodging his legions in two camps in the hills, connecting the camps using an extensive double trench system.

Meanwhile, Vercingetorix's agents had brought the Aeduan tribe over to the Gallic cause with a combination of rhetoric, threats, and gold. With spring just around the corner, a force of ten thousand Aeduans was assembled, armed, and marched down to the Auvergne Mountains. Officially they were coming to reinforce Caesar's legions, but in reality they intended to attack the Romans from the rear. Caesar's famous luck held, because word of the double-cross plan reached him via loyal Aeduans.

Caesar then took the 10th and three other legions and marched twenty-four miles in a day and confronted the Aeduans on the road to Gergovia. At the sight of the legions appearing unexpectedly in front of them, the young Gallic soldiers promptly threw down their arms and surrendered. Caesar not only spared them all, he added them to his force. Giving his troops just three hours' rest, Caesar then turned around and headed back toward Gergovia.

Twelve miles from the town, Caesar was met in the darkness by Roman cavalry bearing news that the two legions left behind outside Gergovia had been under heavy attack from tens of thousands of Vercingetorix's troops ever since Caesar had departed with the bulk of the army, and they'd only just managed to keep the enemy out of their camp. Pounding on through the night, Caesar brought his four legions back to Gergovia a little before dawn, after marching forty-eight miles in a day and a night. Whether his legionaries had been in the camp or on the march, they'd had a rough day.

Caesar then initiated a complicated operation that he later claimed had only limited objectives. He put helmets on his noncombatant mule drivers, then put the mule drivers on his thousands of pack animals and sent them, looking like cavalry, marching off with the 13th Legion as a feint attack on one flank. The plan worked beautifully. Enemy troops were drawn away to cover this force, and Caesar was able to launch an attack on the enemy camps outside Gergovia. Three camps were overrun.

But, according to Caesar, only the 10th Legion then obeyed the "Recall" command. The other legions surged all the way to the walls of the town, led by the men of the 8th Legion. The enemy troops who had been drawn off now rushed back to Gergovia, and there was frantic fighting outside the town walls. A centurion of the 8th and several of his men even succeeded in mounting one of the walls before they were cut down. When Caesar sent the ten thousand Aeduans to the aid of his men trapped by the town, the struggling legionaries mistook them for the enemy. Many panicked, and most began to give ground. Appian was to claim that an entire legion was wiped out here, but Caesar gives an unusually credible on-the-spot accounting in which his legions, principally the 8th, lost more than seven hundred men, including forty-six centurions, before being forced to withdraw.

The victorious tribesmen surged after the retreating legionaries, but the day was saved by the 10th Legion, which Caesar had formed up on a rise in the path of the retreat. The 10th held its ground, and, personally led by Caesar, stopped the advancing enemy in their tracks. Retreating legionaries also joined their stand, and eventually the tribesmen withdrew back to Gergovia, taking numerous captured legion standards with them.

An indication of how desperate the fighting outside Gergovia was comes from a story told by Plutarch. In his day, at the end of the first century, the Averni people showed all comers a sword hanging in one of their temples. It was Julius Caesar's sword, they said, lost by him during the Battle of Gergovia. From other sources Plutarch learned that Caesar was himself shown the sword in the temple at Gergovia several years after the battle, and his officers urged him to reclaim it. But he only smiled and told them to leave it where it was. It was now consecrated, he said.

For the first time in his career, Caesar had suffered a military reverse. Abandoning the siege of Gergovia, he marched his bloodied legions down from the mountains. This gave the rebel tribes great heart, as did the news that General Labienus and his legions had been forced to withdraw from the Seine River after heavy fighting around Lutetia, capital of the Parisii tribe, which occupied the island in the middle of the river where Notre Dame Cathedral stands today. Labienus and his legions had won a major battle beside the Seine, only to have to retreat when tribes massing in their rear threatened to cut them off.

With both Roman armies in retreat, new supporters flocked to the rebel cause in their thousands. As Caesar was rejoined by General Labienus and marched south, Vercingetorix boasted to other Gallic leaders that the Roman commander was abandoning Gaul. Full of confidence, Vercingetorix sent his cavalry against the Roman army on the march, but they were routed by Caesar's cavalry, which had been bolstered by a number of newly arrived German troopers, mercenaries recruited from across the Rhine by Caesar. Not only did the Gauls suffer heavy losses, but several Gallic commanders were taken prisoner as well.

Stung by this, and rather than meet Caesar's legions in the field, Vercingetorix concentrated eighty thousand men at Alesia, modern Alise Saint Reine, on the plateau of Mont Auxois, thirty miles northwest of Dijon. The town of Alesia was then a fortified hilltop stronghold of the Mandubii tribe. On a plateau between the Ose and the Brenne Rivers, it offered a formidable natural defensive position. Caesar wasted no time in swinging his legions around and following Vercingetorix to Alesia. There, Caesar surrounded the hill. The siege that followed became one of the most famous in history.

Caesar's ten legions dug entrenchments around Alesia with a circumference of ten miles and dotted with twenty-three forts. As it became obvious that Vercingetorix was preparing to hold out for some time, Caesar built a second outer line of trenches, walls, and towers, extending for fourteen miles, to defend against attack from any relieving force from the outside. He had now trapped Vercingetorix and his army on the hilltop and sealed his own outnumbered force in around the hill. Vercingetorix's cavalry soon attempted to break out, but in a battle on the plain below Alesia, it suffered heavy losses. In the night, some eight thousand of Vercingetorix's cavalry did finally manage to break out, and galloped off to bring help.

Alerted to Vercingetorix's plight, other tribes now assembled a massive relief column in central France between the Loire and the Saône Rivers. Caesar reckoned they numbered 80,000 cavalry and 250,000 infantry. Knowing his talent for inflation of enemy casualty figures, these numbers are probably overstated to make him look good, but there can be no doubt the army that now marched south was very large indeed, certainly more than 100,000 strong. Among the Gallic commanders marching down to the relief of Alesia was Commius, the man Caesar had made king of the Atrebates. Caesar's onetime ally and envoy during the invasions of Britain had caught the infectious spirit of liberation. Caesar himself had a force in the region of 50,000 legionaries plus large numbers of auxiliary cavalry and infantry. Even so, all told his army wouldn't have exceeded 80,000 men.

When the Gallic relief force arrived at Alesia, its initial attempts to storm the walls of the outer defensive ring were beaten off by Caesar's troops. Then, when 60,000 picked Gauls launched an attack from Mount Rea, Vercingetorix attempted a coordinated attack from the inside at the same time, sending men pouring out of Alesia against Caesar's inner entrenchments.

With Caesar's troops strung out at the forts around the siege works, this two-way attack should have succeeded, but it didn't. Caesar's deputies commanded coolly and intelligently—Generals Labienus, Brutus, Fabius, and a recently arrived colonel, Mark Antony, all playing their part. Caesar describes his troop movements during this final battle in terms of his generals and cohorts, never telling us which of his ten legions did what. In fact, the forces thrown into the breaches were eclectic, with six detached cohorts here going into action, eleven mixed cohorts there, and so on.

As the battle raged, the astute General Labienus sent Caesar a message, urging him to go onto the offensive. The time was right, he said, pointing out where the enemy line was weakest. Caesar seems to have trusted Labienus's judgment implicitly; a number of subordinate generals had come and gone over the past six years, but he had retained Labienus, for his skill and his loyalty. Caesar accepted Labienus's advice, and he himself led the subsequent counterattack. By his own account, his troops and those of the other side were able to identify him by his flowing *paludamentum*, the scarlet general's cloak, in the forefront of the charge.

Following Caesar's lead, Roman cavalry and infantry broke out of the ring then swung about and attacked the rear of the relief force. Carnage ensued. The surprised troops of the Gallic relief force broke and ran. Roman cavalry mowed them down in their thousands and captured many more. Caesar's troopers were still chasing escaping tribesmen after midnight. Witnessing the rout, and seeing the futility of continuing to assault Caesar's fortifications from within, Vercingetorix's men disconsolately withdrew back up the hill to Alesia.

Tens of thousands of prisoners were taken by the Romans—possibly as many as seventy thousand—enough, Caesar claimed, for him to give every single legionary in his force one prisoner each as a slave. He restored another twenty thousand prisoners to their two tribes in exchange for their submission.

With the relief force dispersed and its survivors scurrying home, the men on the hill knew their fate was sealed. Rather than die of starvation, they surrendered. Caesar ordered them to lay down their arms and for their leaders to be brought to him, then seated himself in front of his fortifications for the surrender ceremony. Young Vercingetorix himself came to submit to Caesar. First putting on his richest armor and adorning his favorite horse with golden trappings, the commander of the Gauls rode out the gate of Alesia alone and came down to Caesar's camp, where the men of the 10th and the other legions were lined up in their cohorts, standing as still as statues behind their standards, wearing their plumes and decorations. Only their eyes would have moved as the leader of the Gauls came trotting into their midst.

At the head of the 10th Legion stood Centurion Gaius Crastinus. Not only had he survived all the campaigns since the repulse of the Helvetii, seemingly so long before, but he had been steadily promoted through the grades of centurion, until, almost certainly during the British campaigns, he had been promoted to join the first-rank centurions, the handful of *primi ordines* of the legion's 1st Cohort. And everything points to Caesar personally appointing Crastinus *primus pilus* of the 10th Legion following the tough battle outside Gergovia a few months back. Literally meaning "first spear," this was the post of chief centurion of the legion. With just three years to go before he was due to retire, Chief Centurion Crastinus, now in his early thirties, had risen to the most powerful, most prestigious, most sought-after, and highest-paid rank an ordinary enlisted man could achieve at that time, roughly equivalent in authority to a present-day army captain, but without the status of the modern commissioned officer.

Now, Chief Centurion Crastinus and his men watched in silence—proud, triumphant, and no doubt a little intrigued to see their notorious adversary in the flesh for the first time. On his magnificent charger, the young Gaul completed a full circle of the seated Caesar, then brought his steed to a halt. He dismounted, handed the reins to a Roman groom, then walked to where Julius Caesar sat on a campaign chair in his armor and scarlet cloak. The Roman general was flanked by twelve lictors bearing his fasces of office, the rods and axes, and accompanied by his deputy commanders and staff officers, all standing, as his consular standard probably wafted a little in the breeze behind him.

Without a word, Vercingetorix removed his sword belt and handed it to Caesar. Caesar accepted the sword, then passed it to one of his staff. Vercingetorix removed his helmet, with its distinctive Gallic crest, and passed it over. Then his armor, richly decorated with gold and silver—attendants helped him out of it, and then this, too, he presented to Caesar, who in turn passed it to subordinates. Then Vercingetorix sat himself at Caesar's feet. There, in silence, he watched as his hungry, dejected troops came out of Alesia in a long stream with heads hung low, and piled their weapons and armor before the conquering Romans and were then led away into slavery. Finally, Vercingetorix, too, was bound with chains and taken away.

Kept a prisoner for six years, Vercingetorix would be exhibited at Caesar's Triumph at Rome in 46 B.C., lashed, and then executed in the time-honored manner, garroted behind prison walls in the northwestern corner of the Forum, as the culmination of the triumphal parade through the city's streets.

Other leaders of the uprising had mixed fates. The turncoat King Commius of the Atrebates escaped to the north, but many of his fellow leaders were either executed or submitted themselves and their tribes to Caesar. Some Caesar treated better than others. All were required to offer up hostages to ensure their good behavior in the future, and to provide auxiliaries for the conquering army. These young men from the tribes of Gaul would become the backbone of the auxiliary arm of the Roman armed forces in the decades and centuries to come.

The 10th and Caesar's nine other legions went into camp in Gaul for the winter of 52–51 B.C.. But the Gallic War was not yet over. Some tribesmen needed to be convinced they were beaten. With the defeat in the south, the tribes of the north decided that instead of massing against Caesar, as Vercingetorix had, they should attack his forces at a number of places at once. Guerrilla warfare.

In late December, when Caesar received intelligence at his headquarters at Bibracte, on Mount Beuvray, twelve miles west of Autun, that the Bituriges tribe of Bourges in west-central France was reassembling to launch raids on his forces, he set out on December 29 with the nearest available legions, the 11th and 13th, and in a forty-day campaign took the Bituriges by surprise and ended all thoughts they had of continued resistance. As he returned to Bibracte, in lieu of booty Caesar promised the men of these two legions two thousand sesterces each—almost three months' pay—and two hundred sesterces to each centurion. We never hear whether the promise was kept.

Caesar had been back at headquarters just eighteen days when trouble flared again with the Carnutes, neighbors of the Bituriges. This time he marched with the 14th Legion and a newly arrived legion that had been camped with it, the 6th. The 6th Legion was another Spanish legion raised by Pompey the Great back in 65 B.C. along with the 4th, 5th, 7th, 8th, and 9th. It had operated in eastern Spain all these years while its brother legions had been serving under Caesar. Although he remained at Rome, Pompey had made a deal with Caesar and the elder Crassus, forming what historians later were to call the First Triumvirate, which had carved up the empire, extending Caesar's command in Gaul, giving Crassus command in the East, and Pompey control in Italy and Spain. Caesar asked Pompey for reinforcements in 52 B.C., when the Vercingetorix Revolt blew up and fully stretched his resources. Pompey promptly sent him the 6th, which in 52 B.C. marched up over the Pyrenees and into France from its base in Nearer Spain.

The 6th was a veteran legion, well trained, highly experienced, and, in theory, as good as the 10th or any other in Caesar's army. But Caesar, who was to show a tendency toward pettiness at times, had relegated the newly arrived 6th to guarding baggage trains and harvesting wheat with the understrength and, to Caesar's mind, unreliable 14th Legion, for no reason other than that the 6th was one of Pompey's legions. Caesar only called on it now because the 6th and the14th were the closest units to the latest hot spot. The two legions quickly marched north through appalling winter weather and occupied Orléans, the Carnute capital, as the Carnutes themselves fled in all directions.

Almost immediately, Caesar had more trouble to contend with—news arrived that King Commius had brought together several tribes in eastern France to continue the resistance against Rome. With the 10th Legion the farthest from the trouble, Caesar this time called out the 7th, 8th, and 9th, added the 11th to the task force, and marched against six rebellious tribes gathering to the east.

It was still only February, the weather was icily cold, and the ground wet and difficult to travel, as the three Spanish legions spread out on a broad front and advanced side by side across the French countryside. Behind came the baggage train, with the 11th Legion bringing up the rear. When he found the congregating tribes camped on a hill above marshy ground, Caesar had his legions build a fortress opposite the Gallic camp. His effort was unusually elaborate—its towers were three floors tall, with galleries linking one to the other so there were defenders on two levels. Caesar says this was to make the Gauls think he was afraid of them, but it's just as likely he was only flexing his engineering muscles after they had won him the battle at Alesia.

For days, skirmishes went on outside the camps between foraging parties. Caesar held off assaulting the Gallic camp because he had sent a dispatch to General Trebonius to join him with three legions, which were wintering farther south. When the tribes heard that another Roman army was on the way, they sent away their women, children, and old people and prepared for an all-out battle. In a frenzy of construction activity, Caesar built causeways to higher ground and threw up a new camp. Commius then created a wall of flames in front of his camp one night, and, screened by this, his troops hastily withdrew to a new position ten miles away.

A Gallic cavalry ambush was soon after turned around by Caesar, who had been forewarned of it, and even before the legions could arrive on the scene, the Roman cavalry and auxiliaries had killed thousands of tribesmen. Shaken by this, the tribes now sent envoys asking to surrender. Again Commius escaped, first to Germany, and later to Britain, where he apparently ended his days.

Now the 10th and its fellow legions spent the rest of the year mopping up the final resistance—like stamping out the last flickerings of flame at the edge of a smothered brush fire.

Recalcitrant tribes in the west and southwest were now punished. In the southwest, Caesar successfully besieged the town of Uxellodenum, near modern Vayrac. After it fell, tired of all these little revolutions springing up when his command in Gaul only had one summer left to run, he had the hands of every captured defender sliced off, as a warning to the rest of Gaul. In the north, General Labienus led a large cavalry force of several thousand troopers, who ended opposition from Treveri Germans around Trier.

With the Gallic War finally brought to a conclusion, the 10th and the other legions were quartered in northern France and Belgium for the winter of 51–50 B.C. The new year, 50 B.C., saw peace in Gaul for the first time in many years, peace that allowed Caesar to return to Italy to concentrate on political matters. For the men of the 10th, it was a year without fighting, a year without profit. After so many seasons full of action, many of them were probably bored to tears by the inactivity.

For their senior centurions—men such as Gaius Crastinus, who'd been enlisted back in 65 B.C.—it was a time to plan what they were going to do with their lives once their sixteen-year enlistments expired and their discharge fell due in the new year. For the younger centurions, men of the 61 B.C. enlistment, it was a time to jockey for the positions that would soon be left vacant by the senior men leaving the legion.

What would retirement bring Centurion Crastinus? He would have saved a tidy sum over the years, from his pay, from bonuses paid by Caesar after one campaign and another, from the profits on booty taken from enemy towns, camps, and men he had killed in battle, from the sale of slaves, from furlough fees that enlisted men paid to their centurions to exempt them from duty in camp. He might buy a farm back in Spain, perhaps a tavern. Nothing too shoddy. He was a chief centurion, after all, and that would rank him highly among the working class when he returned to civilian life. He could expect a place of honor in festival day religious processions in whatever place he settled. The highly status-conscious Romans had a saying, "Eagles don't catch flies," and Centurion Crastinus certainly would have felt that applied to him.

It's a safe bet that like most old soldiers, he would miss the occasional good fight. But most of all he'd miss his comrades. He wouldn't miss arrogant young tribunes, fresh from Rome, so wet behind the ears, so stupid they didn't even have the brains to know they were stupid. And generals

whose hands he and his fellow centurions had to hold in the field, fools
who didn't know their ass from their elbow—he wouldn't miss them.

Crastinus would have heard the talk circulating around the legion
camp that fall about the looming possibility of a civil war. Caesar was
being denied his just deserts by the Senate, the men would have been saying. It was all Pompey's doing, they would have said, blaming Pompey for
being jealous of a gifted rival such as Caesar. But Crastinus would probably would not have relished thoughts of Roman fighting Roman. His
father's generation had gone through a civil war, when Caesar was still
only a youth, and too many good men had died for no good end in that
war. Crastinus was probably looking forward to a long life, to dying in his
own bed without a troubled conscience and with his sixty-year-old children gathered around him. And as they spoke of life in retirement, one of
his first-rank centurion friends would have reminded him, with a wink, of
another saying of the time: "Don't make your physician your heir, and
you're sure to live to a ripe old age."

VII

ENEMY OF THE STATE

A s the winter of 50–49 B.C. descended on Europe and his troops in Gaul were generally thought to be going into into winter quarters, Julius Caesar returned to northern Italy from Gaul by way of the Alps. Accompanied by the five thousand legionaries of the 13th Legion stationed in Cisalpine Gaul and his now normal escort of three hundred tall, menacing German auxiliary cavalrymen, he arrived unannounced at the naval base at Ravenna, in northeastern Italy, which was at the southern boundary of his allotted area of responsibility.

The choice of the 13th Legion for this mission had been almost accidental. A couple of years earlier, Caesar had based the 15th Legion in Cisalpine Gaul at the urgent request of its citizens, after bandits had crossed the Alps in his rear and raided the city of Trieste. Then, in 50 B.C., a strange thing happened. Caesar received an instruction from the Senate to hand over one of his legions, to take part in a punitive operation in the Middle East against the Parthians, who had wiped out Crassus, father and son, and their legions, at the Battle of Carrhae in Turkey. Pompey also had been required to hand over a legion for the operation, and as Caesar hesitated, suspecting some plot behind the order, Pompey had allocated the one legion he'd maintained under arms in Italy, the 1st—personally raised by him, and to Pompey what the 10th was to Caesar.

Prompted by this, Caesar decided to hand over the 15th Legion to the Senate, and sent it back to Rome in wary compliance of the Senate's order. Then the Senate suddenly canceled the Parthian plan. It then not only gave Pompey back his 1st Legion, it also gave the 15th over to his command. Both were now in camp in the Puglia region, Roman Apulia, south of Rome. A roundabout way of depriving Caesar of one of his legions and an act that was out of character for Pompey, the scheme had probably been hatched by several of his small-minded supporters just to peeve Caesar. And they succeeded in their objective: Caesar had been incensed by the whole affair.

To replace the 15th on garrison duty in northern Italy, Caesar had pulled the 13th out of central Gaul in 50 B.C., so that this was the legion he picked up as he proceeded down to Ravenna. There, in the fourth week of December, with the legion camped outside the city, Caesar conferred with a tribune of the Plebians—a civil, not military post—one Gaius Scribonius Curio. In his thirties, Curio had been one of his supporters in the Senate ever since Caesar paid off his substantial debts. Curio, a handy man to have in your pocket as the civil tribunes had the power of veto over votes in the Senate, had come galloping up from Rome for the clandestine meeting. Caesar sent Curio scurrying back to the capital. Appian says he covered 270 miles in three days of hard riding. He arrived back at Rome with a written ultimatum from Caesar for the senators, some of whom had been angling to remove him from command in Gaul now that his term of office was due to expire. Caesar said he would give up his army if Pompey gave up his. If not, Caesar would advance into Italy and, in his own words, "Bring succor to my homeland and myself."

It wasn't as if Pompey had been acting like a tyrant. Pompey was much admired, even loved by many of the people of Rome. Certainly he'd used every trick in the book, including strong-arm tactics, to achieve his political ends in the past, but he had mellowed with age, and now the famous general was a benevolent power broker who was as responsible as any man for Rome's preeminent place in the world. Without Pompey's support, Caesar would never have maintained his governorship of Gaul for these past nine years. But Pompey stood in Caesar's way. After years of sharing the empire with Pompey, and with the conquest of Gaul all tied up, Caesar had his eye on bigger things. He wasn't satisfied with just a slice of the cake, he wanted the whole thing. Deny a strong man his due, and he will take all he can get—so, a hundred years later, would write the poet Lucan in his *Civil War*, admirably describing the motivation of Julius Caesar.

In Caesar's path stood a Senate whose members were substantially against him and loyal to Pompey. A Senate that was stunned by the ultimatum delivered to it by Gaius Curio on January 1, 49 B.C. Many senators considered Caesar's "offer" a declaration of war. Despite the protests of Curio and another tribune of the Plebs loyal to Caesar, his friend Mark Antony, and led by the influential, impartial, and respected Marcus Porcius Cato, Cato the Younger, the Senate of Rome now put its support solidly behind Pompey. It appointed him Rome's military commander in chief, voting him the powers necessary to mobilize an army of 130,000 men. And it declared Julius Caesar an enemy of the state.

Julius Caesar stood beside the stream in the darkness, looking pensively into the rippling waters as the first rays of the new dawn pierced the eastern sky. This was the Rubicon River, an otherwise insignificant waterway in eastern Italy that marked the boundary between the province of Cisalpine Gaul and Italy.

The day before, January 10, Caesar had secretly sent a commando force across the Rubicon. According to Plutarch, and apparently on the authority of the written account of Caesar's staff officer Gaius Asinius Pollio, this force was commanded by Colonel Quintus Hortensius. Made up of tribunes, centurions, and picked men of the 13th Legion, the small force had entered Italy with farmers' cloaks disguising their military uniforms and hiding the swords on their hips, and the men had spent the night at the nearest major town, the port of Rimini, or Ariminum as the Romans called it, a little way farther down the coast. That same night, having watched gladiators in training during the afternoon, Caesar had dined at Ravenna with his staff officers.

His companions were men such as the thirty-six-year-old Sallust, who'd recently fled to Caesar after being expelled from the Senate for immorality and who would prove a poor soldier, only to become famous as a writer of influential style. And the blindly loyal Hirtius, who'd recently acted as Caesar's envoy to Pompey and who would later edit his chief's writings. There was Oppius, who'd served with Caesar through much of the Gallic campaign and who would later produce vitriolic works about Caesar's foes. Then there was the Spaniard Lucius Balbus, nephew of his former chief of staff of the same name. And Sulpicius Rufus, whom Caesar would make a general the following year.

Caesar was a solitary man. He knew his own mind, and while he accepted counsel, he never needed it. And, essentially, he trusted few men. About to undertake the greatest venture of his life, Julius Caesar confided his plans only to those who needed to know. Shortly after dusk, with the lie that he was not feeling well and intended getting an early night, he had left the others at dinner, and then, swathed in an ordinary cloak, departed the dining hall.

Waiting for him outside was a small, covered, two-wheeled carriage hitched to two horses. Caesar took his seat in the carriage, and the driver urged his horses into action. So he wouldn't attract attention he first drove west, before pointing his horses down the road to the south, toward Italy proper. According to Suetonius, the carriage became lost for a time in the night. Appian makes no mention of this, telling us only that the carriage linked up with the three hundred German cavalrymen of Caesar's personal bodyguard, who were waiting down the road for him as per his confidential orders.

The cavalry was under the command of twenty-eight-year-old Colonel Gaius Pollio. Appian tells us the troopers then trailed Caesar at a distance as the carriage bumped through the night toward the Rubicon, holding back so no one would link the shadowy occupant of the carriage with the military column and raise the alarm south of the Rubicon that Julius Caesar was heading for the Italian border with his troops.

Despite his promises to the 10th years before that he would make the legion his bodyguard, Caesar had instead come to use big, bearded, physically daunting, and highly mobile Trever and Batavian cavalrymen from the Rhine in that role. They were mercenaries in every sense of the word. While Caesar paid them well, they remained faithful—not to his army, not to Rome, but to Caesar personally—and they would serve him loyally throughout his career. Even when his legions turned against him, he would always be able to count on these troopers from the Rhine. Now, in the early hours of January 11, the Germans waited quietly in the saddle behind him as Caesar stood on the riverbank by a small bridge with the sun beginning to rise out over the Adriatic.

As usual, Caesar had planned this operation down to the last detail. Sealed orders had been sent to his commanders. Two legions that had crossed the Alps and spent the winter in the west of Cisalpine Gaul, the 12th and the 8th, had been ordered to strike camp and join him in Italy. Caesar's deputy, General Titus Labienus, encamped near the Rhine with his main cavalry force, made up of thirty-seven hundred German and Gallic troopers, was also to move out, bringing the bulk of his cavalry down over the Alps to link up with him as he marched on Rome. Caesar's six remaining legions, the 7th, 9th, 10th, 11th, 14th and 16th, which had been camped in Belgium and northern France for the past year, had been brought down into central and southern France with six hundred of Labienus's cavalrymen for the winter. Three of those legions, including the 10th, had based themselves in and around Narbonne, on France's Mediterranean coast, under General Gaius Fabius. From there they could stand in the way of Pompey's six legions based in Spain and prevent them from reaching Italy in support of their commander, while being in a position to reinforce Caesar in Italy if he found the going a little hot.

Many authors have suggested that this pause on the northern bank of the Rubicon in the predawn darkness was to allow Caesar to reflect on the grave act he had in mind before he took an irretrievable step. It's just as likely he was doing no more than waiting for daylight. Caesar, the blinkered pragmatist, had planned this move for many months in advance. He knew that once lost, opportunity, like virginity, can never be regained.

In full armor, helmet, and scarlet general's cloak now—there was no longer any need to disguise himself—Caesar walked to where Colonel Pollio waited with a horse for his commander. The first of Caesar's reinforcements, the men of the 12th Legion, were only several days march away, with the 8th not far behind. Any other general would have waited for them to arrive so that he entered Italy with at least three legions. But not Caesar. Two thousand years later, in 1944, American general George S. Patton would tell U.S. troops gathered in southern England for the invasion of Europe that his motto was "Audacity, audacity, always audacity." The same motto could have been applied to Julius Caesar.

Curio would have informed him that already at Rome it was common knowledge that Caesar's legions were on the move, and that everyone expected him to wait north of the Rubicon until he was joined by his entire army, and from that position of strength threaten his opponents at Rome. In December, when asked what precautions he had taken against an invasion of Italy by Caesar, Pompey had declared that he had ten legions ready. In fact, the only legions he had under arms in Italy were the 1st and the 15th, plus muster rolls to fill another eight with draftees and veterans eligible for recall from retirement. As was to become clear, Pompey never imagined that Caesar would be as adventurous as to go to war with his own country.

So Caesar knew that ahead of him Pompey could field only two experienced legions. Caesar was probably counting on the 15th, a legion he'd raised and trained and that he'd commanded for three of the past four years, coming over to him. He had no fears of any hastily raised, untrained levies Pompey might throw in his path—they could be expected to run at the first charge from his cavalry, in which case he only had the professionals of Pompey's elite 1st Legion to worry about. With the 13th, his cavalry, and possibly bolstered by the 15th, if he could turn it, he figured he didn't have to wait for reinforcements. He could get away with invading Italy with just the one legion.

Colonel Pollio was to write in his *History of the Civil War*, quoted by Appian and Plutarch, that as Caesar mounted up, he heard him make a remark, half to himself, in Greek. There are varying accounts of his actual words. Some suggest he said: "The die is cast." Appian is one of those who reports that Caesar actually repeated a proverb of the time: "Let the die be cast." Either way, it's clear that Julius Caesar had now consigned his future into the hands of the Fates.

With Caesar and Colonel Pollio leading the way and Caesar's personal standard flying proudly from the horse coming along behind him, the German cavalry clattered over the bridge spanning the Rubicon and entered Italy. With this act, Julius Caesar violated the Cornelia Majestatis Law, which made it illegal for a general to lead troops out of the province to which he had been assigned by the Roman Senate. In doing so he was considered to have committed an act of war against the Senate and the people of Rome. There was no turning back from here.

The mounted column pounded down the Aemilian Way to Rimini in the early morning light, and as it approached the main gateway, Colonel Hortensius and the men of the 13th Legion's commando party were ready and waiting inside the city and opened the gates to them. Caesar and his troopers entered the city and took control of it before anyone in Rimini knew what was happening. A courier then galloped back to Ravenna to summon the 13th Legion and Caesar's officers in the wake of his first, bloodless victory of the civil war.

On January 7, the two civil tribunes, Curio and Mark Antony, had slipped out of Rome, in a hired carriage and dressed as farmers, and headed northeast along the Flaminian Way to join Caesar. They found him at Rimini with the 13th Legion several days later. After experience as a cavalry commander under General Aulus Gabinius in Judea and Egypt, Antony, who would turn thirty-two or thirty-three this year, had served as a colonel and then as one of Caesar's junior generals in the last few years of the Gallic campaigns. Antony was related to Caesar via his mother's side of the family, and Caesar always entrusted the greatest responsibility to men he had personal connections with. While envoys dashed back and forth between Caesar at Rimini and Pompey at Capua just south of Rome, carrying offers, counteroffers, demands, and accusations that would have no material effect on Caesar's decision to make war and Pompey's intent to act as the Senate's appointed military commander against him, Caesar gave five cohorts of the 13th to Antony and sent him west across the Apennines to secure Arretium, modern Arezzo, and guard his right flank.

One of the messengers who went back and forth between Caesar and Pompey during January was the younger Lucius Caesar, son of Caesar's cousin, another Lucius Caesar—one of his generals during the latter years of the war in Gaul. Young Lucius went originally to Rimini on personal business; he probably delivered a letter from his father to Caesar. In the letter, the elder Lucius would have informed Caesar of his decision to either support Pompey or stay neutral in any conflict. This news must have stung Caesar to the quick.

While Mark Antony marched west into central Italy, Caesar and Curio proceeded to advance down the east coast with the remaining cohorts of the 13th Legion and their few cavalry, occupying Pesaro, Fano, Ancona, and Iguvium in swift succession. They then turned inland, to occupy Auximum—this acquisition would have given the sometimes petty Caesar particular pleasure, as Auximum was Pompey's hometown, the place where he'd raised his first legion back in 84 B.C., when just twenty-three years of age.

As Caesar pushed on south through the Picenum region, the 12th Legion arrived from northern Italy to join him after a forced march. With fifteen cohorts of his seasoned legionaries now, plus local garrison troops who came over to him in increasing numbers, Caesar continued to advance, and occupied Ascoli Piceno, or Asculum, as the chief town of Picenum was then known, as Pompey's large garrison there fled ahead of him.

All Pompeian resistance north of Rome was now concentrated at the town of Corfinium, on the Aterna River, the Roman Aternus, in central Italy, where Pompey's generals Vibullius Rufus and Lucius Domitius Ahenobarbus brought together eighteen thousand men, mostly new conscripts plus a few of Pompey's old retired legionaries. As the men of the 13th and 12th Legions approached the river in the second week of February, opposition troops were encountered trying to break down the bridge across the Aterna. Caesar's troops beat these men off, secured the bridge, then marched the three miles to Corfinium and made camp outside its stone walls and closed gates—gates possibly made of solid metal, as were those of substantial Italian cities of the time, such as Cremona.

Caesar had sent for Mark Antony, and, when he arrived from Arezzo with his five cohorts of the 13th, immediately dispatched him to take Sulmona, in the upper Pescara River valley, a town that would gain fame the following century as the birthplace of the poet Ovid. Antony took the town in a day, then rejoined Caesar outside Corfinium. Three days later, when the Spanish legionaries of his 8th Legion marched in from the north, Caesar had them build a camp for themselves nearby. His invasion force had now grown to three legions. The following day, realizing that Corfinium intended holding out against him, Caesar began to surround it with entrenchments.

General Domitius had managed to sneak a courier out of the town who had hurried southwest to Pompey at Capua, bearing a message urging him to march over and relieve Corfinium. The same courier apparently sneaked back through Caesar's lines at night, bringing the message from Pompey that he hadn't instructed Domitius to hole up at Corfinium and, suspecting that more of Caesar's legions were drawing closer by the day, he wasn't prepared to risk coming to his aid. He instructed Domitius to pull out and march his cohorts to link up with him south of Rome. But it was too late. By now, Corfinium was surrounded.

General Domitius lied to his men; he told them that Pompey was on the way with a relief force, and urged them to defend the town with all their might. At the same time, he made secret preparations to escape. But not secret enough—word leaked out about the general's planned desertion of his troops. He was nabbed by his own soldiers, in civilian dress, trying to effect his escape. His men angrily made a prisoner of him, then, late in the day, sent a deputation of soldiers to Caesar, offering to come over to his side. At first Caesar seems to have suspected this was some sort of ruse. He had his men circle the town, each man standing within arm's length of his neighbor, and kept them there like that all night with orders to make sure no one escaped from Corfinium.

The next day, February 21, General Publius Lentulus Spinther, Domitius's deputy, came out to Caesar, and they agreed on surrender terms. All the senators and knights at Corfinium capitulated to him, and General Domitius was handed over in chains. When Domitius gave his word not to take any further part in the war, Caesar set him free. All his former troops in the town were then required to swear allegiance to Caesar, which they did. These surrendered troops were soon formed into legions. Combined with cohorts that Caesar also raised locally, there were enough men to make up four new legions, which Caesar called the 17th, 18th, 19th, and 20th. Putting them under the command of Gaius Curio, he would soon dispatch them south to occupy Sicily, sending the trusted Colonel Pollio on ahead with a fast-moving advance force.

Caesar spent seven days engaged in the siege of Corfinium, and by the time it was over he was surprised that General Labienus still hadn't arrived from Gaul with the bulk of his cavalry. Now he was staggered by the news that Labienus had decided that Caesar had overreached himself in going against the Senate, and, while he had brought the Gallic and German cavalry down from the Rhine as ordered, he had offered the services of his troopers and himself to Pompey. Pompey of course welcomed him, appointing him commander of all his mounted forces.

Labienus's defection, on top of that of Lucius Caesar, embittered Julius Caesar. Throughout his career, Caesar tended to be so single-minded that he failed to take into account the grievances of others, or even to recognize the fact that they had a grievance with him until it was too late, as evidenced by the mutinies and desertions of his troops during the civil war and by the assassination plot that resulted in his death.

Typically, Caesar's ego would let him make no mention in his memoirs of how his once firm friend and loyal lieutenant Labienus had defected to Pompey. We simply find Labienus on the other side once battle was joined. Apart from his strong credentials as a professional soldier—he'd been made a praetor and major general by 59 B.C., so would have had seen extensive military service, probably in the East, before his nine notable years with Caesar in Gaul—Labienus was a wealthy, respected, and influential senator who had even established an entire town, Cingulum in Picenum, at his own expense. Stung by Labienus's action, from this point on Caesar would only refer to his skilled and loyal deputy of nine years in the most sneering and derogatory terms. Labienus's character assassination would be completed by Caesar's supporters in their subsequent writings, with the cumulative result that Labienus would be cast into the basement of history. From this point, too, Mark Antony replaced General Labienus as Caesar's deputy commander.

Pompey and the two current consuls had already left Rome, back on the night of January 17–18, joining the 1st and 15th Legions at their camp at Luceria in Puglia. As news of the debacle at Corfinium reached him, his officers informed him that all attempts to raise fresh troops north of Capua were proving fruitless, as much because of Caesar's reputation as his rapid advance, a reputation, according to Plutarch, that credited Caesar with killing a million people during his nine-year conquest of Gaul and of taking another million prisoner and selling them into slavery. At most, said Pompey's subordinates, they could muster three new legions of recruits and retired veterans. In light of this, the fifty-six-year-old Pompey, who had not led an army in more than a decade, made a far-reaching decision. He would abandon Italy, withdrawing to Greece using his strong naval superiority, and there he would regroup and rebuild his army with the half dozen Roman legions stationed in the East and the support of the many eastern potentates who were in his debt.

Pompey and his legions marched out of Luceria, heading for the port of Brundisium, modern Brindisi, on the southeastern coast. Contrary to Caesar's probable expectation, the 15th Legion remained loyal to Pompey and marched with the 1st. Hundreds of senators and knights followed; Plutarch was to say that this was not because of any fear of Caesar, but rather out of loyalty and even devotion to Pompey. In fact, the most famous men of the day, including the great writers and orators Cicero, Cato the Younger, and Varro, all supported Pompey. Pausing briefly at the town of Canusium, probably to add General Labienus and his several thousand cavalrymen to the column, Pompey then hurried south down the Appian Way.

As soon as he heard that Pompey had barricaded himself behind the walls of Brindisi, Caesar marched his forces down to the port city. From Brindisi, while Caesar tried to blockade him on land with major earthworks and on the waters around the harbor using a series of rafts, all manned by the 8th, 12th, 13th, and three new legions raised in southern Italy, Pompey was able in early March to commence an amphibious evacuation. In the first wave, he shipped out two new legions he himself had raised south of Rome, together with General Labienus and his cavalry and the consuls and other leading citizens who had chosen to flee with him, while the 1st, 15th, and another new legion held the city.

The refugees crossed the Adriatic to Durrës, or Durazzo, as the Italians call it, the present-day chief seaport of Albania. Then called Dyrrhachium, the town was Rome's principal port in the Epirus region. Ten days later, Pompey's fleet slipped back into Brindisi, and on the night of March 17–18 began embarking Pompey and the last of his legionaries, who were under strict orders to make absolutely no noise as they withdrew from their positions and boarded the ships waiting at the docks around the antler-shaped inner harbor that gave the city its Latin name—Brundisium meant "stag's head." Only when it was too late did Caesar realize the city walls had been deserted and that the Pompeians were escaping in the darkness. He led the way as his troops scaled the walls and broke into the city. Guided through the blocked and booby-trapped streets by local sympathizers, Caesar reached the waterfront to find that Pompey had outwitted him. Two ships carrying men of Pompey's rear guard were caught at the breakwater, and a few men were found at Pompey's embarkation camp in the town, in their beds and too ill to move—a mystery illness had hit the camp over the winter, almost certainly an influenza epidemic. But their capture was small consolation—Pompey had succeeded in a Dunkirk-like evacuation of twenty-five thousand men from under Caesar's nose, troops who would form the core of his new army.

Caesar had no naval forces to speak of, had no capacity to give chase. So many of his past campaigns had been completed in less than a single season, and, indeed, he had now taken control of Italy within seventy days of crossing the Rubicon. But the short civil war he would have been hoping for was not to be. Now, after putting his stamp on the administration at Rome, he knew that he would have to end the threat at his back posed by Pompey's forces in Spain. Pompey had six veteran legions stationed in the two Spanish provinces, and his commanders there would soon raise a seventh locally.

Planning his troop movements with meticulous care as usual, Caesar sent orders to General Fabius at Narbonne to lead his three legions into Spain and secure the mountain passes across the Pyrenees ahead of his own arrival. The 10th Legion was about to enter onto the civil war stage to play a key part in the second act.

VIII

BROKEN PROMISES

W hile it was camped at Narbonne in the south of France in January, the 10th Legion had said farewell to Chief Centurion Crastinus and his fellow senior centurions. The sixteen-year enlistments of these men had expired, and, thinking the civil war would soon be over, General Fabius had obviously seen no reason why they shouldn't be allowed to receive their discharges and go into retirement. Fabius had been governor of the province of Asia in 58–57 B.C., and, like Mark Antony, had been one of Caesar's subordinates in Gaul since 54 B.C. An unremarkable man who appears to have played things by the book, Fabius may have been in declining health at this time, as indications are he was to die this same year, of natural causes.

The retiring centurions of the 10th were quickly replaced by centurions of the 61 B.C. enlistment, who were promoted up a grade or two by General Fabius to fill their vacant positions, men including Gaius Clusinas, Marcus Tiro, and Titus Salienus.

Where the retiring centurions went after leaving the legion we don't know. Most, if not all, would have been, like Gaius Crastinus, natives of Spain. But Spain was in Pompeian hands at the time, so it's unlikely they went home just yet, as they could be expected to be drafted into Pompey's army. It's more likely they waited around Narbonne until the civil war dust settled.

Between mid-January and mid-March, recruiting officers were busy for Caesar in Italy. Males of military age were drafted in the thousands into thirteen hastily created new legions. Another two new legions would be created the following winter for service in the Balkans. These fifteen new legions were named the 21st through the 35th. Once Caesar turned away from Brindisi empty-handed in the second half of March and decided to take Spain from Pompey's forces, he issued a stream of movement orders as he journeyed to Rome to take over the reins of government. Plutarch was to write that Caesar was gifted above all men with the faculty for making the right use of everything in war, and Caesar's plans for the Spanish operation were detailed and precise as always.

While General Fabius led the 10th and his two other legions from Narbonnne to Spain to pave the way for Caesar, another three legions were ordered to head for Spain from Italy, crossing the Alps and then the Pyrenees on their march. There they were to link up with the advance force. Meanwhile, the six-hundred-year-old city of Massilia, modern Marseilles in southern France, had closed its gates to Caesar's emissaries, and Caesar dispatched a further three legions to lay siege to the city, led by General Gaius Trebonius. At the same time, to make up for the loss of Labienus's three thousand cavalry, Caesar couriered dispatches to all the subject tribes of Gaul, instructing them to send their best mounted fighters to Spain to join his army there, giving each a specific quota and even naming individual nobles of the tribes as men he required to serve.

The upshot of all this was that the 10th and its two fellow legions marched rapidly west and easily cleared the Pyrenees passes of Pompeian guards left there, and as spring blossomed, six legions and three thousand Gallic cavalry congregated in eastern Spain with General Fabius, waiting for Caesar to arrive from Rome to take over operational command. These legions, in addition to the 10th, were the 7th and the 9th, brother Spanish legions of the 10th, plus the 14th, another of Caesar's veteran units from Gaul, as well as the 21st and 30th, two newly raised Italian legions that hurried over the Alps from Italy ahead of Caesar's arrival. To handle the siege of Marseilles, it seems that Caesar allocated his experienced 11th Legion to head the task, supported by another two new legions, almost certainly the 22nd and the 23rd. The last of Caesar's original legions, the 16th, appears to have been left on garrison duty in central France, with the daunting task of keeping all of Gaul in check.

By early spring Caesar was in Rome, and between April 1 and 3 he held a meeting of the much-reduced Senate, appointing a number of new senators to replace the hundreds who had departed the capital with Pompey. During this sitting Caesar settled affairs of state to his satisfaction, including the appointment of governors and military commanders to various regions.

While his focus was now on Spain, Caesar was concerned by reports from the Balkans. Towns in the province of Illyricum, just across the Adriatic, which he'd governed now for a decade, had closed their gates to his officials. Some towns had been taken over by Pompeian supporters, others by local "bandits" professing a desire for independence. So before he left the capital, Caesar set in motion an operation that would send Mark Antony's younger brother Gaius with the new 24th Legion and half the new 28th Legion to make a surprise amphibious landing on the coast of Illyricum and restore Caesar's control of the province. The number of troops involved in the operation, about seventy-five hundred, seems to have been dictated by the number of ships Caesar's supporters could rake together for the landing.

As preparations were set in train for the Illyricum operation, Caesar put Marcus Lepidus in charge at Rome and gave command of all troops in Italy to Mark Antony, who based himself at the key road junction of Placentia, modern Piacenza, on the southern bank of the Po River in central Italy. The legions under Antony's command were strategically placed at Brindisi on the southeastern coast and towns in the Puglia region.

Caesar now set off for Spain. Precisely how long it took him to make the journey we don't know. His journey from Rome to Córdoba carried in a litter in 61 B.C. had taken him twenty-four days. But now he was riding, accompanied by his now constant companions, the three hundred men of his mounted German bodyguard. On one occasion in the past, driving his own chariot, Caesar had made the trip from Rome to southern France in eight days, so, it's likely he reached the Pyrenees within two weeks of leaving the capital. There, holding the passes in expectation of his arrival, were six hundred of Labienus's troopers who had been detached to General Fabius at the beginning of the winter and who had remained loyal to Caesar. Adding these men to his fast-moving cavalry column, he crossed the mountains and advanced into eastern Spain to join General Fabius and his legions.

For some time after the event, Caesar was unable to bring himself to admit that three thousand of Labienus's cavalry had defected to Pompey in Italy and were now in Greece with Labienus and Pompey. Everything points to Caesar dictating many of the chapters of his account of the civil war within days or weeks of their taking place, and to cover up the loss of Labienus's cavalry he initially inflated the number of cavalry he had at his disposal in Spain by three thousand. Later, when dealing with the war in Albania and Greece, his memoirs talk for the first time of Labienus and his German and Gallic cavalry fighting for Pompey.

Riding in with his nine hundred cavalry, Caesar found General Fabius at the Río Segre, the Sicoris River, in northeastern Spain, facing an army of five Pompeian legions. Overall, against the six legions Caesar had sent to Spain were six of Pompey's veteran legions and a seventh, which was hurriedly drafted on the 10th Legion's home turf, the province of Baetica, and called, unimaginatively, the Indigena—the Native or Home-Grown Legion. These Pompeian heavy infantry units were supported by five thousand locally raised cavalry and large numbers of local auxiliaries. Initially in three separate armies, Pompey's forces were now concentrated into two forces. The Indigena was left in western Spain with the governor of Baetica, the famous writer Marcus Terentius Varro, together with the 2nd Legion. The 2nd was one of Pompey's original legions, dating back, like the 1st, to 84 B.C., when it was personally founded and funded by Pompey in the Picenum region of eastern Italy. More recently it had been reenlisted in Cisalpine Gaul.

To meet Caesar in eastern Spain, an army of five legions marched under the mature, plodding General Lucius Afranius and his deputy, hot-tempered General Marcus Petreius. Afranius was an old friend of Pompey's, hailing from the same home territory, Picenum in eastern Italy. He had served under him in Spain and the Middle East at the height of Pompey's military successes in the 70s and 60s B.C., before becoming a consul in 60 B.C. and governor of Nearer Spain in 55 B.C. And he was determined to do his best to defend Spain for Pompey.

General Afranius's legions were the Valeria, another of Pompey's originals, recruited in these times in Cisalpine Gaul; the 3rd, also from Cisalpine Gaul, and the 4th, 5th, and 6th. The latter three were all veteran Spanish legions, whose legionaries, aged between thirty-three and thirty-six, were due to receive their discharge this year, as their sixteen-year enlistments were now up. The 6th was the same legion that had served on attachment with Caesar's army in Gaul in 52–50 B.C., loaned to Caesar by Pompey at the height of the Vercingetorix Revolt, before returning to eastern Spain.

General Afranius decided that the best territory in the northeast for infantry operations was around the town of Lérida, or Ilerda, as it was then known, in the present-day region of Catalonia about eighty miles west of Barcelona. Sitting on a hill, the town was on the right bank of the Segre, not far from where it joined the Ebro River. Moving his forces into the area, Afranius occupied the walled town and also built a fortified camp nearby. By the time Caesar reached General Fabius at the Segre in the second half of April there had already been a number of skirmishes between the two armies, but no major engagements had taken place.

Caesar crossed two bridges over the Segre just completed by General Fabius and marched the army to confront the Pompeian forces outside Lérida, where over the next seventy-two hours his legions built a fortified camp. He then led three of his legions on a surprise mission to seize a small hill that lay between the town and General Afranius's camp, with the objective of dividing the Pompeian forces. Two of the legions involved were the 9th and the 14th. The identity of the third is unknown, but from subsequent events it was probably one of the new, untried Italian legions.

Realizing what Caesar was up to, General Afranius quickly dispatched his on-duty guard cohorts, which occupied the hillock before Caesar's troops could reach it. Afranius soon brought up several legions in support. Caesar's advance guard was beaten back, and then the understrength 14th Legion, occupying one of Caesar's wings, coming under sustained attack and taking casualties, failed to hold its ground and retreated. This caused panic among the ranks of the raw recruits of the other legion, and Caesar had to personally lead up the 9th to stabilize the situation. The charge of the 9th sent Afranius's troops reeling, and the men of the 9th chased them all the way to a ridge at the foot of the hill on which the town of Lérida stood. There, Afranius's troops regrouped, and in a surprise move swept around the flanks and encircled the 9th Legion. The men of the 9th found themselves cut off on the ridge, which was just wide enough for three cohorts to form up side-by-side.

Over the next five hours Caesar tried to fight his way through to the 9th with infantry and cavalry reinforcements, while the men of the 9th fought desperately to hold their ground and not be overrun. Eventually, Caesar's cavalry managed to climb the slope and inject themselves between the 9th and the other side, allowing the men of the 9th to withdraw before the cavalry also pulled out.

Afranius claimed the day's fight as a victory for his side, and messengers hurried away to Italy with the news that Caesar had been bettered. Caesar was to admit to seventy dead in the first encounter at the hillock, including a first-rank centurion of the 14th Legion, as well as more than six hundred wounded, but he didn't reveal how many men he subsequently lost in the five-hour fight outside Lérida. He claimed that the Pompeians lost more than two hundred legionaries that day.

Two days later, a storm brought the heaviest rainfall in memory to the region, washing away the two bridges behind Caesar, over which he was supplied. Afranius then led a raid in Caesar's rear, inflicting more than two hundred casualties on a column bringing up supplies and reinforcements. After failing to repair the bridges because opposition troops occupied the opposite bank, Caesar had his men build light, flat-bottomed boats, of a kind he'd seen in Britain, and was able to spirit troops across the water in the night and drive Afranius's men away from the bridge site. Once he was in occupation of both banks he was able to bridge the river and once more link up with his supply columns and foraging parties.

Slowly, as weeks passed, fortunes began to change at Lérida. Caesar's cavalry cleared the countryside of Afranius's foragers, and the Pompeian troops, locked behind the walls of camp and town, found themselves cut off from resupply, with dwindling resources. On the other hand, with five tribes of the region now voluntarily providing him with supplies, Caesar was sitting pretty. Rather than be starved into submission, Generals Afranius and Petreius agreed that they had to break out and make for the mountains to the north, where tribes loyal to Pompey would supply provisions and reinforcements.

The Pompeians discreetly made their preparations, and then one day in July, carrying enough rations to last them twenty-two days, they took Caesar by surprise and succeeded in their breakout. Initially, Caesar could only harry the column with his cavalry, but, as always, he reacted swiftly, and soon set off after it with five legions. Marching at a cracking pace, he overtook Afranius five miles from the mountains. Both sides built camps, but Caesar then worked his way around, across rough country, giving the appearance of a withdrawal but in reality aiming to skirt Afranius's position in a wide arc and place his forces in the other side's path at the foot of the mountains.

When Afranius saw Caesarian troops between him and his destination he quickly left his camp and marched his troops for the mountains at the double, leaving behind much of his equipment, but Caesar's troops won the race and formed up ahead of him. A force of two thousand auxiliaries subsequently sent by Afranius to take high ground for him was cut off and wiped out by Caesar's cavalry, and the Pompeian army withdrew to the protection of its last camp and regained its equipment.

While Afranius and Petreius were away from their camp, supervising the digging of a line of entrenchments to safeguard their water supply, troops from Caesar's 10th, 9th, and 7th Legions began to fraternize with their fellow Spaniards of the 4th, 5th, and 6th Legions on the other side. Many were fellow townsmen, some were even related, and before long men from Caesar's legions were in the Pompeian camp, sitting and talking and sharing food and camaraderie with their countrymen, all agreeing that it was crazy that they should be fighting each other. Officers from the Pompeian camp even went to Caesar and proposed setting up talks to negotiate the surrender of their army.

When they heard about this, Generals Afranius and Petreius hurried back to their camp. An assembly was called, and Petreius led the army in swearing an oath reaffirming their loyalty to Pompey and vowing that they would not give up the fight. Petreius then ordered men who had troops from Caesar's army in their tents to produce them at once. Those who were given up, men of the 10th Legion among them, were put to death on the parade ground in front of the assembled Pompeian legions.

Generals Afranius and Petreius now conferred on their best course of action. It was obvious that Caesar was not going to let them reach the mountains. One alternative was to try to reach the port of Tarraco, modern Tarragona, on the east coast, where Pompey's fleet could supply them from vast grain supplies being held at Gades, present-day Cádiz, farther south, which was still firmly in Pompeian hands. If need be, they could even be evacuated from Tarragona and join Pompey in Greece. But Tarragona was at least a week's march away under present conditions, and while their legionaries still had a few days' rations, their auxiliaries had already exhausted all their supplies. The generals knew that many of the Pompeian troops were simply not up to a week's march. They had left a little grain back at Lérida, and the other option was to retrace their steps there. This was a short-term option, as once that grain was exhausted, they were no better off. But this was the option the generals agreed on.

So they broke camp and marched their army back the way they'd come. Caesar harried them all the way, so that they covered only four miles on the first morning, before, exhausted, the Pompeian troops set up a new camp. Caesar built a camp of his own two miles away. Now the Pompeians slaughtered all their baggage animals, for food, and because they had no fodder for them.

Caesar began to build earthworks around the opposition camp, with the intention of completely surrounding it, the way he'd surrounded Vercingetorix at Alesia in Gaul three years before. The Pompeians strengthened their defenses and watched the Caesarians work for three days until, at about three o'clock in the afternoon, General Afranius led his whole army out of camp and formed his units up in battle order, his five legions in the first two lines, his auxiliaries behind. Caesar marched out with his legions and formed up facing Afranius. Caesar placed four cohorts from each of his five legions in his front line, and three in each of his second and third lines. Almost certainly the 10th Legion was stationed on Caesar's right wing.

There the two armies stood, staring at each other in silence, with Spaniard unwilling to fight Spaniard and neither side prepared to make the first move, until the sun went down. The two armies then marched back to their respective camps. Over the next few years Caesar would not be so reticent about committing to battle, but at this early stage in the civil war he was apparently very conscious of being accused of taking the lives of fellow Romans. At this point "chivalry," "magnanimity," and "leniency" were still words with a place in his lexicon. Besides, he could see that the men on the other side, out of food and short of water in the baking heat of the Spanish midsummer, many having already demonstrated they'd lost the heart for a fight, were nearing the end of their tether. There had already been surrender overtures; capitulation was obviously on the cards. It was just a matter of waiting.

Caesar didn't have long to wait. The next day, August 2, Generals Afranius and Petreius sent envoys to Caesar, seeking a peace conference. But they wanted the conference to be out of the hearing of their men. Caesar would only agree to discuss their surrender out in the open, within earshot of the troops, and Pompey's generals resignedly agreed, giving up Afranius's son, who was probably in his late teens, as a hostage and token of their good faith.

Caesar marched up to the Pompeian camp, and his legions formed up as if on the parade ground, with helmet crests and shining decorations in place. Afranius and Petreius's troops lined the ramparts of their camp and watched anxiously as their generals went out the praetorian gate and met Caesar in the open. Speeches were delivered by both sides, loud enough for the troops to hear, with Afranius admitting defeat and humbly seeking favorable terms of surrender.

In response, Caesar berated Afranius and his senior officers for taking the side of his enemies, but in the end he stipulated several lenient conditions for surrender: Afranius and his officers were to agree to play no further part in the war, their troops were to lay down their arms, their units were to be disbanded, and they were to go home. Hearing this, the troops behind Afranius and Petreius, who had been expecting Caesar to punish them for opposing him, began to shout their approval of the proposal. General Afranius had no choice. He agreed to the surrender terms.

On August 4, the men of the 4th and 6th Legions, now disarmed, were formally discharged by Julius Caesar and told to go home. The men of both legions had been due for their discharge this year anyway, so this suited them just fine. The discharged men of Pompey's two legions tramped away to their homes in eastern Spain. Before long Caesar also discharged the men of the 5th Legion, but in the meantime he set the 3rd and Valeria Legions on the road to the Var River in southern France. A few miles west of Nice, the river formed the border between Transalpine Gaul and the

two legions' home territory of Cisalpine Gaul. Caesar promised the men of
these two Pompeian legions that once they reached the river, they, too,
would be paid off and discharged.

This column bound for the Var was led by two of Caesar's own legions,
the 7th and the 9th. Caesar chose the escort units quite deliberately. Both
were Spanish legions, they were in their home territory, and both, like the
4th, 5th, and 6th, were due for discharge this year. In fact, they were now
six months past their due discharge date. From subsequent events it is
apparent that when they saw Pompey's Spanish legions receiving their
discharges the men of the 9th in particular began to grumble among
themselves that they couldn't see why they couldn't go home, too. They
considered themselves just as entitled to their discharges, if not more so—
they were on the winning side, after all. But, determined to keep his best
troops in the field as long as it took to defeat Pompey and win the war,
Caesar ignored the unhappy undercurrent and sent the 7th and the 9th to
the Var. They marched with instructions to continue on to Italy once
they'd completed the discharge of the 3rd and Valeria, and to report to
Mark Antony at his headquarters at Piacenza on the Po, there to await
further orders.

The legions Caesar retained with him in Spain for the moment were
the 10th, 14th, 21st, and 30th. The 10th wasn't due for discharge for
another four years, and the 14th not for seven years, while the other two
legions had only been recruited that year, so Caesar knew he could rely
on all of them to serve without the complaints coming from the 9th and
the 7th.

Caesar also now set free General Afranius and General Petreius and
their senior officers, accepting their word that they would take no further
part in the civil war, then turned toward the southwest, setting his sights
on the last two Pompeian legions in Spain, the 2nd and the Indigena at
Córdoba with General Varro. Leaving the 10th and the 14th in the east
with the bulk of the cavalry, he sent General Quintus Cassius Longinus
marching on Córdoba with the 21st and the 30th while he took six hundred cavalry via a separate route. At the same time, he sent messages to
all the major towns of western Spain, urging them to throw out their
Pompeian garrisons.

Meanwhile, Varro, an old friend of Caesar's but also a man who felt
bound by his oath to serve Pompey, decided to march his two legions to
Cádiz to safeguard the grain and shipping there. On the march, the Indigena Legion pulled out of his column and withdrew to Hispalis, modern
Seville. The people of Córdoba behind him and those of Cádiz then threw

out his garrisons, and Varro, left with just Pompey's loyal 2nd Legion and nowhere to go, sent word to Caesar that he was prepared to hand over the 2nd to him. Caesar sent his distant cousin Sextus Caesar to take over the 2nd Legion, and Varro went to Córdoba to meet Caesar and pass over public money and property.

In this way, Caesar's conquest of western Spain was achieved without the shedding of a drop of blood. Assimilating the 2nd and Indigena Legions into his armed forces, he left them to garrison the province together with the 21st and the 30th, under General Cassius Longinus, brother of the Cassius who would be one of Caesar's assassins. Caesar himself acquired a dozen Pompeian ships at Cádiz and sailed up the coast to Tarragona. There, throngs of deputations from throughout Spain awaited him, as did some disagreeable news.

The main account of this episode was removed from Caesar's memoirs by his editors, but from remaining references in his and other works it is possible to piece together what took place. While Caesar had been in the west, Generals Afranius and Petreius had come to Tarragona. At the same time, a squadron of eighteen Pompeian warships commanded by Admiral Lucius Nasidius had pulled into the port.

Admiral Nasidius had been sent from Greece by Pompey with sixteen cruisers and battleships to help the people of Marseilles in southern France hold out against Caesar's legions. The squadron had arrived in Sicily at Messina, which Caesar's commander there, Curio, had left undefended. Taking a warship out of the docks at Messina and adding it to his little fleet, the admiral had then crossed the Mediterranean to Marseilles. There, his ships had joined forces with a squadron of eleven warships built by the people of Marseilles and gone to battle against the Caesarian fleet led by Caesar's longtime naval commander Decimus Brutus. The battle had been a victory for Admiral Brutus, who sank five Marseillaise vessels and captured another four. One of the surviving ships joined Admiral Nasidius's craft, all of which were still intact, after which Nasidius decided to withdraw to Nearer Spain.

The unexpected appearance of the little fleet of friendly warships at Tarragona was a godsend as far as General Afranius was concerned. He and his officers had subsequently hurried around the homes and haunts of the surrendered and discharged men of the 4th and 6th Legions in the region and rounded up some thirty-five hundred of them—enough to make three cohorts of one and four of the other. Contemptuous of their oath of neutrality to Caesar, they loaded the remobilized troops on board Nasidius's warships and set sail from Tarragona to join Pompey in Greece.

Annoyed that Afranius and the others had broken their word to him and that thousands of Pompey's veteran Spanish legionaries had escaped from Spain, Caesar determined to concentrate on the nearest problem, the siege of Marseilles just around the Mediterranean coast, which General Trebonius had yet to bring to a conclusion despite operating against the city with three legions and Brutus's naval forces since April. Leaving the depleted 14th Legion in Nearer Spain, Caesar marched on Marseilles with the 10th Legion.

Never willing to let go of experienced troops, Caesar would have disapproved when he heard that General Fabius had let the senior centurions of the 10th Legion take their discharges back in January. Now, as he marched from Spain with the 10th, Caesar sent out recalls to every one of them. Under the terms of their original enlistment they had to make themselves available for up to four additional years' service if their general required them and had to hand in their names and addresses to the local authorities wherever they went in their retirement.

Legally, these retired centurions had no choice but return to their unit. Many, in fact, were probably itching to get back into harness. Chief Centurion Gaius Crastinus responded to the recall. We don't know exactly where he was when it reached him, but Crastinus was back with the 10th by the time it marched into Brindisi several weeks later.

Caesar and the 10th arrived at Marseilles in early October, just as the city finally capitulated to General Trebonius, and after the Pompeian commander, General Lucius Domitius Ahenobarbus, had escaped by sea. This was the same Lucius Domitius Ahenobarbus who had commanded at Corfinium, the same man Caesar had let go free after accepting his word he would take no further part in the war. Domitius had promptly gone to Marseilles to help the locals against Caesar's forces. After being let down by Afranius, Petreius, and now Domitius, Caesar would not be quick to pardon opposing generals in the future.

Caesar was, of course, delighted to have taken control of Marseilles, but more bad news reached him here. From Appian we know that Mark Antony sent a dispatch from Piacenza to tell him that the 9th Legion, which had joined him at the Po as ordered after escorting the 3rd and Valeria to the Var, was demanding its overdue discharge and a bonus Caesar had promised it at the outbreak of the civil war, and had gone on strike, refusing to obey its officers until its demands were met. The 7th Legion, influenced by the 9th, had then followed suit. Antony told Caesar that nothing he'd done or said had satisfied the two mutinous legions, and now he begged Caesar to come and solve the problem.

That problem had been partly of Antony's creation. Plutarch says he was too lazy to pay attention to complaints and listened impatiently to petitions, and he would have dismissed the grumbles of the 9th without giving them the courtesy of a hearing. It was an attitude that would have fanned discontent until it flared into mutiny.

Before he left Marseilles, Caesar finalized his campaign plans, then issued a mass of troop movement orders. Gaius Curio, holding Sicily with four legions, had already been ordered to invade Tunisia in North Africa by sea, leaving Sicily under the command of General Aulus Albinus. To inspire his troops to rapid success, Curio told them that Caesar had just conquered all of Spain within forty days of first coming into contact with the enemy. It was a flagrant lie; his Spanish operations had taken him months. The tactical value of this North African operation is questionable. Pompey's own forces in the province of Africa, as Tunisia and western Libya were collectively known, were limited, and there was no indication that Pompey's ally King Juba of neighboring Numidia intended sending him further reinforcements in Greece—he'd already sent him several thousand light infantry, and he had internal problems to contend with at home. The operation could have been designed to deny Pompey's strong naval forces based in North Africa, but neither Caesar nor other classical writers offer this as a motive for the invasion. Strategically, however, it would secure a rich wheat-growing area, and add to Caesar's prestige.

Meanwhile, the main target was still Pompey, in Greece. Caesar chose twelve legions and his best cavalry for an invasion of Greece, and soon orders were going out to specific legions to assemble at the embarkation camp at Brindisi. As a part of that operation, the 10th Legion was ordered to march for Brindisi, accompanied by the 11th, which had been part of the siege army operating against Marseilles. The 22nd and 23rd were to stay at Marseilles as a force of occupation, keeping the locals under firm control. The 31st and 32nd, two more new legions, were ordered to eastern Spain, to join the 14th Legion. Marcus Lepidus would take up General Afranius's former appointment as Governor of Nearer Spain. Caesar himself then set off for Rome, via Piacenza.

It was probably when he reached the Po that Caesar received yet more bad news. Mark Antony's little brother Gaius had launched the planned Illyricum amphibious operation, using either Brindisi or Otranto, Roman Hydruntum, as his jumping-off point. But his forty transports had been intercepted on the Adriatic by a fleet of Pompeian warships from the Achaea region of southern Greece commanded by Admiral Marcus Octavius. Led by Centurion Titus Puleio, the men of the 24th and 28th

Legions on board young Antony's ships had voted to go over to the other side rather than fight, and had put into the Pompeian naval base at the Greek island of Corfu.

It's unclear precisely what happened to Gaius Antony. He may have given his parole not to take any further part in the war and was released by Admiral Octavius, or he was kept a prisoner in Greece, being released after Caesar's victories the following year. The former is more likely, as young Antony held no more military commands during the war, next popping up as a civil tribune at Rome three years later. The seventy-five hundred legionaries on the transports were assimilated into Pompey's army in Greece. The men, and equally the ships, would be sorely missed by Caesar.

In a mean mood after digesting the news of this setback on the Adriatic, Caesar called an assembly of the legions encamped at Piacenza with Mark Antony. The men of the 7th and 9th Legions warily fell in, and Caesar stepped up onto the tribunal.

"My soldiers," he began, looking stern. As Appian tells us, Caesar proceeded to remind the mutinous troops of the two legions how quickly he worked, that he was not one to drag his feet. The war was going slowly because the enemy had run away, he said, not because of anything he had done or hadn't done. "You swore to follow me for the whole war, not just part of it," he declared. "And yet now you abandon us in midcourse and mutiny against your officers. No one can doubt how much regard I have held you men in up to now. But you give me no choice. I shall put into practice our ancient custom. Since the 9th Legion chiefly instigated the mutiny, lots will be drawn for every tenth man in the 9th Legion to die."

His audience was staggered. Every tenth man to be executed for the mutiny? No one could remember the last time a Roman legion had been officially decimated like this. A groan of despair went up from the men of the 9th. When the legion's officers came to him and begged him to reconsider, Caesar relented a little. He ordered the 9th Legion's centurions to name the 120 ringleaders of the mutiny. These 120 were then required to draw lots. One in ten of them drew the death card. When it was proved that one of the final 12 condemned men hadn't even been in camp at the time of the mutiny, the vindictive centurion who gave in his name was dragged forward to take his place.

After the 12 men were beaten to death by their own comrades using wooden staves, or clubs, Caesar informed the 7th and the 9th that he had selected them to take part in the next major operation of the war, and ordered them to prepare to march to Brindisi to join the task force assembling there. It seems that the 13th Legion was also at this camp at Piacenza, having probably come up from Brindisi during the spring to give Mark Antony some experienced muscle and to help train new legions. The 13th would have been one of the twelve legions that Caesar had in mind for the Greek operation, but now that he had lost forty ships in the disastrous Illyricum operation, his reduced shipping capacity caused him to reduce the number of the legions allocated to the invasion of Greece by one. The 13th Legion was ordered to join the 14th, 31st, and 32nd in eastern Spain.

Caesar then hurried down to Rome, where he briefly used the title and powers of Dictator, originally a temporary appointment in times of emergency for up to six months. In effect, the exceptional emergency powers of martial law as we know them today were now wielded by Caesar, making him answerable to no one. He spent the next eleven days consumed with business of state at Rome.

In the late fall, accompanied by Mark Antony as well as a host of experienced generals, Caesar left the capital and set off for the embarkation camp at Brindisi, his mind consumed with the minutiae of the operation that lay ahead.

IX

THE RACE FOR DURRËS

In his day, and long after it, men spoke of Julius Caesar's great luck. Caesar wouldn't have felt so lucky as he climbed the tribunal this chill day in December of 49 B.C. and looked out over the thousands of legionaries assembled in front of him at the Brindisi embarkation camp. The only subject of conversation at the camp over the past few days would have been the dreadful news from North Africa. Gaius Curio, his two legions, and his cavalry had been wiped out in Tunisia, primarily by the forces of Pompey's friend and ally King Juba of Numidia.

The men of Curio's legions, almost certainly the 17th and 18th, had been former Pompeian recruits from the Marsi and Paeligni areas of central Italy who had come over to Caesar after the fall of Corfinium in February. The news of their annihilation—probably brought to Caesar by Colonel Pollio, who had been on Curio's staff and was among the few to escape from Tunisia alive—had been so unexpected, and was so potentially shattering to the morale of his men, particularly the new, inexperienced recruits, that Caesar knew he had to address them—and make an impression.

In front of him stood the men of eleven legions plus several hundred cavalrymen. The 10th and 11th Legions had been the last to arrive. They'd had the farthest to march. Some of the other units had been camped here at Brindisi, the rest in the Puglia region, right through the summer and fall. Now they had been divided into two groups. These would be the two waves of his invasion force. At Piacenza, after the news of the loss of Gaius Antony's ships, Caesar would have done a rapid mental calculation and reckoned that with the transports he had left to him he might have to invade Greece in three waves, sending the ships back twice after the initial landing for the subsequent waves. But now it looked as if just two convoys would be required. Hacking coughs coming from the ranks would have been evidence of the cause of change in logistical plans.

The same malady that had affected Pompey's troops at Brindisi in February and March had reappeared in southern Italy in the autumn with a vengeance, and now gripped Caesar's army, laying low his men in their thousands and making the embarkation camp one large melancholy hospital. Few if any tents would have been without a man or two lying, moaning, perspiring, coughing, in his bed. In an era when there were no antibiotic drugs, the sickness had reduced the legions to less than half their normal numbers of able-bodied men.

Caesar had chosen the 10th Legion to accompany him in the first wave of the landing, along with the other veteran troops of the 11th and 12th Legions. The rest of the first wave would be made up of the 25th, 26th, and 27th Legions, and the men of the five cohorts of the 28th Legion left behind when Gaius Antony embarked on his ill-fated Illyricum operation, all of them untried recruits drafted in January and February. Caesar's first wave was a deliberate mixture of youth and experience. The second wave, which would be commanded by Mark Antony, would comprise the mutinous 7th and 9th Legions, plus the reliable 8th, Spanish legions all, and the Italian youths of the newly formed 29th.

"My soldiers," Caesar began. Caesar himself recorded the words he used this day, words that would have been repeated by centurions for those in the rear ranks who could not hear him directly. According to Suetonius, Caesar pitched his voice high when speaking in public, and used impassioned gestures in a theatrical style that impressed his audience. Cicero was to write that he knew of no more eloquent speaker than Caesar, and that his style was grand, even noble.

"We have come almost to the end of our toils and dangers," Caesar went on. "You may therefore leave your slaves and baggage behind in Italy with easy minds. You must embark with only basic kit to allow a greater number of troops to be put on board the ships available. When we win, my generosity in reward will answer all your hopes."

When he asked if his troops were with him, a chorus of agreement would have swelled up from more than twenty-five thousand voices.

In the dead of night, the convoy ran before a favorable wind. Aboard their transports at the forefront of the first wave, the men of the 10th

Legion stood tense and silent in their squads, gripping onto their weapons, to the sides of their lurching ships, to their neighbors. Some were sardined down in the holds; others were crammed on deck. Most would have been seasick. We hear of the prevalent seasickness of troops involved in later amphibious operations, here on the Adriatic and on the Mediterranean, and this crossing would have been no different.

Even though they probably weren't particularly popular with his men, Caesar had a penchant for amphibious landings and night operations. He liked the way an amphibious assault could deliver a mass of troops to one place at one time. He also liked to use the element of surprise that darkness provided, recognizing, as Appian has Caesar say, that "the mightiest weapon of war is surprise." In modern times, Caesar would have been a great exponent of the use of paratroops and the U.S. Marine Corps for troop insertions. Always at night, of course.

It was the night of January 4, 48 B.C. This was before Caesar adjusted the Roman calendar, so it was then running two months behind our own calendar, making January a month in late autumn. Just the same, by all accounts the weather was wintry this January, and the spray coming over the prows of the ships and licking the faces of seasick Spaniards of the 10th as the landing craft bucked through the Adriatic troughs would have been refreshingly icy cold.

This operation was yet another new experience for the men of the 10th. They'd fought in France, Belgium, Holland, Germany, Britain, and Spain; they'd recently marched the length of Italy, the center of the Roman universe, to reach the embarkation camp just days before the year ended; and now they were on their way to invade Greece. What stories they'd have to tell their grandchildren—if they lived that long. These men had been through amphibious landings before. They'd invaded Britain twice, after all. But that had been different. There had been no opposition naval forces lurking in the darkness when they crossed the English Channel. Now, somewhere out there in the night, picket ships of Pompey's navy might appear at any moment. Pompey possessed six hundred warships of various classes, spread among five fleets. And many of them were based here on the Adriatic.

Everyone on board the ships of the convoy was conscious of the fate of Gaius Antony and his men of the 24th and 28th Legions who had been caught on the Adriatic by Admiral Octavius the previous year. But that botched operation and its timing had not been unexpected. At least this time the Pompeians weren't expecting visitors. Sure, everyone on both sides of the Adriatic knew that sooner or later Caesar might invade

Greece, but even the men of 10th would have thought that Caesar would wait until the spring. No one launched a major operation like this on winter's eve. No one except the ever-audacious Julius Caesar.

The darkness was their chief ally. It negated Pompey's naval advantage. If the convoy was spotted, it would be through bad luck. And everyone in his army knew about Caesar's famous good luck. Caesar had planned it so the landing would take place unseen, in the early hours of the morning. The empty transports would then dash back across the Adriatic to Brindisi, clearing the coast of Greece well before dawn, returning the following night with the next wave. And with Pompey's navy none the wiser.

The epidemic had reduced all eleven legions of the task force, so that now fifteen thousand legionaries from the seven legions of the first wave and five hundred German and Gallic cavalrymen were crammed aboard the landing ships, with thousands of their comrades still in their sickbeds back at Brindisi. The intent was that once they recovered, the victims would be ferried over to join their legions in Greece aboard later convoys. As it transpired, those men would remain in Italy, garrisoning the ports of the southeast and southwest, fighting off Pompeian commando raids, and even serving as marines in an Adriatic sea battle before rejoining their legions two years later.

Like foot soldiers in all wars in all times, the men of the 10th Legion wouldn't have been told exactly where they were going. But they would have guessed that the landing zone was somewhere between the Pompeian naval bases at Durrës and Corfu, almost directly opposite Brindisi, near the present-day border between Greece and Albania. Landing there, right under the noses of the enemy, was a dangerous proposition, but the very audacity of it would have boosted the confidence of the men of the 10th.

Caesar had originally intended launching the operation on New Year's Day, and the men of the 10th and the other first-wave units had filed down to the docks through the narrow streets of Brindisi on January 1 and climbed the gangplanks to their ships, only to be told to disembark again after a couple of hours' standing, waiting for the outgoing tide. The weather out on the Adriatic had deteriorated rapidly, and Caesar had reluctantly canceled the operation, forcing the troops to tramp back along the cobbled lanes to the embarkation camp, to wait for a better day. That better day had come.

There was much about Caesar's 48 B.C. amphibious invasion of Greece that would be mirrored by the Allied landing in Normandy two thousand years later, in June 1944, and in the same way that Caesar had to put off the operation because of bad weather, so deteriorating weather conditions would force the Allied commanders to postpone their landing from June 5 to June 6.

As his convoy approached the Albanian coast in the late-night darkness, Caesar's plans had to be altered yet again. The wind changed, swinging around to blast down from the north, driving the invasion fleet farther south than Caesar had intended—right past a Pompeian squadron of eighteen cruisers riding at anchor at Oricum, toward the island of Corfu, and Pompey's main battle fleet based there. Yet Caesar's luck held, and the convoy slipped through Pompey's naval blockade in the inky dark.

In the last, nerve-racking hour of the run, the wild, mountainous coast of the Epirus region of Greece, just to the north of Corfu, loomed out of the night away to the left. The location wasn't ideal. There were no harbors here; in fact, this area was infamous as a graveyard of ships swept by gales onto its rocky shore and wrecked. And Caesar would have farther to march once on shore than he'd originally intended, and over rough country, too. But Caesar gave the order for the landing to go ahead. A signal lantern was quickly run up on his flagship.

The steersmen of the leading ships now shoved their twin tillers hard over, and turned their craft toward the shore. Sailors prepared to take in sail. The legionaries of the landing force tensed for the crunch of *terra firma* under the keels of their transports and listened for the order from their centurions to go over the sides.

It was near Palaeste on the Epirus coast that Caesar ran his ships up onto the rocky shore like latter-day landing barges, enabling the troops to rapidly disembark. It is likely that the men of the 10th were the first to hit the deserted, stony beach. Unexpected and unopposed, the night landing went off without a hitch and without a casualty.

Caesar refloated the ships on the tide, and, with the wind changing to a southeasterly, as it always did during the early morning in these climes at this time of year, he sent them back to Brindisi with General Quintus Fufius Calenus to pick up the legions and cavalry of the second wave waiting anxiously with Mark Antony.

We can imagine the scene as, on Corfu, a servant of Admiral Marcus Calpurnius Bibulus tentatively shook his master's shoulder. The admiral, in his bed, opened his eyes to the news, no doubt told in a hushed voice and in the light of a flickering oil lamp that a picket ship had reported sight-

ing enemy ships off the coast. The picket vessel's captain felt sure a landing was taking place.

Bibulus would have sat up abruptly. Pompey had appointed him admiral in chief of all five of his fleets stationed along the coasts of Greece,
Albania, and Croatia and given him the task of intercepting any Caesarian invasion force. Bibulus was a good choice for the job. Caesar's fellow
consul in 59 B.C., foul-tempered but determined and capable, he'd had
several political confrontations with Caesar in the past, coming off the
worse each time. As a result, he hated Caesar with a passion. Rising now
he would have taken up his scarlet cloak from the back of the chair where
he'd thrown it as he went fully dressed to his bed, as was the Roman
habit. Quickly draping the military cloak around his shoulders, he would
have stormed from his sleeping chamber, issuing a stream of instructions
to bleary-eyed staff officers as his armor-bearers flocked around him with
his personal arms and equipment.

Furious that his captains had failed to intercept the invasion fleet,
Admiral Bibulus ordered the 110 battleships, cruisers, and frigates based at
Corfu to immediately put to sea. As junior officers scurried around the
onshore billets rousing the crews of the fleet, the admiral hurried to the
dockside to board his flagship.

The landing of the troops of the first wave had taken longer than it
should have. The last squadron of Caesar's invasion fleet to depart Epirus
for the return run to Italy had hardly put out to sea when the first rays of
daylight began to peek over the top of the Ceraunian Mountains behind
them. Before long, the strong breeze that traditionally blew from the south
on January nights dropped away. Soon the empty transports were drifting
helplessly, within sight of the coast.

The first to go into action because they had fewer crewmen to round
up, Admiral Bibulus's fast frigates came sliding out of Corfu Harbor with
their timekeepers rapidly pounding the beat for their skilled oarsmen and
with the eyes of their lookouts peeled. Soon spotting the wallowing transports, the frigates rapidly overtook the stranded craft. Thirty of Caesar's
troopships were captured.

Before long, Admiral Bibulus's own daunting battleship came surging
onto the scene—probably a vessel of the *deceres* class, 145 feet from end to
end, with a beam of 28 feet, equipped with three banks of oars up to 40
feet long and a crew of 800 oarsmen, sailors, and marines.

From the deck of his flagship, Bibulus would have surveyed the cargo vessels rolling with their sails struck and their crews looking up at him plaintively, his expression as cold as the morning air. According to Caesar, angry that he hadn't been able to stop the invasion, and knowing that Caesar would attempt to reinforce his landed troops with further legions from Italy, Bibulus decided to make an example of the captured vessels.

"Burn them," he ordered.

"And their captains and crews, Admiral?" a subordinate would have asked.

"Leave them where they are."

The battleship's artillery pieces, trained on the captured vessels, would have been loaded with bolts dipped in tar. The tar was set alight. The burning bolts were fired at the cargo vessels. Soon all thirty were burning fiercely as the crews of the warships all around them watched the spectacle in engrossed, ghoulish silence. Those crewmen on the thirty doomed transports who didn't burn to death were drowned when they jumped into the cold, dark waters to escape the flames. Any who tried to swim to the Pompeian warships were fended off, and they, too, were eventually claimed by the waves.

Back at Brindisi, as the hours passed and the ships of the last squadron failed to arrive, the realization hit Mark Antony and General Fufius that the missing transports had been intercepted. The crews of their remaining ships began to talk fearfully about the risks entailed in making a second crossing now that Pompey's navy had obviously been alerted to the operation.

As the weather deteriorated during the rest of the day, Bibulus cast his warships along the west coast of Greece and Albania like a net, ordering them to anchor in every safe harbor and potential landing place. That night he stayed at sea, beginning the habit of sleeping on board his flagship so he could react more quickly to sightings of enemy ships in the future.

The same day that he landed in Epirus, Caesar began advancing north toward Durrës with the men of the 10th and his six other legions of the first wave. He would have had intelligence that Pompey was keeping large amounts of stores at Durrës for the winter, enough to last him well into the spring, but as the main Roman port on the Adriatic coast and starting point of the Egnatian Way, the Roman military highway to Thessalonika and the East, it always would have been an objective anyway. Once he had taken that, Caesar could ship reinforcements and supplies straight across from Brindisi with some security.

Almost as soon as he landed, Caesar set free a prisoner he'd brought over from Italy with him, to perform a task he probably planned well in advance. Lucius Vibullius Rufus, one of Pompey's officers, had been made a prisoner twice by Caesar; once at Corfinium in February during Caesar's advance into Italy, a second time after he'd fled to Pompey's legions in Spain, only to be caught up in their surrender. Caesar now gave Vibullius Rufus a horse and told him to find Pompey and put a peace proposal to him. The deal was that both leaders were to dismiss their armies within three days and then allow the Senate at Rome to decide a final settlement to their differences. Only an idiot would agree to terms like these—over the past nine months Caesar had filled the Senate with his supporters, and any decision they made would naturally favor Caesar. But he wanted to be seen as the honorable man in this conflict, the man whose hand was continually forced by the forces pitted against him.

As Vibullius Rufus galloped off to fulfill his mission, Caesar advanced up the west coast without meeting any resistance. Town after town threw out its Pompeian commander and small garrison and then opened its gates to the Dictator.

Meanwhile, as Caesar's landing was taking place in the west, Pompey, in northeastern Macedonia, was breaking camp and marching his bolstered army of upward of forty thousand men out of his base at Veroia, heading west to spend the winter on the west coast at Durrës, his main supply base, and as yet totally ignorant of the invasion.

Vibullius Rufus headed north until he reached the Egnatian Way, then turned east and rode as fast as he could, changing horses at every town until he met Pompey on the march on the highway. Breathlessly he gave Pompey the news of the invasion, news that sent ripples of panic through the non-Roman contingents of the army, the troops furnished by eastern allies, and passed on the peace offer, which Pompey promptly and not surprisingly dismissed out of hand. No doubt cursing Caesar for surprising him twice within twelve months—first by crossing the Rubicon with just one legion, now by invading Greece on the eve of winter—Pompey ordered his army to march for Durrës at the double, day and night. If Caesar reached the port first and seized his stores, Pompey would be in deep trouble.

The race for Durrës was on.

X

A TASTE OF DEFEAT

Plutarch quotes Cato the Younger as saying that when, in his younger days, Pompey had done nothing wisely nor honestly, he had been successful, but now that he was trying to preserve his country and defend her liberty, he was unsuccessful. Certainly, in Italy and Spain things had gone against Pompey, but now in Albania he had his first, if minor success—he won the race with Caesar, reaching Durrës first.

Once his army arrived on the west coast he had his men set to work building a large fortified camp below Durrës, not far from the Apsus River. Hearing that Caesar was approaching, the knees of many inexperienced soldiers in Pompey's army began to knock. So, led by Caesar's former deputy General Labienus, Pompey's generals now publicly swore an oath that they would not desert their commander, that they would share Pompey's fate, good or bad. The tribunes and centurions of the legions all followed suit, and the troops then did the same.

Caesar, disappointed, came up and camped his legions on the opposite bank of the Apsus, within sight of Pompey's position, planning to spend the winter there with the hope of being reinforced by Mark Antony in the meantime.

Sure enough, Antony and General Fufius now made another attempt to bring the second wave across from Italy after the weather improved and a good following wind blew up. With the men of the second wave crowded on board, the convoy, reduced by thirty ships now, set sail and tried to make the crossing from Brindisi, even though it would be in daylight. But the frightened crews quickly turned back when blockading warships were sighted. One of the vessels from the convoy failed to see the recall flag flown by Fufius's flagship and sailed on, into the path of Admiral Bibulus's battleship. The troopship was soon captured. Admiral Bibulus executed all on board.

Returning to Brindisi, Mark Antony decided not to risk another crossing. He kept his troopships in port and his men in camp. With just fifteen thousand troops ashore in Greece, Caesar was on his own.

Out of the blue, Admiral Bibulus now sent Admiral Lucius Libo, commander of the Liburnian Fleet, to meet with Caesar to discuss a possible peace settlement. Caesar received him, but as Pompey's admiral pushed for a truce, with the promise that in the meantime any proposals Caesar made would be relayed to Pompey for consideration, Caesar realized that Bibulus was only trying to buy time for more troops to reach Pompey from the East, and broke off negotiations.

It soon became apparent why Admiral Bibulus himself hadn't attended the meeting with Caesar. Never leaving his ship as he plowed through heavy seas and freezing winter rain in his determination to catch Caesar's troopships, Bibulus had come down with what sounds like a case of pneumonia. He refused to see a doctor, and before long died at sea. With his death, Pompey lost one of his more brutal but most dedicated senior officers. Command of the fleets now devolved to their individual admirals. This lack of coordination could only help Caesar. Luck continued to run his way.

In February, Pompey's Admiral Libo made a daring dash across the Adriatic to Brindisi, where he landed a commando force of marines from fifty warships. They sank a number of ships and captured several more, initially causing great panic in the Italian city. But the raiders were soon driven off by Mark Antony's second-wave troops, who were still waiting in the embarkation camp to cross the Adriatic, and withdrew with their limited spoils.

Almost daily, Antony had been receiving dispatches from Caesar in Albania urging him to bring across reinforcements. Caesar later excused Antony by saying that his deputy was reluctant to bring the last troops out of Italy in case Pompey used his ships to cross the Adriatic behind Caesar's back and invade Italy. But several classical authors tell the story—not told by Caesar himself—that he became so frustrated by Antony's failure to reinforce him, despite days and weeks of excellent sailing weather through the latter part of January and into February, that he had his servants hire a twelve-oared fishing boat to take him across to Italy so he could personally stir his subordinates into action. He then boarded the craft disguised as a slave. But soon after the boat began the voyage, the weather changed. As the crew prepared to turn back, Caesar revealed his true identity and urged the fishermen to continue on. But the weather grew steadily worse, and in the face of a howling gale Caesar was forced back to shore, after which he abandoned the idea of the covert trip to Italy.

Finally, in March, inspired by their success against Libo's commandos and feeling the heat of Caesar's increasingly strong-worded dispatches demanding to know why they weren't taking advantage of the favorable winds, Antony and General Fufius embarked ten thousand men of the 7th, 8th, 9th, and 29th, along with eight hundred cavalry, and set sail for Albania with a strong south wind and fingers crossed.

As Antony's fleet of transports approached the coast near Durrës, the squadron of Rhodian cruisers based there under Admiral Gaius Coponius came out after it. But the wind strengthened into a gale, and while most of Antony's ships found shelter in a cove three miles north of the town of Lissus, modern Alessio, sixteen of Admiral Coponius's cruisers were dashed to pieces on the rocky coast.

In the middle of the night, the storm subsided. While Antony landed his troops north of Alessio and pulled Pompeian sailors and marines from the sea, two of his troopships that had ridden out the storm at anchor off Alessio now found themselves surrounded by burning torches on Pompeian small craft from the town. Weakened by seasickness and promised lenient treatment by Pompeian officers, 220 raw recruits of the 29th Legion aboard one ship surrendered. Disarmed, the Italian teenagers were taken ashore, where they were all summarily executed by the Pompeian commander at Alessio.

There were just under 200 experienced legionaries from one of Caesar's veteran Spanish legions on the other ship, men of the 7th, 8th, or 9th Legion with seventeen years' hard service under their belts. Rather than surrender, they forced the ship's master to run their vessel onto the shore, and in the morning landed. The Spanish legionaries fought their way through a Pompeian cavalry detachment sent to capture them, then marched three miles along the coast and joined Mark Antony.

Both Pompey and Caesar received word of Antony's landing at much the same time. Pompey reacted quickly. He broke camp and marched his army south, intent on intercepting Antony's legions and wiping them out. He would avoid battle with Caesar, but Antony was a different proposition; Pompey had no respect for the generalship of Caesar's deputy. Uncharacteristically, Caesar reacted more slowly than his adversary. Seeing Pompey marching south, and then realizing what he was up to, he also gave the order to march, determined to link up with Antony before Pompey could attack him.

Pompey set up an ambush, but local Greeks forewarned Antony as he was marching up the coast. Antony immediately built a camp and stayed put, sending messengers to Caesar to tell him of the situation. As Caesar approached, and unwilling to tackle his main opponent, Pompey had no choice but to abandon his plan. He struck camp and skirted around Caesar, marching back to the Durrës area, establishing a new camp some miles south of the town.

Caesar was now able to reunite with his faithful friend Mark Antony. Combining their legions, Caesar now had an army of twenty-six thousand men. But even if he'd had more troops to draw on back in Italy, he could have kissed them good-bye, because now Pompey's eldest son, Gnaeus, brought the Roman fleet normally based in Egypt ranging along the Adriatic coast in a devastating raid. At one coastal town after another, young Pompey captured or burned Antony's transports as they rode at anchor. Overnight, Caesar lost his capacity for resupply from Italy and was cut off in Albania.

For the first time in his illustrious military career, fortune seemed to have deserted Julius Caesar. Now, if he was to be the victor in this war, he would have to win with twenty-six thousand men. And he would have to do it soon, while he still had supplies.

In Asia, Pompey's father-in-law, Metellus Scipio, had received word that Caesar had landed in Greece. Rapidly now, he brought his two legions into Macedonia. Anticipating this, and receiving deputations from towns throughout the region saying they would come over to him if he had troops in the area, Caesar sent several forces east and south—General Gnaeus Domitius Calvinus with the 11th and 12th Legions, General Lucius Longinus with the 27th Legion, and General Gaius Sabinus with the five remaining cohorts of the 28th, with orders to garrison friendly towns, to forage for supplies, and to screen Scipio's movements.

Caesar says these legions did their job well. First Scipio would advance on one screening force, then wheel around and go after the other. According to Caesar, Scipio expended a great deal of energy for naught, losing a number of cavalry in one skirmish, and was kept from joining up with his son-in-law.

Meanwhile, Caesar followed Pompey back up toward Durrës, then tramped off through the hills to the east. Pompey let him go, thinking he was going in search of wheat. Then it dawned on him what Caesar was up to. Rapidly he broke camp and marched his army north along the coast.

Within a day, his worst fears were realized. By forced march, Caesar had used hill paths to work his way north of Pompey's position through the mountainous terrain. Marching up the road from Apollonia, Pompey came up on Caesar's army digging in along the coast south of Durrës. Now, to reach his food and ammunition stored at Durrës, Pompey would have to go through Caesar's army.

Pompey had his legions build a camp on a rocky mountain slope called Petra, overlooking the coast road and the bay south of Durrës. The bay offered a reasonable anchorage, and he gave orders for his ships to start bringing fresh supplies to him from eastern Greece and Asia via Corfu. At the same time, Caesar sent troops foraging far and wide for grain, with limited success.

Caesar, as much an engineering genius as a master soldier, then began building a double line of entrenchments right around Pompey's camp. By the time he had finished, the inner line ran for fifteen miles and incorporated twenty-four forts. The outer line, set back eleven hundred yards, extended for seventeen miles. The inner line of wall and trench was intended to keep Pompey in, the outer to keep his sailors and marines out. To counter this, Pompey had his chief of engineers, Theosaphanes, a Greek from Mytilene on the island of Lesbos, build a formidable entrenchment line of his own inside Caesar's.

Several times Caesar lined up his troops in the open in battle formation, inviting Pompey to come out and fight. But Pompey didn't accept the invitation. He simply didn't have sufficient confidence in his forces for an all-out battle, and was aiming to win a war of attrition. There were numerous skirmishes during the construction work as parties sallied forth here and there for hit-and-run raids, with a few casualties to both sides, but in the end the result was a stalemate.

All the while, both sides were becoming more and more hungry. Caesar sent a number of raiding parties against the town of Durrës itself, hoping to secure its supplies, but all were repulsed by Pompey's garrison. Both the narrow approaches to the port and numbers were against Caesar—for a full-scale assault he would have had to risk depleting his forces in the encirclement, inviting an attack by Pompey behind his back.

As the months passed, Pompey knew that to survive he had break out of the encirclement. It had been many years since he had last been involved in a military campaign, but he had surprised his men over the past twelve months by taking part in their infantry training and cavalry exercises, showing he was just as agile, just as adept as any of his troops. Nor had the years dulled his brain. A shrewd tactician, he decided to concentrate on just one part of the encircling fortifications, and came up with a scheme to improve his chance of success.

The section of Caesar's narrative dealing with the first part of this operation is missing, probably edited out by one of his friends after his death, as were a number of other incidents that showed that Caesar had blundered—such as the escape from Spain of Generals Afranius and Petreius with the men of the 4th and 6th Legions. This same section is also missing from other, later histories, which rely heavily on Caesar's version of events. Fortunately, from Appian, who took some of his information from the memoirs of Caesar's staff officer Gaius Pollio, we know a little of what took place.

It was probably in mid-June that residents of Durrës stole out of the city and found their way to Caesar, offering to change sides and betray the town to him. They told him to come in the dead of night to one of the city gates, the one near the shrine of Artemis, which was apparently outside the city walls, bringing a small number of picked men. Then, just before dawn, they would open the gates to him so he could seize the city.

This offer was too good to refuse, and, taking a detachment from his German cavalry bodyguard with him, Caesar slipped away from the encirclement and rode through the night to the town to keep the appointment. It seems Caesar was so disappointed with Mark Antony after his slowness in bringing over the second wave that he gave him command of the four legions he'd brought to Albania but not the powers of second-in-command of the whole army. Either that, or Antony accompanied him to Durrës. Either way, in his absence Caesar now left General Publius Sulla, nephew of the famous Sulla the Dictator, in charge of the encirclement of Pompey's army.

Like many towns of the day, Durrës had outgrown its walls, and a number of newer buildings had been built along narrow lanes leading up to the city gates. Here at daybreak, as Caesar approached the gate by the temple of Artemis, Pompey sprung a trap. Caesar's cavalry were ambushed in the lanes by waiting troops, and they had to fight desperately to make their escape, with Caesar himself only just evading capture. Caesar later tells us there were three skirmishes this day at the town, so it is probable he led two counterattacks before withdrawing on receiving news of what had taken place back at the encirclement.

As the sun was rising over the bay at Petra, at the same moment that Caesar was fighting for his life at Durrës, Pompey launched a full legion supported by a large contingent of archers against one of the twenty-four forts on the perimeter of Caesar's encircling trench line. The fort was occupied by a cohort of the 8th Legion commanded by a Colonel Minucius, in the sector under the overall jurisdiction of Mark Antony. To draw potential reinforcements away from Pompey's main target, two other forts were attacked at the same time at different parts of the encirclement, one by a force at legion strength, the other by a German cavalry detachment that was probably led by General Labienus.

It had been a moonlit night, but aided by thick clouds that shrouded the moon, the assault force had crept unseen across no-man's-land and quietly filled in parts of the trenches skirting the fortified wall of the 8th Legion fort. As dawn broke, the spearhead troops surged across the trench, paving the way for archers, who set about raining arrows into the fort. The cohort of the 8th held out for four hours until General Sulla dealt with the feints, then arrived with two legions to relieve them; the 10th may have been one of these units, but we don't know. The appearance of reinforcements prompted Pompey's assault troops to withdraw.

Caesar says his troops killed two thousand of the attackers in this action, but no other account corroborates this figure, which, considering Caesar's track record, is without doubt substantially inflated. He also says that for his side not more than 20 of the fort's defenders were killed in four hours of fighting, again a suspect figure. But he does admit that every survivor was wounded—some 250 to 300 men—with 4 centurions of the 8th Legion cohort losing eyes to arrows.

Among the wounded, according to Appian, was the fort's commander, Colonel Minucius, who also lost an eye and received five additional wounds. When Caesar arrived back from Durrës he was shown the shield of Cassius Scaevus, a junior centurion of the 8th grade who'd taken over command of the fort after Colonel Minucius and the four other more senior centurions were wounded. If we can believe it, the shield had been punctured 120 times in the fight. Caesar also claims that his men collected thirty thousand Pompeian arrows that had been fired into the fort. Centurion Scaevus was promoted to the first rank and received a bonus of two hundred thousand sesterces, a fortune for an enlisted man. All the other survivors of the cohort were later given *duplicarius* status—their wages were doubled—and received extra food and clothing allowances.

Caesar had sent General Fufius south to take command of the force led by Generals Longinus and Sabinus, comprising the 27th Legion and five cohorts of the 28th, and he advanced into the Boeotia region, accepting the surrender of the famous cities of Delphi and Thebes and storming several others. But Fufius's successes in the south weren't helping Caesar at Durrës. With each passing day, the supply situation became increasingly grim on both sides. Caesar's men resorted to digging up the roots of a local plant called "chara," which they mixed with milk to make a kind of bread.

Troops deserting from Caesar's army—and quite a number apparently changed sides—took loaves of this unsavory creation to Pompey as proof of the hard times being endured by Caesar's troops, and Pompey is said to have remarked that the opposition troops were becoming like animals, eating the roots of wild plants. Pompey's own army was little better off for provisions. His men killed all their pack animals, and fed their increasingly weak cavalry horses the leaves of trees. Pompey's cavalry arm was much larger than Caesar's, and, with little confidence in much of his infantry, Pompey was determined to maintain his substantial mounted superiority. As he saw both his men and his cavalry horses dropping, he was forced to set in motion a new plan for a breakout to gain access to his supplies.

Pompey's latest plan came together in early July after two major defections from Caesar's camp. Roucillus and Egus were brothers from the Rhône valley in southeastern France. The sons of Adubucillus, chief of the Allobroges tribe, they had been commanders of Caesar's Gallic cavalry for the past ten years, and even appear to have been enrolled in the Senate at Rome the previous year by Caesar in reward for their service. According to Caesar, when they heard rumors that complaints had been laid against them accusing them of embezzling cavalry funds the pair went over to Pompey, although it's likely Caesar invented this to explain away their change of loyalties.

Whatever their motivation, the two cavalry generals knew Caesar's dispositions, the strong points and the weak points of his encirclement, and the weaknesses of the various units. And Pompey welcomed them. He paraded the two senior defectors around his camp for all his men to see, and he talked with them for hours at a time about Caesar's camp and his army. And then he made careful preparations.

At dawn on the still morning of July 7, the Spanish legionaries of Caesar's 9th Legion manning the western side of the entrenchments, by the sea, found themselves suddenly under sustained attack. Just like the last time Pompey launched a perimeter assault, heavy clouds had hidden the moon, and again legionaries and archers who had crept into position in the predawn darkness were all over Caesar's defenses in moments.

Roucillus and Egus, the high-placed defectors, had told Pompey that the fortifications at this point in the encirclement, just below those manned by the 8th Legion, were incomplete, that the Spanish legionaries of the

9th Legion occupying this sector were overdue for their discharge and not very happy about their continued service, as demonstrated by their mutiny at Piacenza the previous fall, and that the 9th's commander, Major General Lentulus Marcellinus, was unwell and often in his sickbed. These were weaknesses that begged exploitation. Pompey also knew that the sector commander was Mark Antony, and he'd never had any respect for Antony's military abilities.

Now, while some of Pompey's legionaries made a frontal attack, filling in the ditches in front of the Caesarian wall, then bringing up assault ladders and artillery pieces, archers worked their way around the flanks. The only form of missile that the men of the 9th possessed was stones. Pompey's intelligence was so good he even knew this fact, and he'd equipped his storm troops with special wicker coverings for their helmets that created faceguards to protect their faces from flying stones.

The legionaries who carried out this dawn assault stuck to their task and Pompey's well-planned attack overwhelmed the men of the 9th, who were all mature soldiers, in their midthirties or older. Most of their senior centurions fell. The eagle of the 9th was almost gained by the attackers before its dying eagle-bearer passed the standard to other hands. General Marcellinus sent reinforcements, but they were beaten back by Pompey's determined assault force. Urgent smoke signals were sent to Caesar to bring help, and they were relayed from fort to fort around the miles of entrenchments by burning flares.

At the nearest fort, Mark Antony assembled a relief force, then rushed down the hill with twelve cohorts from the 7th and 8th Legions, both of which formed part of his command. These reinforcements stabilized the situation to the south, but Pompey's troops still managed to break out to the sea where they had overrun the 9th Legion. The 9th's fort had been taken and the double walls of the encirclement were breached in numerous places along the shoreline so that Pompey's cavalry could get out and seek fodder, and ships could land supplies.

As Caesar himself hurriedly arrived with more reinforcements, a Pompeian unit of legion strength was seen to occupy a deserted Caesarian camp three hundred yards from the sea; the camp had originally been built by the 9th Legion at Mark Antony's direction weeks before. At the time they had been forced to give it up by constant attack from Pompey's archers and auxiliaries, and the camp, out in no-man's-land, had become untenable for both sides. Things were different now that Pompey had pushed back the 9th from its position on the water's edge; the deserted camp was his for the taking.

It seems that the men who now occupied this camp were from Caesar's former 24th Legion, the unit that the previous year had defected to Pompey at Corfu. As they took up defensive positions on the ramparts of the camp, Caesar could see that these troops would be able to cover supplies coming to the beach. If he was to seal the hole in his encirclement and prevent Pompey from landing supplies coming up from Corfu, he had to dislodge the men now holding that camp.

Caesar, smarting at having been outmaneuvered by Pompey, planned a counterattack. Setting some troops to work very visibly extending defensive walls and trenches to cover his troop buildup in the area, he soon launched a surprise attack on the camp recently occupied by Pompey's cohorts. In two lines, thirty-two cohorts, including legionaries from the 7th and 8th Legions and all the surviving men of the 9th Legion, swept up the slope toward the camp, supported by cavalry.

Pompey's men put up a furious fight from the camp's walls, even though they were outnumbered three to one. Here Caesar gives praise to one of Pompey's officers. Centurion Titus Puleio, who had served bravely with Caesar's legions in Gaul before being assigned to the 24th, had been among Gaius Antony's troops when they were intercepted on the Adriatic. Puleio had been the one who convinced them all to go over to Pompey. Now Puleio fought like a demon, inspiring his men.

Led by Caesar himself, the left wing of his assault force broke into Puleio's camp. But the men of the 8th and 9th Legions on the right wing became lost in the confusing entrenchments. Caesar's cavalry followed the men on the right wing, filing along a narrow passageway between trench walls. At this moment Pompey himself appeared, at the head of five legions, coming to the support of his men at the camp. The 1st Legion was almost certainly at the forefront of this force. Pompey always kept the elite legion close by him. The other four legions were probably the 15th and the three legions recruited in southern Italy before Pompey's withdrawal to Greece.

Encouraged by the sight of their commander in chief coming up with the experienced legions, Puleio and his troops fighting for their lives in the camp regained the initiative and charged Caesar's men, driving them back. Seeing this sudden change of fortune, Caesar's cavalry panicked. They tried to go back the way they had come, down the narrow alley. The troops of the right wing, seeing the cavalry turning and fleeing, seeing Pompey coming with thousands of reinforcements, hearing their comrades inside the camp in trouble, and fearing that they were going to be cut off, jumped into a ten-foot trench that they thought would provide an escape route. Hundreds of Caesar's men were trampled to death in this trench as their own desperate colleagues jumped in on top of them in an attempt to escape.

Seeing the cavalry in wide-eyed flight, Caesar tried to stop them, but they ignored him. He grabbed standards to stem the flood, but the standard-bearers simply let go of them and kept going. Appian even writes of a frantic standard-bearer trying to stab Caesar with the pointed bottom tip of his standard in his desperation to get away—and being cut down by men of Caesar's bodyguard. As the infantry also now flooded in confusion back toward their own lines, the stragglers being overtaken and cut down by the men of Pompey's legions, Caesar had no choice but to retreat himself.

At this point Pompey had the opportunity to turn a success into a victory. With thousands of Caesar's troops retreating, many in panic, he could have continued on with his five legions, and with his cavalry just then starting to come up, he could have overrun the siege works and rolled up Caesar's army. But he ordered his troops not to pursue the fleeing Caesarians. Pompey himself never explained why.

Caesar later speculated that the scope of Pompey's success on the day was far beyond his expectations—Pompey had merely wanted to break out to the sea so his supplies could reach him. Caesar was sure that Pompey was afraid of being led into an ambush. No one had ever seen Caesar's troops run before. It had to be a trap. Some reports have Caesar later belittling Pompey, saying the enemy could have had a victory that day if they'd possessed a general who knew how to gain it.

In this encounter, which historians were to call the Battle of Dyrrhachium, Pompey's troops captured thirty-two standards from the 9th Legion and other units involved in the right wing of Caesar's counterattack and from the Caesarian cavalry. Pompey and his men justifiably celebrated the outcome of the battle as a success. But it could have been so much more.

A chastened Caesar admitted to losing 960 legionaries, the majority of them from the 9th Legion, as well as 36 officers—4 of the rank of general and 32 tribunes and centurions. And he had hundreds more wounded; Caesar never revealed exactly how many, but the number was substantial enough, together with the fatalities, to reduce the effectiveness of the 8th and 9th Legions to the point that Caesar later combined the two. But had Pompey followed up on his success, Caesar could have lost the war. Yet again, Julius Caesar's luck prevailed.

After the unaccustomed experience of failure at Durrës, Caesar decided to withdraw. The siege line had been broken, and Pompey could once again be supplied by sea. It was pointless for Caesar to keep his troops in the trenches, particularly when they were starving. First, with the men in marching order, he called an assembly, and from the tribunal publicly demoted standard-bearers who had fled during the battle.

Then, as his memoirs record, he told the assembled legions: "The setback we have sustained cannot be blamed on me. I gave an opportunity for battle on favorable ground. I took possession of the enemy camp. I drove the enemy out. Through your fear, or some mistake, or some stroke of fate, the victory that was as good as in our grasp was lost. So it falls to you to make an effort to repair the damage, through your valor. If you do, you will turn our loss to gain, as happened at Gergovia."

Well did the listening men of the 10th Legion remember the siege of Gergovia, four years before, Caesar's reverse during the Vercingetorix Revolt in central France. It had been the men of the 10th who'd saved the day for Caesar back then.

Caesar sent the baggage train on ahead just after sunset. As the wagons and pack mules moved out in the darkness, Caesar kept the bulk of his army in camp, with all the visible signs of occupation. In the last hours of darkness next morning Caesar then pulled out his main force. The troops were able to travel light and fast without the impediment of the baggage train, which had a start of eight hours or so. At forced-march pace they hurried east. In Macedonia and Thessaly there were towns friendly to Caesar. They, and their wheat fields, could provide the one thing his troops needed now: food.

Next morning, as soon as he realized that Caesar had pulled out, Pompey set off in pursuit. Leaving Cato the Younger in charge at Durrës with fifteen cohorts detached from his legions, he left his own baggage train behind to make its own progress; this would allow his infantry to make good time, and hopefully catch Caesar on the march. Encouraged by his subordinates, and more confident of the morale of his troops following the success at Durrës, Pompey was more inclined toward a pitched battle now. His confidence spread through the army. His men would have shared jokes about what they would do to Caesar's raw recruits when they got ahold of them.

A detachment of Pompey's cavalry caught up with Caesar's rear guard, which fought them off, and by the middle of the day the two armies prepared to spend the night at camps in eastern Albania. Again Caesar had a trick up his sleeve. Just when a number of Pompey's troops departed from his camp and marched out of sight to provide an escort for their baggage train, which was straggling up from the coast, Caesar suddenly set off again with his entire force. They covered another eight miles before making a new camp that night, leaving Pompey in their wake.

Each day after that, Caesar would send his baggage on ahead in the night, then follow later with the army. After four days of trying to pursue Caesar, Pompey gave up the chase. Instead, he diverted east to Thessaly to link up with his father-in-law, Metellus Scipio, who was camped with his two legions at the town of Larisa on the Peneus River.

Caesar made a halt at Apollonia, modern Pollina, then a famous center of learning. This stop was just long enough for Caesar to leave his wounded behind—several thousand men, mostly from the veteran Spanish legions that had been fighting for him for the past thirteen years. Detaching a total of eight cohorts of fit legionaries, almost certainly from his newer Italian legions, he spread them between Apollonia and two other towns to maintain his hold on the region. He then continued east and linked up with the veteran legions under his general Domitius Calvinus, the 11th and 12th, which had been screening Scipio's two legions in Thessaly.

Gomphi, a town in Thessaly, had gone over to Pompey after the news of his success at Durrës, and Caesar decided to make an example of it, to ensure the cooperation of other Greek communities. A little rape and pillage wouldn't do the damaged morale of his men any harm, either. Surrounding the town, he sent his legions against its walls. They began the assault in the early afternoon. As the sun was setting, they broke into the town. Caesar gave his troops permission to plunder Gomphi. It was destroyed, and every one of its inhabitants killed.

The victorious troops drank the town dry, with, according to Appian, Caesar's German cavalrymen in particular ending up disgustingly drunk. Germans in general, Appian remarked, had no head for drink, especially wine. A similar observation would be made by Tacitus a century later.

Leaving Ghompi a smoking ruin, Caesar marched on to the town of Metropolis. At first it closed its gates to him. Then news reached the townspeople of the fate of Gomphi. Metropolis quickly opened its gates to Caesar. Before long, he moved on.

A little east of Metropolis, Caesar crossed the Enipeus River. Just to the north of the river, on a plain covered with ripening wheat, he made camp. The town of Pharsalus, modern Farsala, was on a hill some way off in the distance. Several miles to the northwest, the plain was fringed by the foothills of Mount Dogandzis. Here Caesar was determined to do two things: cut down the wheat as soon as it was ripe so his men could get some fresh bread in their bellies again, and then offer Pompey battle.

A few days later, Pompey marched into Thessaly and linked up with Scipio, father of the beautiful young Cornelia, his fifth wife. Cornelia, widow of Publius Crassus, youthful commander of the 7th Legion who had impressed many in Gaul before dying with his father at Carrhae, was waiting on the island of Lesbos to the east with Pompey's youngest son, nineteen-year-old Sextus Pompey. Already couriers were on their way to Cornelia with news that her husband had achieved a great success at Durrës and he was now in hot pursuit of Caesar. The message-bringers assured Cornelia that Caesar's ultimate defeat was now just a matter of time.

As the legions of Pompey's two armies combined with cheers of greeting, and as friendly banter was exchanged between the ranks, Pompey honored Scipio by appointing him his co-commander. Giving up his tent to him and pitching a new one for himself beside it, he also issued orders for the trumpeters who sounded the changes of watch every three hours to do so from outside Scipio's quarters, as a mark of respect.

The combined army resumed the pursuit of Caesar, finding him on the plain of Farsala. Pompey chose a camp site three miles to the northwest of Caesar with the advantage of higher ground, making his camp in foothills fringing the plain to the west, with Mount Dogandzis rising behind him.

Pompey was still reluctant to commit to a full-scale battle. Despite his success at Durrës, and even though he outnumbered Caesar, he had little confidence in the majority of his infantry. He knew that Caesar had by far the most experienced legionaries, and when it came down to it, experience would win out over numbers. Pompey's plan now was to avoid a major encounter and wear Caesar down through a war of attrition. Few of the generals and senators with him were of the same view, as they repeatedly informed him. This was the big difference between Pompey and Caesar, and why Pompey had so much popular support—he would listen to others, although for now he put off their demands for a decisive battle by saying the time was not yet right. But, says Caesar, so sure were members of Pompey's party that victory was just around the corner that they began to argue among themselves about who should receive what official appointment after Caesar had been defeated.

Pompey called a council of war. He told his colleagues to be neither overconfident nor impatient, but assured them that they would indeed do battle with Caesar in due course, and that when the armies met he would defeat Caesar before the two battle lines even came together. The secret, he confided, lay with their cavalry.

In his memoirs, Caesar disparaged General Labienus, his former deputy and now Pompey's cavalry commander, claiming that at this war council Labienus assured his fellow Pompeian generals that all Caesar's best troops were dead and that the bulk of the Caesarian soldiers now were inexperienced, poor-quality levies from Cisalpine Gaul and Transalpine Gaul. This claim by Caesar is just plain silly. From highly placed deserters such as Roucillus and Egus, Labienus and his fellow commanders knew precisely what the makeup of Caesar's army was, knew about his four veteran Spanish legions, including the 10th, knew that just two of his legions, the 11th and 12th, were from Cisalpine Gaul, and that they were made up of highly experienced men. Besides, both Pompey's best legions, the 1st and the 15th, were from Cisalpine Gaul.

From other sources we know what Labienus actually said that day. He did encourage his colleagues, but not by putting down Caesar's troops. All Romans were highly superstitious and much influenced by omens, and Labienus, probably a member of several priesthoods, assured his fellow commanders that all the omens were auspicious and pointed to a victory for Pompey. General Labienus then led all present in an oath that once they went out to fight they would only return to camp as victors. Pompey's supporters enthusiastically took the oath, and left the meeting in high spirits.

XI

THE BATTLE OF PHARSALUS

G aius Crastinus moved among his men, checking their equipment. He was no longer chief centurion of the 10th. That role had gone to a younger centurion the previous year, on Crastinus's retirement. But on his recall, Caesar had welcomed Crastinus back to his legion with the rank of first-rank centurion, and for this operation had placed him in charge of 120 volunteers of the 1st Cohort of the 10th Legion, putting them in the front line. Caesar had once more placed the 10th Legion on his extreme right wing, the attacking wing. Much would depend on the 10th today.

Crastinus assured his comrades that they had just this one last battle to face as he moved along the line. He would have noticed a change of attitude among the men of the 10th since his return to its ranks. A lot of them had probably complained that Caesar no longer valued the 10th, that he treated it no better than the new Italian units with their raw, weak-kneed recruits. He'd broken his promise, and used the Germans as his bodyguard, not the 10th.

Now aged between thirty-four and thirty-seven, Crastinus had served Caesar for twelve of his seventeen years with the legions and was fanatically loyal to his general. He would have been quick to remind his comrades that Caesar had chosen the 10th to accompany him in the invasion's first wave and now given them place of honor on the right wing. But there were apparently many in the 10th who sympathized with their countrymen in the 7th, 8th, and 9th, who were now eighteen months past their due discharge date and yet, as they complained, Caesar had not said a word about when they could go home.

"Remember what Caesar told us at Brindisi before we embarked," Crastinus would have been telling his men. "One last campaign, one last battle."

113

Caesar himself records Crastinus saying: "After today, Caesar will regain his position, and we our freedom."

It was midmorning on August 9, 48 B.C. As Centurion Crastinus took up his position on the extreme left of his front-line detachment, he faced across the field of swaying, ripening wheat to the army of Pompey the Great formed up some 450 yards away. Ever since the two sides had arrived on the plain of Farsala several weeks earlier, each had felt the other out, with cavalry skirmishes bringing a handful of fatalities on both sides, including one of the Allobroges brothers who'd defected to Pompey. More than once, Caesar had formed up his army in battle order in the wheat field, encouraging Pompey to come down off his hilltop and enter into a contest. Each time, Pompey stayed put. And each time, Caesar edged a little closer to the hills.

Then, early this morning, Caesar had broken camp. According to Plutarch, he was planning to march to Scotussa. Caesar himself says he'd decided to keep constantly on the move, seeking supplies for his army and leading Pompey a merry dance until the ideal opportunity for a battle presented itself. Even as his legions' tents were being folded away and packed onto the baggage train, cavalry scouts came to Caesar to tell him that there was movement at Pompey's camp. And as the lead elements of Caesar's column marched out the front gate of his camp, more scouts arrived with the news that Pompey's troops were beginning to come down from their hill and line up in battle formation—on the plain, giving up the advantage of higher ground. This was an obvious invitation to Caesar, and he accepted it.

"Our spirits are ready for battle," Caesar says he declared. "We shall not easily find another chance." He quickly issued orders for his red ensign to be raised as the signal for battle, and for the army to wheel about and form up on the plain opposite Pompey's troops. According to both Appian and Plutarch, Caesar called out to his men, "The wished-for day has come at last, when you shall fight with men, not with famine and hunger."

Summoning his senior officers to a brief conference, he'd ordered the same dispositions as the last time the army formed up for battle. Then, turning to General Publius Sulla, who would command the division on the right wing of the battle line, he told him to call for volunteers from the 10th to form the front line and lead the charge, knowing the untried legions in the center would be inspired by the performance of the famous 10th.

Some 120 men had quickly volunteered, among them Centurion Crastinus, which was why they now stood at the front of the 10th Legion's formation on the extreme right of Caesar's army, the cohorts stretching back in a total of three battle lines. Beside the 10th, making up the rest of the right division, stood the men of the 11th and 12th Legions. General Sulla had already taken up his position on the right with his staff.

Caesar's center was commanded by General Domitius Calvinus, who had previously led the screening force in eastern Greece. As was the custom, the weakest troops took the center. In this case the central division was made up of three of the new legions raised in Italy the previous year, the 25th, 26th, and 29th.

The left wing was commanded by Mark Antony, once again holding the post of second-in-command of the army. With him stood the experienced Spanish legions he'd brought over from Brindisi and commanded at Durrës. The 9th was on the extreme outside, with auxiliaries and slingers filling the gap between them and the Enipeus River. The 8th was stationed next to the 9th. Both legions had been so depleted by the flu epidemic and then the casualties at Durrës that Caesar had ordered them to work together during this action and operate as one legion. Next to them stood the men of the 7th Legion, adjacent to the central division. All told, leaving just two cohorts guarding his camp and the baggage, with his 27th and 28th Legions absent in southern Greece, now under General Fufius, and eight assorted cohorts garrisoning three towns on the west coast, he was able to field nine legions in eighty understrength cohorts, totaling twenty-one thousand foot soldiers.

To counter Pompey's cavalry massing on his right, Caesar deployed his own thousand-man cavalry, Germans and Gauls, supported by auxiliaries, extending from the 10th Legion's position. His mounted troops and the auxiliaries had cooperated well in skirmishes against Pompey's cavalry in the week or so leading up to the battle, and Caesar was hoping they would do the same again today to counteract Pompey's significant superiority in cavalry.

Facing him, at Caesar's estimation, Pompey had forty thousand infantry and seven thousand cavalry. As he came down onto the plain that morning, Pompey left seven cohorts drawn from a number of his least experienced legions to guard his camp, supported by auxiliaries from Thrace and Thessaly. General Afranius, who'd escaped from Spain to join Pompey, had come under severe criticism from Pompey's other generals for losing seven legions to Caesar in Spain, despite the fact that he'd managed to bring thirty-five hundred men of the 4th and the 6th with him to Greece, and he'd been given the humble job of commanding the defenders of the camp, accompanied by Pompey's eldest son, Gnaeus, who was probably in his midtwenties at this point.

Young Gnaeus would have been hugely frustrated at being left in the comparative safety of the camp, with the second-rate troops and thousands of noncombatants. He'd proven his bravery and military skill when he'd commanded the fleet from Egypt that had destroyed Caesar's shipping along the Adriatic coast during the winter. But his father was obviously anxious to protect his son and heir. This act is indicative of the negative mind-set of Pompey on the day of the battle. Forced to agree to the battle by his impatient supporters at the meeting two days before, he still had little confidence in most of his infantry.

According to both Plutarch and Appian, Pompey had been awakened by a disturbance in his camp in the early hours of that morning: just before the last change of watch, excited sentries had witnessed a fiery-tailed meteor race across the sky from the direction of Caesar's camp and disappear beyond the hills behind their own. Once awake, Pompey confided to his staff that he'd been dreaming he was adorning the temple of Venus the Victorious at Rome. Julius Caesar's family claimed descent from the goddess Venus, and Pompey's supporters were delighted by the dream, seeing it as an omen that Pompey soon would be celebrating the defeat of Caesar. Pompey wasn't so sure; the dream could also be interpreted that he was saluting Caesar as victor.

Unbeknownst to Pompey, the previous evening Caesar had issued as his army's watchword, or password, for August 9, "Venus, Bringer of Victory," quite unaware that Pompey planned to bring on a battle next day.

A new watchword was issued every day in Roman military camps. Polybius tells us the watchword was issued for the next twenty-four hours by the commanding officer just before sunset. The tribune of the watch then distributed it on wax sheets to his legion's guard sergeants, who in turn passed it on to the duty sentries in a strictly regulated process that required the prompt return of the wax sheets. Anyone trying to enter a Roman camp without knowing the watchword for the day was in trouble.

In battle, especially at times of civil war like this, with both sides similarly equipped, as well as in night fights, a watchword was often the only way to identify men from your own side. There are several instances of watchwords being hurriedly changed just before a battle in case deserters had passed on the latest watchword to the enemy overnight.

Watchwords could be a single word or a phrase. In imperial times, the emperor always issued the watchword to the Praetorian Guard if he was at Rome or to the army if he was in camp with them. Claudius frequently gave lines from epic poems. Nero famously issued "The Best of Mothers" in honor of the mother he later murdered. Dio and Seutonius say Caligula teased a particularly macho Praetorian tribune who came to dread the days when it fell to him to ask the emperor for the watchword; Caligula would call him a girl and give him watchwords such as "Love" and "Venus"— goddess of love. Dio also says that the night before Emperor Marcus Aurelius died in A.D. 180 he gave as the next day's watchword "Go to the Rising Sun, I Am Already Setting."

On August 8, 48 B.C., Pompey the Great, knowing the new day would bring the battle he'd been avoiding for a year and a half, had issued "Hercules, the Unconquered" as his watchword for August 9. Like mighty Hercules, Pompey had never been defeated in battle, and he was hoping it would stay that way.

Now that the day had arrived, despite his misgivings, Pompey made his troop dispositions with care. Marshaled by their centurions, the men of his elite 1st Legion confidently took up their assigned positions as the first heavy infantry unit on his left wing. Like Napoleon's Imperial Guard 1,860 years later, the men of the 1st considered themselves the *crème de la crème* of their general's army. Yet, as Pompey knew, despite the 1st's proud record, most of the men of this enlistment of the legion had never been involved in a major engagement.

Beside the 1st stood Caesar's former 15th Legion. The men of the 15th had six years' experience behind them, four of those fighting for Caesar in Gaul, and were probably Pompey's best troops in terms of experience. Since being given to Pompey by the Senate two years back, the legion had served him without question. Caesar now refused to call it the 15th. Instead, being rather petty, he would refer to it as the 3rd—because, it seems, the 15th came from the same recruiting ground in Cisalpine Gaul as the 3rd, which was one of Pompey's legions that Caesar had captured in Spain and disbanded. But, deep in his heart, Pompey must have wondered whether, when it came to the crunch, the 15th could be trusted, whether the legion's old association with Caesar would impact on its reliability in the heat of battle.

Next to the 15th stood two of the newly recruited legions that Pompey had brought out of Italy the previous year, made up mostly of youths in their late teens. This left-hand division of four legions came under the command of General Domitius Ahenobarbus. This was the same General Domitius who had lost Corfinium and Marseilles, but Pompey was a great respecter of rank, and Domitius outranked just about everyone else in his party, so he'd been given this command despite his past failings.

Pompey's father-in-law, Scipio, held the middle of the line with his two Italian legions, raised five years earlier, survivors of Carrhae who had subsequently been stationed in Syria, plus the third of the new legions made up of untried Italian recruits which had escaped from Brindisi with the 1st and the 15th.

Commanding the division on Pompey's right wing, General Lucius Lentulus, a consul the previous year, had long been a violent opponent of Caesar and was a dependable commander. Pompey had stationed auxiliaries and 600 slingers all the way to the Enipeus River. The riverbanks dropped down sharply to the Enipeus, like small cliffs, and couldn't be scaled by either infantry or cavalry, so Pompey knew that he couldn't be outflanked on his right, allowing him the luxury of leaving this wing without cavalry cover. The veteran soldiers of the seven Spanish cohorts of the 4th Legion and the 6th Legion that had escaped from Spain to join Pompey now held his right wing, behind their own eagles but working together, facing their countrymen of Mark Antony's 8th and 9th across the wheat field, units that had been similarly combined because of their lack of numbers.

Beside these Spanish cohorts stood the Gemina Legion, the "twin," so called by Pompey after he'd made up a single legion from two raised in Italy by Cicero in 51 B.C., and taken by him to Cilicia when he was governor there for a year, then left behind on garrison duty after he returned to Rome in 50 B.C. The remaining cohorts of those two original legions were still stationed in Cilicia. Between the Gemina Legion and Scipio's troops, the seventy-five hundred men of the 24th and 28th, the former Italian legions of Gaius Antony that had come over to Pompey with Centurion Puleio and performed well at Durrës, formed up behind two eagles. Caesar, stung by their defection, would never refer to these two legions by name, simply calling them "some of Gaius Antony's old troops."

Pompey had called up another two thousand men, retired veterans who'd settled in Macedonia and on the island of Crete, originally thinking of forming them into a separate legion; but they were no longer young men and were out of practice, so he split them into cohorts and spread them among his other units.

On paper, Pompey had 12 legions made up of 110 cohorts. Caesar would have only considered several of these any threat—the 1st, 15th, the Spanish cohorts of the 4th and 6th, perhaps the Gemina, and probably the two battle-hardened Italian legions Scipio had brought from Syria. Pompey had even less faith in these units than his opponent, and was pinning his hopes of victory solely on his cavalry. He had told his supporters that the cavalry would bring them victory before the infantry could even come to grips. This was wishful thinking. Pompey dreaded the prospect of pitting his infantry against Caesar's, as he was certain his were not up to the task. So now all seven thousand of his cavalry formed up on his left wing, ready to undertake the tactical strike he had planned for them.

As Pompey and his staff prepared to take their position on the left, behind the 1st and 15th Legions, he and General Labienus parted company. Labienus rode to where his massed cavalry waited on Pompey's far left wing. He would not have been surprised to see the 10th Legion allocated to Caesar's right, facing him. He may have even thought that Caesar was becoming predictable. But he would not have taken the 10th lightly. The 10th Legion was by now universally considered, in the words of Plutarch, the stoutest of Caesar's legions. Labienus had personally led the 10th in Gaul, and he knew what the Spanish legion was made of. Who could forget the day Labienus had sent the 10th splashing back across the Sambre to save Caesar from the Nervii? Overcome the 10th, he knew, and the rest of Caesar's legions would be likely to buckle. In fact, Plutarch tells us that Pompey's cavalry were given the explicit task of cutting off the 10th Legion from the rest of Caesar's army and destroying it.

Behind General Labienus spread his massive mounted force. The twenty-seven hundred long-haired German and Gallic cavalrymen Labienus had brought over to Pompey from Caesar's army formed the core of his cavalry. Five hundred Italian troopers had been brought up to Greece by sea by Gnaeus Pompey from where they'd been stationed in Egypt as a part of the bodyguard of young King Ptolemy XIII and his sister Cleopatra. King Deiotarus of Galatia had brought Pompey six hundred cavalry. The remaining cavalrymen had been supplied by various rulers from throughout the East, and both their quality and their loyalty were questionable. The main responsibility for the success of the operation lay with Labienus's own men.

As had become his usual practice, Caesar had decided to station himself on his right wing, usually the hottest place in any battle, the place where victory and defeat were most decided. As he was moving to his position, he saw Pompey's cavalry spreading directly opposite, saw Pompey himself on that wing, with six hundred slingers and three thousand auxiliary archers from eastern states forming up behind him. Colonel Pollio and other staff officers would have warned their commander that Pompey was aiming to outflank him on the right, but Caesar had already seen the danger for himself. He immediately devised a counter.

"Have one cohort taken from each of the legions in the third line," he instructed. "Form them into a fourth line, behind the Tenth, where they are to await the order to charge the enemy's cavalry." He passed on a particular tactic he wanted this fourth line to employ, then added that the day's victory would depend on their valor.

The exact number of men taken out of the third line for this special reserve is debatable. The implication, from Caesar himself, is that nine understrength cohorts were involved, one from each of his legions. Plutarch says there were six cohorts, and both he and Appian say they totaled 3,000 men; but in their day six *full-strength* cohorts numbered close to 3,000 men—2,880, to be precise—and none of Caesar's units was anywhere near approaching full strength. It's probable that about 2,000 men were actually involved. From what Appian says, it's likely that these men were ordered to lie down to conceal their presence, in the same way the Duke of Wellington would, at the 1815 Battle of Waterloo, order his Foot Guards to lie down behind a ridge and await his signal to rise to the charge, a tactic that turned the battle against Napoleon's advancing Old Guard.

Now, as Centurion Crastinus stood with his men of the 10th Legion in the front line, a familiar voice away to his right called him by name.

"What hopes for victory, Gaius Crastinus? What grounds for encouragement?"

This incident is recorded by several different classical sources, including Caesar himself. The centurion's head whipped around, to see Caesar riding along the front line toward him accompanied by his staff officers. "Victory will be yours, Caesar," said Crastinus. According to Plutarch, he reached out his right hand toward his general in a form of salute, adding, "You will conquer gloriously today."

Caesar would have smiled in response to the centurion's confident prediction and wished the men under Crastinus's command good luck, then spurred his horse on. In his memoirs he relates how several times he stopped along the front line to give a short speech, moving on to repeat the same sentiment several times, making separate reference to the glorious record in his service of the individual legions in front of him, then adding, "My soldiers, I call on you, every man, to witness the earnestness with which I have sought peace up till now." He went on to list the missions of various peace envoys and his failed attempts to negotiate a settlement with Pompey, then said, "It has never been my wish to expose my troops to bloodshed, nor to deprive the state of this army or of that which stands across the field from us today. But I have been given no choice."

Then he issued his battle orders. The first two lines were to charge on his signal. The third line was to wait for his flag to drop a second time. Men of the front line were to let fly with their javelins as soon as the enemy was within range, then quickly draw their swords and close with the other side. Each time he gave his speech, it was met by a roar from the legionaries within earshot.

Across the wheat field, Pompey the Great was doing the same, pumping up his troops as he rode along their front line, with a speech he likewise would repeat several times. At their council of war two days earlier he'd told his officers that the battle they had all urged on him was at hand and it was up to them to bring the victory they so eagerly sought. According to Appian, he now told his troops, "We fight for freedom and for homeland, backed by the constitution, our glorious reputation, and so many men of senatorial and equestrian rank, against one man who would pirate supreme power." He urged them to picture their success at Durrës as they advanced to the battle they had been demanding, with high hopes for a final victory. And here, too, the roar of thousands of soldiers rent the air of the summer's morning in response to their general's harangue.

As he returned to his position on the right wing, Caesar passed Centurion Crastinus once again. "General," Crastinus called out as he went by, "today I shall earn your gratitude, either dead or alive."

Caesar acknowledged him with a wave and cantered on. In Caesar's mind was probably the morning's sacrifice to the gods, prior to ordering his army to march, prior to Pompey inviting him to do battle, when the priest conducting the ceremony had informed him that the entrails of the first sacrificial goat indicated that within three days he would come to a decisive action. A little later, the augur had added that if Caesar thought himself well off now, he should expect worse, while if unhappy, he could hope for better.

With the departure to the rear of his commander in chief, Crastinus would have fixed his gaze on the soldiers immediately opposite—men of the 1st Legion, men from Cisalpine Gaul. He would have been glad of that, glad the 10th wasn't facing the 4th or the 6th. He would not have enjoyed killing fellow Spaniards. But he'd killed plenty of Gauls in his time. He could kill these fellows quite happily, even if they were Roman citizens.

Never before had so many Roman troops faced each other on a single battlefield. Never before had two of Rome's greatest generals fought it out like this. Pompey, conqueror of the East, fifty-seven, a former young achiever who had made history in his twenties, a multimillionaire, an excellent military organizer, a master strategist, coming off a victory, with the larger army. Caesar, conqueror of the West, who had celebrated his fifty-second birthday only three weeks before in the month that would eventually bear his name, who had been nearly forty before he made his first military mark, an original tactician and engineering genius with a mastery of detail, a commander with dash, the common touch, luck, and the smaller but more experienced army.

Plutarch was to lament that, combined, two such famous, talented Roman generals and their seventy thousand men could have conquered the old enemy Parthia for Rome, could have marched unassailed all the way to India. Instead, here they were, bent on destroying each other.

It probably occurred to Centurion Crastinus that he might know some of the 1st Legion centurions across the field, might have served with them, might have drunk with them and played dice with them somewhere on his legionary travels. He would have watched them talking to their men, animatedly passing on instructions. They were easy enough to spot; like him, they wore a transverse crest on their helmets. It made them easy to identify for their own men, and marked them as targets for the opposition. Centurions were the key to an army's success in battle. Crastinus knew it, and Caesar knew it. The 10th Legion's six tribunes were back between the lines. Young, rich, spoiled members of the Equestrian Order, few had the respect of the enlisted men. From later events it is likely that one of the 10th's tribunes, Gaius Avienus, had done nothing but complain since they set sail from Brindisi that Caesar had forced him to leave all his servants behind.

This day would be decided by the centurions and their legionaries, the rank and file, and as Crastinus had told Caesar, he was determined to acquit himself honorably. Four hundred fifty yards away, men of the first rank of the 1st Legion would have been looking at Crastinus and setting their sights on making a trophy of his crested helmet. The man who took that to his tribune after the battle, preferably with Crastinus's severed head still in it, could expect a handsome reward. Without doubt they looked confident, these legionaries of the 1st. Crastinus may have imagined they thought they were something special, Pompey's pets. Crastinus would see how confident they looked in an hour or so.

Around the centurion, his men would have been becoming impatient, knowing in their bones that this day would not be like the others when they'd stood and stared at their opponents for hours on end before marching back to camp at sunset. This day the air was electric, and the tension would have been getting to some of them, wanting to move, to get started.

As if in answer, trumpets sounded behind the ranks across the field. Many of Pompey's men were more than nervous; the centurions of the newer units were having trouble maintaining their formations, so Pompey decided not to waste any time. Moments before, the thousands of cavalry horses banked up on the extreme left of Pompey's line had been waiting restlessly, some neighing, some pawing the ground, some fidgeting and hard to control. Now, with a cacophony of war cries, their riders were urging them forward. Within seconds, seven thousand horses and riders were charging across the wheat field.

Behind Crastinus, trumpets of his own side sounded. In response, Caesar's German and Gallic cavalry lurched forward to meet the Pompeian charge, with their auxiliary light infantry companions running after them. The Battle of Pharsalus had begun.

On Pompey's side, his thirty-six hundred archers and slingers dashed out from behind the lines and formed up in the open to the rear of their charging cavalry. On command, the bowmen let loose volleys of arrows that flew over the heads of their galloping troopers and dropped among Caesar's charging cavalry.

The infantry of both sides remained where they were in their battle lines, and watched with morbid fascination as their cavalry came together on the eastern side of the battlefield. General Labienus would have been at the head of his German and Gallic cavalry, cutting down any Caesarian trooper who ventured near him, and issuing a stream of orders.

For a short while Caesar's cavalry held its ground, but with their men falling in increasing numbers, they began to give way. At least two hundred of Caesar's cavalrymen were soon dead or seriously wounded, and Labienus saw the time had come to execute the maneuver that Pompey had planned. Leaving the allied cavalry to deal with Caesar's troopers, probably under the direction of his colleague General Marcus Petreius, he led his German and Gallic cavalry around the perimeter of the fighting and charged toward the exposed flank and rear of the 10th Legion.

Caesarian auxiliaries scattered from the path of the cavalry, and the men of the 10th Legion on the extreme right were forced to swing around and defend themselves as Labienus's troopers surged up to them. As Labienus urged more squadrons to ride around behind the 10th and as they came to the legion's third line, Caesar, not many yards away, barked an order.

Trumpets sounded, and the reserve cohorts of the fourth line suddenly jumped to their feet and dashed forward behind their standards, slamming into the unsuspecting cavalrymen before they even saw them. The men of the reserve cohorts had been given explicit instructions not to throw their javelins but to use them instead like spears, thrusting them overarm up into the faces of the cavalrymen. According to Plutarch, Caesar said, when issuing the order for the tactic, "Those fine young dancers won't endure the steel shining in their eyes. They'll fly to save their handsome faces."

Now Caesar's shock troops mingled with the surprised Germans and Gauls at close quarters, pumping their javelins as instructed, taking out eyes, causing horrific facial injuries and fatalities with every strike. The congested cavalry had come to a dead stop, compressed between the rear ranks of the 10th and the reserve cohorts. There were so many of them there was nowhere for the riders to go; they merely provided sitting targets for the men of the reserve cohorts as they swarmed among them.

As many as a thousand of Labienus's best cavalrymen were killed in this counterstroke. The panic that was created quickly spread to the allied cavalrymen behind them. Seeing the carnage, with Labienus's big, long-haired riders falling like ninepins or reeling back and trying to protect their faces from the javelin thrusts instead of pressing home the now stalled attack, the allied riders disengaged from Caesar's cavalry, turned, and galloped from the battlefield, heading in terror for the hills.

This allowed Caesar's cavalry to join the reserve cohorts against Labienus's men, and despite the general's best efforts to rally his troopers, the combination of infantry and cavalry was too much for them and they broke and followed the allied cavalry toward the high country. Labienus had no choice but to pursue his own men, with hopes of trying to regroup.

As Caesar's cavalry chased Labienus and his troopers all the way to the hills, Pompey's left flank was exposed. With a cheer, Caesar's reserve cohorts spontaneously rushed forward to the attack in the wake of their victory over the cavalry. All that stood in their way were Pompey's archers and slingers. These men of Caesar's strategic reserve, high on their bloody success against the mounted troops, quickly crossed the ground separating the two groups, neutralizing the effectiveness of the archers' arrows and the slingers' lead shot. The slingers were armed merely with their sling-shots. The archers, men from Crete, Pontus, Syria, and other eastern states, were armed, apart from their bows and arrows, only with swords. In close-quarters combat they were no competition for legionaries whose specialty was infighting. As the slingers ran, the archers bravely stood their ground and tried to put up a fight, but they were soon mowed down like hay before the scythe.

Now Caesar issued another order. His red banner dropped. The trumpets of the first and second infantry lines sounded "Charge."

In the very front rank, on the right of Caesar's line, Centurion Crastinus raised his right hand, clutching a javelin now. Caesar would later be told of his words. "Come on, men of my cohort, follow me!" he bellowed. "And give your general the service you have promised!"

With that, he dashed forward. All around him, the men of Caesar's front line roared a battle cry and leaped forward, javelins raised in their right hands for an overarm throw when the order came to let fly.

Ahead, to the surprise of Crastinus and his comrades, Pompey's front line didn't budge. Pompey's men were under orders to stand still and receive Caesar's infantry charge, instead of themselves charging at Caesar's running men, as was the norm in battles of the day. According to Caesar, this tactic had been suggested to Pompey by Gaius Triarius, one of his naval commanders. Pompey, lacking confidence in his infantry and anxious to give them an edge in the contest, had grabbed at the idea, which was intended to make Caesar's troops run twice as far as usual and so arrive out of breath at the Pompeian line.

Caesar was later scathing of the tactic. He was to write that the running charge fired men's enthusiasm for battle, and that generals ought to encourage this, not repress it. In fact, Pompey's tactic did have something going for it, as his troops would present a solid barrier of interlocked shields against Caesar's puffing, disorderly men, who had to break formation to run to the attack. It may have been effective against inexperienced troops, but in the middle of the battlefield Centurion Crastinus and his fellow centurions of the first rank drew their charging cohorts to a halt. The entire charge came to a stop. For perhaps a minute the Caesarian troops paused in the middle of the wheat field, catching their breath; then, led by Crastinus, they resumed the charge with a mighty roar.

On the run, the front line let fly with their javelins. At the same time, in Pompey's front line, centurions called an order: "Loose!" The men of Pompey's front line launched their own javelins with all their might, then raised their shields high to receive the Caesarian volley. Then, with javelins hanging from many a shield, they brought them down again, locking them together just in time to receive the charge. With an almighty crash Caesar's front line washed onto the wall of Pompeian shields. Despite the impact of the charge, Pompey's line held firm.

Now, standing toe to toe with their adversaries, Caesar's men tried to hack a way through the shield line. On Caesar's right wing, Centurion Crastinus, repulsed in his initial charge, was moving from cohort to cohort as his men tried to break through the immovable 1st Legion line, urging on his legionaries at the top of his voice above the din of battle. Crastinus threw himself at the shield line, aiming to show his men how to reach over the top of an enemy shield and strike at the face of the soldier on the other side with the point of his sword. As he did, he felt a blow to the side of the head. He never even saw it coming. The strength suddenly drained from his legs. He sagged to his knees. His head was spinning. Dazed, he continued to call out to his men to spur them on.

As he spoke, a legionary of the 1st Legion directly opposite him in the shield line moved his shield six inches to the left, opening a small gap. In a flash he had shoved his sword through the gap with a powerful forward thrust that entered the yelling Gaius Crastinus's open mouth. According to Plutarch, the tip of the blade emerged from the back of Crastinus's neck. The soldier of the 1st withdrew his bloodied sword and swiftly resealed the gap in the shield line. His action had lasted just seconds. No doubt with a crude cheer from the nearby men of the 1st Legion, Centurion Crastinus toppled forward into the shield in front of him, then slid to the ground.

It was a stalemate at the front line. Neither side was making any forward progress. But on Caesar's right, the reserve cohorts, fresh from the massacre of Pompey's archers and slingers, were swinging onto the flank and rear of the 1st Legion.

Pompey had seen his cavalry stroke destroyed in minutes, had seen the cavalry he'd been depending on for victory flee the field. And now his ever-dependable 1st Legion was in difficulty. If the 1st couldn't hold, no one could. Without a word, he turned his horse around and galloped back toward the camp on the hill. A handful of startled staff rode after him.

Plutarch says that as Pompey reached the camp's praetorian gate, looking pale and dazed, he called to the centurions in charge, "Defend the camp strenuously if there should be any reverse in the battle. I'm going to check the guard on the other gates."

Instead of going around the other three gates of the camp as he'd said, he went straight to his headquarters tent, and there he remained. He hadn't wanted this battle, he had known the likely outcome, especially if it came down to a pure infantry engagement. But expecting something and then actually experiencing it are two different things. In a military career spanning thirty-four years Pompey the Great had never once experienced a defeat. And never once, in all probability, had he put himself in the shoes of men he'd defeated, and imagined what defeat might feel like. It would have made the emptiness of failure all the more difficult to comprehend.

The men of the 1st, fighting now on three sides and outnumbered, were in danger of being surrounded and cut to pieces. No orders came from Pompey—he'd disappeared. None came from their divisional commander, the useless General Domitius. Pompey had failed to maintain a reserve, which might have been thrown into support the 1st now in its time of need. With no hope of reinforcement, and with self-preservation in mind, the officers of the 1st decided to make a gradual withdrawal, in battle order, in an attempt to overcome the threat to their rear. Orders rang out, trumpets sang, and standards inclined toward the rear. Their pride and their discipline intact, the 1st Legion began to pull back in perfect order, step by step, harried all the way by the 10th Legion and the reserve cohorts.

Beside the 1st, the 15th Legion did likewise. Away over on Pompey's right, General Lentulus, seeing the left wing withdrawing, and with his own auxiliaries and slingers already in full flight, ordered his legionaries to emulate the 1st Legion and make an ordered withdrawal, for if they attempted to hold their ground, the center would give way and the right wing would be pressed against the Enipeus and surrounded. Like their comrades of the 1st, the Spanish veterans of the 4th and 6th Legions maintained their formation as they slowly edged back, pressed by their countrymen of the 8th and 9th. But in the center, the inexperienced youths of the three new Italian legions began to waver. They tried to follow the example of the legions on the flanks, but their formations, like their discipline, began to break down.

Now Caesar issued another order. Again his red banner dropped. Again trumpets sounded "Charge." Now the men of his third line, who had been standing, waiting impatiently to join the fray, rushed forward with a cheer. As the fresh troops of the third line arrived on the scene, the men of the first and second lines gave way and let them through. The impact of this second charge shattered what cohesion remained in Pompey's center. Raw recruits threw down their shields, turned, and fled toward the camp on the hill they'd left that morning. Auxiliaries did the same, and the entire center dissolved. It was barely midday, and the battle was already lost to Pompey's side. It was now just a matter of who lived, and who died, before the last blows were struck.

The 1st Legion stubbornly refused to break, continuing to fight as it backpedaled across the plain pursued by the men of the 10th Legion and reserve cohorts. The 15th Legion appears to have broken at this point, with its men turning and heading for the hills. Over by the Enipeus, General Lentulus deserted his men and galloped for the camp on the hill. The

4th and 6th Legions, cut off from the rest of the army, withdrew in good order, fighting all the way, following the riverbank, which ensured they couldn't be outflanked on their right. Mark Antony pursued them with the 7th, 8th, and 9th, and, apparently, with a charge was able to separate two cohorts of the 6th from their comrades. Surrounded, these men of the 6th, a little under a thousand of them, resisted for a time, then accepted Antony's offer of surrender terms.

Meanwhile, two cohorts of the 6th and three of the 4th continued to escape upriver, with their eagles intact. Antony would later break off the pursuit and link up with Caesar at Pompey's camp. These five cohorts of Pompey's Spanish troops later found a ford in the river, slid down the bank, crossed the waterway, then struggled up the far bank. That night they would occupy a village full of terrified Greeks west of the river before continuing their flight west the next day.

At the camp on the hill, several thousand more experienced legionaries of the 15th, the Gemina, and the two legions from Syria had been regrouped by their tribunes and centurions to make a stand outside the walls. But as tens of thousands of Pompey's newer troops and auxiliaries swamped around them, a number without arms, their standard-bearers having cast away their standards, and with Caesar's legions on their heels, they abandoned their position and withdrew to make a stand on more favorable ground in the hills. Behind them, many of the men flooding through the gates began looting their own camp. It seems that the camp's commander, General Afranius, had already escaped by this time, spiriting away Pompey's son Gnaeus, probably as prearranged with Pompey.

While Pompey's guard cohorts and their auxiliary supporters from Thrace and Thessaly put up a spirited defense of the camp, the overwhelming numbers of the attackers forced them to gradually withdraw from the walls. With fighting going on inside the camp, young General Marcus Favonius found Pompey in his headquarters tent. A friend of Marcus Brutus and an admirer of Cato the Younger, Favonius, who'd been serving on Scipio's staff and just been made a major general, was a fervent supporter of Pompey. Now, horrified by the state in which he found his hero, the young general tried to rouse his commander from his stupor. "General, the enemy are in the camp! You must fly!"

Pompey looked at him oddly. All authorities agree on Pompey's words at the news: "What! Into the very camp?"

Favonius and Pompey's chief secretary, Philip, a Greek freedman, helped their commander to his feet, removed their general's identifying scarlet cloak, replacing it with a plain one, then ushered him to the door. Five horses were waiting outside the tent. According to Plutarch, three of the four men who accompanied Pompey as he galloped from a rear gate before Caesar's troops could reach it were General Favonius; General Lentulus, commander of the right wing division; and General Publius Lentulus Spinther. The fourth man would have been Pompey's secretary, Philip.

The five riders galloped north toward the town of Larisa, whose people were sympathetic toward Pompey. On the road, they encountered a group of thirty cavalrymen. As Pompey's generals drew their swords to defend their leader they recognized the cavalry as one of Labienus's squadrons, intact, unscathed, and lost. With the troopers gladly joining their commander to provide a meager bodyguard, the thirty-five riders hurried on.

Many of the men who had found a temporary haven in the camp now burst out and fled toward Mount Dogandzis, where a number of their colleagues were already digging in. The 1st Legion, in the meantime, appears to have withdrawn east. With Caesar summoning the 10th Legion to help him in the last stages of the battle at the camp, the 1st was able to continue to make its escape. It appears to have swung around to the south in the night and then, substantially intact and complete with most of its standards, including its eagle, marched west to the coast and Pompey's anchored fleet.

Leaving General Sulla in charge of the continuing fight at the camp, Caesar regrouped four legions, his veteran 7th, 8th, 9th, and 10th, and set off after Pompey's men who had fled to the mountain. Upward of twenty thousand in number, mostly armed, and well officered still, these Pompeians continued to pose a threat. As scouts reported that these survivors had now left the mountain and were withdrawing across the foothills toward Larisa, Caesar determined to cut them off before they reached the town and its supplies.

Caesar took a shortcut that after a march of six miles brought his four legions around into the path of the escaping troops in the late afternoon. He formed up his men into a battle line. Seeing this, the Pompeians halted on a hill. There was a river running along the bottom of the hill, and Caesar had his weary troops build a long entrenchment line on the hillside above the river, to deprive the other side of water. Observing this, the men on the hill, all exhausted, hungry, and thirsty, and not a few wounded, sent down a deputation to discuss surrender terms. Caesar sent the deputation back up the hill with the message that he was willing to accept only an unconditional surrender. He then prepared to spend the night in the open.

XII

THE SOUR TASTE
OF VICTORY

At dawn on August 10, Pompey's troops on the hill came down to Caesar, lay down their arms, then prostrated themselves before him and begged for their lives. Caesar told them he would spare them all and instructed his troops to treat the prisoners leniently, then told the 10th and his other three Spanish legions to prepare to march on Larisa as he gave chase to Pompey.

What transpired now appears to have gone along the following lines. To his astonishment, tribunes now came to Caesar to say that the men of the Spanish legions refused to march another step for him. The revolt probably began with the 9th Legion. Its troops had never forgotten the way Caesar had decimated its ranks at Piacenza the previous autumn. Nor had they forgotten his promise of one last battle. Well, they'd fought the battle, and they'd defeated Pompey, as they'd promised. Now they wanted Caesar to keep his promise. They wanted their overdue discharge, they wanted the bonus he'd been promising his legions for eighteen months, said by Suetonius to be as much as twenty thousand sesterces a man, a fortune for legionaries with a base pay of nine hundred sesterces a year.

It's likely that the men of the 8th quickly joined the 9th. They would have reminded their general that their continued service was illegal. They had signed enlistment contracts in 65 B.C., and so had the state. Their discharges had been due two winters back. They had served well past their discharge date as a favor to Caesar, but now that they had done what he'd asked of them, they just wanted to go home. The 7th Legion, always slow to join the others when they ventured into disputes, would have then followed suit.

Shocking Caesar even more, the men of the 10th came out in sympathy with their countrymen, apparently demanding their bonuses before they took another step toward the enemy. They had lost their most fanatical centurions in the previous day's battle, and now, free of their influence, they could express their frustration and disappointment with the general who never seemed to keep his promises.

Caesar, furious, was determined not to be blackmailed by his own troops after he'd just won the greatest victory of his career. If these legions weren't prepared to obey orders, he had others that would. He sent couriers galloping back to his main camp by the battlefield, with orders for four of his other legions to march at the double to his present location and replace the Spanish legions. When these units arrived, about midmorning, together with more of Caesar's cavalry, he sent the 7th, 8th 9th, and 10th back to the Enipeus with Mark Antony, escorting the Pompeian prisoners. Intending to deal with the leaders of the mutiny when he returned, Caesar prepared to march on Larisa with the newly arrived troops.

Typically, in his own narrative, Caesar makes no mention of the revolt by his troops after the Battle of Pharsalus. Of this initial flare-up and its consequences, he merely says that he decided to send the four legions that had accompanied him from the battlefield back to camp to rest.

A messenger now reached him from Larisa, bearing a letter from Marcus Brutus. The previous night, a number of senators with the Pompeian troops on the hill had slipped away in the darkness and reached Larisa, and Marcus Brutus had been among them. About thirty-seven years of age, Brutus was a handsome and erudite senator with much influence among his peers as the nephew of Cato the Younger and also because of his natural talents and a winning personality. His mother was Servilia, Cato's sister. Years before, Servilia had fallen in love with Julius Caesar when both were only teenagers, she being a young widow at the time. Their relationship ended when she remarried, but before long it was apparent she was pregnant. Many classical authors were to write that when Marcus was born Caesar felt sure the boy was his. While Caesar was only fifteen when Brutus was born it's not impossible that they were father and son. Romans started their sex lives early—females could legally marry at twelve, while males officially came of age in their fifteenth year. Whatever the biological facts, for the rest of his days Caesar treated Brutus like a son.

Caesar had been staggered to learn at the outbreak of the civil war that like so many of those near and dear to him, Brutus had taken Pompey's side. Caesar's surprise was exacerbated by the fact that Pompey had executed Servilia's new husband and Brutus's "father," Marcus Junius Brutus, some years before, and was never on friendly terms with the young man. But Brutus was a republican at heart, and believed in the values espoused by Pompey. Since the previous year Brutus had been serving on the staff of Pompey's governor of Cilicia, but, bored, had come of his own accord to join Pompey in Thessaly.

When Caesar had learned that Brutus was in Pompey's camp, he'd issued orders to his officers that nothing was to happen to the young man if they encountered him. If he surrendered of his own free will they were to bring him to Caesar. If he refused to surrender, they were to let him escape. Now, Caesar was overjoyed that the young man was alive and well, and he hurried to Larisa with his cavalry, leaving the replacement legions to follow at their own pace.

In his letter, Brutus had probably told Caesar that the people of Larisa wished to submit to him; when he arrived, the town opened its gates to the conqueror. There, he embraced Brutus, and immediately pardoned him. A little later, as they walked in private together, Caesar asked where Brutus thought Pompey might go. Pompey hadn't confided his intentions to Brutus, but, according to Plutarch, Brutus guessed that Pompey would seek support in Egypt.

Spending the night at Larisa, having learned that Pompey had stopped only briefly at Larisa the previous day before continuing on to the east coast, and with intelligence that he had since escaped by sea, Caesar turned around and marched back to the plain of Farsala with his four legions and cavalry, to look after unfinished business.

Arriving in the afternoon, he went first to Pompey's former camp. Colonel Pollio was with him as he surveyed the scene. Caesar sneered at the way Pompey's officers had left the camp, with artificial arbors, tents of generals spread with fresh turf and decorated with ivy, their tables laid with vast amounts of silver plate in readiness for the victory banquet they'd expected to celebrate after the battle, all of which offended Caesar, who had a soldier's taste and expected a military camp to look like a military camp, not a bordello.

The camp was littered with thousands of bodies, which would have already been beginning to bloat and reek in the summer heat. According to Colonel Pollio, who was at Caesar's shoulder as usual and would note his chief's words for use in his later memoirs, some of the dead here were soldiers, but most had been unarmed Pompeian noncombatants who had been killed by the indiscriminate blows of Caesar's troops as they overran the camp the previous day.

Caesar shook his head. "They brought this on themselves," he said disdainfully. "They forced it on me. I, Caesar, after succeeding in so many wars, would have been condemned to a similar fate if I'd dismissed my army as they wanted."

He moved down to the battlefield on the plain. Here men of both sides still lay where they had fallen. Mass graves were dug for most of the dead, but when Caesar learned that Centurion Crastinus of the 10th had perished in the battle, he had his body found and buried separately. Before his body was interred, Caesar laid several bravery decorations on the dead centurion's chest.

With grim satisfaction Caesar surveyed the trophies of the battle, 180 captured Pompeian standards piled untidily on the trampled corn, nine of them the eagles of legions. He was to claim that just 200 of his men had died in the battle, including 30 centurions. It was a lie. Indications are that he lost 200 cavalry alone. Plutarch and Appian agree that his actual losses at Pharsalus were 1,200. Caesar also claimed that 15,000 of Pompey's troops were killed and 24,000 captured. But this distortion was to hide the fact that so many escaped—18,000 in all. Many of Pompey's troops would reach Buthrotum, today's Buthroton, in southwestern Albania, opposite Corfu.

When Cato, at Durrës, heard of the defeat in Thessaly, he also came down to Corfu. Pompey's ships that had been anchored at and near Corfu subsequently shipped many thousands of Pompeian escapees to North Africa, among them men of the 1st, 4th, and 6th Legions, as well as General Labienus and sixteen hundred of his German and Gallic cavalrymen.

Colonel Pollio made a liar of his chief by revealing in his memoirs that the actual Pompeian losses in the battle were a maximum of six thousand soldiers, not fifteen thousand, plus an unknown number of noncombatants. Ten officers of general rank on Pompey's side died, along with some forty colonels. But, like Pompey himself, many of his senior generals escaped: his father-in-law, Scipio, Afranius from the camp with Pompey's son Gnaeus, as well as Generals Labienus, Petreius, Lentulus, Spinther, and Favonius. The only senior Pompeian general to fall was the ill-starred Domitius Ahenobarbus, commander of the left wing. Trying to escape the camp and reach Pompeian troops digging in on Mount Dogandzis, General Domitius had collapsed, exhausted, and was overtaken and killed by Caesar's cavalry.

With Pompey still alive and as many as eighteen thousand troops still armed, loyal, and on the loose, Caesar wanted to give chase, but now there is a sudden gap in his story, which is only explained by later events. The gap is caused by the revolt initiated by his Spanish legions. We can only speculate about precisely what took place next, but it likely that it was at dawn the next day, August 11, that Caesar called the traditional postbattle assembly of all his troops and doled out praise, promotions, pay raises, and decorations to his men on the recommendation of their tribunes and centurions. We know from Appian that Caesar now announced that once the war was at an end every man could look forward to substantial rewards, both in terms of money and grants of land, but he didn't go into detail.

Indications are he then advised that as soon as the army was ready to march, they would be going east, to chase Pompey. But before they could do that, he was forced to punish the four legions that had disobeyed his orders on the road to Larisa on August 9. The war was not yet over, and would not be over until Pompey and his adherents were soundly defeated, he would have said, and there was no room for disobedience. Therefore, as an example to all, he was going to decimate the 10th Legion.

The men of his legions would have looked at Caesar in astonishment. They all knew that his victory two days earlier had come chiefly as a result of the efforts of the 10th Legion. If the 10th hadn't forced the 1st Legion to retreat, Pompey's line wouldn't have given way. The men of the 10th were probably dumbfounded, but howls of protest rose up from the men of the 8th and 9th, and then the 7th. Then the 11th and the 12th joined in. This wasn't justice, they cried. The men of the Spanish legions began to renew their demands for their discharge and their bonuses, swearing once again to not march another mile for Caesar. They knew that they had the strength of numbers. Without his army, Caesar was nothing, and they knew it. Perhaps a chant began. "Discharge! Bonuses! Discharge! Bonuses!"

And now they were joined by the men of the other legions, the recruits from Italy, also demanding their bonuses before they followed Caesar any farther. He'd made an error in sending the Spanish legions back to camp while he'd gone to Larisa. It had only allowed the mutinous spirits to inflame the passions of their colleagues even more. And when they were rejoined by the other legions, they'd shared their grievances with them and won their sympathy and support. Besides, the legions would have suspected that Caesar had secured Pompey's pay chests and could afford to pay them. Men demanded more than empty promises. Give them their money now, they cried. Discharge the men who were being kept in the ranks illegally! And if Caesar was going to give them grants of land, they told him to make sure it wasn't confiscated land with disgruntled former owners living right next door. Yelling, chanting, jeering, the troops were becoming ugly.

Caesar's officers now probably warned Caesar not to call on the men of the 10th to decimate their own, or to call on other legions to decimate the 10th, because if they refused he would have a full-scale revolution on his hands, and in that case they could not vouch for his safety.

Inflamed by the disloyalty and hardly able to believe that he, victor of the Battle of Pharsalus, should have to deal with such behavior from his own troops, Caesar must have angrily declared that if his own legions wouldn't march with him, then he'd recruit soldiers from Pompey's surrendered ranks and use them for the rest of the war instead. The mutinous cries continued. Probably after annoucing that he would give his legions the night to think it over, Caesar left the tribunal, and the legions were dismissed.

Caesar would have been genuinely shaken by what had just taken place. Assured by his cavalry commanders that he had the loyalty of his eight hundred surviving German and Gallic mounted troops, he probably allocated the bulk of the cavalry to guarding the prisoners overnight, in case the ringleaders of the mutiny tried to set them free. He also sent officers through the POW camp beside the Enipeus, seeking volunteers from among Pompey's men to join new units fighting for Caesar. And he would have stationed the German troopers of his bodyguard around his own quarters and the pay chests.

With the morning of August 12, Caesar would have stepped up in front of a new assembly of his troops. If he were to now ask those men who were prepared to continue marching with him to step forward, and few did, the damage to his prestige would be incalculable. His authority was on the line, and he dare not risk it. So, to maintain control, Caesar apparently announced that he was sending all his own legions back to Italy with Mark Antony, and that he was continuing the pursuit of Pompey with the cavalry and a legion of volunteers from the ranks of the surrendered Pompeian troops. In language he would repeat later, he would have declared that once he had beaten Pompey he would come and deal with the question of discharges, bonuses, and other rewards. But not before. He then stepped down and angrily strode away, leaving his men open-mouthed. He'd called their bluff.

The legion Caesar referred to was in fact the two cohorts of the 6th Legion that had surrendered beside the Enipeus on August 9. Caesar always preferred Spanish legionaries above all others, and would have had his officers approach them first of all in the POW camp. These men of the 6th, little more than nine hundred of them, made a deal with Caesar—a short-term deal, based around financial incentives. Perhaps they agreed to march with him for six months, or twelve. But agree to march for Caesar they did. The only other condition stipulated by the proud Spaniards seems to have been that they continue as the 6th Legion, marching behind their own eagle, and not be assimilated into another Caesarian unit.

Within hours, Caesar rode away from the Enipeus with his eight hundred cavalry, heading northeast. Suspecting that Pompey would try calling in debts in Asia and Syria before heading for Egypt as Marcus Brutus had surmised, Caesar was bound for the Dardanelles, and the eastern states beyond. He himself tells us that at the same time he dispatched orders to General Fufius in the south of Greece to send him his five cohorts of the 28th Legion—twenty-three hundred men by Caesar's reckoning, recruited in Italy the previous year, with limited experience, but unaffected by the mutiny at Farsala and probably even unaware of it.

Over the next few days, while Caesar's legions mooched around camp, his quartermaster, General Quintus Cornificius, rearmed the 900 men of the 6th Legion and loaded a baggage train with the best kit, supplies, and ammunition available. The 6th Legion then set off, marching northeast to keep their part of their bargain with Caesar.

When he wrote his memoirs, Caesar could not bring himself to reveal the details of the mutiny of his entire army, and attempted to explain away the fact that none of his own legionaries marched with him after the Battle at Pharsalus with the excuse that all twenty thousand survivors had been overcome by their wounds in the battle or by the toil of their long march to the battle site—even though they'd been there several weeks before the battle, had plenty of time to recover from the march, and completely ignoring the fact that the men of the 6th had arrived after his troops and had less time to recover, yet were still fit to follow him.

Over the coming days, another ten thousand of Pompey's surrendered men in the POW camp accepted the terms offered by Caesar's officers. They swore loyalty to Caesar and volunteered to serve in two new Caesarian legions created there on the plain of Farsala, the 36th and the 37th. Once they were rearmed and ready to march, these two new legions set off after Caesar. By early October they would be encamped in Asia, where they awaited further orders. The remaining POWs marched for the west coast in company with Mark Antony and Caesar's nine legions, including the 10th.

One of those prisoners heading west with Antony was a veteran soldier of seventeen years' service by the name of Titus Flavius Petro, whose hometown was Sabine Reate in central Italy. Originally joining one of Pompey's legions in the mass enlistments of 65 B.C., he'd distinguished himself fighting for Pompey in the East in his youth. Probably a centurion by the time of his retirement early in 49 B.C., he'd soon been recalled by Pompey, and shipped out of Brindisi in the March evacuation. Serving with one of the three new Italian legions, he'd fought at both Durrës and Farsala before his surrender on August 9. Centurion Petro had seen enough fighting, and didn't volunteer to serve under Caesar. Pardoned and allowed to go home once he reached Italy, he became a debt collector at Reate after the war and raised a family. His son would work as a farmer's agent in Asia in his youth, later returning home to Reate to set up in business as a small-time moneylender. Centurion Petro's grandson would also become a soldier. Rising to the rank of lieutenant general, that grandson would subsequently become the ninth emperor of Rome, Vespasian.

In July and August, a Pompeian fleet under Admiral Decimus Laelius had lain siege to Brindisi, but when news of Pompey's defeat in Thessaly arrived, it withdrew. Admiral Laelius soon reconciled with Caesar, so it's possible he helped bring Mark Antony, his legions, and POWs back across the Adriatic from Epirus. One way or another, once Pompey's ships evacuated his fleeing troops from Buthroton to Tunisia, the Pompeian naval threat on the Adriatic ended until a raid by Admiral Marcus Octavius the following year, giving Antony a clear run back to Italy during these days of the late summer of 48 B.C.

Once they were shipped over to Brindisi, the disgraced legions were dispersed. The 11th and the 12th seem to have soon lost their passion for revolt and were sent overland to Illyricum with General Cornificius to carry out the mission Gaius Antony had failed to accomplish the previous year. The three Italian legions, the 25th, 26th, and 29th, stayed in southern Italy, in the Puglia region. The Spanish legions, the 7th, 8th 9th, and 10th, all marched up the Appian Way to Rome with Mark Antony and set up camp on the Field of Mars just outside the city, where Antony could keep an eye on them.

Antony was apparently under strict orders not to let the men of the four Spanish legions left behind in their sickbeds the previous year, and who'd since recovered and fought off enemy raids on Brindisi and Vibo, where they were now based, mix with the Pharsalus mutineers and be polluted by their rebellious ideas. Meanwhile, the men of the 10th and three other legions now at Rome were told that Antony didn't have the authority to give them their discharge or bonus payments. Only Caesar could do that. And Caesar was busy right now. Chasing Pompey.

XIII

THE MURDER OF POMPEY THE GREAT

Captain Peticius was the master of a grain ship. Typically 90 feet long, with a beam of 28 feet, Roman grain ships could carry 250 tons of cargo and 300 passengers. At dawn on the morning of August 10, 48 B.C., Captain Peticius had neither cargo nor passengers. His empty vessel lay at anchor in Thermaikos Bay, a little south of Katerini, off the northeastern coast of Greece. With the Greek wheat harvest about to take place, Captain Peticius and his crew had come looking for a consignment of grain. As the sun rose over the Aegean and the men of his crew were taking down the hide covers strung over the ship's deck each night to provide shelter and catch rainwater, in preparation for weighing anchor, Captain Peticius was telling them about a dream he'd had the night before.

"So there I was, sitting with Pompey the Great, discussing affairs of state. . . ."

"Why would Pompey the Great discuss affairs of state with you?" one of his seamen asked with a grin.

"I don't know why," Peticius replied with annoyance. "He just was."

"Have you ever met Pompey?"

"Met him? No. But I saw him, several times, in my youth. I could have almost reached out and touched him, he was that close. A fine figure of a man. A fine figure. So, as I was saying, here we were, Pompey and me, and he dressed like a common traveler, and looking in a very dejected state of affairs. . . ."

"Captain," another crewman interjected.

"What now?" Peticius demanded.

"There's a riverboat coming out. The people on it seem to want to attract our attention." The seaman pointed toward the shore.

138

The ship was anchored a little way off Paralia. A small port town at a river mouth, it was one of the few landing places on a coast of sand dunes and salt pans. Looking out over the port side, Captain Peticius saw a small boat, powered by several oarsmen, making its way toward his ship from the shore. The little craft was crowded with passengers, and two men were standing in the bow, waving cloaks back and forth and calling out to the ship. Intrigued, Captain Peticius and his crew crowded the rail. But as the boat drew closer they saw that some of its occupants were armed soldiers, and they suddenly became afraid.

"What do you want?" Peticius called worriedly.

"Pompey the Great requires the use of your ship," came the reply.

In astonishment, Peticius and his crewmen looked at the occupants of the boat, and then, as a round-faced man swathed in a cloak of cheap cloth looked up, Peticius recognized him. "Pompey! It is you!" He slapped himself on the forehead and turned to his companions with a dazed smile. "What did I tell you?"

Excited and flustered, Captain Peticius ordered a boat lowered, then a rope ladder, then called out to Pompey that he was a Roman citizen and knew who he was, and that his ship was at his service. Pompey was brought aboard, looking ashen-faced, and with him his three generals, his secretary, and his small bodyguard. This, as described by Plutarch, inclusive of Captain Peticius's dream, was how Pompey escaped from Greece.

The captain upped anchor, raised his sail, and set a course for the island of Lesbos. The tubby merchantman—Romans called them "round ships," because they were so broad of beam—was soon coasting south along the east coast of Greece, with snowcapped Mount Olympus, home of the Greek gods, away to its right. After passing between the islands of Voriai and Sporadhes, the craft swung due east and crossed the Aegean, arriving at Mytilene, modern Mitilini, capital of Lesbos, where Pompey's wife, Cornelia, and son Sextus were waiting for him. The last that the young, beautiful Cornelia had heard, Pompey was about to complete the defeat of Caesar. So when a fearful messenger knocked on the door of her villa at Mitilini with the news that her husband had arrived in the harbor—with just a single commandeered round ship and not the fleet of six hundred sleek warships that had sailed for him a week before—she realized what had happened before she was even told of Pompey's defeat, and fainted with shock.

With just four heavy cruisers he acquired after he picked up his wife from Lesbos and half a dozen frigates he encountered along the way, Pompey made a fateful decision. Instead of trying to link up with his powerful naval forces west of Greece, he remained in the East, planning to raise new support in the region, starting with Syria. But when he reached the island of Cyprus he heard that Syria was firmly against him. Having sent Generals Lentulus and Spinther to Rhodes to raise support there, he himself set sail south, bound for Egypt, just as Marcus Brutus had predicted.

Pompey headed for Egypt because Roman troops were based there, including men from legions he'd led in the past—he'd acquired five hundred of his cavalrymen from that force the previous year—and he was confident of gaining the support of the teenaged King Ptolemy, who had sizable, well-trained, and well-equipped armed forces.

In addition to his wife, Cornelia, Pompey was almost certainly accompanied by his younger son Sextus, who'd been with Cornelia on Lesbos. Plutarch was to report that within days of events in Egypt, Cato the Younger would encounter Sextus Pompey with a small flotilla off the North African coast, and from Sextus he would learn of Pompey's fate. General Favonius appears to have also remained at his commander's side. Plutarch says that young Favonius was so devoted to Pompey that he cared for all his needs during their flight, like a personal servant.

Pompey dropped anchor in a shallow bay off Pelusium, on the northeastern coast of Egypt, on September 28, 48 B.C. The next day he would celebrate his fifty-eighth birthday. Young Ptolemy XIII, no more than sixteen years of age, had been in conflict with his elder sister Cleopatra for the past few months, and he was camped here at Pelusium with an army of twenty thousand infantry and two thousand cavalry while Cleopatra camped in Syria to the north, trying to gather an army of her own around her.

News of Pompey's defeat in Thessaly reached Ptolemy before Pompey did. Knowing that Pompey was on the run, and seeing his pitifully small fleet, the king's advisers decided to turn against Pompey to stay in Julius Caesar's favor. A Roman tribune named Lucius Septimius, who was a commander with the cohorts stationed in Egypt for years to keep Ptolemy and his late father in power, was made a proposition by the Egyptians. Septimius had served under Pompey during the 66 B.C. campaign against Cilician pirates as a young centurion commanding a century in one of his legions, and consequently knew Pompey on sight. The Roman troops in Egypt had been there for years, had forgotten Roman rules and discipline, had acquired local wives and children. Men such as Colonel Septimius knew where their best interests lay. Or thought they did. He agreed to the proposition.

After Pompey sent several officers ashore to discuss the question of assistance from the king, Ptolemy in turn sent a small boat out to Pompey's flagship. From the boat stepped Ptolemy's general, the Egyptian Achillas, as well as Colonel Septimius and one of his subordinates, a Roman centurion named Salvius. It's possible that Septimius wore Egyptian-style clothing, because Pompey didn't seem to recognize him as a Roman at first. The pair told Pompey that they'd been sent to bring him ashore to meet the king. Pompey looked at the small boat unhappily, but decided that if he didn't accept the invitation he risked offending the Egyptians. And right now he needed them. So he bid farewell to his unhappy wife, Cornelia, who didn't want him to go ashore. After assuring her that all would be well, he climbed down into the boat alongside, wearing his best armor and a scarlet general's cloak once more.

Pompey was accompanied by Philip, his secretary; Scythes, a slave who'd probably been in Cornelia's entourage on Lesbos; and just two armed companions, a pair of centurions of the legion he'd left in Cilicia when creating the Gemina—they'd brought a detachment of legionaries to join him at Pamphylia, on the southern coast of modern-day Turkey, when he'd been on his way from Lesbos to Cyprus. Pompey and his centurion bodyguards seated themselves in the boat, and General Achillas, Colonel Septimius, and Centurion Salvius took seats opposite. As the boat pulled away from Pompey's cruiser and slid across the bay toward the beach, where the young king was sitting waiting on a throne with his army drawn up in rank after serried rank behind him, Pompey's wife, consumed with dread, watched from the ship's deck with his son Sextus and Pompey's small staff.

Plutarch and Appian both record in detail what followed. Looking up at Colonel Septimius opposite as the boat moved across the water, Pompey began to frown. The officer's face was beginning to look familiar. "Don't I know you, fellow soldier?" Pompey asked.

Septimius nodded but didn't say anything. Pompey looked away, perhaps thinking about his changed circumstances and harking back with regret to his recent poor decisions. Plutarch wrote that Pompey had complained to his companions on the voyage to Egypt that he blamed himself for being talked into the battle at Farsala, and for not taking the precaution of having the navy stand off the east coast of Greece to provide support. Had he not done the former, or had he done the latter, he wouldn't have been here now, about to beg the help of a boy.

As the boat came gliding into the beach, members of the young king's retinue walked to the water's edge, all smiles. The keel ground into the sand. Philip the secretary stood and offered his hand to his general. Pompey rose up and turned to step to the front of the boat. At the same time, his two bodyguards also came to their feet and turned with him. Behind them, Colonel Septimius drew his sword, stepped forward, and before any of Pompey's companions could prevent him, plunged it into the general. As Pompey fell forward, General Achillas and Centurion Salvius slid their swords from their scabbards and slit the throats of Pompey's centurions; then they, too, struck Pompey.

A woman's scream echoed across the water—Cornelia had witnessed it all. Still alive, Pompey dragged his scarlet cloak over his head, so that his face was hidden from spectators in his dying moments. As Pompey's two servants watched in terror, Colonel Septimius then stepped up, and wielding his sword like an ax, severed Pompey's head with several blows. Reaching down with his left hand, he grabbed a handful of his victim's graying hair and lifted the head up for those on shore to see. There was a roar of approval from the Egyptians. Septimius dropped the head, then reached down and roughly removed Pompey's signet ring, which contained his personal seal, the image of a lion with a sword in its paw.

The body was quickly stripped, then thrown into the shallows. After a throng of Egyptians had insulted the remains, Philip, his secretary, was left on the beach with his master's naked, bloody corpse. Already, Pompey's few ships were rowing back out to sea as fast as they could go to preserve the lives of Pompey's wife and son, as the crews of Egyptian ships in the bay began to man their battle stations to give chase. The Egyptian king was marching away with his army, and with Pompey's signet ring and severed head, heading back to his camp, feeling satisfied with his day's work.

Philip sank down beside the headless body. According to Plutarch, Philip cremated the remains on the beach, and both servant and ashes were found there the following day when General Lentulus, commander of Pompey's right at the Battle of Pharsalus, arrived by sea in search of his commander in chief after an unsuccessful trip to Rhodes. Lentulus was himself seized by the Egyptians and later put to death in prison by Ptolemy.

Four days after the assassination of Pompey the Great, Julius Caesar arrived at Alexandria, hot on his adversary's trail. The Egyptians proudly informed him of Pompey's inglorious fate. He refused to look at Pompey's severed head when it was presented to him by the Egyptians, but did accept his signet ring. Some classical authors say that Caesar cried at the meanness of Pompey's end. Perhaps he did. Nowhere, in any account of Caesar's life, is there any suggestion that he'd ever wanted Pompey dead. He merely wanted to remove an obstacle to achieving his ambitions.

According to Appian, Pompey's remains, either bones or ashes, were buried there on the Pelusium shore, and a memorial built over them inscribed "Rich Was This Man in Temples, but Poor Now in His Tomb."

Pompey's burial place soon fell into disrepair. Dio says that 170 years later, on a visit to Egypt, the emperor Hadrian made a point of locating Pompey's forgotten grave and restoring his memorial.

XIV

THE POWER OF A
SINGLE WORD

Caesar is here! Caesar is here!" The word swept through the camp
like fire before a hot north wind. As the men of the 10th Legion
emerged from their tents on the Field of Mars, the trumpets of
the legion began sounding "Assembly."

More than a year had passed since they'd seen Caesar riding out of the
camp on the plain of Farsala for the last time, in pursuit of Pompey. He'd
spent nine of the past thirteen months in Egypt locked in a life-and-death
struggle with the Egyptians, who, after he'd arrived there on October 2,
had decided to eliminate him the way they'd eliminated Pompey. Reacting
quickly, Caesar had kidnapped young King Ptolemy. Joined by Ptolemy's
sister and rival Cleopatra, Caesar and his small force had barricaded themselves in part of the royal palace at Alexandria. Trapped, and with just his
eight hundred cavalrymen, the nine hundred men of the 6th Legion, and
the twenty-three hundred inexperienced legionaries of the 28th, Caesar
had battled King Ptolemy's twenty-two thousand troops for months, the
contest involving savage street fighting and desperate battles for control of
the dock area. He'd sent to Asia for the 36th and 37th Legions, the two
units created using former members of Pompey's army after the Battle of
Pharsalus, but the 36th was caught up in strife in Pontus, and only the
37th answered his call. Later, Caesar's friend Mithradates of Pergamum
had marched to his relief with an army made up of allied troops plus the
27th Legion, the unit that had remained stationed in southern Greece all
this time. In a battle beside the Nile, Caesar had defeated Ptolemy's army.
The king himself drowned while trying to escape, allowing Caesar to
install Cleopatra, by now his mistress, as queen of Egypt. Caesar had then
marched with the 6th Legion cohorts and his cavalry to Pontus, where,
adding the 36th Legion and the remnants of two units of King Deiotarus

144

of Galatia to his force, he'd confronted the army of King Pharnaces, who'd recently occupied Pontus.

At the Battle of Zela on August 2, 47 B.C., almost exactly a year since his victory at Farsala, Caesar had crushed the charioteers and hapless infantry of Pharnaces. It was after this victory that Caesar sent his famous message back to Rome: "I came, I saw, I conquered." Only then could he turn his attention to Mark Antony's problems at Rome.

Those problems had started with the 10th Legion. Month in, month out, they had waited for Caesar to return to Rome, kicking around the camp beside the Tiber, bored, frustrated, and increasingly angry. Almost a year went by. Finally the patience of the men of the 10th snapped. Ignoring the commands and then the pleas of Mark Antony, and encouraged by two of their own tribunes, Gaius Avienus and Aulus Fonteius, and by several of their centurions, who all agreed with the men that they had been deprived of their just rewards, the men of the 10th had burst into the city and began looting the homes of the rich. Their thinking was obvious enough: if Caesar wouldn't give them what he owed them, they'd take it for themselves. The 8th and 9th Legions had promptly joined them, but the 7th had stayed loyal to its officers and kept apart from the other legions.

According to Plutarch, the mutineers killed two former major generals in their rampage, the ex-praetors Cosconius and Galba, although no other author confirms their murders.

When Antony ordered the 7th to cordon off the city, the legion had obeyed. Rather than come to blows with their comrades, the men of the 10th, 9th, and 8th then turned away from the capital and went on a looting spree in the wealthy Campania region, south of the capital. The three out-of-control legions had then returned to camp with their spoils, not long before Caesar slipped back into Rome unnoticed.

Caesar had gone directly to see Antony, to obtain a firsthand account of the revolt. Over recent months he'd received countless letters from the leading citizens of Rome begging him to come home and bring his legions back into line, and few if any of the authors had been complimentary about the way Antony had handled the affair. Assured by Antony that he'd done everything in his power to keep the lid on the problem—which had been of Caesar's creation, after all—and that these troops were in a murderous mood, Caesar began by having a detachment from the loyal 7th Legion surround and protect his own house on the Sacred Way in the heart of the city—the official residence of the *pontifex maximus*, high priest of Rome, which he'd occupied since his election to the post for life in 63 B.C.

Reluctant to stand before these men whose help he'd sworn he no longer needed when he left them on the plain of Farsala and admit that he'd been wrong, Caesar sent one of his deputies, Gaius Sallustius Crispus—Sallust—to talk to the mutineers on his behalf. Sallust, whom Caesar would make a major general in the new year, was authorized to promise the men four thousand sesterces each to return to their standards and march to Sicily for the next stage in Caesar's war against the Pompeians, an invasion of North Africa.

But when Sallust couldn't come up with these four thousand sesterces on the spot, along with the money Caesar had promised them at the start of the war, plus the vague rewards he'd mentioned after the Battle of Pharsalus, including grants of land, he was rejected by the angry legionaries, most of whom wanted to go home just as much as they wanted their money. According to Appian, Sallust was to claim he only just escaped from the Field of Mars with his life.

Caesar had told these men that he didn't need them, and for a year he'd stubbornly stuck to his word, employing Pompey's former troops and the youngsters of the 27th and 28th to conquer Egypt and then regain Pontus. But intelligence reports that were now reaching him said that Scipio and King Juba of Numidia could muster fourteen legions between them, supported by tens of thousands of cavalry and auxiliaries and something like 120 war elephants. Like it or not, Caesar needed his best legions if he was to triumph in this war. He knew he had no option but to speak to the recalcitrant 8th, 9th, and 10th himself. And talk them around to his way of thinking. But what would he say?

Now, as the men of the mutinous legions answered the call to assembly, no doubt deliberately standing in loose formation rather than precisely in their ranks and files, a lean, balding, middle-aged officer in the scarlet cloak of a general appeared in their midst with several other officers. Walking purposefully to the tribunal, he climbed its steps. The troops instantly recognized the bareheaded man on the speaker's platform.

He is said to have been hailed by the men in the traditional manner, but perhaps it was only legionaries of the loyal 7th who spoke up. With many soldiers no doubt standing with arms folded defensively, eyeing their commander with a mixture of guilt and suspicion, he looked around the sea of faces, waiting for everyone to fall silent. And then, when the mumble of voices faded away, with perhaps just the faint sound of a light breeze rippling around them and the distant hum of life from the city that never slept, he paused a little longer still, stretching the tension as the thousands of soldiers wondered what he would say to them. Then, at last, he spoke. According to Appian, this is what transpired.

"What is it you want?" Caesar began. "State your demands."

No one answered at first. Appian says that none of them had the courage to ask for money and so one or two men began to call out for their discharge. They had been detained in the legions illegally, they said, and they wanted to go home. There were loud choruses of agreement.

"Very well," Caesar responded, "I discharge you. All of you."

There was a stunned silence.

"And," he went on after a judicious pause, "I will pay you everything I promised you, *after* I win this war with other legions, and after *they* have had their just rewards."

The men looked at him in astonishment, waiting for him to say more. But he didn't. He just looked out at them, his face expressionless. The strained silence was painful, so painful that his staff officers standing beside the tribunal begged Caesar to say something more, not just dismiss with a few harsh words these troops who had been through so much with him over the years.

Caesar nodded slowly, then began, with a single word: "Citizens . . ."

The thousands of upturned faces were expectant. The men waited for him to continue, but Caesar paused, and waited. And as he paused, the true effect of that lone word sunk into his troops. Normally, generals began addresses to their troops with "Soldiers" or "Fellow soldiers." Caesar habitually began with "My soldiers." And now he was addressing them as citizens, as if they were no longer soldiers, just men off the street.

"No!" men began to cry out. "We're still your soldiers, Caesar!"

The cries grew into a deafening tumult. Caesar turned to leave the dais, but legionaries crowded around the steps and wouldn't let him step down.

"Stay, Caesar!" the voices chorused. "Punish the wrongdoers among us. The rest are ready to serve."

He turned back to the assembly and raised a hand. The voices faded away. In the new silence he began again. "I will not punish any man here," he declared. He turned his gaze to the familiar faces of the men of his favorite 10th Legion. "I am," he said, "pained that even the 10th Legion, which I have particularly honored over the years, could be involved in agitation of this kind. This legion alone I discharge from the army. But when I return from Africa after defeating the Pompeians, I shall reward the men of the 10th Legion along with the rest, just as I have promised. And the land I distribute to my soldiers will not be confiscated property, but public land, and my own land, and land bought for the purpose of distribution to my veterans."

All the men of the 9th and the other mutinous legions clapped and cheered, but the men of the 10th were far from happy at being left out.

Their centurions called for Caesar to have the men of the 10th draw lots, and every tenth man would be put to death for mutinying, as he had proposed at Farsala. After making an appearance of reluctance, he said that he would not even punish the men of the 10th, and he would allow them to continue to march with him. Now the men of the 10th cheered and applauded as well.

The men of the three legions had just allowed themselves to be artfully talked into fighting, and perhaps dying, in yet another campaign, and they were pleased about it. As Tacitus was to write, the turnaround had been achieved by a single word. That, and the personal charisma of Julius Caesar.

XV

THE NORTH AFRICAN CAMPAIGN

I n the fall of 47 B.C. the legions began to assemble in Sicily for Caesar's next big amphibious operation. Why didn't the civil war end with the death of Pompey? Quite simply, he had been elected Rome's military commander in chief by the majority of the Senate, to fight the rebel Caesar, and on his demise the exiled senators merely elected a new commander in chief, Pompey's father-in-law, Scipio, to continue the struggle against Caesar. And now Scipio had assembled an army in North Africa theoretically large enough to reclaim Rome. Caesar could wait for them to invade Italy, or he could take the war to them by invading North Africa. As always, Caesar would take the initiative.

With a long march ahead of them through southern France and Italy, the 13th and 14th Legions set off from eastern Spain, where they'd been stationed since Caesar's victory there in the spring of 49 B.C. Ahead of them, also marching from Spain, went Spanish cavalry accompanied by the 5th Legion. Pompey's 5th had been disbanded by Caesar in 49 B.C., but he'd enrolled a new enlistment of the legion in western Spain shortly after. Always a fan of Spanish legionaries, he'd summoned the new 5th for his next offensive.

The two legions that had been garrisoning Sicily for some time, the 19th and the 20th, were not to be included in the invasion force. Made up mostly of former Pompeian troops who'd surrendered at Corfinium in February of 49 B.C., they'd been left behind when Gaius Curio had taken their two ill-fated brother legions to Tunisia and led them to their destruction by the Bagradas River. After that performance, Caesar showed no interest in the two untried units. One had been based for some time at Messina, on the island's northeastern coast—somewhat belatedly after

Admiral Nasidius's unopposed visit—and as the legions of the invasion force began to arrive at Sicily, the other joined it at the Messina garrison.

Legions hardened by battle experience and emboldened by success, this was what Caesar wanted. The 25th, 26th, and 29th, legions that had taken part in the mutiny after the Battle of Pharsalus, were brought down from their bases in southern Italy, sailing from Reggio to Messina, then marching along the northern coast of Sicily. Caesar had initially left the 28th Legion in Egypt with the 27th and the 37th after he'd placed Cleopatra on the throne, but this legion was now shipped from Alexandria to Sicily to join the task force. And the 7th, 8th, 9th, and 10th Legions packed up their tents on the Field of Mars and began the march from Rome. Meanwhile, the men of the 10th Legion who'd been left behind in their sickbeds at Brindisi in January of 48 B.C. and had been stationed at Brindisi and Vibo in southern Italy after their recovery, now also headed for Sicily. With a head start of a week or so on the main body of the legion, these troops reached their destination before the rest of the 10th.

Caesar had lost faith in Mark Antony, particularly after the inept way he'd handled the mutiny of the 10th, 9th, and 8th Legions at the capital. Antony's high and mighty attitude annoyed Caesar and many others. Typically, Antony had contracted to buy Pompey's former house at Rome after it had been confiscated by Caesar, but complained bitterly when required to pay up—he thought Caesar should make a gift of it to him. (The house, in the "Keels" district, would subsequently come into the possession of the emperor Augustus and become an imperial residence used by, among others, Tiberius prior to his becoming emperor.) Antony was sidelined by Caesar, who now appointed himself and Marcus Lepidus as the consuls for the next year and left Antony behind as he set off to commence his latest military campaign. According to Plutarch, Antony later wrote that he'd chosen not to go to North Africa with Caesar, with the excuse that his former services hadn't been recompensed as they deserved.

Other officers also had come to displease Caesar, while others still had parted company with him to take up senior appointments in the territories he now controlled. But three of his faithful staff officers—Oppius, Pollio, and Sallust—were to accompany him to Africa.

Nothing ever happened quickly enough for Julius Caesar. At least part of his audacity can be attributed to impatience. On December 17 he arrived at the embarkation point, Marsala, Roman Lilybaeum, on the west coast of Sicily. He pitched his tent on the beach, then fretted increasingly as the days passed. The weather was unfavorable. His legions were arriving in Sicily in dribs and drabs, with the majority of his best troops still days and weeks away. The supplies ordered by his new quartermaster, General Granius Petro, were coming in too slowly. And he was limited by insufficient transports to ship his entire force across the Mediterranean to North Africa in one hit. Yet, despite all this, he was determined to commence the offensive on the eve of winter, when the other side wasn't expecting him. Within a week, good weather arrived. That was all Caesar needed. He launched the operation immediately, just as the year was ending.

It was December 25, 47 B.C., following the Saturnalia, a religious festival that would become Christmas in the Christian era, when all Romans traditionally did no work and spent carefree time at leisure. Caesar set sail from Sicily with his German cavalry bodyguard and elements of six legions, including the cohorts of the 10th Legion that had joined him from southern Italy.

There are many parallels between the civil war of 49–45 B.C. and the Second World War of A.D. 1939–1945. The amphibious landings, the amphibious evacuations. And here was another. On July 10, 1943, at Licata, a little east of Marsala, the Allies began the invasion of Sicily from North Africa, the reverse of Caesar's invasion of North Africa from Sicily.

Caesar endured a slow crossing of the narrow stretch of the Mediterranean separating Sicily from North Africa, caused by indifferent winds that also scattered his fleet. On December 28 he landed unopposed on the east coast of Tunisia near the small port of Sousse, Roman Hadramentum, with just 3,150 men. Anxiously he waited for his other ships to arrive with the rest of his invasion force, as Pompeian cavalry began to move along the coast toward him.

Sousse closed its gates and the residents prepared to defend their walls, but when the rest of his fleet still didn't arrive after thirty-six hours Caesar moved on, posting his best men, his few 10th Legion cohorts, as rear guard. A large force of Numidian cavalry now arrived at Sousse and gave chase. But when Caesar's handful of cavalry charged into them, the Numidians scattered.

On the first day of the new year, Caesar set up camp outside the town of Ruspina. Some two miles from the nearest port, it would become his operational headquarters for the campaign. Today the ruins of Ruspina lie three miles to the west of the modern Tunisian town of al-Munastir. Caesar set up a supply base a few miles away, at Leptis Minor on the coast, and sent his warships looking for the missing transports of the invasion fleet. Early on January 4, most of the missing troopships arrived and disembarked their troops at Leptis Minor. Caesar now had four full legions ashore, the 25th, 26th, 28th, and 29th, as well as most of the 5th and several cohorts of the 10th. The main contingent of the 10th Legion, along with those of the 7th, 8th, and 9th, had yet to reach the embarkation camp in Sicily; they were all still marching down from Rome.

Reinforced, and having come across from Sicily with limited rations, that same day Caesar took 30 mixed cohorts of infantry, including his men of the 10th Legion, supported by 400 cavalry and 150 archers, and advanced inland to cut ripened wheat from the wheat fields that covered the plain around Ruspina. Colonel Pollio accompanied Caesar on several later sorties from Ruspina, so it is probable he also went along on this mission as his second-in-command, and it was from his memoirs that Appian and Plutarch took their version of events on this particular day.

Just before 11.00 A.M., and three miles from his base, Caesar was caught in the open by a large enemy flying column led by his former good friend and deputy and now his implacable enemy Major General Titus Labienus. After commanding Pompey's cavalry at the Battle of Pharsalus, Labienus had regrouped sixteen hundred of his Gallic and German troopers and taken them to Buthroton, from where they'd been among the first of Pompey's troops evacuated to Tunisia. Labienus's force here on the Ruspina plain consisted of his regular cavalry plus local light infantry and archers.

Caesar's troops, caught tramping along with their helmets slung around their necks, shields over their shoulders, and packs on their back containing scythes and wicker baskets for harvesting wheat, hurriedly donned their helmets on Caesar's command and formed a skirmish line as Labienus lined up his troops in front of them. For a long time there was a stalemate, with each side trying to stare down the other, before Labienus's cavalry suddenly spurred their steeds into action and tried to envelop Caesar's flanks. At the same instant, his Numidian light infantry dashed forward to attack in the center.

The fight dragged on for hours, with Caesar's force surrounded. Every time one of his cohorts made a sally against Labienus's cavalry they advanced too far and were almost cut off, so Caesar ordered his men to advance no more than four feet from their line. In the end he had to form an *orbis*, the circular formation of last resort.

General Labienus rode up and down his line bareheaded, cheering on his men. As recorded by the author of *The African War*, the work possibly written by and certainly edited by Caesar's staff officer Aulus Hirtius and added to Caesar's memoirs, Labienus occasionally yelled caustic comments to Caesar's troops.

"What do you think you're doing, recruit?" the general called, fixing his gaze on one particular short, fresh-faced legionary in Caesar's line. "Little fire-eater, aren't you? Are you another one who's had his wits befuddled by Caesar's fine words? I have to be honest with you, he's brought you into a desperate situation. I'm sorry for you."

"I'm no raw recruit, Labienus," the soldier called back. "I'm a veteran of the Tenth!" A veteran who must have served under the general in Gaul, what was more.

"The Tenth?" Labienus retorted with a laugh in his voice. "I don't recognize the standards of the Tenth anymore. Let's see what you're made of!"

"You'll soon see what I'm made of," the 10th Legion man angrily declared, ripping off his helmet. "Here! See my face? Remember it!" With that, he flung the javelin in his right hand with all his might.

The range was extreme, and as the combatants watched the javelin's flight, as if in a dream, it appeared it would fall short of the target. Instead it plunged into the chest of General Labienus's charger. The horse reared up in pain and fear, throwing the unprepared Labienus from the saddle. He landed heavily.

A cheer rose from Caesar's men.

"Maybe that'll help you recognize a soldier of the Tenth in the future, Labienus," the legionary called, bringing laughter from his 10th Legion comrades.

As General Labienus lay prostrate on the ground, men of his bodyguard hastily gathered around him. He was moving, dazed, and hurt by the fall as he was carried away. The general's men continued the attack after he'd gone, but in his absence their enthusiasm waned a little. But at the same time most of Caesar's surrounded troops were losing heart. The men of the newer legions were constantly looking around for Caesar as he strode around the inside of the circle directing the defense, and many now merely dodged opposition missiles without going on the offensive themselves.

Realizing he had to seize the initiative, Caesar formed his thirty cohorts up so he had fifteen facing one way and the fifteen behind them facing the other. Both groups then charged forward at the same time, on his command, splitting the attacking force in two and breaking the encirclement. Caesar then called his men back, and before the other side could re-form he quickly advanced through one of the gaps he'd opened up and marched for Thapsus at the double.

Caesar's column had gone only a few miles, harried by Labienus's troops all the way, when another opposition force swept into its path. Led by the fiery General Marcus Petreius, who'd escaped from Spain with General Afranius and then from Greece with Labienus, this force of sixteen hundred picked Numidian cavalry and a number of light infantry cut off Caesar from his base. Caesar had no choice but make a stand, and to gain the advantage of high ground he edged his beleaguered force to a low, bare hill, the only rise on the otherwise monotonously flat plain.

The battle lasted all through the afternoon, with Caesar surrounded and taking heavy casualties. It was looking like Julius Caesar's last stand. At one point the eagle-bearer from one of the new legions broke ranks and tried to flee, but Caesar personally grabbed him and spun him around. Plutarch says that Caesar angrily yelled, "Look, that's the way to the enemy!" and pushed the soldier back toward the fighting.

Aulus Hirtius, who was made a major general this year by Caesar, himself admitted that he hadn't served in the African campaign. He said that part of what he knew of the campaign he learned from later conversations with Caesar, although he hadn't made notes, as he had no plans at the time to put the story on record. Hirtius's other Caesarian writings are at times more deliberately one-eyed than merely inaccurate, and this episode in *The African War* is no different—it has Caesar's troops escaping back to Ruspina late in the day after seriously wounding Petreius and victoriously driving off the enemy.

In contrast, Cassius Dio writes that many of Caesar's men were killed in this action, while Appian says that Caesar's troops were routed on the plain. Dio's and Appian's versions ring truest. Appian also states that Caesar was only saved when, late in the day, as the sun was setting, General Petreius instructed his troops to disengage, adding, "Let's not rob our commander Scipio of the victory."

So the Pompeian troops pulled out, and Caesar and his surviving men gratefully stumbled back to their camp in the darkness, carrying their numerous dead and wounded among them. Caesar's notorious luck had held good yet again. Seventy-five years later, Nero's chief secretary, the philosopher Seneca, would say that luck never made a man wise, but Julius Caesar learned from his lucky escape on the Ruspina plain. After discovering the inadequacies of the men under his command—other than his few 10th Legion veterans—he wisely decided not to allow himself to be dragged into another major engagement until reinforced by his best legions.

With the winter just around the corner, the two forces faced off. Scipio advanced his army to the vicinity of Thapsus and penned Caesar in an area of six square miles. Over the coming months there were occasional skirmishes, with General Labienus losing a number of German and Gallic cavalrymen in one engagement, but although Scipio frequently lined up his army in battle order, Caesar would not come out and play his game. He kept his troops behind the walls of their defenses and awaited the arrival of reinforcements. Impatient as always, according to the author of *The African War* he was forever looking out to sea for the arrival of the next convoy, even accusing the navy and the army of deliberately putting off its sailing. In particular Caesar was waiting for his veteran legions. He had little confidence in the newer units, which had already shown their lack of fighting qualities in the battle on the Ruspina plain at the beginning of the month.

In the third week of January a second convoy finally arrived from Sicily and landed the seasick 13th and 14th Legions plus cavalry, auxiliary light infantry, and badly needed supplies. The bloody nose Caesar's forces had received on the plain outside Ruspina and stories about a huge Pompeian army complete with elephants had caused many of Caesar's young soldiers to start talking of mutiny rather than take on Scipio's forces, but now the arrival of these veteran reinforcements bolstered flagging spirits.

Several ships of the second convoy fell into enemy hands, including a troop-carrier with two colonels aboard and a cruiser carrying another pair of colonels, a centurion and the last contingent of young Spanish recruits of the 5th Legion, and a centurion and veterans of the 14th. Most of the senior men were put to death, while the enlisted men were pressed into Scipio's army.

King Juba was now forced to withdraw most of his troops to put down a rising back in Numidia. Despite his reduced numbers Scipio was prepared to take on Caesar in a full-scale battle, but still Caesar preferred to wait for his favored Spanish legions before he ventured too much too soon. He was moving camp every few days, slowly advancing down the coast toward the town of Uzitta, daily fighting off attacks by detachments of Scipio's troops. In mid-February, a third convoy arrived, this time bringing the rest of the 10th Legion and the men of the 9th.

Caesar had been seething about the way the 10th had turned against him after Pharsalus and then led the mutiny and looting rampage at Rome. Never one to forget, yet no doubt conscious of warnings from his staff that it might rebound on him if he were to punish the men, he was still determined to make an example of the 10th. So he chose instead to single out several of the legion's officers for special treatment, having been given a list of the officers who'd encouraged their men to mutiny. One of the culprits seemed particularly determined to earn his commander's censure—Colonel Gaius Avienus had taken one of the ships in the latest convoy and loaded it with his personal slaves and horses, bringing not a single soldier of the legion with him across from Sicily.

The men of the 10th had gone through a lengthy, hazardous voyage during which their water supply had run out after the convoy shied away from the Tunisian coast on seeing warships in their path. They'd barely had time to reunite with the cohorts of the legion who'd preceded them in the first convoy when, the day following their arrival, Caesar called an assembly of the tribunes and centurions of the 10th and all his other legions now in North Africa. Once the officers, upward of six hundred of them, had lined up, Caesar strode from his praetorium, then stepped up onto the tribunal, looking severe. His words are quoted in *The African War*.

"I would have thought," he began, "that people might at long last have put an end to their impertinence and insubordination, and ceased to take advantage of my leniency, moderation, and patience. But since they won't themselves set any bounds or limits, then I'll make an example, in accordance with military practice, to teach the others to mend their ways."

He then called out two tribunes and three centurions of the 10th Legion by name. Looking puzzled and not a little worried, the five nominated officers stepped forward and lined up in front of the tribunal. As they did, they probably noticed the centurions of the guard cohorts on duty taking up positions close by with hands on sword hilts.

"Gaius Avienus," Caesar now began, glaring down at the spoiled, rich young colonel, "whereas you did in Italy incite the troops of the Roman people to action against the state and did plunder various municipalities, and whereas you have been of no service to either myself or the state, but have, instead of troops, embarked your own slaves and livestock, and have thereby caused the state to be short of troops at a time of crisis—for these reasons, I discharge you with dishonor from my army and order you to remove yourself immediately from Africa."

Avienus had probably blanched white, while, beside him, the other officers were sweating profusely.

Caesar turned his attention to the second colonel, another wealthy young man in his twenties. "Aulus Fonteius, whereas you have, as a tribune, incited my soldiers to mutiny, and as a citizen, have been disloyal, I dismiss you from my army."

Now it was the turn of the trio of centurions. All three would have been promoted by General Fabius on the retirement of Centurion Crastinus and other senior centurions of the 10th back in early 49 B.C., but as far as Caesar was concerned not one of them had deserved their promotions. From what he'd come to hear, they'd blatantly curried favor with Fabius to get where they were. "Titus Salienus, Marcus Tiro, Gaius Clusinas, whereas you have obtained your ranks in my army by favor, and not through merit, have shown yourselves neither brave in combat nor loyal in peace, and have directed yourselves to inciting the men to mutiny against their commander rather than to respectful and obedient conduct, I judge you unfit to hold rank in my army. I dismiss you from my service and order you to leave Africa immediately."

Caesar turned to the centurions of the guard and instructed them to escort these men to a ship. The discharged officers were each permitted to take one personal slave with them but nothing else. And they were to leave the province's shores that same day.

Caesar was feeling more confident now. He had two of his four best legions with him, plus another seven legions. And the young Spanish recruits of the 5th Legion had sent their tribunes to him to say they wanted the honor of taking on Scipio's elephants when battle was finally joined. Caesar didn't hesitate to accept their offer, which made the men of the other units feel a whole lot better about what lay ahead.

In stages of a few miles each day Caesar now advanced down the coast toward Thapsus, a port town that sat on a cape overlooking the sea, about five miles from present-day Teboulba in Tunisia. After each move, he would have his men build a new fortified camp. The troops' amenities were basic. The latest convoy had replenished their food supplies, but Caesar had made his soldiers come across from Sicily with only basic gear so he could cram as many men as possible on his few ships. Most didn't even have tents to sleep under, and rigged up flimsy shelters using clothing and pieces of wood.

By the beginning of March, King Juba had returned to Tunisia, bringing three of his four legions back with him to bolster Scipio's force. Now, outside the village of Uzitta, the opposing armies drew up in lines facing each other, with about 450 yards separating them, in battle order and ready for a full-scale fight. Caesar would have learned from prisoners after the Battle of Pharsalus that Pompey and General Labienus had expected him to place the 10th Legion on the right wing on that occasion and made their dispositions accordingly, so now, as Caesar formed his battle line, he allotted the 10th to the left wing, with the 9th on its immediate right, just to keep Scipio on his toes.

For hour after hour, 130,000 men stood glaring at each other under the North African sun, with neither commander, not Caesar, not the bearded, severe Scipio, wanting to be the one to make the first move. They stood there from morning until late afternoon until finally Caesar began to withdraw his troops to his camp, unit by unit, in formation.

Suddenly General Labienus led the entire Pompeian cavalry force in the direction of Caesar's camp, as if to cut off his line of retreat. Before Caesar could order any counteraction, some of his cavalry and auxiliary light infantry launched an attack from his left wing of their own accord. A swift fight ensued, before the Pompeians sent Caesar's men into retreat, killing twenty-eight and wounding a number of the others. Nightfall saved Caesar from any further embarrassment. Scipio let him withdraw into his camp. The stalemate continued.

In mid-March Caesar welcomed the men of the 7th and 8th Legions as they arrived in the next convoy from Sicily. Now he had all four of his fractious veteran Spanish legions back with him. Knowing how inexperienced the men of his newer legions were and after the reverse he'd suffered at the Battle of the Ruspina Plain back in January, he personally led the newer units in a new training regime.

Described in *The African War* as acting like the trainer of new gladiators, Caesar showed the young legionaries exactly how many feet to retire before they suddenly wheeled around as a group and counterattacked, how to advance and retire alternately, how to make feint attacks, and how to defend themselves in close-quarters combat. When drilling them on throwing their javelins, he would mark a spot on the ground as their target. To help the men of the 5th Legion accustom themselves to anti-elephant tactics, he shipped four or five elephants over from Italy, animals originally taken to Rome by Pompey some years before. While the youngsters of the 5th trained with the beasts at every opportunity, Caesar had no intention of employing his own pachyderms in battle—he is said to have considered the lumbering, tusked bull elephants a menace to both sides.

On March 21 Caesar led his army in the Lustration Exercise, the religious ceremony performed by the Roman military in March of each year during which the standards of the legions were purified, dressed in garlands, and sprinkled with perfumed oil. Traditionally this ceremony marked the beginning of the annual campaigning season, and the men of the legions considered it bad luck if the Lustration wasn't performed prior to launching the latest campaign. Now Caesar began his offensive in earnest. Taking the village of Sarsusa, he slaughtered its small Pompeian garrison. The next day, shadowed by Scipio, he marched on the town of

Thysdra, but it was well defended, and without a water supply in the vicinity he decided against a siege and withdrew to Aggar.

Despite the risk of being intercepted by patrolling enemy warships, Caesar's troopships continued to maintain a shuttle service from Sicily, and another convoy now arrived, bringing four thousand men from all his legions who'd previously been on the sick list or on leave, plus four hundred cavalry and a thousand archers and slingers. Adding these reinforcements to his task force, Caesar formed up his army two miles from Scipio's camp, near the town of Tegea. Again Scipio brought his army out in battle order, but following a stuttering cavalry action with first one side retreating, then the other, Caesar withdrew his main force to camp at about 4:00 P.M. after seeing no advantage.

On April 4, in the small hours of the morning, in one of his typical night marches Caesar hiked his legions sixteen miles down the coast from Aggar, making camp within sight of Thapsus as dawn broke. He then began digging trench lines with the intention of cutting off the town's Pompeian garrison from Scipio and the rest of his army.

To relieve the town, Scipio marched his forces up from the south to within eight miles of Thapsus and established two large camps covering a corridor between an extensive salt lake, the Marsh of Moknine, and the coast—one camp for his army, the other for King Juba's Numidian troops. The next day, leaving some troops with General Afranius at his camp, Scipio moved most of his forces closer to Thapsus. After swinging west around the lake in the night, his men were seen to be busy setting up a new camp as the sun came up, about a mile and a half from Caesar's fortifications. Tactically this was a clever move—Scipio could now trap Caesar on the peninsula, between the camps of Juba and Afranius at the southern end and his new position, which covered access from the west.

Caesar being Caesar, he was quick to turn a disadvantage into an advantage. Seeing the construction work under way at Scipio's camp, Caesar decided to attack immediately, before the Pompeians could finish their defenses. He quickly formed three battle lines outside Thapsus. This time he returned the 10th Legion to its customary right-wing position, placing the 7th beside it. (Not the 2nd, as *The African War* records at one point. The 2nd Legion was in western Spain throughout this period. A copyist at some stage erroneously wrote II instead of VII when identifying the legion beside the 10th.) The 8th and 9th Legions went on his left wing. It was a given that the less experienced legions would take the center as always, but now that he had the luxury of deploying eleven legions, Caesar strengthened his center with the veteran 13th and 14th. If he maintained the lineup he'd used several weeks before, Caesar placed the 25th and the 29th to the left of these two legions and the 28th and the 26th on the other side, next to the 7th. As he had planned for some time, the 5th Legion was split in two—half its cohorts went on each extreme wing, along with cavalry and slingers, ready to take on King Juba's sixty elephants. (The *African War* says Caesar left two entire legions guarding his camp, but this is probably propaganda. Auxiliaries would have guarded the camp.)

Caught still building his latest camp, Scipio had little choice but to send his army into the field or risk his incomplete fortifications being stormed. Scipio's exact deployment is unknown. He placed his ten legions and King Juba's three legions in the center of his line, distributing his cavalry and light infantry on the wings along with his war elephants—thirty of which were placed on each side. These beasts were complete with armored howdahs on their backs, or "castles" as the Romans called them, each containing two to three javelin throwers. A Numidian mahout, or driver, sat, sidesaddle, at each elephant's neck, driving his charge with a long crook that looked like a modern-day hockey stick.

Among Scipio's legions were the 1st, which had escaped almost intact from Greece, and the three cohorts of the 4th and two of the 6th that had escaped with it. Scipio, and Cato the Younger, who had taken command at the provincial capital, Utica, modern Utique, along the coast, had recruited twelve thousand locals into their existing legions, some of them former slaves, and this insulted the proud Spaniards of the 4th and the 6th to the extent that some of them had defected to Caesar over the past few weeks in disgust.

Scipio also had the two locally raised legions of General Publius Attius Varus that had participated in the brief campaign that had wiped out Caesar's two legions under the overconfident Gaius Curio two years before. Scipio's remaining five legions were also made up of locally recruited men, many of them slaves, who had no combat experience whatsoever. The men of King Juba's three legions were highly experienced and supremely confident. Principally responsible for Curio's defeat, the Numidian legionaries boasted haughtily to the men of the 1st, 4th, and 6th that they had fought forty-two battles over the years without suffering a single defeat.

In addition to his sixty elephants, Scipio also had tens of thousands of lightly armed Numidian auxiliaries and upward of ten thousand cavalry. Some fifteen hundred of these cavalrymen were General Labienus's tough German and Gallic troopers who'd served with him for years and come through the campaign in Gaul and the Battles of Dyrrhachium and Pharsalus with him. Another fifteen hundred were Numidians trained and led by General Petreius using Roman-style equipment and tactics, while the rest, seven thousand of them, were wild Numidians riding without either saddles or bridles, which made them of questionable value in a battle against Roman heavy infantry. Pitted against them, Caesar had at least three thousand cavalry of quality, his Germans, Gauls, and now, too, Spaniards.

From subsequent events it is likely that the 1st Legion took Scipio's right wing, not facing Caesar's 10th as it had at Farsala. The inexperienced legions and Juba's troops would have held the center. The 4th and the 6th Legions probably took the left of the line. In part compensation for desertions from the 4th and 6th, Scipio had taken several hundred men of the 5th and the 14th Legions prisoner after their troopships had been captured, and they now stood in his front line. But how well they would fight, looking across the void separating them from their friends and relatives in their own legions as they did now, would have been anyone's guess. Like most Roman legionaries on the battlefield that day they would have silently said the legionary's prayer, then gritted their teeth and waited for "Charge" to be sounded.

Even though Scipio had thirteen legions at his disposal and his total force numbered in the region of eighty thousand men, only the four thousand or so legionaries of the 1st, 4th, and 6th Legions had the sort of experience that Caesar's best troops possessed. Only troops of one of Caesar's legions, the new recruits of the 5th, had never seen action, while the men of the 10th and their fellow Spanish legionaries had achieved legendary status in Roman military circles.

Exactly where in his line General Scipio located himself we don't know. He probably kept well away from King Juba. The king was a cruel, arrogant brute of a man who'd shown Scipio and most of his fellow noble Romans little respect. Juba's only friend among the Roman ranks was General Petreius, a man with a similar abrasive nature. After his troops had annihilated Curio's army, Juba had been contemptuous of Roman force of arms. Weeks before, when he'd seen Scipio wearing his scarlet general's cloak, Juba had exploded with indignation and declared that only he was entitled to wear scarlet cloaks. Scipio, himself a proud and arrogant man, knew he needed Juba if he was to overcome Caesar. So, swallowing his pride, he lay aside his scarlet cloak and took to wearing a white one, which he sported today.

Scipio, like his son-in-law Pompey before the Battle of Pharsalus, knew that to win he could not rely on his infantry. Like Pompey, he decided to focus on his cavalry superiority. His battle plan earlier, outside Uzitta, had been to outflank Caesar's outnumbered infantry with cavalry, then surround them and pick them off, the way his cavalry general Labie-nus had almost terminated Caesar's career weeks earlier on the bare plain outside Ruspina. It seems that he had a similar plan here at Thapsus. But here, his freedom of movement was restricted. His line, as it extended in front of Thapsus, was hemmed in by the sea on one side and the salt lake on the other. And part of his army was still frantically working on camp defenses, as Caesar and his officers were well aware—they could see men rushing in and out of the open camp gateways in disorganized confusion.

Plutarch quotes two quite different accounts of Caesar's activities on the day of the Battle of Thapsus. One goes like this. Caesar had dismounted. He was walking along his front line, exhorting his troops to fight well when the time came. But his men were so keen to come to grips with the Pompe-ians, seeing the obvious consternation in their rear, that cohorts started to advance of their own accord, and their centurions had to hurry out in front of them to stop them. Caesar himself yelled to these impatient legionaries that the battle would not be won by an impromptu advance—the men had to wait until he judged the time and the circumstances right. Then, men of the 10th on the right wing made their trumpeters sound "Charge." The troops here surged forward, and the rest of the line followed suit. Realizing he couldn't stop the snowball, Caesar signaled "Good luck" to his men—how, we're not told—then mounted up and charged into the fray himself.

Plutarch says that several other sources had it that Caesar was in fact immobilized on the morning of the battle by one of his epileptic fits. It was said to have struck just as the battle was about to begin, and, feeling it coming on, he quickly had himself taken back to his camp, leaving his subordinates in charge of the battle. Depending on their type, epileptic fits usually strike without warning. But Caesar also suffered from severe headaches, and these may have served to warn him of an impending attack. And, in partial epileptic attacks, the victim remains conscious. Whatever the nature of Caesar's particular affliction, he was highly self-conscious about these fits, the first of which had hit him while he was at Córdoba some years earlier. People of the time associated epilepsy with insanity, and Caesar never spoke or wrote of his affliction himself.

Most of his officers likewise respected his memory and made no men-tion of his illness in their writings, particularly if it meant revealing he was incapacitated at the commencement of one of his greatest battles. The facts that the battle began almost accidentally and that the officers weren't able to rein in the troops suggest that perhaps Caesar was indeed not present at the outset, that he was laid low by his epilepsy and only came back onto the scene later.

One way or another, the attack began with an unauthorized charge by Caesar's troops. On the extremities of the two wings, Caesar's slingers disconcerted the mighty elephants with their lead projectiles; then the men of the 5th Legion charged into the cavalry and elephant formations. On Caesar's right wing, Scipio's left, the elephants turned and stampeded ahead of the charge of the 5th and then the 10th Legion, trampling the auxiliary troops lined up behind them. The Numidian cavalry formed up farther back broke up and fled as the elephants careered in through the unfinished gateways of Pompey's camp and began to trample everything and everyone in their path.

This left the way open for cohorts of the 5th Legion to get behind Scipio's left wing while the 10th attacked from the front. Virtually surrounded, it was Pharsalus all over again for the men of the legions on the Pompeian left. Up against the tough, disciplined 1st Legion, the progress of the 8th and 9th Legions on the far wing wasn't as dramatic, but it didn't have to be. As the Pompeian left swiftly unraveled, the rest of Scipio's line dissolved, with groups of soldiers fleeing in all directions, some into Scipio's new camp, many to the camps of Afranius and Juba to the south of the peninsula.

At the Battle of Pharsalus, those inexperienced troops who had sought safety in the camp had paid the price. It was the same here. Caesar's legionaries swept in through the open gateways of Scipio's incomplete camp and massacred everyone they found, soldiers and unarmed camp followers alike. Caesar's troops then pushed on to Juba's camp and eventually smashed their way in there, too.

Thousands of Pompeian soldiers in Juba's camp threw down their arms and tried to surrender. But they, along with colonels and generals, were butchered, whether armed or not. Caesarian troops ignored their officers' orders to stop, killing in an indiscriminate frenzy of blood. Several of Caesar's own colonels were killed or wounded here by their own troops, who angrily labeled them "agitators." It's possible these were officers who'd worked against the mutineers at Farsala and Rome and that their assailants included men of the 10th who were settling old scores.

Despite the apparent simplicity of the action, like the Battle of Pharsalus before it, the Battle of Thapsus raged all day, lasting until nightfall, with a series of actions taking place all over the coastal plain around Thapsus. Some accounts say that fifty thousand Pompeian troops were killed. The more authoritative reports put the number at five thousand to ten thousand, with Caesar's losses ranging from fifty to several hundred. In anyone's language it was a comprehensive victory for Caesar.

As at Farsala, most of the Pompeian generals escaped. Farther up the coast, the port town of Utique was still in Pompeian hands, under the firm command of Cato the Younger. Thousands of soldiers as well as numerous generals and senators flocked to it to escape on the many ships sheltering there. Once all the leading figures had escaped, along with the 1st Legion, which had withdrawn to Utique substantially intact, the principled Cato took his own life. Caesar was later to write a bitter condemnation of him in his *Anti-Cato*.

General Afranius escaped west into Mauretania with a thousand troops, possibly including men of the 4th and 6th Legions, aiming to get away to Spain. His small force was ultimately ambushed, and most of its members, including Afranius, were taken prisoner. It appears that Caesar subsequently had Afranius executed for breaking the parole he'd given after surrendering in Spain. Officially, Afranius was killed by Caesarian troops who got out of hand, along with the young Lucius Caesar, Caesar's second cousin who'd acted as an envoy between Pompey and Caesar just after Caesar crossed the Rubicon.

As Caesar mopped up all resistance in Tunisia, with one town after another surrendering to him over the next three weeks, King Juba fled to Zama, one of his two capitals, in Numidia, accompanied by General Petreius. With Caesar's cavalry patrols everywhere, the pair hid in farmhouses by day and traveled at night. But when they reached Zama the inhabitants closed the city gates to them. Juba and Petreius dined together that night, then fought a fatal duel. The survivor committed suicide.

General Labienus, Pompey's cavalry commander, who had recovered from the fall outside Ruspina, managed to escape from Tunisia by sea and head for Spain, as did the chief Pompeian commander, Scipio, and a number of other officers, including General Publius Varus. Scipio's convoy of twelve undecked ships was soon caught in a storm and blown into the harbor at Annaba, also known as Bône—Roman Hippo Regius—on the coast of Algeria, only to find a large number of Caesar's warships also sheltering there. Trapped, Scipio took his own life. But Generals Labienus and Varus succeeded in reaching the Balearic Isles off the Spanish coast, together with the 1st Legion.

Prior to the Battle of Thapsus, Gnaeus, Pompey's eldest son, had tried to take Mauretania with a motley force of two thousand men, many of them slaves. Repulsed by the garrisons of the local monarchs, he'd sailed to the Balearic Isles, joining his younger brother Sextus, who was hiding there. Now, landing at Cádiz in southwestern Spain with the 1st Legion and other escapees from Africa, the Pompey brothers declared that there, in Spain, they would continue the war against Caesar.

XVI

CAESAR'S LAST BATTLE

aesar returned to Rome by the end of July 46 B.C., after wrapping up Pompeian opposition in Africa and leaving four legions there. Back in the capital he attended to business and enjoyed the adulation of the crowds in a series of Triumphs for his victories in Egypt, Pontus, and Africa, and, by some accounts, also for Gaul. Because a Triumph could only be celebrated over foreign enemies, Thapsus was called a victory over King Juba of Numidia.

But worrying news had reached Caesar from Spain. When the Pompey brothers landed in Farther Spain, Caesar's two legions based there, the 2nd and the Indigena, both former Pompeian units, had deserted Caesar's commander, General Trebonius. They'd gone over to the brothers, linking up with the one Pompeian legion that had escaped from North Africa, the 1st. As Caesar recalled General Trebonius to Rome, his three other legions in Nearer Spain, the 21st, the 30th, and a new enlistment of the 3rd Legion raised in Cisalpine Gaul for Caesar and now led by General Pedius, Caesar's relative and a subordinate in the Gallic campaign, together with General Quintus Fabius Maximus, were instructed not to engage the Pompeys until Caesar reached the scene with reinforcements.

The Pompeys quickly took Córdoba and were in the process of occupying most of Andalusia, attracting large local support and enrolling new recruits daily—their father had been widely popular in Spain. Caesar had reacted with a stream of movement orders. The 5th, 7th, 8th, 9th, 10th, and 13th had all been shipped back across from Tunisia and were by this time camped in southern Italy. The 28th also had been brought out of Tunisia, but, being just five cohorts strong, it went to Syria. According to Appian, Caesar was already thinking about an operation against Rome's old enemy in the East, Parthia, once he'd dealt with the Pompeians, and the 28th arrived in Syria with orders to commence preparations for that operation. The other six legions transferred out of North Africa were

165

ordered to march to Spain. Meanwhile, the two cohorts of the 6th that had fought so well for Caesar in Egypt and Pontus had been resting in Italy, probably at Rome, where they would have participated in his triumphal parades, and they, too, were ordered to Spain.

It wasn't until late December that Caesar himself set off. Appian says he made the journey to Spain in twenty-seven days. When he arrived in January, it was accompanied by just his staff officers and personal attendants. Almost certainly he made the last leg, from Marseilles to Tarragona, by sea, avoiding a crossing of the Pyrenees. But in doing so he'd been forced to leave behind his faithful German cavalry bodyguard, so he had dispatched a courier ahead to Generals Pedius and Fabius in Spain with orders to send him a cavalry detachment to act as his bodyguard once he arrived. Camped east of the Guadalquivir River, or the Baetis, as it was called in Roman times, the generals had barely received the message by the time Caesar landed.

Without waiting for an escort, or for his main cavalry force, which was still on its way from Italy with General Nonius Asprenas, Caesar hurried south and joined the legions camped on the border of Nearer and Farther Spain. His rush had been necessitated by stunning news awaiting him in Tarragona: when his veteran legions reached Spain as ordered, after marching from Italy and through southern France, three of them had defected to the Pompey brothers.

Caesar had blundered in sending Spanish legions back to their homeland, legions now four years past their discharge date, legions sick of promises of rewards that never materialized and with no wish to fight their own countrymen, legions that had already mutinied several times over the past few years. Probably inspired by the news that the 2nd and the Indigena had gone over to the Pompeys, the 8th and 9th Legions deserted Caesar and went over to the other side to fight for their own people in their own country. The 13th, the legion that had crossed the Rubicon with Caesar, followed them. Why, it's unclear. The 13th's enlistment wasn't up for another three years. Maybe its legionaries from northern Italy were simply sick of Caesar's endless unfulfilled promises. No doubt to Caesar's great relief, his crack 10th and 7th Legions remained loyal to him.

The Pompeys were as surprised as Caesar by the defections. To be on the safe side, the younger Pompey, Sextus, who was now twenty-two, kept the 9th and 13th Legions with him at Córdoba. Only the 8th Legion joined his elder brother Gnaeus's field army.

In late January 45 B.C., Caesar crossed the Guadalquivir River and advanced deep into Andalusia with the 3rd, 5th, 6th, 7th, 10th, 21st, and

30th Legions and local cavalry. As the Pompeian forces fought a series of delaying actions, gradually withdrawing ahead of Caesar's legions, he drove relentlessly toward Córdoba, his provincial capital sixteen years earlier, scene of his first command, and the place where he'd raised the 10th Legion.

Southeast of Córdoba, in the Salsum River valley, Gnaeus Pompey and General Labienus, the irrepressible cavalry commander from the campaigns in Albania, Greece, and North Africa, tried to hold Caesar back by camping between the hill towns of Ategua and Ucubi and building fortifications across the river. As Caesar surrounded Ategua and began to lay siege to the town, there was a series of engagements along the valley floor. After one such encounter, the people of Ategua slit the throats of Caesarian POWs and threw their bodies from the town wall. The war was becoming dirtier by the day. But Caesar's pressure told, and on February 19 the town surrendered.

Pompey and Labienus moved their camp closer to Ucubi, and Caesar followed. Men were by now deserting from both sides daily, although the tide was increasingly in Caesar's favor. A few men from the recalcitrant 8th Legion actually deserted back to Caesar at this point. A battle now took place for a hill in the valley, five miles from Ucubi. It had no name that anyone recorded. It was like a hill in the Korean or Vietnam Wars of the twentieth century—it had no real strategic value, but it was there, and both sides decided they wanted it. On March 5 a desperate battle was fought on the slopes of the anonymous hill in southwestern Spain. Young Gnaeus Pompey's forces took the hill, and held it against all Caesar's counterattacks. Both sides suffered more than five hundred casualties. The Pompeians' success was to give them the courage for what followed.

From his right wing, Caesar took a long, thoughtful look from the back of his horse out over the helmeted heads of the men of the 10th Legion in front of him as March 17 dawned still and warm. Satisfying himself that the Pompeian units across the valley had settled into their final positions, he turned to his cavalry commander, General Asprenas, who had by this time arrived from Italy with the German, Gallic, and Spanish cavalry and now commanded eight thousand riders, the largest mounted force Caesar ever put into the field. Caesar would have told him that he intended trying to turn the enemy's left wing, using the 10th Legion, and instructed Asprenas to be ready to go in with his cavalry and capitalize on the gains made by the 10th when the time came. Asprenas acknowledged his instructions and then rode to his position on the wing.

For two weeks Gnaeus Pompey had given ground, burning several towns as he retreated. The previous day, he'd set up camp on the plain not far from the hill town of Munda. Caesar had arrived with his legions after nightfall and set up his own camp, five miles away. Then in the early hours of the morning, Caesar was awakened with the news that young Pompey was forming up his troops in battle order. As Caesar rose he would have noted that young Pompey had chosen the festival day of the god Liber, the Liberalis, for his great battle. This was the day that young Romans who had come of age traditionally donned the *toga virilis*, the symbol of manhood, for the first time. Perhaps Gnaeus had hopes of coming of age as a general on this day. Not if Caesar could help it.

Certainly, Pompey was not shy about pitting himself against the mighty Caesar. Pompey would have been conscious of the fact that his father had made his name at his age. Son of a general and grandson of a general, young Gnaeus had already shown he had military skill and daring—a few years back, he'd been the one who'd commanded the fleet that had devastated Caesar's shipping at its Adriatic anchorages, cutting off Caesar in Greece. Gnaeus had proven to be a young man with an old head on his shoulders. And it seems he'd had enough of these backpedaling skirmishes that only sapped the enthusiasm of his troops and strained the loyalty of the locals. Thirty years later, the Roman poet Horace was to write, "Seize today, and put as little trust as you can in tomorrow." On the retreat, and with more and more Spanish towns expressing doubts about the Pompey boys' ability to beat Caesar, Gnaeus Pompey had decided to seize the day and settle the matter with a full-scale battle, before he lost his grassroots support.

Caesar had been glad to oblige, and ordered his flag to be hung out, the symbol for battle. As the trumpets sounded "To Arms" throughout Caesar's camp, he'd issued a new watchword for the day: "Venus." His watchword on the day of his victory over Pompey Sr. at Pharsalus had been "Venus, Bringer of Victory," so he was sticking with a good thing and hoping that Venus would bring him his famous luck yet again. For his part, young Pompey had issued the watchword "Piety."

The men of the 10th Legion stood in their now customary position on Caesar's right wing. Unlike the 8th and 9th and like the 7th, they'd remained loyal to Caesar; they hadn't deserted. To them, demanding what was due to them was one thing, but deserting to the enemy was out of the question. Their numbers were well down according to the author of *The Spanish War*, a work likely to have been written by a junior officer in Caesar's army—a veteran centurion, it's been suggested, a distinct possibility judging from the language and tenor—before being edited by Hirtius and Balbus. Typically, Hirtius edited out the circumstances of the defection of the 8th, 9th, and 13th Legions. In *The Spanish War* they suddenly materialize on the other side in Spain, fighting against Caesar.

The 10th Legion, which was due for discharge this very month, was probably at considerably less than half strength after the toll taken on it by the Gallic campaign and the civil war. Its surviving battle-hardened veterans, perhaps two thousand of them now, were aged between thirty-three and thirty-six, and they would have been hoping that this would be their last campaign, that unlike their former comrades of the 8th and the 9th they would be allowed to take their discharge now that it was due. Just one last battle, they would have told themselves, echoing the words of Chief Centurion Crastinus three long years before.

The 5th Legion had been positioned on Caesar's left. It was the "famous 5th" now, after its daring deeds against Scipio's elephants at Thapsus. Following the battle, Caesar had granted the 5th the right to bear the elephant symbol on its shields and standards, and according to Appian two hundred years later the 5th Legion would still be famous for Thapsus, would still bear elephants on its standards. Beside the 5th stood the new recruits of the 3rd Legion from Cisalpine Gaul. Caesar's remaining four legions filled the line between the 3rd and the 10th. On his flanks he'd positioned the cavalry and several thousand auxiliaries. All told, he fielded eighty cohorts of legionaries and auxiliaries, although many of the legionary cohorts were, like those of the 10th, well understrength. There were literally only hundreds of 6th Legion men here, last survivors of the legionaries who had signed up with Caesar after Pharsalus and gone on to cover themselves in glory at Alexandria, the Nile Delta, and Zela. The total number of Caesar's infantry was no more than thirty thousand men.

All around them were rolling hills, but here on the valley floor the terrain was flat, good for both infantry and cavalry maneuvers. But first Caesar's men had a long hike to reach the enemy. In their path lay a shallow stream that dissected the plain. Well away to the right, the stream drained into a boggy marsh. The author of *The Spanish War*, an eyewitness on the day, indicates he and his fellow Caesarians felt sure the Pompeians would come down off the hill and meet them in the middle of the plain. If not, Caesar's troops would have to cross the stream, then traverse another stretch of flat, dry turf to reach the hill where the other side waited.

Because he'd chosen the battlefield, young Pompey had taken the high ground. For added support, the town of Munda was on the hill behind him, surrounded by high walls dotted with defensive towers manned by locals. Gnaeus Pompey had lined up his men on the slope below Munda. Estimates of his total troop numbers vary between fifty thousand and eighty thousand. His most experienced legions were the 1st and the 8th, and they probably took each wing, supported by the 2nd and the Indigena.

His center was occupied by nine legions of raw recruits drawn from throughout western Spain and Portugal, mere teenagers with no experience and little training. Pompey's wings were covered by cavalry supported by six thousand light infantry and the same number of auxiliaries. Pompey himself commanded, with General Labienus as his chief deputy. General Varus, who'd escaped from North Africa with Labienus, commanded one of the divisions, probably the Pompeian left, opposite the 10th.

The author of The Spanish War says that Caesar's men were both delighted that the longed-for opportunity for a decisive battle was being given to them and apprehensive about how Fate would treat them over the next hour or so.

Both generals delivered their traditional prebattle addresses, and although we don't know their exact words, Caesar apparently told his men to stay in tight formation and not under any circumstance charge before he gave the order, a command stimulated by the undisciplined opening to the Battle of Thapsus. Then, at last, he gave the command to advance. His flag inclined forward, and the trumpets of the legions sounded "Advance at Marching Pace."

Caesar's legions marched in step across the plain as, on the flanks, the cavalry also moved forward, at the walk. Caesar himself and his staff officers rode in the middle of the 10th Legion's formation. Ahead, Pompey's troops didn't budge, didn't advance to meet them in the normal fashion, a repeat of Pompey Sr.'s tactics at Farsala. Caesar's men splashed across the stream.

When his front line reached the base of the hill, Caesar unexpectedly called for a halt. The advance froze. As his men then stood, waiting to go forward to the attack, and enemy formations on the hill reshuffled to meet them, Caesar ordered his formations to tighten up, to concentrate his forces and limit the area of operation. The order was relayed and obeyed. Just as his troops were beginning to grumble impatiently, Caesar gave the order for "Charge" to be sounded. With a deafening battle cry, Caesar's eighty cohorts charged up the hillside.

With an equally deafening roar, Pompey's men let fly with their javelins. The volley of missiles, flung from above, scythed through the air and cut swathes through Caesar's ranks. The charge wavered momentarily, then regained momentum. Another volley blackened the blue sky. And another, and another. The attackers in Caesar's front ranks, with their dead comrades lying in heaps around them, out of breath, and still not within striking distance of the enemy, stopped. The following lines of breathless, perspiring men followed suit. The entire attack ground to a halt.

Swiftly dismounting, Caesar grabbed a shield from a startled legionary of the 10th in a rear rank in front of him, then barged through his troops, up the slope, all the way to the front rank, with his staff officers, hearts in mouths, jumping to the ground and hurrying after him. Dragging off his helmet with his right hand and casting it aside so that no one could mistake who he was, he stepped out in advance of the front line.

According to Plutarch, he called to his troops, nodding toward the tens of thousands of raw teenaged recruits on the Pompeian side: "Aren't you ashamed to let your general be beaten by mere boys?"

Greeted by silence, he went on to cajole his men, to berate them, to encourage them. But none of his panting, sweating, bleeding legionaries took a forward step. Then he turned to the staff officers who'd followed him.

"If we fail here, this will be the end of my life and of your careers," Appian says he told them, before he drew his sword and resolutely strode up the slope, proceeding many yards ahead of his troops toward the Pompeian line.

On Pompey's side, men within range of Caesar loosed off a volley of javelins in his direction—so many that not even the famously lucky Julius Caesar could possibly survive the hail of missiles. His men held their breath.

Caesar dodged some missiles, and took others on his shield. They jutted from the ground all around him and hung limply from his shield—two hundred of them, according to Appian. But, amazingly, Caesar himself remained unscathed. He turned back to his watching troops. "Well, what are you waiting for?" he demanded.

"Come on!" one of Caesar's staff officers called to his companions—probably Colonel Pollio—and the officers all grabbed shields from 10th Legion men in the ranks or from corpses lying at their feet and ran up to join Caesar, forming a protective wall of shields around him.

This movement forward was a catalyst for the necessary courage and momentum along the whole front line. With a roar, Caesar's troops charged up the slope once more. Men of the 10th swept past Caesar and his officers, and closed the gap between them and the enemy. With a crash of shields, the opposing lines came together. Pressed forward by those in the rear ranks pushing up the hill behind them, those in front had no choice but to go forward.

Soon it was a stalemate along the line, with neither side gaining an advantage—except on Caesar's right wing. Caesar himself was in the thick of it all with the legionaries of the 10th, wielding his sword, urging his men forward. They had a reputation to uphold, and with Caesar there on the spot urging them to superhuman efforts, fighting uphill, toe-to-toe, shield-to-shield, the veterans of the 10th gradually pushed back the Pompeian troops opposite, one bloody step at a time.

To counter this and bolster his hard-pressed left, and probably urged by the alert General Labienus—just as he'd advised Caesar on the time and place of crucial troop movements at Alesia and other battles in the past—Gnaeus Pompey gave the order for one of his other legions to swing across from the opposite wing.

Ever the opportunist, and seeing this move under way, Caesar ordered one of his staff officers to find General Asprenas, his cavalry commander, and tell him he was to concentrate his cavalry on the opposite wing, where it had been weakened by Pompey's withdrawal. The young colonel pushed his way though the sea of soldiers, back down the hill. Finding the cavalry commander, the colonel passed on the message. General Asprenas personally led several thousand cavalry in a wheel against young Pompey's weakened right.

Meanwhile, as Pompey's legion was moving over from his right wing to his left, the inexperienced young troops in Pompey's center, not knowing the strategic purpose of the move, misread it as a retreat. More and more teenagers in the center ceased to fight. Before long, thousands were streaming back up the hill, many throwing away their weapons. Panic spread among the Pompeian recruits. The center of the line dissolved as men fled in their thousands, some to Munda, others out onto the plain.

Some units, like the proud 1st Legion, survivors of Pharsalus and Thapsus, stood and fought, even though they soon were surrounded and cut off. Outnumbered, these men either died or surrendered. Most died. Like Napoleon's Old Guard at Waterloo in 1815, the 1st Legion went down fighting. And if they were offered quarter, many veterans of the 1st probably uttered the cry familiar to every man in the ranks, "*Abi in malam crucem!*" (Go and be hanged!).

It was estimated that thirty thousand of Pompey's rank and file were killed in the rout outside Munda, and up to three thousand officers. Among them, the feisty General Labienus—surrounded, and cut down from his horse, he died there outside Munda, fighting to his last breath, as did General Varus. Both were buried on the battlefield, minus their heads, which, according to Appian, were presented to Caesar. As for Caesar's losses, they were estimated at a thousand. Many of these would have died in the early stages of the battle, when the outcome was still uncertain.

For Caesar, Munda was, as Wellington was to remark about Waterloo, a near run thing. Both Plutarch and Appian report that later, in the wake of the battle, Caesar confessed to his officers and friends, "I have often fought for victory, but this was the first time I fought for my life."

Gnaeus Pompey was wounded but managed to escape, accompanied by a bodyguard of 150 cavalry and infantry. But he was in the minority. With thousands of Pompeians taking refuge in the town of Munda, and the last of the enemy being dealt with on the plain by pursuing cavalry, Caesar ordered the town surrounded by entrenchments. To convince the 14,000 sheltering in Munda to surrender, he had the bodies of Pompeian soldiers killed in the battle heaped one on top of the other as part of the entrenchments, forming a gory wall around the town. Just to add to the sickening sight, the heads of many of the dead were lopped off and placed on sword points facing the town. Leaving a small force to seal off Munda, the victor marched the bulk of his army off to Córdoba to finish the business.

Gnaeus Pompey hurried south toward the port of El Rocadillo, then called Carteia, not far from present-day Gibraltar, where he had warships and a garrison. But Pompey had been wounded in the shoulder and the leg, and also had sprained an ankle. Eventually too weak to ride, and unable to walk, he was eight miles from his destination when he could go no farther under his own steam and a litter was sent for him from El Rocadillo. He was carried into the town.

A few days later, young Pompey sailed with ten warships, but after three days' sailing he was forced to put into the Spanish coast for water and supplies. After his little fleet was trapped there by Caesar's admiral Gaius Didius, Pompey fled inland with several hundred men. Admiral Didius pursued him with men from his ships, surrounding his position in the rocks. During hectic fighting, Pompey, who'd been immobilized by his wounds, was cut off from most of his men. Tipped off by a prisoner, Didius's men located Gnaeus hiding in a gully. They killed him on the spot. The severed head of Pompey the Great's brave but doomed eldest son was subsequently put on public display in Seville.

Ironically, Admiral Didius, the man who ended Gnaeus Pompey's life, was himself killed by Pompey's men, who kept fighting for several more days despite the death of their leader and caused considerable damage and mayhem before they were mopped up by Caesar's forces.

Caesar subsequently took Córdoba, the provincial capital, which was being held by two of his former legions, the 9th and the 13th. The 13th defended the town, but the 9th went back over to Caesar at the last minute and began fighting their former comrades in the city. Caesar's forces won the day and the city, with twenty-two thousand supporters of the other side dying in Córdoba. Sextus Pompey managed to slip out of the city before it fell, but if he had thoughts of regrouping the Pompeys' supporters for a renewed offensive, he was to be sorely disappointed. The momentum of the campaign had swung Caesar's way, powerfully, irrevocably, and the heart went out of the Pompeian resistance. One by one, the last Spanish towns in Pompeian hands were stormed or surrendered. Munda, too, surrendered. Caesar spared the lives of all fourteen thousand sheltering there.

After Gnaeus Pompey's death, his brother Sextus disappeared into the countryside with a handful of followers, determined to continue a guerrilla war, and pursued by Caesar's aide Colonel Pollio. In a peace deal set up by Mark Antony the following year, the Senate would pay Sextus fifty million sesterces in compensation for his father's lost estates and give him command of a Roman fleet. For the time being this ended the influence of the Pompey family on Roman history. But not for long. In time Sextus would use the fleet to his own advantage, becoming a pirate and a thorn in the side of Roman administrations, eventually trying to seize Sicily. After some initial success he would be killed by one of Mark Antony's generals when forced to flee to the East, ten years after the Battle of Munda.

With the end of resistance in Spain that summer of 45 B.C., the civil war, which had cost hundreds of thousands of lives, came to a close. Julius Caesar was now ruler of all he surveyed.

As summer drew to an end, the men of the 10th Legion were allowed to take their discharge, which had become due in the spring. Like all the legionaries who had remained loyal to Caesar, they received substantial bonuses now that the war was over. According to Suetonius, it was twenty-four thousand sesterces per man—the twenty thousand initially promised, plus the four thousand promised the previous year outside Rome. They also received land grants in Spain. The previous fall, Caesar had put the necessary legislation before the Senate to provide land for all his veterans in Italy and Spain, and now the process began.

At the same time, Caesar ordered that a new enlistment be raised to fill the ranks of the 10th and all his other legions then undergoing discharge. Plutarch says he was well into the planning of his next military operation, an invasion of Parthia, to punish the Parthians for wiping out his fellow triumvir Crassus and his legions at Carrhae eight years before, and even had his eyes on India. As recruiting officers bustled around western Spain drafting new enlistments of young recruits, some veterans of the 10th decided that farming was no life for them. They signed on for another sixteen years with the legion. All those men staying with the legion were allocated to the leading cohorts, the 1st, 2nd, and 3rd. This would become standard practice in the future, with those men volunteering to serve a second or even a third enlistment going into the leading cohorts.

The 10th Legion remained in Spain for the time being as its new recruits were assembled, equipped, and trained. Before long the legion would come under the command of Lieutenant General Marcus Lepidus, consul with Caesar the previous year, who would shortly become Governor of Nearer Spain, with four legions under his immediate control.

Caesar was on his way back to Rome. According to Appian, when friends urged Caesar to "have the Spanish cohorts as his bodyguard again"— a reference to the 7th Legion, which had lately been transferred to Italy as part of the buildup for the Parthian offensive, and which had acted as Caesar's bodyguard in Rome in 47 B.C. at the time of the rampage of the mutinous 10th, 9th, and 8th Legions. Caesar declined, saying there was no worse fate than to be continuously protected, for that meant a person was constantly in fear, a sentiment expressed by many a leader down through the ages.

Caesar left Colonel Pollio in western Spain with two legions to continue the search for Sextus Pompey. Although he failed to catch young Pompey, Pollio would be made a major general by Caesar in 44 B.C. He would become a consul in 40 B.C., conduct a successful campaign against tribes in the Balkans in 39 B.C., and live to the age of seventy-eight or seventy-nine, dying in A.D. 4 a wealthy and respected general, statesman, and writer.

Caesar was back in the capital by September of 45 B.C. and was soon granted the title of Dictator for Life by a cowed Senate. Republican ideals had given way to rule by one man. And even though Caesar spurned the title and trappings of a king, there were many who felt he was now the king of Rome in everything but name. And they were not happy about it.

Six months later, in the middle of March 44 B.C., at a time when he was finalizing preparations for his invasion of Parthia, Caesar called a meeting of the Senate in Rome. The sitting was to take place in a meeting hall at the eastern end of a theater complex built on the Field of Mars by Pompey the Great, and would be the last before Caesar departed Rome four days later to take command of the army of six legions now waiting in Syria in readiness for the Parthian operation.

Sixty senators were a party to what followed, among them some of Caesar's closest associates, including General Trebonius; Servius Galba, who had been one of his generals in Gaul; and Caesar's chief admiral and appointee as Governor of Transalpine Gaul, Decimus Brutus Albinus; and men he had pardoned and promoted, such as Pompey's admiral Gaius Cassius.

At about ten o'clock on the morning of March 15, Caesar left his home on the Sacred Way and was carried in a litter toward the Forum, heading for the Pompeian Meeting Hall and the gathering Senate. There was a legion in the city at this time, without doubt the 7th, quartered on the island in the middle of the Tiber River, and as one of Caesar's best and most loyal units almost certainly preparing to accompany their commander in chief to Syria for the Parthian campaign. But as he had shunned armed guards, Caesar went without an escort apart from his twenty-four lictors, attendants who cleared the way bearing his fasces of office.

He was joined on the journey across the Forum by Mark Antony. As in the past, Caesar had forgiven Antony for his transgressions and welcomed him back into his fold. Antony had been the first to go out and greet him on the Aurelian Way as he returned to Rome from Spain, and had been appointed consul with Caesar for 44 B.C.

According to Appian, Caesar paused *en route* while the city magistrates sacrificed a goat and examined its entrails for omens, as was required before each sitting of the Senate. When the omens were not good, Caesar ordered a second sacrifice. Again the augurs reported ill omens. Ignoring their caution about the advisability of attending the meeting, just as he had dismissed a soothsayer's warning about this day, Caesar, impatient to have the business of government over so he could return to his military planning, resumed his journey.

As Caesar climbed from his litter outside the meeting hall, Mark Antony was waylaid by Albinus and Trebonius, who deliberately detained him in conversation. There were those among the conspirators who had wanted Antony to share the fate they had planned for Caesar on this, the

Ides of March, but wiser heads had convinced them that to retain popular support for what they were about embark on they must be seen to strike down the despot alone, as a blow for democracy. Anything more would leave them open to accusations of acting in vengeance on behalf of the late Pompey the Great, which would without question turn Caesar's fiercely loyal legions against them and sign their own death warrants.

Caesar, dressed in his quasi-regal scarlet robe and laurel crown of a Triumphant, as was required for the magistrates' ceremony, went on alone, carrying a pile of petitions handed to him on the ascent of the meeting hall steps by a throng of waiting citizens. On top of the pile was a letter penned by Artemidorus of Cnidia, a teacher of Greek logic. As the scholar passed it over, he'd urged Caesar to read it in private. The letter contained details of a plot to murder Caesar, even naming the chief conspirators. It remained unopened as Caesar strode into the crowded meeting hall. Plutarch, Appian, and Suetonius all describe in complementary detail what followed.

The waiting senators rose to their feet as the Dictator entered and walked toward his throne of ivory and gold, which faced the semicircle of benches. As he did so, handing the petitions and the unread written warning to a secretary, a number of senators crowded around him. Senator Tillius Cimber pressed a petition on him as Caesar took his seat, pleading that his brother be allowed to return from exile. As other senators added their petitions in support of Cimber, Caesar impatiently advised that he would not consider leniency for Cimber's brother, admonishing the petitioners for wasting his time and telling them to resume their seats. It was then that Cimber suddenly reached forward and pulled Caesar's scarlet robe down over his arms, pinning them.

According to Suetonius, the astonished Caesar exclaimed, "This is violence!"

At the same moment, at Cimber's side, Senator Publius Servilius Casca produced a dagger. He struck at Caesar's neck. The blow was not well aimed and caused only a superficial wound. Caesar looked around at Casca in astonishment.

"Vile Casca!" Plutarch says Caesar cried, as he shook himself free of Cimber's restraining grasp and grabbed at the knife to prevent Casca from striking a second time, and adding, "What's the meaning of this?"

Casca, panicking, looked around for his brother, a fellow senator. "Brother, help!"

Casca's brother and a score of others were drawing weapons from under their garments. They came at Caesar with blades raised, each determined to fulfill a vow to strike a blow against the Dictator. Twenty-three con-spirators plunged swords or daggers into Caesar. Among them was Marcus Brutus, the young man Caesar had treated like a son and whose life he had spared after the Battle of Pharsalus.

Suetonius writes of some authorities claiming that as Brutus struck, Caesar gasped in Greek, "You, too, my child?" A line that would inspire Shakespeare.

In their frenzy, several of the assassins wounded each other. Caesar rose, staggering as he tried to escape the blows, attempting to strike back with his writing stylus, a mere pen-knife, according to Suetonius. At a later autopsy, Suetonius tells us, the physician Antistius concluded that a blow to the chest had been the fatal one—a blow by Brutus, Suetonius says, although Appian records that Brutus struck Caesar in the leg.

According to Plutarch and Appian, as the meeting hall emptied in a panic-stricken rush, Caesar fell at the foot of a statue of Pompey. And, like Pompey, he tried to cover his face with his cloak in his last moments. There, in his fifty-fifth year, and almost seventeen years to the day since he'd raised the 10th Legion and commenced his march to power, Gaius Julius Caesar, Dictator of Rome, perished.

XVII

MARK ANTONY'S MEN

The father of the legion was dead. The 10th had been created by Caesar, and had marched for him throughout its entire seventeen-year existence. Suddenly its leader, and in many ways its reason for being, had gone. The men of the legion would have been stunned by their leader's murder, but as Rome's premier legion, Caesar's finest, it would be expected to play a prime role in the tumultuous events that followed Caesar's bloody end.

In the months after Caesar's assassination his murderers advocated a return to the old republican system, where Rome was governed by the Senate. But other men felt that the day of the autocrat was there to stay, and several factions emerged as leading men of the state jockeyed for position. Mark Antony now saw himself as a legitimate successor to Caesar. In the division of the postwar empire, he'd been given the governorship of Macedonia, and allocated five legions to police the province.

The 5th Legion, we know, was sent from Spain to Macedonia to join this force of Antony's. Just as Caesar's legions due for discharge had their ranks filled with new recruits, so the former Pompeian legions in Spain were also reenlisted. The 4th, finally defeated by Caesar at Thapsus in Tunisia, had been reenlisted in Spain, and it marched with the famous 5th to Macedonia. Of the other legions in Spain as the civil war came to an end, the 7th soon marched to Italy and was at Rome at the time of Caesar's murder, *en route* to join the Parthian expedition. But for the time being the 10th was one of the legions that remained in Spain.

Within a few months of Caesar's death, Antony was feeling too far from the action, and asked the Senate to give him another province, Cisalpine Gaul, on Rome's northern doorstep. It was then being governed by Marcus Decimus Brutus Albinus, one of the assassination conspirators, and Antony suggested that the Senate swap their provinces. Albinus didn't want to make the transfer. So, late in the summer of 44 B.C., with things

179

moving too slowly for him, Antony took the initiative, shipping four of his legions back to Italy via Brindisi. The fifth was to follow shortly after. Technically this was an act of war against the Senate, in the same way that Caesar's crossing of the Rubicon had been five years earlier.

Brutus and Gaius Cassius, another leader of the assassination plot and a onetime admiral, had been serving as praetors, and in the new year they were due to take up provincial governorships previously allotted to them by Caesar—Macedonia for Brutus, Syria for Cassius. But since Caesar's death Antony had convinced the Senate to take these appointments away from the pair and give them lesser posts, to their great dissatisfaction. In September they fled Rome in fear of Antony. Reaching Macedonia, they claimed their former appointments given to them by Caesar, and summoned the six legions stationed in Syria by Caesar in the buildup for his planned Parthian campaign. In the face of this military muscle, by the following February the Senate would appoint them to jointly command all Rome's eastern possessions, from the Adriatic to Syria.

In November, as Antony marched his army up through Italy to the Po to take Cisalpine Gaul from Albinus by force, and with the Senate having met at Rome and declared him an enemy of the state for his precipitous and illegal action, two of his legions deserted him—the 4th and the Martia, the latter, it seems, being the legion left by Pompey in Cilicia in 49 B.C. when he created the Gemina from two existing units. Shrugging off this setback, Antony pushed on with his three remaining legions and lay siege to Albinus and his four legions at the city of Mutina, modern Modena, just north of the Po River on the Aemilian Way.

With Antony pushing his luck too far, a coalition quickly formed against him. An unexpected key player in this coalition was Caesar's eighteen-year-old great-nephew Gaius Octavius, who, according to the terms of Caesar's will, had become his adopted son and heir on his death and who was now legally known as Gaius Julius Caesar Octavianus, or as we know him, Octavian. He had hurried back to Italy from Apollonia in Greece, where he'd been studying for the past six months in preparation for joining Caesar on his eastern military expedition. The youth proved a surprisingly able political performer, attracting many of Caesar's former followers to him. By the spring of 43 B.C., empowered by the Senate and supported by the two current consuls, Generals Aulus Hirtius and Gaius Vibius Pansa, and with a force of five legions, including the 7th as well as the recently defected 4th and Martia Legions under General Sulpicius

Galba, Octavian marched from Rome to Albinus's relief. At the same time, Marcus Lepidus marched from Spain into southern France to occupy Transalpine Gaul and so deny it to Antony, leading the legions then based in Spain, including the 10th, across the Pyrenees.

On April 14 and 21 of 43 B.C., in successive battles near Modena, Antony was defeated by Octavian's legions, suffering 50 percent casualties. Among the fatalities on the other side were the two consuls, General Hirtius, Caesar's aide for so many years and editor of his writings, and General Pansa, who died a lingering death. Antony, taking his surviving troops, retreated west across the Alps into Transalpine Gaul. As he did, Lepidus marched east to confront him with seven legions—units he'd brought from Spain plus at least one of the legions then based in Transalpine Gaul.

The two armies came together at a river, almost certainly the Var, border between Cisalpine and Transalpine Gaul, and camped on opposite banks. To indicate a lack of aggressive intent, Antony purposely didn't build the normal fortifications around his camp, instructing the substantially outnumbered men of his three legions to merely set up their tents in the open. Before long the men of the two armies began to fraternize, and on their own initiative built a bridge of boats to link their camps.

In Lepidus's camp, the men of the 10th Legion, who'd been commanded by Antony several times during the civil war, began speaking favorably of him to their fellow legionaries. This caused Lepidus to fret that his men might desert him, so, according to Appian, that night he divided his legions into three divisions and sent them on tasks that were designed to test their loyalty. The plan backfired, with the men of the last watch opening his camp gates and admitting Antony and his troops. Lepidus, by all accounts a weak man both physically and emotionally, quickly came to an accommodation with Antony, with the result that the 10th and his six other legions transferred their allegiance to Antony, although nominally Lepidus was still in command.

Antony's force was also soon reinforced by three legions led by Publius Ventidius, one of the new consuls for the year, which came over to him with their commander, so that he now had a formidable force of thirteen legions. By November the astute young Octavian had drawn Antony and Lepidus into a three-way pact. Their junta, called by latter-day writers the Second Triumvirate, took the official title Board of Three for the Ordering of State. At a meeting at Bononia, modern Bologna, they decreed death sentences on numerous opponents, including the orator Cicero, and divided the empire among them. Antony was to take the East as his personal fiefdom. But there was a small problem: Brutus and Cassius controlled the East, and, determined to resist the Triumvirate and restore the

Republic, they had assembled a formidable army of twenty legions in Macedonia—the six from Syria; two more that Brutus raised in Macedonia; and another twelve brought together from their bases throughout the East by Cassius, including the four left by Caesar in Egypt to support Cleopatra's reign since his departure in 47 B.C.

By the summer of 42 B.C., leaving Lepidus, now bestowed with Caesar's former lifelong post of *pontifex maximus*, and a consulship, in charge at Rome, Antony and Octavian set off to invade Greece. Jointly they would take their legions, including Antony's 10th, against Brutus and Cassius, who had based themselves in Macedonia at a town on the military highway between Durrës and the eastern provinces. A town called Philippi.

XVIII

PHILIPPI AND ACTIUM

P hilippi, the modern Filippoi, was probably already several hundred years old when King Philip II of Macedon fortified the town in 356 B.C. to protect neighboring gold mines. The town lay about eight miles from the port of Neapolis, present-day Kavala, where Brutus and Cassius established their supply base in 43 B.C. The two renegade generals built separate camps for their legions two miles west of Philippi township, each on a hill about a mile apart. They had chosen their positions so they could straddle the Egnatian Way, the military highway from Thessalonika in the east to Durrës on the Albanian coast in the west, with their positions partly protected by marshland. Once the camps were completed, they built fortifications from hill to hill that linked the two. And there they waited for the triumvirs and their armies.

In the midsummer of 42 B.C., Antony and Octavian sent an advance force of eight legions across the Adriatic from Italy. Led by Generals Lucius Decidius Saxa and Gaius Norbanus Flaccus, this force skirted around Philippi and occupied the passes east of Brutus and Cassius, cutting them off from reinforcement and overland supply by their supporters in the East. Now, in the last days of summer, Antony and young Octavian chanced their arms against their opponents' powerful fleet of 240 warships, and, driven by strong winds, successfully brought a second convoy to Greece's shores and landed a further 20 legions.

Octavian, who would turn twenty-one on September 23, was frequently unwell in his youth, and during the voyage to Greece he fell seriously ill. So, leaving the feverish young man at Epidamnus to recover, Antony took control of their joint forces, including the 10th Legion, and advanced into Macedonia to confront their enemies. Finding the town of Amphipolis occupied by friendly local forces, Antony left one legion there with his heavy baggage, then continued to advance toward Philippi.

In mid-September, Antony came marching up to Philippi, and, to the surprise of his opponents, built a camp on unfavorable ground on the dusty plain not far from their position. The ailing Octavian joined his army ten days later, arriving on a litter, too weak to walk. In the meantime, the two armies had begun facing off, lining up daily to confront each other across the plain. Each day, both sides formed up nineteen legions and twenty thousand cavalry in battle order. Many of the legions confronting each other on the plain at Philippi had until recently fought on the same side. For Antony and Octavian, legions including the 4th, 5th, 7th, and 10th faced legions such as the 27th, 28th, 36th, and 37th fighting for Brutus and Cassius.

Brutus and Cassius were reluctant to join battle, hoping instead that their opponents would run out of supplies, so they kept their troops on higher ground and refused to let them come down onto the plain. For ten days this went on, and all the while Antony had a detachment secretly building a path through the tall reeds of the marsh toward Cassius's fortifications.

Once the path was complete, Antony sent a unit along it on a commando raid that seized several opposition outposts, to the surprise of Brutus and Cassius. To counter and outflank this pathway they started building a line of entrenchments. Then, one day in early October, close to noon, as their troops were on the verge of cutting off the commando force with their creeping trench line, Antony unexpectedly led his legions forward in a charge at the defenses below the hill occupied by Cassius's camp. Antony not only surprised the opposition; he also surprised Octavian's legions, which were lined up in battle order in front of their camp at the time. They stood and gaped as their comrades of Antony's nine legions charged the enemy.

Like Caesar, Antony would have valued his Spanish legionaries above all others. Almost certainly, Antony followed Caesar's practice and put the 10th Legion on his right wing this day. The unit charging forward on the extreme left of Antony's line was the Spanish 4th Legion, which had been given back to him by Octavian after the formation of the Triumvirate. Some of the 4th Legion's men were former Pompeian legionaries who'd signed on for a new enlistment under Caesar after the legion's defeat at Thapsus. Most were new recruits raised in Spain since 45 B.C.

In giving the left to the 4th Legion, Antony was paying it a high compliment. The legions on an army's extreme wings were always considered its best. Appian was to describe the 4th Legion as being of the highest quality at this time, ironically in tribute to the unit's performance against Antony in the Modena battles the previous year.

Brutus was preparing for battle when the unexpected charge came on his right. He'd placed the legion he considered his best on his right wing—we don't know its identity—under the command of General Marcus Valerius Corvinus Messalla. Surviving the battle and the war, Messalla would later write of this day's events in his memoirs. Reconciled with Octavian after Philippi, Messalla served under him at Actium, after which he was made a consul. His memoirs, consulted by classical authors including Plutarch, have not come down to us. According to Plutarch, Messalla noted that when Antony's charge came, Brutus was busy organizing his cavalry and supporting infantry, while at the same time his orderly sergeants were still going about their legions handing out the *tesserae*, small wax sheets containing Brutus's hastily revised watchword for the day. Many of Brutus's men went into action even before the new watchword reached them.

No one could say that Mark Antony was a coward—he'd proven his courage time and again in numerous battles. Equally, he was to show in numerous battles that he was an inept if not appalling tactician. He could be assessed as a poor general served by excellent lieutenants. Now, in leading this unexpected charge, he certainly grabbed the initiative and had the element of surprise on his side. But in taking his line forward against Cassius's position he exposed his left wing to Brutus's troops—the men of the 4th Legion had to run past Brutus's battle line, inviting the opposition to swing in on their rear.

Brutus's eager troops on his right wing couldn't believe their luck. Anticipating General Messalla's orders, his legion launched an attack on the 4th Legion before he or Brutus even gave the word. They drove in around the 4th, attacking it from the flank and rear and cutting down its men in droves. As more of Antony's troops came up in support of the 4th, more of Brutus's legions joined Messalla's unit and increased the pressure on Antony's left.

The men of the 4th, conscious of their reputation, put up a ferocious fight, but their wing was eventually overwhelmed by superior numbers. General Messalla's legion and another fighting beside it excitedly swept on to Octavian's troops as they stood in their lines watching the battle, outflanked them, and cut their way through legion formations and those of Greek auxiliaries. They reached the camp of Antony's and Octavian's army and overran it, killing everyone they found, and looted it.

Appian tells us that Octavian was to write in his memoirs—which were never published but kept in the imperial archives at Rome, where only those with permission to do so could consult them, and where they and all other official records were destined to be destroyed when Rome was sacked by invaders in later centuries—that the night before the battle he'd had a dream that had warned him not to stay in camp. So he had himself removed to a safer place earlier in the day. Plutarch says that it was a friend of Octavian's, Marcus Artorius, who'd had the cautionary dream. Either way, the fact that Octavian took heed of this dream enabled him to escape the bloody fate of others caught in his camp.

In the meantime Antony, unaware of the disaster on his left, had broken through Cassius's line on his right. Probably with the 10th Legion in the vanguard of his attack, Antony personally led the assault on Cassius's camp, driving through three legions in his path and smashing down the camp gates. According to Plutarch, Antony himself now withdrew, leaving his troops to an orgy of destruction and pillage in the camp.

All around him, Cassius's troops fled in terror. As his cavalry dispersed and galloped off toward the sea to the east, his infantry began to give way as well. Grabbing a standard from a fleeing standard-bearer, Cassius planted it in the ground, determined to become the focal point for a stand. But he had difficulty rallying even the men of his personal bodyguard and in the end was forced to mount up and withdraw up the hill behind his camp.

Trying to observe the course of the battle from the hilltop with just a few remaining supporters, Cassius could see little because of a huge dust cloud roused by the feet of 160,000 combatants and 40,000 horses, in what was the largest battle of the era. All he could see with any clarity was Antony's legions overrunning his camp below and killing everyone in it.

Cassius was no military novice. A little older than Brutus, he'd been quartermaster in Crassus's army at the Carrhae debacle in 53 B.C., and had been primarily responsible for the fact that some ten thousand Roman troops had managed to survive that battle and escape back to Syria. He'd successfully commanded a fleet for Pompey in the early years of the last civil war. And over the past year he'd defeated two legions led by General Publius Dolabella on an abortive invasion of Syria on behalf of the triumvirs, then invaded and occupied the island of Rhodes in a series of sea and land battles. But now, for all his military experience, Cassius assumed the worst: Brutus was dead, his troops overrun, their mutual cause lost.

Seeing cavalry galloping toward his hill, he sent a staff officer named Titinius riding down to determine their identity. When Titinius reached the cavalry he found they were from Brutus's forces. Recognizing him, the cavalrymen surrounded him, embracing him, and patting him on the back. But from his hilltop vantage point, it looked to Cassius as though his friend had been overwhelmed and made a prisoner.

Most classical historians agree that there are two accounts of what followed, and none is sure which to credit as the truth. One account has the desolate Cassius ordering his servant Pindarus to kill him with his sword, while the other version says that Pindarus murdered him. Either way, Cassius died there on the hilltop on the day of the battle, which, coincidentally, was also his birthday.

Brutus was neither dead nor defeated. The end result of the battle was something of a stalemate, with both armies losing camps but remaining reasonably intact. According to both Appian and Plutarch, the latter quoting General Messalla, Brutus's army had the better of the encounter, leaving only eight thousand dead on the field, while Octavian and Antony lost sixteen thousand men. Among the dead were a great many legionaries of the 4th Legion. In Appian's narrative of the battle, Brutus was to boast to his troops the next day that they had "completely destroyed the famed 4th Legion." Not quite, but the badly mauled 4th probably played little part in further operations against Brutus. As to the 10th, its casualties are not mentioned.

If anything, Antony and Octavian can be said to have suffered a reverse in the First Battle of Philippi. Not only did they lose twice as many men as their opponents on the battlefield, but also, out on the Adriatic that day, another convoy sailing from Brindisi to bring them reinforcements—the Martia Legion and one other, plus cohorts of the Praetorian Guard—was intercepted by 130 opposition warships, which swarmed all over the heavily laden transports. Many troopships were sunk and thousands of legionaries and Praetorians died, some consumed by flames in burning vessels, others drowning in the Adriatic, others still dying of thirst in succeeding days as they clung to wreckage. Weeks later, a number of survivors were found on deserted islands.

Yet, the republican cause took a body blow with the death of the well-respected Cassius. The morale of the troops opposing the Triumvirate had to be affected, not to mention that of Brutus. And three weeks later, at three o'clock in the afternoon of October 23, Brutus, likening himself to Pompey at Farsala, was dragged unwillingly into a second Battle of Philippi near the location of the first by his officers, who included his close friend and Pompey's dedicated follower General Marcus Favonius.

This time Brutus's dispirited forces were routed by Antony and Octavian. At first Brutus led his left wing in a successful charge, but his right wing quickly gave way, allowing Antony's and Octavian's legions to swing around into Brutus's rear and steamroll his troops from behind, much as Brutus had devastated the 4th Legion a few weeks earlier. Among the fatalities were Brutus's deputy, General Antistius Labeo, and Flavius, his chief of engineers, both of whom died before his eyes, and his cousin Marcus Cato, son of Cato the Younger.

When Brutus's surviving four legions refused to continue the fight, he was forced to flee with just a handful of supporters. Shortly after, he took the honorable way out. His head was sent to Rome for display on the Gemonian Stairs, the traditional fate of traitors. His chief surviving followers, including Favonius, were led off in chains to an uncertain fate. With the death of Julius Caesar's "son" and chief assassin, hostilities came to an end.

There was still work for the men of the 10th Legion in the coming years. First there would be soldiering against the Parthians with Antony, who was determined to carry through Caesar's planned invasion of Parthian territory, and then the great confrontation between Octavian and Antony and Cleopatra that, in the summer of 31 B.C., would bring the 10th to a promontory on the west coast of Greece called Actium.

Details of the Battle of Actium are in part sketchy. The battle was a long time coming, but it was inevitable. Between 42 and 33 B.C., Antony and Octavian became increasingly at odds. By 36 B.C., Lepidus had been pushed out of the Triumvirate after foolishly trying to convince Octavian's legions on Sicily to throw their support behind him. Lepidus played no further part in Rome's government. By some accounts retaining just his post as *pontifex maximus*, according to Suetonius he lived out the rest of his days in exile on the coast of southwestern Italy, at Circeii, today's village of San Felice Circeo, then an isolated summer resort popular with the Roman elite. This left Antony, in control in the East, and Octavian, in charge at Rome, to fight over who would eventually rule the empire.

In the 30s B.C., Antony's legions had success against the Parthians in Armenia. Although most of the credit was due to his deputy, General Ventidius, that didn't stop Antony from riding in a pseudo Triumph through the streets of Alexandria. At the same time, Antony developed an amorous relationship with Queen Cleopatra of Egypt that scandalized Roman society. Already married, and at a time when Romans could not legally marry foreigners anyway, he treated Cleopatra as his consort and partner, his wife in all but name. His stocks in Rome fell even lower when he gifted Roman territories in the East to her. The latest power-sharing agreement between Antony and Octavian was not renewed when it expired in late 33 B.C. Hostilities were just a matter of time.

Antony wasn't without his supporters in Rome. As the war clouds gathered in 32 B.C., judging the mere slip of a boy Octavian unfit to lead them, both consuls for the year and more than two hundred senators departed Rome and fled to the fifty-year-old Antony in Egypt. But Octavian retained the loyalty of the legions in the West, who saw him as the legitimate heir of Julius Caesar, the commander they'd come to venerate. With an army the equal of Antony's and an organizational ability and tactical sense that Antony never possessed, Octavian had the tools to win this contest.

Both sides prepared for war, but in different ways. Many of Octavian's legions had been raised by Caesar in Italy at the outbreak of the civil war in 49 B.C. and were due to undergo their sixteen-year discharge this year, 33 B.C. But rather than lose these experienced veteran troops Octavian kept them in service, promising them big rewards once the conflict with Antony was settled.

In the East, a number of Antony's legions were also due for discharge, but he let most of his veterans retire, replacing them with recruits drafted in the territories under his control, being effectively cut off from the recruiting grounds of some of his legions such as the 3rd, a unit that had been recruited in Cisalpine Gaul for the last few enlistments, and the 4th, a Spanish legion. He raised new recruits for several of his legions, including the 3rd, in Syria, which had been made a Roman province by Pompey thirty-one years before. Meanwhile, letting those surviving Spanish legionaries of the 4th who wished to retire do so—he had no desire to bring on a repeat of the mutiny of Spanish legions under Caesar that had damaged his own reputation—Antony filled their places with new recruits from Macedonia. The 10th Legion had more than three years of its current enlistment to run, so Antony still had the Spanish veterans of his best legion marching with him.

In 31 B.C., to bring their conflict to a head, the two opponents began issuing each other challenges. Octavian offered Antony a beachhead in Italy, with space for a camp, where their two armies could fight it out. Antony replied with a challenge of his own—single combat, just the two of them, like the heroes of Greek legend. When Octavian turned down that flamboyant invitation, Antony issued another, this time for a pitched battle between their armies at Farsala, site of Caesar's victory over Pompey. Octavian declined this challenge, too.

Antony and Cleopatra established a major naval base at Actium on the Ambracian Gulf in the west of Greece. In the summer, Octavian surprised his adversaries by arriving there out of the blue with a troop convoy and a vast fleet of 400 warships, almost all of them light, fast frigates, dropping anchor just up the coast from Antony's position.

As Octavian's admiral, Marcus Agrippa, seized strategic points around the Gulf of Corinth to cut Antony's supply lines, Octavian himself landed with forty thousand legionaries and set up camp. With Cleopatra's Egyptian flotilla of 60 battleships, Antony retained a naval force here of 230 warships and 50 transports. Although, overall, Antony's land forces outnumbered Octavian's—one hundred thousand men in 19 legions to Octavian's eighty thousand—Antony's units were spread throughout the East, from Greece to Egypt, and it seems he had only a third of his legions here at Actium. What was worse, according to Cassius Dio, these men had been camped in an unsuitable location for some time, so that in both winter and summer they were seriously affected by disease, almost certainly dysentery and malaria, reducing their effectiveness.

Outnumbered here on land, and no doubt now regretting that he'd permitted his best troops to go into retirement, Antony allowed Cleopatra to talk him into engaging Octavian in a sea battle, to break out of Agrippa's blockade and withdraw to Egypt, where Antony had another seven legions encamped.

Antony's and Cleopatra's warships were mostly battleships and cruisers. These huge craft could accommodate numerous marines, who would be used to board opposition ships. In addition, says Dio, Antony had high turrets built on the decks of the warships and embarked a large number of men from his legions "who could fight as it were from battlements." Plutarch put the number at twenty thousand marines and legionaries and two thousand archers aboard Antony's and Cleopatra's ships. This left about twenty thousand of Antony's legionaries and an unknown number of his total complement of twelve thousand cavalry on shore, cheering on the maritime contestants.

The identities of individual legions involved at Actium haven't come down to us, so we can only speculate on which units were actually there, and where. It would be surprising if the men of the 10th Legion weren't present for Antony, with their experience, their fame, and their display of loyalty to him at the Var. They would either have been on his warships or lined up on the shore, where the two land armies faced each other while the sea battle took place, with Antony's land forces commanded by Lieutenant General Publius Canidius Crassus, and Octavian's by Lieutenant General Titus Taurus Statilius.

According to Dio, when Antony addressed his troops prior to the battle and informed them of his plans, he told them, "You yourselves are the kind of soldiers who can conquer even without a good leader, and I am the kind of leader who can win even with inferior soldiers." History shows he was half right.

Plutarch tells of a battle-scarred centurion of one of Antony's legions, perhaps the 10th, who had fought for Antony for many years. With orders to board a ship for the coming battle, he asked his commander in chief to let his legionaries do service on land, where they knew how to fight. But Anthony waved away all objections; he had made up his mind, or Cleopatra had made it up for him—Actium would be decided on water, not on land.

During the morning of September 2, 31 B.C., the two navies lined up, each in two main lines, with Octavian's fleet to the west, blocking Antony's path. Accounts vary as to the identity and location of the commanders. Plutarch doesn't mention Octavian's subordinates apart from Agrippa, but from other sources we know they included Admiral Marcus Lollius and General Valerius Messalla. Plutarch puts Octavian on his own right wing, with Agrippa controlling his left, and he says that Antony himself commanded his right, supported by Admiral Publicola. Admiral Marcus Insteius and Admiral Marcus Octavius had command in his center, and Admiral Coelius his left. In the center, Cleopatra formed up her squadron of sixty ships, including vessels carrying their joint treasury, to the rear of Antony's line. Although some authors, like Plutarch, have characterized what followed as flight, it seems that Antony's intent all along was to break out of the encirclement rather than achieve a decisive victory on the day, and then regroup in Egypt. That was certainly the impression of several classical authors, including Dio.

At about noon, with sails stowed so they couldn't be set alight by enemy artillery, and relying only on his oarsmen, Antony advanced his left wing, hoping that Admiral Coelius would draw Octavian into action and open a break in his line. But Octavian's frigates backed water, and drew Antony's ships out into open water. Antony's left wing engaged, and soon, all along the line, ships of both sides were locked in battle.

Octavian's Admiral Agrippa had issued tactical orders to the frigates of his fleet to avoid single close contact with Antony's much larger vessels, whose marines and legionaries would overwhelm their small crews if they managed to board. Instead, two and three frigates at a time were to surround a single battleship or cruiser. These tactics proved highly successful, but even so, a gap opened up in the center of Octavian's line.

Seizing her opportunity, Cleopatra ordered the ships of her squadron to make for the opening. With Cleopatra's flagship, the battleship *Antonias*, leading the way, the Egyptian ships powered through the gap with flashing oars and turned south for Egypt. Raising their sails and with a strong northwesterly behind them, they sped away from the scene of the battle.

Transferring from his beleaguered battleship to a fast cruiser in a small boat, Antony hurried after her. As many of his ships as possible tried to break off action and do the same, and up to eighty of them made their escape with Antony. But the rest of his warships, about a hundred of them, were hemmed in.

Now, with three and four frigates surrounding each stranded larger ship, like ants around a crippled beetle, every one of Antony's remaining craft was either captured or surrendered, although, says Dio, Antony's marines and legionaries continued fierce hand-to-hand fighting with Octavian's boarding parties long after their commander's departure. Plutarch says bitter fighting lasted until about 4:00 P.M., while Suetonius says it was well into the night before the battle was finally terminated—so late, in fact, that Octavian spent the rest of the night at sea.

Many of Antony's surrendered warships would be burned, but some, those of sound Egyptian construction—the Egyptians were far better shipbuilders than the Romans—would still be serving in Rome's navy fifty years later. Five thousand of Antony's men died in the battle. The surviving legionaries, marines, and crewmen taken from the ships all swore allegiance to Octavian.

Antony's legions on shore held out for days, staying in their camp, until, after a week, their general, Canidius Crassus, fled in the night. The disillusioned legionaries he left behind all now went over to Octavian, and he assimilated their units into his army.

Not counting the Battle of Dyrrhachium, which the men of the 10th would have assured you was nothing more than a strategic withdrawal, this was the first defeat that the 10th Legion had ever been involved in. It was certainly the first time the 10th surrendered. And the last.

At an assembly of his army following the battle, as Octavian stood before his troops to congratulate and reward them, the men of the numerous legions who were well past their discharge date clamored to be released from service, to be paid the bonuses they were owed, and to be given the land grants they'd been promised. Upward of twenty legions in Octavian's army had been raised or reenlisted in 49 and 48 B.C. and were between one and two years past their due discharge by this time.

Octavian silenced them with a single look, so says Tacitus. He then discharged the men of legions raised in Italy who were due for it, and assured them their bonuses would be paid and their promised land grants handed over in due course. Suetonius says that in abolishing several legions that were demanding their overdue discharges at this time Octavian failed to pay them their promised bounties. Technically this was true—his treasury was almost bare, and he simply didn't have the capacity to pay his discharged troops at the time.

But Octavian knew that if he didn't pay them eventually, they could rise up in revolt and march behind anyone who promised them enough to take up arms again. To provide some men with land immediately, he set in motion a series of confiscations, taking over the land of communities in Italy that had previously supported Antony, for redistribution among his retiring troops. As for his legionaries' bonuses, there was only one way Octavian could find that sort of money: It would have to come from the fabulous horde of gold, silver, and jewels that Cleopatra was reputed to keep in Alexandria.

Octavian gave orders for his remaining legions, now including the 10th and other Antonian units, to prepare to march on Egypt. Octavian's future now depended on his not only eliminating Antony but also getting his hands on Cleopatra's treasure, if it did indeed exist. If he failed in either objective, the youthful leader was doomed.

Following the Battle of Actium, Octavian rapidly marched across Greece, giving chase to several of Antony's legions pulling out of the north of the country and trying to reach their commander in Egypt. He overtook them in Macedonia, where they, too, came over to him, without a fight.

Octavian's army spent the winter in Greece. He himself returned briefly to Italy, landing at Brindisi in January 30 B.C. to personally administer the distribution of confiscated land to retired legion veterans. Retirees had lost patience with his promises and had been on the verge of an uprising as they agitated for their just rewards. Octavian even offered to sell his own property and that of his friends and put the proceeds toward the veterans' bounties. The offer placated the former legionaries, especially when he assured them that the treasure of Egypt would soon be in his hands and every legionary would be more than well rewarded if they continued to be patient a little longer.

Come the spring, Octavian rejoined the troops in Greece. Once he'd performed the rituals of the Lustration Exercise, he led his army, consisting now mostly of Antony's former legions such as the 10th, to the Dardanelles, shipped them across to Asia, and marched down into Syria, where local rulers such as King Herod of Judea sent him vows of loyalty, and thousands of their own troops in support of their vows.

With the arrival of summer, Octavian marched into Egypt. Antony was prepared to do battle with his seven legions, outnumbered more than two to one by Octavian. But in the end Antony's last legions refused to fight their comrades and to a man deserted to Octavian.

In August 30 B.C., as Octavian arrived outside Alexandria, Mark Antony committed suicide. Shortly after, in the best tragic tradition, Cleopatra followed suit. In Cleopatra's treasury at Alexandria, Octavian found a treasure so vast even he was astonished. From the proceeds, he was able to pay all his troops their outstanding pay and the war bonuses he'd promised them. Tens of thousands of retired troops in Italy ultimately went on such a spending spree that there was a shortage of goods of all kinds, and moneylenders had to reduce their interest rates from 12 percent to 4 percent to attract business. Octavian was also able to personally pay the salaries of the legionaries of his postwar army for the next several decades.

As Cleopatra was laid to rest by Octavian, side-by-side with Antony in the same tomb at the Egyptian capital, the civil war was at last at an end. It was with the prospects of bulging purses that the men of the 10th Legion now began thinking about their retirement in the new year when their 29 B.C. discharge fell due.

XIX

IN THE NAME
OF THE EMPEROR

Octavian was to prove himself the greatest administrator in Rome's history. Granted the title by the Senate in 27 B.C. by which we know him as Rome's first and arguably best emperor—Augustus, meaning "revered"—he transformed every aspect of Roman civil and military life. He wasted no time reforming and remodeling the army. At the time of the Battle of Philippi in 42 B.C., he, his ally Antony, and his opponents Brutus and Cassius had a total of fifty-nine legions among them, all of which Octavian was to inherit. This was far too large an army for Rome to support on an ongoing basis, and he'd started the reduction process in 31 B.C. by sending home all the men of the Italian legions who were due for retirement. Most of the units they departed were officially abolished, and on the death of Antony the following year Octavian further reduced his army by amalgamating several legions.

He ended up with twenty-eight legions, numbered 1 through 28, all made up of Roman citizens from areas throughout the empire other than Italy south of the Po. Until the reign of Nero a hundred years later, when he recruited the 1st Italica Legion in Italy proper, the only Roman troops recruited from that region were the men of the Praetorian Guard. All the existing Spanish legions remained—the 5th, 6th, 7th, 8th, 9th, and 10th. And another Spanish legion, the 21st Rapax, was created. This appears to have come about when the Spaniards of Pompey's former Indigena Legion, renamed the Rapax, or "rapacious," took the number of the old 21st Legion, whose Italian legionaries had retired.

Octavian didn't too look kindly on the 10th Legion. This famous unit, which had once been Caesar's favorite and most loyal legion had, after all, gone over to Antony and marched against Octavian, and it seems that when the 10th's discharge fell due in 29 B.C. he held off sending the men of the 10th home. According to Suetonius, they rioted to press their demands, after which Augustus dishonorably discharged the entire legion.

But this wasn't the end of the 10th Legion. As a non-Italian unit, the 10th would continue, in name at least, as one of the twenty-eight legions in Octavian's new army, and he must have immediately issued orders for a fresh enlistment of the legion to be raised without delay in its old Spanish recruiting grounds.

Octavian was determined to make his new legions lean, mean, killing machines. As recruiting officers scurried around western Spain rounding up new recruits for the 10th Legion in 29 B.C., some basic administrative changes were put in place. As with the other remaining legions, the 10th Legion's numbers were reduced. Cohorts now contained 480 men, not the 600 of Julius Caesar's day, with the 1st Cohort being of double strength. The legion also now included a small cavalry unit for reconnaissance, courier, and escort duties made up of 120 of its own legionaries in 4 squadrons of 30 troopers, commanded by 4 decurions, or lieutenants, who each had an *optio*, or sergeant major, from the ranks as his deputy. The main cavalry role would be left to mounted auxiliary units in *alae*, or wings, some of 500 troopers, some of 1,000.

The legion still had 60 centurions—fifty-nine in ten grades, plus the *primus pilus*, the chief centurion. And the duties of its six tribunes were radically changed. Octavian had seen that in practice the legion was commanded in battle by its centurions, and that the rank and file had little respect for the wealthy young colonels who were supposed to command the legion and the cohorts. Now, five of the six tribunes of every legion would be officer cadets, tribunes of the thin stripe. Staff officers, they would work at headquarters and act as colonels of the watch and aides to the legion commander, but in battle they would have no power of unit command. Serving a six-month cadetship from age eighteen, these lieutenant colonels would then move on to the next step on the promotional ladder.

By the reign of the emperor Claudius, who came to power in A.D. 41, that promotional ladder had been formalized. After serving their cadetships as junior tribunes, young men of the Equestrian Order would become prefects, with the equivalent rank of colonel, commanding auxiliary troops. Initially they had command of an auxiliary infantry cohort. Every legion now had its own attached auxiliary light infantry cohorts and auxiliary cavalry squadrons, but some auxiliary units also served independently of legions. Later the ambitious prefect could be appointed to command an auxiliary cavalry wing, or a mixed unit containing both auxiliary infantry and cavalry.

After commanding a cavalry unit, a prefect could be promoted to the rank of senior tribune, tribune of the broad stripe, a senior colonel who was second-in-command of a legion. The journey from junior tribune to senior tribune customarily lasted ten to twelve years. A tribune of the broad stripe was called a "military" tribune, to distinguish him from the post of civil tribune, the tribune of the plebs, at Rome. Names of the units with which a Roman officer served as a senior tribune and prefect might be listed on his tombstone, but the unit with which he trained as a junior tribune was not identified.

Octavian also implemented the process whereby each legion now had its own dedicated commander of general rank. The legate, equivalent to a modern brigadier general, was normally a young senator in his early thirties who'd climbed the promotional ladder to senior tribune before entering the Senate at age thirty. Under Octavian—or Augustus, as he became—the legion commander's tour of duty would last one to two years before he moved on to another assignment. In the reigns of later emperors, legion commanders frequently kept their commands for up to four years.

The next step up the ladder was appointment as a praetor, which would involve service in Rome as a magistrate or a prosecutor, and, because a praetor had the equivalent military rank of major general, it could be followed by a senior military role. A praetor aimed for appointment to consul, which brought with it the equivalent military rank of lieutenant general. Once he'd served a consulship, a lieutenant general could be appointed to govern a province, which entailed command of all military units in that province, or to the command of a field army.

We don't know the name of the brigadier general who became the 10th Legion's first permanent commander, but we do know that the 10th was left disdainfully in the East by Octavian following the death of Antony and Cleopatra, as one of four legions stationed in the province of Syria; the 4th Legion was one of the others, and it's likely that all were former Antonian units. As the 10th's new recruits marched overland from Spain in 29 B.C. to join the legion in Syria, Augustus began operations in the Cantabrian Mountains of northern Spain, personally leading seven legions—units that had remained loyal to him in the conflict against Anthony—on what he hoped would be a short and profitable campaign that would finally bring all of Spain under Roman control. That campaign, although ultimately successful, would drag on for ten years.

The 10th moved into a new permanent winter base at Cyrrhus in northern Syria, not far from Commagene and the Euphrates River—stationed there quite deliberately with a sentinel's eye to the old enemy the Parthian Empire east of the river.

The legion had a relatively quiet time of it in Syria during this enlistment. Most of the surviving veterans enlisted by Caesar himself back in

Córdoba in 61 B.C. had left the 10th in its ignominious discharge of 29 B.C., but several centurions would have been brought back for a third enlistment. Aged between forty-nine and fifty-two, these tough veterans had an incredible record behind them—they'd marched with Caesar in Portugal as raw recruits, they'd conquered Gaul, invaded Britain twice, then fought throughout the civil war for Caesar: the lightning campaign in Spain, the Battles of Dyrrhachium and Pharsalus, Thapsus and Munda. They'd fought for the triumvirs at Philippi and for Antony at Actium. And yet they still had plenty of service left in them—a centurion of the 1st Italica Legion the next century was well into his third enlistment when he died, still in harness, at age sixty-six.

The 10th was still stationed in Syria in the winter of 14–13 B.C., leading up to its latest discharge and reenlistment. During that winter the discharged Spanish legionaries of the legion settled at the ancient city that was to grow into the modern Lebanese metropolis of Beirut, which was then in the province of Syria. Going back to Old Testament times, the city, whose Canaanite name was Be'erot, meaning "wells," sat on the Mediterranean coast between several hills where underground wells provided ample fresh water. It was granted Roman colony status by Augustus in 14 B.C. to accommodate the discharged 10th Legion veterans. Augustus dedicated the colony to his wife, Livia, officially the empress Julia Augusta, giving the town the name of Colonia Julia Augusta Felix Berytus—literally, "Julia Augusta's Fruitful Colony of Beirut."

Ten years later, in 4 B.C., on the death of King Herod the Great, there was considerable unrest in his former kingdom of Judea. The Governor of Syria, Lieutenant General Publius Quintilius Varus, assembled three of his four legions, including the 10th, and marched down to Jerusalem from Antioch to restore order. Once the unrest was quelled, and leaving the 10th Legion with his deputy, Procurator Sabinus, to garrison Jerusalem, General Varus returned to Syria with the other legions.

Trouble soon brewed again, as troops from the late king's army joined with Jewish partisans in an uprising. The men of the 10th Legion and three thousand royal Jewish troops who remained loyal to Rome found themselves cut off and under siege inside the Antonia Fortress, beside the Jewish Temple, in company with Procurator Sabinus. After Sabinus managed to slip mounted messengers away at night who galloped up to Syria, General Varus put together a relief force apparently made up from the 4th, now known as the 4th Macedonica, the 6th Victrix (the original Spanish 6th Legion, which apparently was given this sobriquet, meaning "Conqueror," by Augustus in about 25 B.C. for its work in the Cantabrian War), and 12th Legions, plus auxiliary infantry and four squadrons of cavalry, and hurried south to Judea.

As General Varus and his force approached Jerusalem, burning villages in his path, the partisans besieging the Antonia Fortress melted away, and Varus was able to link up with the 10th Legion without difficulty. With the situation corrected, and leaving the 10th stationed permanently in Jerusalem, Varus took the other legions back to Syria.

In A.D. 4, as the 10th Legion underwent its latest discharge and reenlistment, its new recruits in western Spain found themselves signing up for a twenty-year enlistment, as opposed to the old term of sixteen years. Back in 6 B.C., Augustus had decided to extend the enlistment period of all twenty-eight of his legions, and the longer enlistment was introduced to each legion as its discharge fell due in subsequent years. By now, too, the enlistment age for all legionaries was twenty, raised from the minimum of seventeen of Caesar's day. A legionary was still paid the same, just nine hundred sesterces a year, but this was an era when inflation was unheard of and there was no need to keep pace with rising costs—the prices of goods and services remained the same for a hundred years.

The 10th Legion remained in Jerusalem until A.D. 6, when Judea was made a Roman province by Augustus. To mollify the Jews, who apparently had no liking for the 10th after its ten years in their homeland, Augustus transferred it out, sending it back up to Syria, and replaced it with the 12th Legion, in a reversal of roles that saw the northern Italians of the 12th march down from Syria to Judea and make their headquarters at the newly designated capital of Roman Judea, Caesarea. (See appendix C for details of the uniqueness of the legion commands in Egypt and Judea.)

In the winter of A.D. 18, a new commander in chief for the Roman East arrived in Syria—Germanicus Caesar, grandson of Mark Antony, and in many respects the JFK of his day. Adopted son and heir of his uncle the new emperor Tiberius, who'd replaced Augustus when he died in A.D. 14, and grand-nephew of Augustus, Germanicus was a charismatic and talented thirty-three-year-old lieutenant general. He was famous throughout the empire and beyond it for his dashing performance in the Pannonian War of A.D. 6–9, when he'd led flying columns with spectacular success while still only in his early twenties, and more recently for his three-year *blitzkrieg* in Germany against the German rebel leader Arminius, or Hermann, as the Germans called him.

To cap his military skills, good looks, and charming personality, Germanicus was a talented poet and playwright. And not only did his family background give him blood ties to both Mark Antony and Julius Caesar, he also had an intelligent, supportive wife in Agrippina the Elder, daughter of Augustus's great general and admiral Marcus Agrippa and a granddaughter of Augustus himself.

But most of all, Germanicus was famous for giving Romans back their pride. In A.D. 9, Hermann had wiped out three entire legions—identified as the 19th and two others, probably the 25th and 26th Legions—in the Teutoburg Forest east of the Rhine, legions led by the same General Varus who'd commanded the 10th Legion as Governor of Syria a decade before, legions that were never re-formed, so great was the disgrace of their destruction. Teutoburg was the biggest Roman defeat since Carrhae. Germanicus had gone on to reclaim two of the eagles of Varus's annihilated units and devastated the Germans in several major battles at the head of eight legions, paying the German tribes back for the humiliation of the Varus disaster. And now he was heading for a new headquarters in Syria. Tiberius had given him supreme command in the Roman East.

Such was Germanicus's repute that even the much-feared Parthians would soon send ambassadors to him, offering to sign a formal peace treaty. His power in the East should have been unchallenged, but even before he reached Syria he was embroiled in a bitter feud, not with foreigners, but with the Roman governor of the province of Syria, Gnaeus Calpurnius Piso.

Piso, in his sixties, a consul in A.D. 7, was an irascible and haughty lieutenant general who bowed to no man. And from the outset he seemed determined to make life difficult for Germanicus. According to many at the time, Piso did so at the prompting of Tiberius, who was jealous of his popular heir, having been forced to adopt him by Augustus. Piso ignored Germanicus's orders to send several Syrian-based legions, including the 10th and the 6th Victrix, marching up to Armenia to back him in his planned coronation of a new Armenian king.

Accompanied by just his personal staff, Germanicus nonetheless marched into Armenia, which had long been a country disputed over by Rome and Parthia. There, in the capital of Artaxata, his authority guaranteed by nothing more than his reputation, he crowned a king friendly to Rome, Zeno, son of the king of Pontus, naming him King Artaxias. For this deed, and for organizing neighboring Cappadocia and Commagene into Roman provinces *en route*, the Senate was to vote Germanicus an Ovation, a lesser form of Triumph where the celebrant rode on horseback through the streets of Rome rather than drove in a *quadriga*—he'd already celebrated a Triumph in Rome the previous May for his German victories.

Arriving in Syria a few months ahead of Germanicus, Governor Piso had gone around the four legions of the Syria command to win their loyalty and support, removing their stricter tribunes and centurions and replacing them with men who were in his debt or who would follow his wishes for a price. Piso then had legion discipline relaxed, allowing the legionaries based in the province to lead an easy life inside and outside camp. The more dissolute legionaries began to call Piso "father of the legions," and the men of the 6th in particular showed strong allegiance toward him.

Meanwhile, Germanicus completed his business of state in Armenia and marched down into Syria, sending Piso an instruction to meet him at the winter quarters of the 10th Legion at Cyrrhus. The shabby, lazy legion Germanicus found at Cyrrhus was a far cry from the elite and famous 10th of Julius Caesar's day.

The pair sat down at the legion's permanent base in what was outwardly an amicable meeting. But behind closed doors Germanicus wanted to know why Piso had disobeyed orders. They parted coolly. Their relationship only went downhill from there.

Antioch, Germanicus's new center of operations, was the empire's third-largest city after Rome and Alexandria, with a population of several hundred thousand, including forty thousand Jews. A crossroads between East and West, it was a commercial hub, a prosperous city boasting fine buildings in brick, stone, and marble; broad avenues; and lush gardens. Prevented from decorating his own kingdom of Judea by the religious constraints of Judaism, King Herod had bestowed lavish gifts on the city, including golden paving decoration from which we derive the saying about streets being paved with gold.

The Governor of Syria had his palace in Antioch, and living here in A.D. 18 with Governor Piso and his wife, Plancina, as their guest was Vonones, a former king of Armenia. A Parthian who had been raised in Rome as a hostage, Vonones had been expelled from Armenia by King Artabanus of Parthia a few years back and had ambitions to reclaim his throne. Vonones showered expensive gifts on the governor's wife, and plotted with Piso for a return to Armenia. Their plans were thwarted by Germanicus. Not only did he place the son of the king of Pontus on the Armenian throne, he also soon had Vonones removed to Cilicia and kept under house arrest. Vonones escaped, but was caught and killed by a retired legion veteran.

Piso was already fuming at being dressed down by Germanicus and at having to play second fiddle to him. Germanicus even superseded him as chief judge in Syria, so that Piso had to watch the young prince dispense justice in his stead, doing so, according to Tacitus, with a sour scowl on his face throughout the court sittings. And now Piso's plans for power-broking in his region had been destroyed.

Piso's growing hate of Germanicus came exploding out at a banquet given by the king of Nabataea, who presented Germanicus and Agrippina with heavy golden crowns, and lesser ones to Piso and the other Roman officials present. Throwing his crown to the ground, Piso jumped up and raged that the banquet was being given to the son of a Roman emperor, not of a Parthian king, before launching into a lengthy diatribe against luxury. Germanicus patiently let him rant, which probably annoyed Piso even more.

Early in A.D. 19 Germanicus visited Egypt as a private citizen, touring the historic sites like a modern-day tourist. This provoked outrage among Tiberius's closest supporters in Rome, because Germanicus was breaking the laws of Augustus that prevented Romans of senatorial rank from entering Egypt without the emperor's express permission. As men spoke against him in the Senate, Tiberius himself publicly acknowledged his displeasure with Germanicus for his act.

On his return to Antioch, Germanicus found that all his decrees regarding provincial government and the activities of the legions of the East had been ignored or countermanded by Piso in his absence. Germanicus apparently finally lost his cool with Piso, displaying a rare bout of temper. It was obvious that before long one or the other would have to go. One way or another.

Germanicus tried to calm the waters, inviting Piso to a banquet in his palace at Epidaphna outside Antioch and giving him the most honored place on his dining couch beside him. Shortly after the dinner, Germanicus fell gravely ill. Merchants traveling by sea to Italy took tidings of his illness to Rome. Just as the assassination of JFK stunned the world, so this news stopped Romans in their tracks. People throughout the empire waited anxiously to hear more about the state of his health, and there was universal relief when reports arrived that he had recovered fully.

But before long Germanicus was again floored by an illness that had all the hallmarks of a poisoning. And then the thirty-four-year-old prince died, in great pain, with his wife and friends at his palace bedside vowing to seek vengeance. Just before he died, Germanicus dismissed Piso from his post as governor. Although Piso and his wife, Plancina, were the chief suspects in what Germanicus's friends were sure was a case of murder after incriminating evidence was found at the governor's palace, the accused couple was already sailing away when Germanicus died. Piso lingered at the Greek island of Cos, and there loyal centurions from legions of the Syria command, including the 10th, caught up with him bearing the news he had apparently been waiting to hear.

Piso openly celebrated, and made plans to return to Syria and take back his command. To be on the safe side, he sent General Domitius Celer, one of his friends, ahead in a cruiser to prepare the way. But as soon as Celer stepped ashore in Syria, he was arrested by the commander of the 6th Victrix Legion. So Piso decided to take back his command by force. Landing on the coast of Cilicia, in southern Turkey, he established himself at the castle of Celenderis and pulled together a rough-and-ready force.

He armed his own slaves, brought in auxiliaries from allied kings in the region, and waylaid a group of recruits marching by on their way to join their unit in Syria. We aren't told which unit they were bound for, but as this was the winter of A.D. 19 and two of the legions stationed in Syria—the 4th Macedonica and the 6th Victrix—were due to undergo their latest discharge and reenlistment in the new year, these were probably Greek or Spanish recruits for one or the other of these legions who were roped in by Piso.

In all, Piso managed to bring together five thousand men at Celenderis. As he was assembling his little army, Lieutenant General Gneius Sentius, a close friend of Germanicus who had been at his deathbed and taken command in Syria on his chief's demise, marched up to Celenderis with a force comprising the 6th Victrix Legion, almost certainly the 10th, and possibly also elements of the 4th Macedonica. After a brief skirmish outside the walls of the fortress, Piso surrendered, and was sent back to Rome to face trial in the Senate for Germanicus's murder.

Piso would die, apparently committing suicide, in the middle of the high-profile trial the following year, just as it emerged that his wife, Plancina, had for some time been on intimate terms with the emperor's mother, Julia Augusta, who arranged to have Piso's wife pardoned. There were many, including the historian Tacitus, who would go to their graves convinced that Piso was murdered before he could implicate the emperor in Germanicus's death. But there was no way of proving the widely held suspicion.

Ambition was not a quality associated with Germanicus. Cassius Dio was to say that he was one of the few men of all time who had neither sinned against his fortune nor been destroyed by it. Despite this, in the immediate future, links with Germanicus would not prove beneficial, and within a few years most of his friends had either been destroyed by Tiberius or his Praetorian commander Sejanus or deserted Germanicus's family to save themselves. But the ordinary people never forgot their hero and in due course transferred their affections to his descendants. After the death of Tiberius eighteen years later, Germanicus Caesar's son Gaius—Caligula, as we know him—Germanicus's brother Claudius, and his grandson Nero would each successively become emperor of Rome. But as much as the people of Rome hoped for it, not one of his kin proved to be a Germanicus.

XX

KNOCKED INTO
SHAPE BY CORBULO

Many considered Lieutenant General Gnaeus Domitius Corbulo one of Rome's finest soldiers since Caesar. He was certainly the toughest. When he arrived in Germany in 47 B.C. to take command of Rome's Army of the Lower Rhine, he summarily executed a legionary who was digging a trench without wearing his sword belt. After centurions read aloud to their men the regulation requiring troops to be armed at all times while on duty, a soldier was found digging a fortification wearing his weapon belt and nothing else. Corbulo had no sense of humor—the naked legionary was also put to death, for insubordination.

General Corbulo arrived in the East in A.D. 54 to take up an assignment as Governor of Galatia and Cappadocia, but with a secret brief from the new emperor Nero and his chief ministers Seneca and Burrus to return Armenia to the Roman fold after the Parthians had installed their own king in the mountainous country. Tacitus describes Corbulo as "an old and wary general" at this juncture. It's likely he was promoted to major general prior to A.D. 21, making him in his sixties by the time he took up his eastern appointment.

Some modern historians have postulated that a Domitius Corbulo mentioned by Tacitus in about A.D. 21 may have been General Corbulo's father. This Corbulo, a "former praetor," was affronted by a young noble who had not given place to him at a gladiatorial show, and demanded and received an official apology. Tacitus says this Corbulo also objected to the state of Italy's roads, which he blamed on the dishonesty of contractors and the negligence of officials, and went on to personally take charge of road maintenance. The roads of Italy were soon no longer in ruin, but the determined Corbulo managed to ruin numerous Italians previously involved in the road business by attacking their property and credit through a series of convictions and confiscations. So if he was Corbulo's father, it seems his son inherited many of his traits, but it's just as likely this was none other than the pragmatic general himself.

In any case, General Corbulo arrived in the East with a reputation for ruthless efficiency in both civil and military administration. Determined to keep his preparations low-key, he quietly recruited new auxiliary units in the region. Some were destined to support Corbulo's legionary army; others were stationed at a series of border forts, with orders not to provoke trouble in Armenia. And Corbulo chose two legions currently with the Syria command to spearhead his Armenian project—the 6th Victrix and the 10th.

That both were Spanish legions was probably no coincidence. As we know from Josephus, the reputation gained by Julius Caesar's Spanish legionaries had lingered long after their exploits had seen them labeled Rome's best troops in the 1st century B.C. But General Corbulo was in for a shock. He obviously chose the legions before he saw them.

What Corbulo found when he arrived at the base of the 10th Legion at Cyrrhus were lame fifty-five-year-old second-enlistment men lazing around barrack rooms. The younger thirty-five-year-olds were busy in town running businesses and standing over the locals. "Sleek moneymaking traders," Tacitus calls them, perhaps echoing Corbulo's own remarks. The disease of indiscipline introduced by Piso all those years before had become an epidemic facilitated by decades of inactivity. "Demoralized by a long peace" is how Tacitus describes the legionaries Corbulo discovered in Syria.

Many soldiers of the 10th Legion had sold their helmets and shields. There were second-enlistment men of the 10th who in all their time with the legion had never dug a trench or thrown up the wall of a marching camp, who had never done picket duty or stood guard in the lonely hours of the night. Corbulo soon fixed that.

General Corbulo dismissed the sick and the lame, and the remaining men of the legion were very quickly pulled back into line. Transferring the two legions up from Syria to his base of operations in Cappadocia, the general implemented a training regimen that would have seen his flabby legionaries doing twenty-five-mile-route marches day after day, digging entrenchments, undergoing hour after hour of weapons drill. When the winter arrived he marched the men of the 10th and the 6th Victrix up into the mountains of Cappadocia and made them camp out in their flimsy tents until the spring, on ground covered with ice and swept by bitter winds. It was so cold that some men suffered from frostbite. Several froze to death on night guard. Deserters, when caught, were executed immediately, and not given a second or a third chance, as in the past. The desertion rate within Corbulo's units quickly plummeted.

But Corbulo endured the same hardships he imposed on his men. He camped with them through the snow and the blizzards. He marched on foot and bareheaded at the head of the column wherever he took them. He would have eaten what they ate, and presumably if they didn't eat at all because of supply problems, then neither did he. Tacitus says that throughout this period Corbulo had praise for the brave, comfort for the feeble, and was a good example to everyone. And as the legionaries toughened up, they acquired a grudging admiration for their old son-of-a-bitch general.

Corbulo spent four years building the two legions into a crack fighting force, until, in the spring of A.D. 58, he launched his Armenian offensive. His unheralded drive from Cappadocia east into Armenia involved two forces in a classic pincer movement. Taking the enemy completely by surprise, Corbulo led one force made up of the 10th Legion and auxiliary and allied support that swept through the middle of the country and went against the major Parthian fortress at Volandum, which is believed to have been to the southwest of Artaxata and just north of Mount Ararat.

His deputy, Brigadier General Cornelius Flaccus, took the second force against several lesser forts farther south. His battle group was made up of his own 6th Victrix Legion and six cohorts of the 3rd Augusta Legion under Camp Prefect, or Major, Insteius Capito, who had come up from their bases in Judea—where they'd left their remaining four cohorts on garrison duty. Corbulo had personally trained the tough little Syrian legionaries of the 3rd Augusta when they'd been stationed with him on the Rhine a decade earlier, and he was well aware of the ferocious capabilities of these worshipers of the Syrian sun god Baal—or Elagabalus, as the Romans were to call him. General Flaccus's troops proceeded to overrun one enemy fortress after another—three on a single memorable day.

Volandum looked to be a tougher nut to crack. Urging his men to win themselves both glory and spoils, General Corbulo divided the 10th Legion into four divisions for the Volandum assault. He had undertaken a careful engineering survey of the defenses, and now he personally led one group in an attack beneath a *testudo* of shields, against a section of the outer wall considered the most vulnerable to undermining. While this group labored at the base of the wall, two more went against other parts of the rampart with scaling ladders. The fourth group covered the other three with dense artillery fire from prepared artillery mounds.

The assault lasted eight hours. By the time they had finished, the men of the 10th had stripped the walls of their defenders, had overthrown the fortress's gates, and had scaled its fortified bastions and taken them one after another. The 10th Legion massacred the adult defenders of Volandum to a man. All the nonmilitary survivors were auctioned off to the traders following the army. During the attack, Corbulo's units had suffered a few wounded, but not a single fatality. Now the men of the 10th were allowed to plunder Volandum to their hearts' content.

The two assault groups then linked up to the south of the Armenian capital, Artaxata, a walled city not far from Lake Sevan that sat in a formidable position beside the Avaxes River, the modern Aras River. Archaeologists suggest that Artaxata was actually on an island in the middle of the river, but this is not mentioned by Tacitus, who indicates only that it was reached by just a single bridge. The last Roman general to venture near Artaxata had been Germanicus, forty years before.

Crossing the Aras well downstream, Corbulo led his task force on Artaxata from the southeast. As they advanced along the Aras valley floor in battle order, with elements of the 10th Legion in the center, the 3rd Augusta cohorts on the right flank and the 6th Victrix on the left, the Romans were shadowed by tens of thousands of mounted Parthian archers led by Tiridates, the Parthian prince who had taken the Armenian throne.

At any moment the Romans expected the fearsome Parthians to attack. Many in the 10th would have remembered how General Crassus and his legions had perished at the hands of mounted Parthians like these at Carrhae back in 53 B.C., and they would have shuddered at the thought that history might be about to repeat itself. But apart from a Roman cavalry lieutenant on the right wing who ventured too close to the archers and was drilled with arrows, there was no blood spilled this day. As night fell, the enemy melted away. The Parthians, daunted by the reputation of General Corbulo and his by now crack legions, didn't have the stomach to take them on.

Artaxata fell without a fight. The city opened its gates to Corbulo, just as it had to Germanicus four decades before. But knowing he could be cut off and destroyed here if he tried to hold the 250-year-old Armenian capital, the pragmatic Corbulo gave the residents a few hours to collect their valuables and flee, then burned the city to the ground. Having decided that the more accessible southwestern city of Tigranocerta would make a better capital, he led the army down through central Armenia toward it.

The men of the 10th had only one complaint as they tramped through Armenia—the task force ran out of grain, and the troops were forced to eat meat. There is an old joke, put into writing by Juvenal, that Romans could be kept happy on a diet of bread and circuses, and it was true. Roman legionaries loved their daily bread.

Arriving at Tigranocerta on the Nicephorius River, General Corbulo installed a king of Rome's choice on the Armenian throne, Tigranes, a Cappadocian prince, making the substantial 120-year-old city his capital. For the next four years, a cohort from the 10th Legion and one from the 6th Victrix were stationed at Tigranocerta as bodyguard to the king, supported by fifteen hundred auxiliaries.

In A.D. 62 the Parthians invaded Armenia and laid siege to Tigranocerta. In response, Corbulo, who was now given the wide-ranging powers of a modern field marshal by Nero, promptly sent a relief force across the border. Led by Brigadier General Verulanus Severus, latest commander of the 6th Victrix, the force was made up of the balance of the cohorts of the 6th and the 10th. The Parthians rapidly withdrew from Tigranocerta, but their king, Vologases, began to make preparations to invade Syria.

To defend Syria, the field marshal dug in along the Euphrates River. Retaining his best units, the 10th and the 6th Victrix, he once more brought six cohorts of the reliable 3rd Augusta Legion up from their station in Judea to add to his force. At the same time, to help Corbulo, Lieutenant General Caesennius Paetus was sent out to the East by the Palatium, Rome's combined White House and Pentagon. General Paetus, a man apparently afflicted with both a squint and a massive ego, subsequently led the 4th Macedonica and 12th Legions into Armenia against the Parthians.

The Parthians avoided a full-scale battle and withdrew ahead of this advance, unaware that neither of these units had benefited from Field Marshal Corbulo's personal training, unlike the 10th, the 6th Victrix, and the 3rd Augusta.

General Paetus had boasted that he would show Corbulo how to deal with the Parthians, but the omens for his operation were not good from the start—as he was crossing a bridge over the Euphrates into Armenia, the horse carrying his lieutenant general's standard bolted and galloped to the rear.

While Paetus overran several outposts, the main Parthian forces kept a wary distance for months, and with the weather deteriorating, the inept Paetus made camp for the winter at Rhandeia in northwestern Armenia beside the Arsanias River, the modern Murat River. He let many of his troops go on leave, sending a message to the emperor at Rome declaring that he had as good as won the war against the Parthians.

Meanwhile, King Vologases was ready for his invasion of Syria; he led his Parthian army in a full-scale assault against Field Marshal Corbulo on the Euphrates. The 10th and the men of the other two legions dug in along the eastern bank of the river, the 3rd Augusta and the 6th Victrix, fought off one desperate attack after another. To increase his firepower, Corbulo threw a wooden bridge across the river, and on the bridge he built towers, and on the towers he installed heavy artillery, which raked the Parthian cavalry whenever they came near. In the end, unable to penetrate the defenses of the 10th and its fellow elite legions, the Parthians gave up on their assault along the Euphrates, and turned north against General Paetus at Rhandeia. They swiftly surprised and surrounded his army at their camp on the Murat.

With his quickly demoralized troops putting up a halfhearted defense from their camp walls, Paetus sent desperate pleas to Corbulo for help, and the field marshal carefully prepared a relief force inclusive of men of the 10th and a column of camels from the Dromedary Wing carrying tons of grain—he was determined that his men wouldn't run out of bread the way they had four years before. Only when he was satisfied that all was in readiness did he march up from Syria and through Commagene and Cappadocia. Just as Corbulo was about to cross the Euphrates into Armenia, he met Paetus coming the other way, withdrawing with his disheveled army. To escape with his life, Paetus had agreed to humiliating peace terms with the Parthians—he'd made his legionaries build the enemy a bridge across the Murat, and he'd left his fortress at Rhandeia intact for them, inclusive of his artillery, heavy equipment, and baggage train. His men were forced to leave behind all personal possessions apart from what they could carry on their backs.

As Paetus returned to Rome in temporary disgrace—he would be forgiven by Nero and given important posts by a later administration—Field Marshal Corbulo prepared a new Armenian offensive. The Palatium sent him reinforcements, the 15th Legion from the Balkans, along with its attached auxiliary light infantry and cavalry. He also brought his reserve unit, the 5th Legion, down from Pontus. Leaving the dependable 10th dug in along the Euphrates defense line to cover his rear, Corbulo swept into Armenia early in A.D. 63 with the 3rd Augusta, 5th, 6th Victrix, and 15th Legions and sent the Parthian army scampering out of the country, as much by his fearsome reputation as any shedding of blood. He then settled the Armenian question by putting on the throne Tiridates, a Parthian prince who swore fealty to Nero, emperor of Rome.

Following this campaign, the 10th returned to base in Syria and prepared for its next discharge and reenlistment in the new year. This would be the legion's eighth enlistment since Caesar raised the legion in 61 B.C. Already the recruiting officers, the *conquisitors*, were out looking for recruits in the legion's home province if Baetica, Farther Spain, and a contingent of 10th Legion centurions would have now set off from Syria to take charge of the product of their efforts.

Precisely how the legion's latest enlistment day played out is not recorded, but all the evidence points to something very much like the following. On a fall day at the beginning of December A.D. 63, in the ninth year of the reign of Emperor Nero, who would turn just twenty-six in several weeks' time, thousands of young men gathered on the sands of the amphitheater at Córdoba, capital of the province of Baetica. To ensure that none of the youngsters tried to go home, fully armed auxiliary infantrymen from the military base outside the city would probably have circled the perimeter of the amphitheater, which they normally used for their training drills, when gladiatorial contests weren't taking place there for the pleasure of the local populace.

Roman citizens all, the youngest men in the arena had just turned twenty. City boys, country boys, the sons of blacksmiths, shopkeepers, farmers, and fishermen. Their heads would have been full of tales they'd heard about bloody battles and brutal legion discipline, tales of fabulous adventures told by retired legion veterans that invariably involved wine, women, plunder, and crushing victories over barbarian hordes. Some were volunteers—the out-of-work, even a few petty criminals. Most were draftees. All were about to enroll in the Roman army's 10th Legion.

They would sign a binding contract with the state to serve for an enlistment period of twenty years, during which time they were not permitted to marry—although many would form relationships with female camp followers and father children out of wedlock in years to come. In return, they could expect to be paid nine hundred sesterces a year—increased to twelve hundred sesterces a year by the emperor Domitian twenty years later—plus bonuses and booty, and the legion would feed, clothe, and house them. On retirement, they were guaranteed a discharge bonus of twelve thousand sesterces plus a small grant of land, although the location of that land would be at the discretion of the government. After their retirement, they would also be required to make themselves available in times of emergency for service in the Evocati, a militia made up of retired legion veterans. Once they signed that contract, as a legionary they would no longer be subject to civil law. But they would have to follow rigid legion regulations and obey their officers' commands without question, on pain of death. And they would have to swear allegiance to the emperor, a vow they would renew every January 1, and put their lives on the line for him time and time again.

To reach this stage, the recruits would have passed physical inspections by the recruiting officers, who sent home the lame, the obese, the mentally deficient. Ninety years earlier, Augustus had set the basic requirements for Rome's legion recruits before the Senate. According to Cassius Dio, they had to be "the most active men in the population, those who are in their physical prime."

Members of a party of 10th Legion centurions recently arrived from Syria would have moved among the recruits. They would have separated several score of them from the rest, men who professed riding skills—they would go to the legion's own small cavalry unit. The centurions then quickly, roughly sorted the rest into groups of eight. No discussion, no argument, lining them up with a gap of perhaps three feet between each man. Each group of eight was a *contubernium*, a squad. Unless he perished or was promoted, a man would spend the next twenty years in this squad. Its members would share a tent and sleep together, cook together, eat together, relieve themselves together, train together, march together, fight together, and, if need be, die together.

In 1963 Lieutenant General Sir Brian Horrocks, a British corps commander during World War II, remarked that in an average group of ten fighting men two will be leaders, seven will be followers, and one just doesn't want to be there. It's not unlikely that a similar generalization applied to the men of a Roman legion *contubernium*.

Having created their squads there on the sand at Córdoba, the centurions would have lined up ten squads, one after the other. This was a century. Then another ten squads. The two centuries formed a maniple, 160 men strong, the equivalent of the modern company. Then they created another maniple, and another, leaving places in each century for a centurion and his two deputies, an *optio*, or sergeant major, and a *tesserarius*, an orderly sergeant. Together, the three maniples created a cohort, or battalion, of 480 men.

The centurions would have made up as many cohorts as required, as many as seven or eight. The local recruiting officers would have received orders from the Palatium to enroll a specific number of recruits to fill the gaps in the legion's ranks left by illness and battle casualties and by the men who would soon retire from the legion after serving out their twenty-year enlistments. Some veterans of the 10th would have already volunteered for a second enlistment, probably about 1,500 of them, and those men would go into the legion's senior cohorts after the retirees departed. So about 4,000 new legionaries would have been enrolled here at Córdoba to fill the vacancies and meet the legion's requirement of a total of 5,345 enlisted men and NCOs. With its 72 officers, the full-strength legion would number 5,417 men.

Once the cohorts had been formed, a senior centurion of the 10th would have stepped up onto the rostra in front of his new Spanish *tiros*, as recruits were called. The centurion may not himself have been Spanish; by this time centurions transferred from one legion to another as they went up the promotional ladder, changing legions as much as a dozen times in their careers. Probably in his forties, he would have been garbed in dress uniform—blood red legionary tunic; shinguards; shining segmented metal armor that covered his chest, shoulders, and back; a helmet complete with a transverse crest of eagle feathers that signified his rank; and with his bravery decorations on display across his chest. On his right hip he would have worn a dagger, on his left a sword, both in scabbards richly decorated with gold and jet inlay. Apart from the segmented armor, which had replaced the cuirass of iron mail ringlets worn by his first-century B.C. predecessors, he would have looked little different from Centurion Gaius Crastinus of the first enlistment of the 10th Legion.

The centurion would have addressed the silent, apprehensive recruits. He would have told them that they were joining Rome's most famous legion, Julius Caesar's "old faithfuls," and that they had a lot to live up to, reeling off the 10th Legion's long list of battle honors since the day in 61 B.C. when it had been personally founded by Caesar. The centurion would have told them about the legions' "buddy system," whose existence we know of from Tacitus. The Roman army encouraged every legionary to team up with a comrade from his squad, a comrade who would literally stand at his back when the fighting got tough, who would witness his will, and who would bury him if necessary when the time came. It's easy to imagine that the day would come when these rookies would need their legion buddy like a baby needs its mother.

Before long, the centurions of the 10th were leading their new recruits out of Córdoba. Unless taking part in an amphibious assault of the type for which Caesar had been famed, the legions invariably traveled by foot wherever they had to go. Over the next several weeks, the 10th Legion's *tiros* tramped all the way across Spain, through France, northern Italy, the Balkans, Greece, and Turkey to reach the unit's station in Syria, using the straight, paved Roman highways built primarily to permit the rapid transit of the legions, and commandeering supplies *en route* in the name of the emperor.

Early in A.D. 64, the 10th Legion underwent its latest discharge and reenlistment at Cyrrhus. The youngsters who'd marched all the way from Spain paraded at Cyrrhus with the men of the last enlistment who were staying on. Now the recruits were in red woolen tunics and shining armored cuirasses. Not a single toga was to be seen—it was a formal, ceremonial garment akin to our tuxedo today and rarely worn. The tunic was the everyday garb of Romans of all walks of life, and was made of two pieces of cloth sewed together, with openings for the head and arms, and short sleeves. It fell to just above the knees at the front and a little lower at the back, with the military tunic being a fraction shorter than that worn by civilians. In cold weather it was not unusual for several tunics to be worn on top of each other. Augustus habitually wore up to four tunics at a time in winter months.

Just as a Scotsman is asked if he wears anything beneath his kilt, so the question is still asked by scholars about what the legionary wore beneath his tunic. There is no documentary evidence, but most Romans are believed to have worn a loincloth, although it is suggested that climate and ethnic background could have meant that at least some legionaries, such as those based in the East, went without undergarments in the heat of summer.

No matter what the weather, and irrespective of the fact that auxiliaries serving in the Roman army, both cavalry and infantry, wore trousers of some sort, legionaries didn't begin wearing full-length trousers until the fourth century. Trousers were considered foreign and vulgar by educated Romans. Comfort did begin to win out over fashion toward the end of the first century, when legionaries commenced the habit of wearing short breeches under their tunics.

Over the tunic the soldier of A.D. 63 wore an armored cuirass of segmented metal plates that covered chest, shoulders, and back and wasn't unlike today's bulletproof vest. Heavy but effective, the *lorica segmentata*, introduced in about A.D. 30, relegated the mail-covered leather jacket of Caesar's day to use by auxiliary units only over time.

Each man wore a helmet, kept in place by a leather strap that tied under the chin. With a protruding neckguard, it looked a little like a modern fireman's helmet, except that it had the added protection of flexible cheek flaps. The helmet was adorned with a removable parade plume of yellow horsehair—2nd-century Roman governor, general, and author

Arrian describes the plumes worn by his troops as yellow, and archaeological evidence suggests yellow plumes were universal. Not worn in battle since early in the first century, the plume would be kept with the rest of the soldier's kit when the legion was on active duty.

At the throats of the new recruits would have been tied the legionary neck scarf, so fashionable that auxiliaries wore them as well, even though they didn't have to protect their necks from the chafing effects of heavy armor. And on their feet, hobnailed army sandals, the *caligulae* from which the emperor Caligula's nickname derived when he was a child living with his parents, Germanicus and Agrippina, among the troops on the Rhine. His actual name was Gaius.

On his right hip each man wore a double-edged, sharp-pointed twenty-inch mild steel sword, the *gladius*. In 150 B.C. Polybius called the Roman legionary's sword the "Spanish sword." Spanish swordmakers were reputedly the best in the Roman world. Even if by the time of the A.D. 63 recruitment legionary swords were sometimes produced in other parts of the empire to the same design, there is no doubt that a legion recruited in Spain would have sourced its sidearms there. The swords of most of the Roman soldier's adversaries had rounded ends, making them effective in just the slashing mode. The legionary's sword, the Spanish sword with its sharp point, could be used to both jab and slash, putting the legionary at a distinct advantage in the confines of close-quarters combat.

On the new legionary's left hip hung a dagger—the arrangement of a legionary's sword and dagger were opposite to that of his centurions. To complete his outfit, every man also carried heavy arms—a javelin in his right hand and a rectangular shield in his left bearing the proud bull emblem of the 10th Legion, made to an effective design that hadn't changed in hundreds of years.

Almost certainly, Field Marshal Corbulo would have come up from Antioch for the swearing in of the 10th's new enlistment. He would have welcomed the new recruits with an earthy speech, and, as tradition required, presented the standard-bearers of the maniples and cohorts with their new standards. Men leaving the legion took their old standards with them, and would march behind them in their Evocati units. Only the legion's eagle standard remained; it never left the legion. The field marshal would then have led the new men in swearing the oath of allegiance to emperor, legion, and officers.

The retiring veterans of the legion were probably already on their way to their new homes. As it happened, the 10th Legion was the only one of Rome's now twenty-five legions that underwent its discharge this particular year, and the Palatium apparently decided it wanted to settle more veterans along the Rhine in A.D. 64, almost certainly in the wake of the recent activities of hostile German tribes east of the Rhine. So the men of the 10th who retired that year were given land on the west bank of the Rhine, and had to travel all the way to Germany to take up their grants.

We know this because, five years later, as a new civil war engulfed the empire in the wake of the demise of the emperor Nero, the reliable Tacitus describes retired veterans of the 10th Legion marching from the Rhine in their Evocati militia cohorts as part of an army of the aspiring emperor Vitellius, led by General Aulus Caecina. They were combined with other Evocati militiamen of the 4th Macedonica and 16th Legions who were also living along the Rhine in their retirement, and veterans of three of the four legions based in Britain. Those 10th Legion veterans defeated the army of the emperor Otho in the Battle of Bedriacum at the town also known as Betriacum near Cremona in northern Italy in A.D. 69, and five months later were defeated themselves at the Battle of Cremona by troops loyal to General Vespasian.

The surviving 10th Legion vets from Vitellius's defeated army would have been pardoned and permitted to go home to their farms along the Rhine after the war, in A.D. 70. But before these events took place, their comrades still serving with the 10th Legion had a problem of their own to contend with in the Middle East, one of the bloodiest campaigns in the legion's history to date: the Jewish Revolt.

XXI

ORDERS FROM
THE EMPEROR

On a lazy day in January A.D. 67, guards on duty in the towers at the decuman gate of the 10th Legion's base at Cyrrhus would have peered down the road to Antioch to the south as a legion courier came galloping toward them.

The base at Cyrrhus was a permanent installation. Back in 30 B.C., Augustus had required permanent winter camps to be established for all the legions of his new standing army, throughout the empire. Augustus stipulated that there was to be a maximum of two legions at each base, although from the Greek geographer Strabo we know that the main legion base in Egypt, at Babylon Fossatum, just up the Nile from Alexandria and today the site of Cairo, was occupied by three legions when he visited there in 25 B.C. Probably one of these legions was just passing through at the time, heading west or northeast to a new station.

The buildings at the Cyrrhus base in A.D. 67 may have been wooden, standing behind a wall of earth and timber and punctuated by wooden guard towers, giving it the appearance of a fort of the nineteenth-century American Wild West. Or it may have originally been built from stone, like other permanent structures of the region. Before the century was out, all the legion bases throughout the empire would be upgraded to be constructed of solid stone buildings behind formidable stone walls and featuring cleverly engineered granaries and luxuries such as vast bathhouses. The layout of the legion marching camp was preserved in these permanent bases, with neatly set-out barrack rooms lining the camp streets instead of rows of tents, as well as workshops, stables, and a *praetorium*, the legion headquarters complex.

Occupying the praetorium at Cyrrhus in January A.D. 67 was a colonel, the 10th Legion's deputy commander, a senior tribune in his late twenties.

Like so many legions, the 10th would have seen its commanding general depart late the previous year, moving on to a fresh assignment elsewhere in the empire or perhaps back at Rome, and the unit was now awaiting the arrival of a new commander for the next campaigning season beginning in the coming spring.

The colonel of the 10th received important news via several sources. The most regular was the *Acta Diurna*, or *Daily News*, the world's first daily newspaper. Founded by Julius Caesar in 59 B.C. when he was consul, by imperial times it was produced by industrious secretaries working in one of the departments of the Palatium in Rome. The handwritten copies of the *Acta* were distributed to Roman officials in every corner of the empire in the satchels of the couriers of the *Cursus Publicus*, the remarkably efficient state courier service also run by the Palatium. The *Acta* contained details of official decrees and appointments; birth, death, and marriage notices; sports results—the outcomes of the latest gladiatorial contests and chariot races at the capital; and even news of traffic jams and house fires in Rome.

It's likely that once he and his senior officers had perused the *Acta*, the legion commander posted the latest copy on a notice board in the camp, as they were in Rome itself, for all the men to read. Even in far-off Judea, this news from Rome would still have been quite current. Regularly changing horses at way stations every six to ten miles along the military highways that crisscrossed the empire, the carriages and mounted couriers of the Cursus Publicus covered an average of 170 miles a day. This compares favorably with the 180 miles-per-day average of the short-lived Pony Express of the United States in 1860–1861. Cursus Publicus inspectors made sure the horses, way stations, and highways were always in top condition.

News that more directly affected the 10th Legion arrived from regional headquarters at Antioch and was carried by legion couriers. Since republican times it had been a tradition that couriers bearing good tidings, such as news of a Roman victory on the battlefield, adorned their javelins with laurel. The guards who watched the courier dismount outside the decuman gate on this particular day—it was forbidden for even a Roman general or a foreign king to ride within a Roman camp—would have been hopeful of news of a victory over the Jewish rebels who had been embarrassing the Roman army down in Judea since the previous summer. But his javelin was unadorned.

The dusty courier wouldn't have needed to be told where to go. The layout of the camp of every legion had been the same for hundreds of years; he probably could have found his way to the *praetorium* with his eyes closed. Passing between the prescribed complement of four sentries at the *praetorium* door—Polybius sets out the precise number of sentries at each post within a legion camp, a formula that seems to have been adhered to by the legions for centuries—he would have entered the headquarters pavilion, removed a roll of parchment or vellum from his dispatch case, and handed it to the legion's colonel in charge.

Almost certainly, the dispatch, in the form of a scroll, would have borne the *Sardonychis*, the wax Palatium seal depicting a profile of the emperor Augustus, which had been used by every emperor of Rome since Augustus. It would continue to be used by all emperors but one at least up to and including Severus Alexander in the third century, and possibly much later. The exception was Galba, briefly emperor in A.D. 68–69, who used his family seal of a dog looking over the prow of a ship.

Accepting the dispatch, the colonel of the 10th would have broken the seal or seals and unraveled the document, to find it set out in pages of two parallel columns written neatly in Latin by an imperial secretary of the Palatium staff.

As the colonel read, other officers probably crowded into the *praetorium* to hear their orders. They would have been anticipating instructions to march, were no doubt straining at the leash to go into action after what had recently taken place to the south. The previous year, the Jews of Jerusalem had laid siege to the single cohort of the 3rd Augusta Legion based in their city, and after days of vicious fighting had killed every man except the cohort's commander, Camp Prefect Metallus, most after they'd surrendered. At the same time, members of the Zealot sect had tricked their way into the fortress of Masada on the Dead Sea and massacred the 3rd Augusta cohort based there. Another band of rebels had done the same at the fortress of Cypros, overlooking the city of Jericho. The rebels had then flooded into the countryside and occupied Judea and much of Idumaea and southern Galilee. A cohort of the 3rd Augusta had managed to escape from its fortress at Machaerus and reach the provincial capital, Caesarea. Another 3rd Augusta cohort holding the port city of Ascalon had fought off attackers but had been cut off there ever since.

A punitive operation against the Jews had been called for, and Field Marshal Corbulo should have been the man to lead it. The problem was, Corbulo had recently been recalled to Rome under a cloud of suspicion. His son-in-law, Brigadier General Vinianus Annius—some ancient authorities call him Vinicianus—onetime commander of the 5th Moesia Legion in Corbulo's Armenian task force, had foolishly become involved in a plot against the emperor.

New conspiracies against Nero were regularly being discovered in Rome and being put down by the Praetorian Guard in these increasingly conspiratorial times. The year before, the widespread "Piso plot" had even implicated Nero's retired chief secretary, the famous writer and philosopher Seneca, who'd been forced to commit suicide for merely associating with conspirators, including his nephew, the poet Lucan. In the same way, as Vinianus now met his death, his father-in-law's position was looking precarious. In the new year, guilt by association would see Corbulo also forced to take his own life, the act causing Rome to lose arguably her best general at the worst of times.

Corbulo's replacement as Governor of Syria, Lieutenant General Cestius Gallus, achieved his appointment on seniority, not ability. After a delay of three months, Gallus had reluctantly marched with a force of twenty-eight thousand men to restore Roman control in Judea. Among the units he chose for his task force were four cohorts of Syrian legionaries of the 3rd Augusta and four of the 22nd Primigeneia, a legion traditionally recruited in Galatia to the north. But the core of Gallus's force had been eight cohorts of the 12th Legion. The 12th Legion was due to undergo its twenty-year discharge in the new year—its youngest legionaries were thirty-nine, while most of those of its senior cohorts were fifty-nine and would have been enthusiastically looking forward to their looming retirement. But General Gallus was supremely confident that when it came down to it, the resistance of the Jewish partisans would dissolve at the sight of a Roman legionary army and that his men would not have to lift a sword against them.

How wrong Gallus turned out to be. Making a leisurely progress down through Galilee, burning everything in his path, he turned up outside the walls of Jerusalem in November, with winter just around the corner and with the partisans determined to resist Rome's might. After a desultory five-day siege, Gallus had inexplicably ordered his troops to pull out. In the Beth-horon valley, trying to retrace its steps back down the road to Lod and the coast it had traveled only a week before, General Gallus's column was surrounded and very nearly wiped out by the partisans. Only by leaving behind a four-hundred-man suicide squad of volunteers was Gallus able to extricate the rest of his troops in the night. When the task force staggered back into Caesarea, it was without six thousand of its men and numerous standards, including the eagle of the 12th. Among the dead was Brigadier General Priscus, commander of the 6th Victrix Legion, who'd apparently been acting as Gallus's chief of staff for the operation.

Gallus himself died shortly after; some said of shame. It had been all for naught—Judea was still in Jewish hands.

The dispatch from the Palatium would have informed the colonel of the 10th that the emperor had appointed Lieutenant General Gaius Licinius Mucianus to replace Gallus as Governor of Syria. It also would have said that Nero had appointed Lieutenant General Titus Flavius Vespasianus—Vespasian, as history would come to know him after he became the ninth emperor of Rome—to head a special task force to end the Jewish Revolt in Judea. And the colonel would have nodded approvingly as he read the emperor's orders for the 10th Legion—the 10th was to mobilize immediately and march south to General Vespasian's task force assembly point at Ptolemais on the Mediterranean coast, a little north of Caesarea. There it would join the 3rd Augusta Legion, the 5th Moesia Legion, the 15th Legion, and numerous allied and auxiliary units for Vespasian's Judean operation.

What was more, the emperor had appointed a new commander to take charge of the 10th for the offensive—Major General Marcus Ulpius Trajanus, or Trajan, father of another future emperor of Rome.

Nero had been visiting Greece in December when the news of the Gallus disaster reached him. General Vespasian had been a member of the entourage accompanying him. The son of a moneylender and grandson of an enlisted man who'd fought for Pompey at the Battles of Dyrrhachium and Pharsalus, Vespasian had commanded the 2nd Augusta Legion in the emperor Claudius's A.D. 43 invasion of Britain. This had been the first return of Roman legionaries to England since the 10th Legion last set foot there, in 54 B.C. But this time the invaders didn't go home. Vespasian had led the 2nd Augusta in overrunning much of southwestern England. For this deed, Claudius had presented the young major general with Triumphal Decorations, an award usually reserved for lieutenant generals, and also bestowed on him several prestigious priesthoods. Vespasian had gone on to be a valued military adviser to both Claudius and Nero.

A consul in A.D. 51 at age forty-one and Governor of Africa in A.D. 63, Vespasian was liked and respected by the legions because he'd come from common stock like themselves and because he was a good soldier. He was infamous for being tight with the government purse, but his personal commercial dealings up to this point had been disastrous. He'd invested heavily in a business that ran mule farms, and with government contracts to supply the army with pack animals, it should have been a license to print money. But inexplicably the owners of the business had mismanaged it woefully and sent it bankrupt. To cover his debts and maintain his membership of the Senate, Vespasian had been forced to mortgage his family home on Pomegranate Street in Rome's 6th Precinct to his elder brother Flavius Sabinus.

Vespasian's unfortunate personal finances had no bearing on his military credentials—he was the ideal choice for the task in Judea, an unpretentious, no-nonsense general who could get the best out of his men. And Nero knew it. According to Suetonius, Vespasian had fallen asleep during one of Nero's poetry recitals on the Greek tour and been dismissed from court. He was keeping out of the way in a quiet Greek backwater when news of his appointment to lead the Judean task force arrived.

Probably as the 10th Legion marched out of Cyrrhus and headed south to Ptolemais on the Mediterranean coast, just above the border between the provinces of Syria and Judea, in present-day Lebanon, it was joined by its new commander, Major General Trajan. Born at the town of Italica in Farther Spain—the 10th Legion's home territory—like Vespasian, General Trajan is also likely to have been traveling with the emperor's party in Greece at the time of his appointment. In his late thirties or early forties, capable and reliable, he would have been a popular choice with the men of the 10th, as it was extremely rare for a legion to be commanded by a general who came from the same area as its legionaries. At this time Major General Trajan's son, the future emperor, was only fourteen and probably still living back in Spain, where he'd been born.

It was unusual although not unheard of for a major general to command a legion. This was normally a role filled by a less senior brigadier general. But there appears to have been a scarcity of suitably qualified and experienced generals in the East at the time. With the death of its commander, Brigadier General Priscus, in the Gallus disaster, the 6th Victrix Legion, for example, located not far from the 10th's Cyrrhus base, at Zeugma on the Euphrates, would be led for the next few years by its senior tribune and second-in-command, Colonel Gaius Minicius, who took up his post in A.D. 67 at age twenty-seven after promotion from command of an auxiliary unit. Likewise, the 12th Legion, also based in Syria, appears to have been commanded by its second-in-command throughout this period, even when it, too, was eventually brought into the Judean offensive.

The new supreme commander in the East quickly came overland to Antioch. There, Lieutenant General Vespasian made careful logistical preparations for his Judean operation before joining his troops. At the same time, his eldest son, Titus, took a fast frigate from Greece and sailed down to Alexandria on his father's orders. Titus, who'd just turned twenty-seven, had served in the army as a colonel commanding auxiliary units but had left the military and was working as a lawyer at Rome when his father invited him to join him for the emperor's trip to Greece. Suddenly Titus was back in uniform.

The 15th Legion, one of the units selected for this operation, had been based in Egypt since Corbulo's last Armenian campaign, and Titus had been sent to get it. The old Augustan laws still made it illegal for a member of the Senate to enter Egypt, but as Titus wasn't yet old enough to sit in the Senate, he was able to enter the province. As the 10th Legion arrived at the assembly point at Ptolemais, Titus brought the 15th marching up the coast from Egypt. At the same time, six cohorts of the 3rd Augusta came up from Caesarea, aching to revenge the deaths of more than fifteen hundred of their Syrian comrades at the hands of the Jewish rebels, and the 5th Legion came down from its base in Pontus. By the late spring the army numbered forty-five thousand men, including auxiliaries and troops supplied by allied kings in the region. All impatient to go to war.

XXII

OBJECTIVE JERUSALEM

As General Vespasian left Antioch in the late spring of A.D. 67 to join his task force at Ptolemais, he knew from informants who'd escaped the Jewish capital that a power struggle among the Jewish leadership at Jerusalem had seen the partisans divide into three factions, which had occupied different parts of the city and which were now locked in bloody internecine conflict. And people who tried to leave Jerusalem to escape the madness either saved their skins with gold or were killed by members of any of the three factions.

Vespasian's staff urged him to march directly on the Jewish capital, but the gruff, coarse Vespasian was a thoughtful, careful man by nature. He hadn't survived in the service of three temperamental emperors by taking risks. He decided to let the Jews in Jerusalem exhaust themselves killing each other before he wasted any time, effort, or legionary blood trying to take the city. There was even a possibility that one or other of the factions might come over to the Roman side if he waited long enough. For the time being, Vespasian would concentrate on subjugating the countryside north of Jerusalem.

It was June by the time the Roman army moved out of Ptolemais. The 10th Legion marched in the vanguard of the column. We saw most of its legionaries on the sands of the Córdoba arena three years before when they were just raw recruits. The men of its senior cohorts had been recruited in A.D. 44; these were the men knocked into shape by Field Marshal Corbulo, the hardened troops who'd whipped the Parthians.

Vespasian turned left and swept inland, determined to methodically knock over the Jewish strongholds in Galilee one at a time. Gabara, in southwestern Galilee, just across the Syrian border from Ptolemais, was lightly defended and was stormed before the sun set on the first day of fighting.

Jotapata, modern Jefat, was a different story. The Jewish resistance leader for the region was the thirty-year-old partisan Joseph, who later took the Roman name Josephus Flavius. It's from his writing that we know most about the Jewish War. Originally given his regional command while at Jerusalem, where he'd left his parents, Josephus had first gone to Tiberias. Now, alerted to the Roman troop movements, he hurried down from Tiberias and slipped into Jefat late one afternoon in June, just before it was surrounded by Vespasian's mounted advance force, joining more than forty thousand Jewish people sheltering there.

The town was well sited for defense, with sheer cliffs on three sides and a massive wall in the fourth. Vespasian himself soon came up with the main force and surrounded the hill with two lines of infantry and an outer ring of cavalry. Auxiliary archers and slingers continually cleared defenders from the city wall, but for five days in a row Josephus's partisans ventured out from the fortress in assault groups to attack the Roman lines in hit-and-run raids before hastily withdrawing.

So Vespasian had a massive earthbank constructed in front of the wall as an artillery platform, then brought up 160 artillery pieces and sited them on the bank. Metal bolts, stones up to a hundred pounds in weight, firebrands, and arrows—all were hurled at Jefat for hours on end in methodical volleys. The front wall was eventually cleared of defenders by this barrage, as was a large area behind it. Still the Jews launched counterattacks, surging from the town unexpectedly and striking at the artillery platform, driving the artillerymen from their weapons. Roman counterattacks retook the bank. The Jews would again seize the bank, the Roman troops would regain it. But in the meantime, other partisans, working feverishly around the clock, added another sixty feet to the height of the town wall.

Because the wall offered only a limited front to operate against, Vespasian couldn't use all his units at once, so for much of the siege he rested two of his legions. He'd carefully selected the units he summoned for this offensive. Before its Egyptian assignment, the 15th Legion had come from its longtime Pannonian station in the Balkans to serve under Field Marshal Corbulo in his second Armenian campaign, and the unit's legionaries, men from Cisalpine Gaul, northern Italy, were solid and dependable. The Syrian cutthroats of the 3rd Augusta were anxious to revenge themselves on the Jews, but their unit had been severely reduced by their casualties at the hands of the rebels in the early stages of the revolt, so Vespasian held them back for use as shock troops.

According to Josephus, both the 10th and the 5th Legions were "world-famous" at this time. The 5th was still known throughout the empire as the legion that had beaten Scipio's elephants at Thapsus, and even though the current enlistment had been raised in Moesia, modern Bulgaria, the unit's legionaries still carried the elephant symbol and the reputation that went with it. The Spaniards of the 10th still bore the reputation their forebears had earned the legion as Julius Caesar's best troops, and since they'd been knocked into shape by Corbulo and savaged the Parthians, they'd once more earned their elite status. As a result, most of the hard work of the siege of Jefat fell to the 5th and 10th Legions.

Both legions built siege towers and mantlets—siege sheds on wheels—which were run up against the wall, and from the protection of these some legionaries set their battering rams to work while others tried to undermine the wall. At one point the constructions of the 5th were set alight by Jewish firebrands, so the siege buildings were dragged away, the fire extinguished, and their wooden roofs covered with earth to fireproof them before they were wheeled back into position and the siege works resumed.

Another time, the Jewish defenders poured boiling oil down on men of both the 5th and the 10th who were working at the wall face under the cover of *testudos* of raised shields, causing horrible burns to troops involved. This was history's first recorded use of boiling oil by defenders of a besieged fortification, a tactic that would frequently be emulated in the Middle Ages. Not that the maimed men of the 10th would have appreciated the gruesome way they entered the history books. This was certainly not the sort of fate they would have imagined for themselves when they joined the legion at Córdoba a little over three years before.

Shortly after, General Vespasian was himself wounded in the foot by an arrow fired from the city wall. First on the scene was his son Titus, as the general's officers and bodyguard crowded anxiously around. But to the relief of his troops, the general's wound was only minor, and soon he was back on his feet.

Knowing the defenders had limited water, Vespasian halted the assault for several weeks in the hope they would be driven to capitulate by thirst, but when the Jews would not surrender, he resumed the attack. On the forty-seventh day of the siege, after a furious artillery bombardment lasting several hours, the legions launched a night assault. Led by Vespasian's son Titus, legionaries swarmed over the town wall in the darkness and overwhelmed the defenders.

After Jefat fell, forty thousand Jewish bodies were found; twelve hundred prisoners were taken, among them the Jewish commander, Josephus. He was later to claim that he saved himself by prophesying to Vespasian that both he and his son Titus would become emperors of Rome. He accompanied the army for the rest of the campaign, providing advice and information on his former comrades-in-arms.

Even though it was only mid-August, but probably assured by Josephus the collaborator that the Jewish leadership in Jerusalem was so rent by internal fighting that the different factions were likely to destroy themselves if given enough time, Vespasian now withdrew most of his troops to Caesarea, planning to winter there and restart the campaign the following spring. For three weeks he enjoyed the hospitality of his ally King Herod Agrippa II of Chalcis, great-grandson of the famous Herod the Great. With Rome's consent and support, Herod Agrippa ran a small kingdom covering today's northern Israel and part of Lebanon. It was at his capital, Caesarea Philippi, near the headwaters of the Jordan River, that news reached Vespasian of large numbers of partisans concentrating at Tiberias on the southern tip of the Sea of Galilee, and that nearby Tarichaeae had closed its gates. Vespasian ordered a resumption of military operations.

The Roman army descended on Tiberias, which quickly surrendered, but not before its defenders escaped to Tarichaeae, a little farther around the lake. As the legions marched on Tarichaeae, young Titus led a large cavalry force on ahead. He succeeded in capturing the town after bloody fighting, much of it actually on the Sea of Galilee in boats and on rafts.

While Titus then went north to Antioch on a secret mission to General Mucianus, Governor of Syria, Vespasian continued the advance, moving out into the Jordanian desert, east of the Sea of Galilee, to assault the town of Gamala, which clung to a steep hillside described by Josephus as being like a huge camel's hump jutting from the desert. But progress was slow. One assault by the 3rd Augusta went awry when roofs the troops were climbing over caved in and buildings collapsed down the slope like houses of cards.

When Titus returned from Antioch he led a commando raid at night that removed Jewish sentries from a section of the town wall. Vespasian then brought the waiting legions hurrying on his son's heels, and they took the city.

It was now December, and while Vespasian took most of the army back to the coast to wait out the winter, Titus led a cavalry force to deal with the town of Gischala, the last Jewish holdout in Galilee. It soon fell, as the Jewish commander, John of Gischala, escaped and fled to Jerusalem. All of Galilee was once more under Roman control.

By the spring of A.D. 68, with the Jews still fighting each other in Jerusalem but showing no signs of capitulating to him, General Vespasian
ordered the offensive to resume. Over the winter his force had been
reduced by the Palatium's transfer of his six 3rd Augusta cohorts at Caesarea to Moesia, modern Bulgaria, to reinforce the two legions stationed
there who were coming under increasing pressure from raiders from across
the Danube—a thousand men from one of the resident legions, the 7th
Claudia and 8th Augusta, were lost to enemy action during this period.
But as the 3rd Augusta cohorts marched away for the long journey overland to the Danube, Vespasian would have consoled himself that he still
had more than enough troops at his disposal to finish the job in Judea.

In March he conducted the ceremonial lustration of the legions' standards, then gave the order to move out. As he departed Caesarea and
marched south down the coast with the 5th and 15th Legions, Vespasian
received news that Julius Vindex, governor of one of the provinces of
Gaul, had revolted against the emperor Nero. According to the sycophan-
tic historian Josephus, this news spurred Vespasian to speed up his campaign so he could wrap it up quickly and relieve the empire of this worri-
some situation in the East.

Maybe so, maybe not. It's possible that Vindex had written to Vespasian prior to launching his rebellion, seeking his support, just as we know
he wrote to Servius Galba, Governor of Nearer Spain, with the same
intent. Young Titus's secret mission to Antioch the previous year may
have been spurred by such a letter. General Mucianus, Governor of Syria,
hadn't been on friendly terms with Vespasian for many years, but he liked
Titus. According to Suetonius, Mucianus was homosexual, and he implied
that he was attracted to the handsome young colonel and this was why
Titus became an acceptable intermediary. Quite possibly, Mucianus, who
commanded the four legions stationed in Syria, also had been contacted
by Vindex, and Vespasian had sent his son to discuss whether Mucianus
and he would support the rebel governor. If this was the case, they must
have decided against throwing their legions behind Vindex, but a door
had been set ajar that both generals would before long open wide. Whatever his thoughts about Vindex's rebellion, Vespasian kept them to himself and pushed on south into Judea.

While the main force advanced down the coast, the 10th Legion took
a different route. After spending the winter near the Jordan River at the
friendly inland city of Scythopolis, a place inhabited by people of Greek
heritage and described as oppressively hot in summer but tolerably mild in
winter, the 10th Legion crossed the Jordan before General Trajan led it

down the river's eastern bank into the Peraea district. It then recrossed the river opposite Jericho, destroying towns and villages in its path. The 10th then lay siege to Jericho. The town had neither the situation nor the manpower to hold out as long as Jefat, and it and the nearby fortress of Cypros were stormed by the 10th Legion in May. Among the partisans who died in the assault was the Jewish commander for the Jericho region, John ben Simon.

The capture of Jericho and Cypros would have given the men of the 10th Legion particular satisfaction. On a dusty bluff overlooking Jericho, the old Herodian fortress of Cypros was where the rebels had massacred five hundred legionaries of the 3rd Augusta the year before. Rome's vengeance was not necessarily always swift, but it was sure.

Vespasian's main force quickly advanced down the coast to Antipatris, then to Lod and Jamnia, before swinging inland and marching up into the hills along the infamous Beth-horon road as far as Emmaus. There a major fortification was built, blocking the coastal approach to Jerusalem. Leaving the 5th Legion stationed at Emmaus, Vespasian took the remainder of his force and returned to the coast, ravaging the northern part of the Idumaea district.

Then he returned to the hills, passed through Emmaus, and overran a number of hill villages before marching down to Jericho, five miles from the Jordan River and sixteen from Jerusalem, where he linked up with General Trajan and the 10th Legion. As the 10th set up camp for the winter at Jericho, smaller forces of auxiliaries circled around through the hills and cut off escape routes to the south of Jerusalem. The Jewish capital was now effectively surrounded. Vespasian continued on to the Dead Sea, just a day's march south of Jerusalem; not for any strategic reason, but to satisfy his curiosity. The lake, thirteen hundred feet below sea level and the lowest stretch of water on earth, was famed around the civilized world.

The taciturn general stood looking at the still, dark waters. To test its famous buoyancy, he had several Jewish prisoners tossed into deep water with their hands tied. He was suitably impressed when they floated. No doubt so were the prisoners involved. It's not unlikely these prisoners came from the Essene community at Qumran, Jewish guardians of the so-called Dead Sea Scrolls. The Qumran monastery, on a cliff above the lake, had only recently been overrun by Roman auxiliary cavalry, and the buildings burned. A small Roman military post was established among the ruins, garrisoned by auxiliaries. Nineteen centuries later, in 1947, the Dead Sea Scrolls would be discovered in eleven caves behind the Qumran settlement, where they'd been hidden by priests of the sect before Vespasian's troopers swept into the monastery.

In that same month of May a dispatch arrived from Rome bearing the news that the rebel governor in Gaul, Vindex, was dead—his revolt had been quickly and ruthlessly terminated by the legions of the Rhine after just two months, and Vindex had committed suicide. On the heels of this news, Vespasian heard that despite Vindex's fate, General Galba in Spain had declared himself emperor, even while Nero still ruled at Rome, and was levying Spanish troops in preparation for a march on Italy to seize the throne by force. Throughout the provinces, some officials and military officers were speaking up in favor of Galba and against Nero. A new civil war threatened the stability of Rome.

With the empire in turmoil, General Vespasian took stock of his situation. It was late spring, and only Jerusalem and a few out-of-the way fortifications such as Masada remained in Jewish hands. Jerusalem was surrounded, with, it was said, more than a million people behind its walls. This was a figure given by Josephus, who was on the scene at the time. Tacitus, who wasn't there but was a more reliable historian in many ways, put the number at six hundred thousand. Either way, there were a lot of mouths to feed. Vespasian knew that many of the partisans were still fighting among themselves. Early heroes of the revolution had either been murdered or had fled south to the Zealots at Masada. New leaders vied for control in the Holy City while their people scrambled for food.

In comparison, Vespasian had supplies aplenty, and he had time. And patience. He could starve the citizens of Jerusalem into submission if he had to. Not that Jerusalem was his chief concern now. Vespasian's mind was in Rome. Who would win in this contest between Nero and Galba? And where would Vespasian stand, depending on the outcome? Officially, Vespasian now decided to await further orders from Rome. Suspending offensive operations, he took the 15th Legion back to his operational headquarters at Caesarea and told the 10th and the 5th to sit tight in their forward bases at Jericho and Emmaus.

And then something happened that rocked Vespasian and the empire.

In the second half of June, a messenger arrived at General Vespasian's headquarters at Caesarea with the astonishing news that the thirty-year-old emperor Nero Claudius Caesar Augustus Germanicus was dead. It was said that on June 9 Nero had taken his own life at a villa owned by Pheon, one of his freedmen, four miles outside Rome. Officially, Nero had simply disappeared, but the story going around the capital and later repeated by Suetonius was that, with the help of his secretary Epaphroditus, Nero had stabbed himself in the throat after being deserted by the Senate and the Praetorian Guard, and that his Christian mistress Acte had performed burial rights and cremated his remains. Vespasian knew firsthand that Nero had long professed a desire to give up the reins of empire. Now, it seemed, he had done just that.

Before long, the elderly Galba arrived in Rome at the head of a legion newly raised in Spain, Galba's 7th. A unit separate from and additional to the original 7th Legion, the 7th Claudia, but raised in the same recruiting grounds, Galba's 7th Legion would within several years become the 7th Gemina, in combination with another of the civil war legions created by Galba. With legionary steel to back his claim, Galba took the throne, endorsed by the Senate and supported by the Praetorian Guard.

For months, Vespasian waited for orders from Rome, orders that never came. In the meantime, with the Roman army inactive behind the walls of its camps in Judea, one of the Jewish leaders at Masada, Simon ben Gioras, went on the offensive against the inhabitants of the region, leading a force of twenty thousand partisans as he raided villages and towns in southern Judea and Idumaea and occupying the ancient city of Hebron, just to the south of Jerusalem, driving off the small contingent of Roman auxiliaries in the vicinity. Reckoned even then to be twenty-three hundred years old, Hebron was by tradition the burial place of Abraham, a figure destined to be revered by three of the world's great religions, Judaism, Christianity, and Islam. Simon then surrounded Jerusalem. Killing anyone who attempted to leave, he forced those in the city to elect him their new leader. He, and his partisans, then joined the multitude inside Jerusalem.

At Caesarea, Vespasian had tired of waiting for orders from new emperor Galba. So early in the new year, as soon as the seasonal winds were favorable, he dispatched his son Titus, and Herod Agrippa, king of Chalcis, to take his respects to Galba at Rome and seek the emperor's direction. In February 69, while Vespasian's two envoys were coasting past Greece in fast warships, they heard news when they put into port that Galba had been murdered in Rome in January, that thirty-six-year-old Marcus Otho had been put on the throne by the Praetorian Guard, and that the legions on the Rhine had declared not for Otho but for their own general, Aulus Vitellius. The forty-one-year-old Herod Agrippa decided to continue on to Rome anyway and pay his respects to Otho, but Titus turned his frigate around and headed back to Caesarea at full speed to convey the news of Galba's death to his father.

Meanwhile, annoyed by the activities of Simon ben Gioras, Vespasian decided to tighten his grip on Jerusalem. With the arrival of the new spring he marched out of Caesarea with the 15th Legion and occupied several towns in the hills north of Jerusalem, then sent Brigadier General Sextus Cerialis from Emmaus with a detachment from his 5th Legion and cavalry support to circle around to the south of the Jewish capital. Burning one town and accepting the surrender of another, General Cerialis came to the city of Hebron. After his Moesian legionaries easily stormed the city and eliminated its Zealot defenders, he burned ancient Hebron to the ground. The noose around Jerusalem had once more been tightened.

Outside of Jerusalem, the rebels now held only Masada, Herodeum, and Machaerus, and each was cut off from the other. There would be no more exploits like Simon's rampage through the countryside. As Vespasian hesitated to launch an all-out assault on Jerusalem, his son sailed back into Caesarea's harbor with the news of Galba's death, Otho's accession, and Vitellius's claim to the throne. According to Plutarch, both Vespasian and General Mucianus in Syria now sent letters to Rome vowing their allegiance to and support of Otho.

In that same spring of 69, General Vitellius sent two armies marching down from the Rhine to Italy, among them the retired veterans of the last 10th Legion discharge who were living on the great river. In mid-April, at Bedriacum, Vitellius's forces defeated Otho, and the short-lived young emperor took his own life. Vitellius was now emperor, and in July he would triumphantly enter Rome.

Vespasian, who had deliberately stalled operations in Judea to see how affairs in Rome panned out, was being repeatedly urged to consider making a bid for the throne himself by those around him, including, now, his son Titus. All accounts suggest he resisted at first. As Dio says, Vespasian was never inclined to be rash. But then in the middle of the year, under the guise of a visit to a religious shrine, he held a secret meeting on Mount Carmel, just north of his headquarters at Caesarea, with General Mucianus, who came down from Antioch. The two men sealed an agreement, with Mucianus giving Vespasian his backing for a tilt at the ultimate prize.

Tiberius Alexander, Prefect of Egypt, also supported Vespasian. If he wasn't at the Mount Carmel meeting he was certainly aware of it and the agreement that came out of it and was a party to both the meeting and the agreement. For the movement to make Vespasian emperor to appear to be spontaneous, the first step was taken by Alexander. On July 1, A.D. 69, he led the troops of his Egyptian garrison—the 17th Legion and four cohorts of the 18th—in hailing Vespasian as emperor of Rome.

The three legions in Judea followed suit several days later—first the 15th at Caesarea, then the 10th at Jericho and the 5th at Emmaus. By July 15, Mucianus had also sworn all four legions of his Syrian command for Vespasian. These were the 6th Victrix, the 12th, and as can be best ascertained, the 23rd and the 24th.

Vespasian hurried to Beirut, where he met with Mucianus and received deputations of potentates from throughout the East. With the nine legions of the East vowing their allegiance to Vespasian, plans were agreed for Mucianus, given the authority of a field marshal, to lead a task force to Italy to take the throne for Vespasian. That task force would consist of the 6th Victrix Legion as well as large numbers of auxiliaries and recalled militia veterans. While Vespasian headed south, Field Marshal Mucianus chaired a conference of officials at Beirut that set in motion all the necessary arrangements for the call-up of thirteen thousand retired legion veterans living in Syria and eligible for Evocati militia service, the production of arms and ammunition, the acquisition of baggage animals, and the coining of currency to pay for it all.

Vespasian gave command of the legions in Judea to his son Titus, with the brief to take Jerusalem in the coming spring, while he transferred his own headquarters to Alexandria, from where he could control the supply of grain going to Rome—the capital's lifeblood.

Major General Trajan now parted company with the 10th at Jericho, probably after calling an assembly of the legion and thanking its men for their bravery and loyalty while serving under him. It seems Trajan journeyed south to Alexandria, to join Vespasian's staff and to commence planning for a possible invasion of the province of Africa, modern Tunisia and part of Libya, using the one intact legion remaining in Egypt, the 17th, to gain control of the grain coming out of that province as well. That operation was soon made unnecessary by rapidly changing events in Europe. Once emperor, Vespasian would make Trajan his coconsul for A.D. 70, and within several years appoint him to govern Syria, then Asia. Major General Trajan was replaced as commander of the 10th Legion by Brigadier General Larcius Lepidus.

Vespasian's son, and successor in Judea, twenty-nine-year-old Titus, until recently a mere colonel but now with the authority of a field marshal, accompanied his father to Alexandria for the moment. There, Vespasian appointed the Prefect of Egypt, Tiberius Alexander, as his son's chief of staff. Alexander, probably in his fifties at this point, was intended as a mature and experienced adviser to the young general. Two decades earlier Alexander, a former Jew, had served as Procurator of Judea for several years. He'd also served on Field Marshal Corbulo's staff during his Armenian offensives. So he had considerable regional knowledge and military experience to offer Titus.

Titus and Alexander marched back up to Caesarea from Alexandria. Tacitus tells us they brought with them reinforcements from the 18th and 3rd Augusta Legions. These were four cohorts of new African recruits for the 18th Legion that had been stranded in Egypt by the Jewish Revolt, and the lone cohort of the 3rd Augusta Legion, which had been holding Ascalon on the coast south of Jerusalem since A.D. 66. As can be deduced from Tactitus, in A.D. 66 the 18th Legion was transferred from its long-term assignment in Egypt to the Rhine. Since 42 B.C. the legion had been recruited in Illyricum, but Tacitus indicates that for the new enlistment of A.D. 67 the Palatium gave it two new recruiting grounds, Africa and Narbon Gaul. At the same time, its brother legion, the 17th, also from Illyricum, had its recruiting ground changed to Asia. Cohorts enrolled in Gaul reached the 18th Legion's new Rhine station on schedule, but the recruits from Africa had only marched as far as Egypt by the time news of the Gallus disaster reached Alexandria in late A.D. 66, and they were held there pending further orders, probably on Vespasian's instructions.

According to Josephus, these five cohorts from two legions were put under the command of Colonel Heternius Fronto, who would have been commanding either the 18th Legion cohorts or the 17th Legion in Egypt up to this time. Josephus says that Titus and Fronto were old friends, and it's likely that both had commanded auxiliary units attached to the 2nd Augusta Legion in Britain at the same time earlier in their careers.

The buildup for the renewed Judean offensive continued in earnest. At the beginning of the new spring of A.D. 70, the 12th Legion marched down from its base at Raphanaeae in Syria, apparently led by its second-in-command, and three thousand legionaries based on the Euphrates, almost certainly from either the 23rd or the 24th Legion, or both, came down to perform rear-echelon duties out of Caesarea.

In April, Roman operations in Judea finally wound back into gear. Wearing the purple cloak of a Roman commander in chief that his father had worn before him, Titus led the 12th and 15th Legions and the 3rd Augusta and 18th Legion cohorts out of Caesarea and up into the Judean hills toward Jerusalem. At the same time, couriers rode to the 5th at Emmaus and the 10th Legion at Jericho. Both were ordered to march on Jerusalem.

Titus's main body from Caesarea was the first to reach Jerusalem, camping in the hills just north of the city. Riding ahead of his legions and taking his staff and an escort of six hundred cavalry with him, Titus reached the summit of twenty-seven-hundred-foot Mount Scopus to the northeast of the city, which provided a panoramic view of the Jewish capital. From the mountain, where a university and a hospital stand today, Titus studied the rugged lay of the land—Jerusalem was and is located among several hills, twenty-five hundred feet above sea level, although today's barren hills were then tree-covered.

He took particular note of the three walls surrounding the city, the outer walls twenty feet high, the inner thirty feet high and fifteen feet thick, with a number of defensive towers dotted along their length— ninety on the Third Wall, fourteen on the Second, and sixty on the First or Old Wall. Eerily, there was not a sign of Jewish defenders anywhere.

Seeing that the walls were deserted, Titus suddenly spurred his horse forward, planning to go down the slope to take a closer look. Most of his cavalry escort had halted on the reverse side of the hill, so that as he went down the slope, Titus was accompanied by just his staff and immediate bodyguard, leaving the surprised cavalry force behind. Reaching the bottom of the slope, Titus became caught up in gardens. At this moment, thousands of Jewish partisans rushed out the Women's Gate in the outer Third Wall.

The wildly yelling partisans swiftly cut off Titus and his party, and almost ended the young general's career in the dust there that spring day. Titus and most of those with him did manage to fight their way out and rejoin the cavalry, but a straggling bodyguard was hauled from his horse by partisans who cut his throat, and another who dismounted to fight was overwhelmed and killed. It was a lesson for young Titus not to take anything at face value at Jerusalem.

That night, the Moesians of the 5th Legion arrived from Emmaus. The next morning the 12th and 15th Legions set about building a camp on Mount Scopus, and, at Titus's direction, the 5th built another for itself six hundred yards to the rear of that of the 12th and 15th. Later in the day, the 10th Legion marched in from Jericho, and Titus ordered it to build a camp on the Mount of Olives, due east of the city and separated from it by the Kidron valley.

General Lepidus, the 10th's new commander, hadn't witnessed his commander in chief's brush with death the previous day and was unaware of the surprise tactics of the partisans. Without setting guard pickets down the slope, he put his legion to work building entrenchments on the Mount of Olives. During the afternoon, as his 10th Legion men wielded entrenching tools in the hot April sun, and with ramparts of the city walls deceptively empty, thousands of armed Jews suddenly swarmed out of the Lower City and across the Kidron, splashed through the stream flowing along the bottom of the mountain, then surged up the slope toward the toiling legionaries.

Taken by surprise and armed with just their swords and entrenching tools, the men of the 10th fell back up the mountain in disorder. It just so happened that Titus was nearby at the time, and he rushed to the spot and rallied the troops. Organizing them into their cohorts, he led them against the partisans, who were driven back into the city.

Titus instructed General Lepidus that in the future he was to deploy large numbers of fully armed legionaries to protect their comrades laboring on defenses. As Titus was standing with a group of officers discussing dispositions, the Jews suddenly burst out of the Lower City again and launched a second attack. Once more they swept up the slope unhindered, as again the men working on the incline hurriedly withdrew. But Titus didn't budge. Drawing his sword, he ordered his colleagues to do the same.

The partisans quickly surrounded Titus and his party, but already the centurions of the 10th were arming their men with shields and forming them into their cohorts. As the legionaries came running down the hill to support their general, Titus led his party in a charge at their assailants. Again the partisans were put onto the back foot, and again they fled across the Kidron and into the city. It was another lesson for the 10th. These tricky partisans were unlike any adversary they'd ever faced before. As Boy Scouts were to learn in modern times, the legionaries had to be prepared. For anything.

Titus and his senior officers held a council of war. Some advocated a siege, to starve the Jews into submission. In times past, this is what Titus's father would have done; it was the prudent course. But Titus wanted a quick victory, so he could turn his attention to his father's campaign to win the throne. Time was all-important. After hearing his subordinates' opinions, Titus announced to his generals and colonels that he intended to conduct a massive assault at several different parts of the city and overwhelm the defenders quickly.

Because of the lay of the land, armies assaulting Jerusalem in times gone by had been forced to do so from the north. Titus had his own ideas. But first he needed to break through the Third Wall, which the Jews had only recently completed. Choosing a place for an assault on the Third Wall thought by modern scholars to have been just to the north of the Jaffa Gate, Titus gave instructions for the ground leading up to it to be leveled, and for trees to be felled throughout the region to provide clear fields of fire for the artillery and to provide timber for siege equipment. Before they had finished, the legionaries would denude the Jerusalem area of all its trees.

At the same time, Titus set men to work improving the defenses on their own camps, because the Jews several times fought all the way to the camps in surprise raids from the city. He also moved his own headquarters several times, finally settling on a location west of the Old City, close to where the King David Hotel stands today.

Within the walls, two of the Jewish factions fighting each other in their protracted civil war agreed on a truce and combined to fight the Romans. The third faction, while fighting the Romans, continued to fight the other factions at every opportunity.

As Jewish bands unexpectedly sallied from this gate or that gate to fall on Roman work parties, or decoyed green Roman troops into ambushes under the wall, Titus was forced to deploy a large part of his army just defending his work parties. Several ranks of infantry and cavalry circled the city, and with them, archers to cover men digging and carting and felling and building.

The preparation took several weeks. Finally Titus brought up his artillery, and the assault troops prepared their heavy equipment. As the soldiers of the Roman army went to their beds on May 9, all was in readiness.

XXIII

THE END OF
THE HOLY CITY

At dawn on May 10, A.D. 70, the full-scale Roman assault on Jerusalem began. Ravines three hundred feet deep dropped away from the southern, eastern, and southwestern sides of the city, so the young Roman commander had chosen to concentrate on a section of the city's Third Wall, to the northwest. While assault troops tried to get to the wall and breach it using *testudos*, mantlets, siege towers, and battering rams, the combined artillery of the legions raked the wall in this locality to keep defenders off the ramparts.

Simon ben Gioras was in charge of defenses in this sector, and he tried to counter the Roman efforts with frequent sallies beyond the walls by raiding parties and with 340 artillery pieces of his own mounted on the wall. Ironically, the Jewish gunners were using Roman artillery, captured from the 3rd Augusta, 12th, and 22nd Primigeneia Legions at the taking of the Antonia Fortress and the Battle of Beth-horon four years earlier.

But the Jews didn't have the training or the skill of their Roman counterparts, and the artillery of the 10th Legion played a leading role here in the assault on the Third Wall. Its artillery comes in for particular mention from Josephus, who says the 10th possessed the most powerful spear-throwing Scorpions and the largest stone-throwing *Ballistas* of all the legions. The former Jewish commander, now with Titus's party, writes of the prodigious rate of fire of the 10th's quick-firing dart launchers, and tells of how the legion's biggest stone-throwing weapons—possibly Onagers, heavy *Ballistas*—could hurl stone shot weighing a hundred pounds more than four hundred yards and kill not only men on the front lines in its whooshing progress but also continue on, to mortally wound others in the rear as well. Josephus writes of one Jewish fighter who had his head taken clean off by a Roman artillery shot—the man's head was later found

238

hundreds of yards from his torso. At the earlier siege of Jefat, he says, a single Scorpion bolt skewered several Jewish defenders at once.

Roman gunnery was no hit-or-miss affair. The 10th Legion artillerymen set their ranges with precision. The science of guided missiles—ballistics, as we call it—derives from the catapult, the original missile launcher. To make their gunnery so precise, the artillerymen of the 10th and the other legions at Jerusalem measured the distance from artillery platform to city wall with lead and line.

Josephus tells of how, at the height of the assault on the Third Wall, Jewish spotters on nearby towers were able to yell warnings to their comrades in specific areas to take cover when Roman artillery shot came whizzing toward them with a cry of "Baby coming!"

Partisans in the target area would then hit the dirt. This was made easier by the fact that the Roman artillerymen were using Judean stone for their projectiles, which was quite light in color, almost white. To counter the spotters, the legions' artillery commanders had their men coat their ammunition in black pitch, making it harder to see.

Under fire all the way from the Jewish defenders, three massive Roman siege towers were rolled over the leveled ground and into position against the Third Wall. A tower had been built by each of three legions—the 5th, 12th, and 15th—and while the 10th concentrated on its artillery expertise, these three units now competed to see which could be the first to breach the wall.

Each wooden tower was covered in protective metal plate and had three levels. From the top level, archers and slingers tried to keep defenders at bay. Catapults operated from the next floor down. At ground level, teams of legionaries operated a battering ram slung from the framework of the tower. The ram consisted of a heavy metal head on a long pole, which was swung back and forth to pound away at the base of the wall. Battering rams acquired their name from the metal ram's head attached to the business end of the length of pole.

The din made by the three rams pounding relentlessly away at the Third Wall was an ominous sign. It forced all three Jewish factions to unite—for the moment. Defenders concentrated their efforts in the sector where the Romans were conducting their siege operations. But apart from a corner of a tower being loosened by the ram operated by the 15th Legion, no damage was done by the siege towers in the first week.

At one point the Roman cavalry protecting the towers was withdrawn. Seizing the opportunity, a large band of Zealots led by John the Idumaean, a senior resistance commander, rushed out a concealed gateway and set fire to one of the towers. Titus personally led a cavalry squadron that drove the partisans back the way they had come. It was a costly foray for the defenders—among the Jewish dead was the Idumaean, killed by an arrow. The fire on the tower was soon extinguished.

As the rams kept up their work, day in, day out, the Jewish defenders inside the city walls, who slept in their armor, went to sleep with the sound of the pounding in their ears, and awoke to it again the next day.

On day fifteen of the assault, May 25, the wall began to give way to all three rams. Cohorts of Roman shock troops moved into position. As the wall crumbled close by the gate, legionaries scrambled up the rubble like so many ants, overwhelmed and slaughtered any partisans who stood in their way, and opened the gate. Thousands more legionaries poured in through the gateway.

The defenders fled to the nearby Second Wall. Dating back before 37 B.C., this wall was much higher and thicker than the Third. It didn't possess as many towers, but it incorporated the bastions of the Temple to the east and Herod's Palace on the western side of the city.

The assault now moved into its second phase. While he left the camp of the 10th Legion where it was, Titus quickly moved the 5th, 12th, and 15th Legions closer to the city, consolidating their quarters in an area, still on the western outskirts, called the Camp of the Assyrians. It had acquired its name from its use by King Sennacherib and his Assyrian army during their siege of Jerusalem back in 701 B.C. Sennacherib had called off that siege after the people of Jerusalem paid him a huge ransom. The city was not to be so lucky this time.

While his troops threw up their new camp, Titus maintained the momentum of the success at the Third Wall by immediately resiting his artillery to attack the northern part of the Second Wall and by sending one of his siege towers against the central northern tower of the Second Wall. Partisans venturing out in raids against the tower were quickly beaten back by supporting infantry and cavalry.

A few days into the operations at the tower, a Jew named Castor and ten others appeared on the ramparts nearby and indicated that they wanted to surrender. Titus suspended siege operations and offered to let the eleven men come down from the wall unharmed. They then appeared to fight among themselves, with some deciding not to surrender. An archer on the Roman side then let loose an arrow that hit Castor in the nose, and this brought a halt to the fighting. Pulling out the arrow, Castor protested to the Romans. Titus asked Josephus the defector to speak with Castor, but he declined, saying the men on the wall were up to something. When Titus sent a Jewish deserter named Aeneas to the foot of the wall with a legionary escort, to parley, Castor threw a stone at Aeneas, missing him and wounding one of the legionaries of the escort. As Aeneas and his party hastily withdrew, and Castor and his companions yelled mocking comments at the Romans, Titus ordered the ram to resume work against the tower. The tower collapsed from the pounding of the ram shortly after. Castor and his men set fire to the ruins and then committed suicide by jumping into the flames.

From dawn till dusk the legionaries continued to pound away at the Second Wall. Like all Romans, the men of the legions rose before dawn, the Roman day being dictated by whatever could be achieved in daylight hours. The troops slept in their uniforms and frequently in their armor, being summoned from their tents by the trumpets sounding reveille and ending the last watch of the night at the camps.

Five days after battering operations had begun against the Second Wall, on May 30, a section of the wall adjacent to the ruined tower collapsed. The Jewish defenders retreated to the First Wall, ignoring Titus's suggestion that they come out and fight in the open like soldiers, or surrender. All who capitulated would be treated honorably, Titus had assured them, and would even be allowed to retain their property. In response, the armed defenders threatened death to the hundreds of thousands of refugees still sheltering within the remaining sections of the city if they dared attempt to surrender.

Ordered into the attack, legionaries went climbing over the rubble at the breach in the Second Wall. Surging triumphantly into the city, they found themselves in a maze of narrow lanes flanked by the walls and barred doors of houses. Suddenly gates opened in the First Wall and thousands of partisans rushed into the streets. The leading legionaries were overwhelmed and cut down. Their comrades hurriedly retreated to the gap in the Second Wall, but in the frantic crush few could squeeze out at any one time. There were numerous Roman casualties before the legionaries were able to withdraw. The gleeful Jews regained control of the Second Wall, convinced God was on their side and that the Romans were fated never to penetrate any farther.

Titus launched new, sustained ramming operations on the Second Wall. Three days later, on June 2, legionaries poured through several new breaches, and the defenders were again forced to retreat to the First Wall. This time Titus had his troops demolish every building between the two walls. Soon a clear, dusty space was opened.

Now Titus suspended the siege. In an attempt to awe the defenders, he paraded his legions in full-dress uniform, and over the next four days ceremoniously doled out the pay of every legionary, in full view of the people of Jerusalem who crowded the walls and windows of the city to watch the process. One at a time, every man had to come forward in parade dress and full equipment and sign for his pay. Cavalrymen were required to lead up their horses adorned with full decorations.

When this didn't have any visible effect on the morale of the partisans, the young Roman general sent Josephus to attempt to negotiate a surrender from the defenders. Josephus had a very personal reason for wanting the city to capitulate—both his mother and his father were among the refugees still inside Jerusalem. Standing behind cover near the First Wall, Josephus called out to his fellow Jews that Rome would treat well all who surrendered.

There was no immediate response. But over the succeeding days many people did manage to escape from the city and reach the Roman lines. As the days passed, some Jews inside the city secretly bargained with Roman soldiers outside to buy food. In the night they lowered baskets containing gold to legionaries below the wall. When they hauled the baskets back up again, expecting to receive food, all they found was straw. It would have been highly amusing to the legionaries, but a bitter disappointment to the starving people on the wall. The rate of Jewish desertion rapidly increased, to five hundred a day. But even at that rate it would have taken years for the city to be cleared.

To speed defections, Roman troops even roasted goats under the walls. As the aroma of cooking meat was carried into the city on the breeze, some starving refugees inside apparently went crazy. One demented Jewish woman was said to have even cooked and eaten her own baby. Armed bands roved the city searching for hidden reserves of food, killing anyone who resisted. Families fought each other over scraps; parents supposedly took food from the mouths of their children. When the widow of former high priest Jonathan couldn't buy food despite her wealth, she threw her gold into the street in disgust. People died from hunger even as they were attending the funerals of friends and relatives.

Jews caught by Roman troops foraging for food outside the walls were whipped, then crucified. Soon there weren't enough crosses to accommodate all the victims, so instead of crucifixion, many prisoners had their hands lopped off before being sent back to the city.

Once his surrender terms were rebuffed by the Jewish leadership, Titus set in motion the third phase of the assault. He assigned a different sector to each of his four main legions, no doubt conscious of the poet Ovid's observation that a horse never runs so fast as when he has other horses to catch and outpace. The young general intended to use the spirit of competition that always existed among the legions as a spur to a rapid completion of the assault.

From officers such as Colonel Alexander, who knew Jerusalem well as a former administrator of Judea, Titus would have learned the city's strong points, those key bastions he would have to take if the city was to fall. He also would have been able to draw on the firsthand knowledge of 3rd Augusta men who had been stationed in the city in the past. From the advice he received, Titus knew that he had to concentrate on the Antonia Fortress and the adjacent Temple, and, on the western side of the city, the massive castle that was Herod's Palace.

The 10th Legion was assigned a section at the northeastern corner of the First Wall near the Amygdalon, the Almond Pool, next to Herod's Palace. The 15th's sector was forty-five feet away, opposite the High Priest's Monument. The 5th was assigned the northwestern tower of the Antonia Fortress. The men of the 12th were just 30 feet away. Each legion was instructed to build an embankment of earth against the sixty-foot wall. With a gentle slope from base to top, each embankment would be just wide enough for a siege tower to be rolled along it to the wall. The rams would then go into action against the upper works of the wall.

It took fifteen days to build the embankments. All four competing legions finished work at much the same time. But the defenders hadn't been idle all this time. One of the their commanders, John, who had escaped to Jerusalem from Gischala, led a team that dug a tunnel out under the First Wall from the Antonia Fortress, using a natural underground water conduit as a starting point. The miners supported the walls and roof of their tunnel with wooden uprights. As the Romans finished work on the two embankments above, the partisans coated the tunnel supports with pitch and bitumen, then withdrew, setting fire to the timbers. Once the fire had consumed the wooden supports, the tunnel roof caved in, and the embankments above collapsed, to the horror of the troops about to push their siege engines up the slopes.

There was consternation in Roman ranks at the embankment collapse over by the Antonia, but at their sector the men of the 10th and the 15th were able to push their siege towers up their ramps all the way to the wall. Just as the legionaries were congratulating themselves on their efforts, a Jewish raiding party dashed out a nearby gate, overwhelmed men at the two towers, then set fire to wicker palisades around the towers.

Reinforcements were urgently summoned from both legions to save the towers from the flames, but even as legionaries of the 10th strained to drag their massive metal-sheathed tower free of the burning palisades, partisans pulled in the other direction, ignoring the heat and fire, even grasping hold of red-hot metal. Determined to see the towers destroyed, the Jews won the day. The legionaries had no choice but back off as flames roared up inside the pair of wooden structures, and both towers were consumed.

Then the jubilant Jews went on the offensive, chasing the Roman troops all the way back to the camp walls at the Camp of the Assyrians. There the legionary pickets held the attackers until reinforced, and the legions drove the partisans back to the First Wall. Just the same, the day's work was a morale-boosting success for the defenders of Jerusalem and a crushing blow for Titus and his troops.

The quick victory that had been on the cards up till now had eluded Titus, and he called a meeting of his commanders and staff to discuss a revision of tactics. As mime writer Publius Syrus had noted a century before, it is a bad plan that admits of no modification. And Titus was open to suggestions. Some of his officers advocated an all-out frontal attack from one end of the First Wall to the other. Others advocated settling in for a long siege, to wait for the Jews to either starve or surrender. Titus's cautious father would have chosen the latter, and now Titus was inclined the same way. He decided to prepare for a long siege, without giving up on the idea of breaching the First Wall in several places simultaneously.

Titus now ordered his legionaries to surround Jerusalem with a wall of their own, a so-called wall of circumvallation. One of the factors that set the Roman military apart from its opponents over many centuries was its engineering skill. Caesar had been as much an engineer as a soldier, and the men who inherited his empire inherited his practices. This Roman wall was designed to seal the Jews within their city. Their daring raids outside the city walls before now had been more than a hindrance—several times they had driven all the way to the Roman camps.

Titus had no idea how many fighting men the Jews actually possessed inside the city, and how many they could therefore throw into a major sally outside the walls. He'd been told there were 600,000 to 1.2 million people in the city. Most were refugees, but even refugees can throw stones. They were starving, but supposedly starving men had just dug a tunnel and burned his siege towers, so he could never be sure whether the Jewish fighters hadn't maintained food reserves for themselves while they let the rest of the city starve. Throughout the siege, even though he did extract information from prisoners and defectors, Titus would never have been entirely sure what he was up against in Jerusalem.

Then there were his lines of communication. Titus had to bring every-thing to his siege camps from miles away. His troops had already cut down every tree within a twelve-mile radius, so even wood for the legionaries' cooking fires had to be brought in from far off. Water was of prime impor-tance. There was plenty of water inside the city—that was why it had been built in this desolate location in the first place, its fresh-water cis-terns keeping the occupants supplied. Outside the walls, there was no water for many miles. So Titus had to bring in fresh water for sixty thou-sand troops and perhaps as many noncombatants in hundreds of water wagons every day. As well as food and ammunition.

The principal supply base for the offensive was back at Caesarea on the Mediterranean, so the road that clawed up into the hills from the maritime plain must have been one constant sea of wagons and mule trains during the months of the siege, bringing in supplies and ammuni-tion and taking out wounded. In quarries somewhere behind the lines, workers were chipping out massive white Judean rocks, rounding them to the satisfaction of their supervisors, who would then have them swung onto waiting wagons for the lurching journey to the front lines, to feed the insatiable Roman artillery pieces.

All this made Titus and his task force vulnerable. The Jews had proven themselves masters of guerrilla warfare. If they managed to get a large force out of Jerusalem that could cut his supply route to the north, Titus would be in trouble. All the more reason to seal in the Jews.

His troops quickly began work building the wall of circumvallation. They astonished the Jews by completing the five miles of trench and wall, inclusive of thirteen forts built along its length, in just three days. This construction feat was a record for the Roman army. Not even Julius Cae-sar had built so much so rapidly. Erection of Titus's wall at Jerusalem would become legendary within the Roman military. To achieve these results, Titus had again treated the project as a competition, with each legion assigned its own section of wall to construct and with Titus making nightly inspections to praise, encourage, and reward his troops.

The breached Third Wall would have come in handy as legionaries cast about the barren, dusty landscape for building materials. Today there is little trace of the Third Wall. Without doubt, the toiling legionaries would have plundered it for building material. The wall of circumvallation ran within about two hundred yards of the First and Second Walls, fol-lowing the Valley of Hinnon to the south, running along the bottom slope of the Mount of Olives to the east, and inside the Third Wall in the north, cleaving through the middle of the Betheza district, the so-called New City. On the western side of the city, Titus's wall ran down past the Serpent's Pool, at the foot of his headquarters at the Camp of the Assyrians.

Inside the surrounded city, civilians now became even more depressed, and partisans turned on each other once more. John of Gischala murdered Eleazar the Zealot. On the wall, Simon the Zealot executed Mattathias, one of the chief priests, for the Romans to see, having first killed the priest's three sons in front of him. When Jude, one of Simon's lieutenants, began to talk of surrender, Simon killed him, too.

Seeing this disarray among the opposition, Titus sent Josephus to once more call for a Jewish surrender. According to Josephus, this time he was hit on the head by a stone thrown from the walls, and knocked out cold. The rebels cheered with delight, thinking Josephus had been killed. A Jewish party was sent out to collect his body, but Titus had already sent a strong legionary detachment to his aid, and he was brought back to the Roman lines and revived. He returned to the wall to resume his peace efforts, but the Jews, disappointed that the traitor had survived after all, sent him away.

Titus now decided to concentrate all his offensive activities on taking the Antonia Fortress. All four legions began building new embankments against the Antonia's northern walls. Work was hampered by lack of timber, and several times new embankments gave way for lack of wooden support. For the first time, the spirits of the legionaries began to sag. This hot, unrewarding work was now in its third month.

On July 20, all four siege towers were rolled up into position against the Antonia, their progress unimpeded by a hail of missiles from the fortress. John of Gischala led another sortie outside the walls with firebrands, hoping to repeat the fiery success of the attack on the earlier towers of the 10th and 15th Legions. But this time the legionaries were expecting the attack—compressed tightly together and with their shields locked, they created an impenetrable barrier around their towers. Meanwhile, accurate Roman close artillery support cut down attackers in droves. The surviving partisans retreated inside the First Wall, and the battering rams began their pounding of the northern wall of the Antonia.

The massive fortress of the Antonia, which dominated the Temple the way the Temple in turn dominated the city, resisted the rams, so infantry came up under cover of their shields, in a *testudo*, and undermined part of the wall by hand, dislodging four massive stones with their crowbars. Unbeknownst to the assault troops, this happened to be right over part of the tunnel built earlier by John of Gischala. In the night, the tunnel collapsed beneath the weakened section of wall. As if by a miracle, a breach appeared in the wall. But with the dawn the Roman troops saw that the Jews had built yet another wall, using piles of rubble, inside the First Wall. The legions would have to start all over again.

Seeing his men dejected by the prospect, Titus called an assembly of his elite troops, telling his generals to send him the best legionaries from each legion. As the picked men sat on the dusty ground in front of him, he climbed onto a tribunal to address them. Josephus also was there, and he recorded Titus's speech.

"My fellow soldiers," the young general began, "it would be scandalous for men who are Romans and my soldiers, in peacetime trained for war, in war accustomed to victory, to be outshone by these Jews in strength or determination. And on the brink of success and with Jupiter to help us!" He went on to say that death in battle was glorious, and that Roman soldiers who died in this battle could look forward to their souls being set free amid the stars. The taking of this wall was a dangerous enterprise, he conceded, but he would not insult Roman soldiers by asking them to take risks and expose themselves to danger—risks and danger were commonplace to a legionary. This was just another job that had to be done. And for those who succeeded, he promised, the rewards would be great. Then he called for volunteers to attack the new wall.

A Syrian legionary named Sabinus, from the task force's single cohort of the 3rd Augusta Legion, now came to his feet. His unit was famed as one of Rome's fiercest, bravest legions. The six cohorts of the 3rd Augusta recently sent to Europe from Judea had immediately added to their reputation after their arrival in Moesia—on a single icy winter's day they had wiped out an entire raiding party of ten thousand Sarmatian cavalrymen who had crossed the Danube, and with barely a casualty of their own. These same cohorts of the 3rd Augusta had subsequently spearheaded the bloody, unrelenting drive through Italy that had taken Cremona and Rome and secured the Roman throne for Vespasian.

But according to Josephus, the little, shriveled, dark-skinned Syrian legionary who now stood before Titus looked like anything but a soldier. Almost certainly a second-enlistment man, he would have been fifty years of age, having joined his legion in the 3rd Augusta's enlistment of A.D. 40. Inspired by his example, eleven other legionaries from various units now also came to their feet, volunteering to join the Syrian for what was likely to be a suicide mission.

"If I fail, General," Josephus says Legionary Sabinus declared, "I have chosen death with my eyes open."

That morning at dawn, like all the men of the 3rd Augusta in all parts
of the Roman world, Sabinus would have bowed down to the sun as it
crested the eastern horizon, just as he had every day of his adult life, saluting and offering prayers to Baal, his patron deity. Tacitus describes how
the Syrians of the six cohorts of the 3rd Augusta that took part in the
Battle of Cremona the previous year broke off at dawn to salute the rising
sun before returning to the fight. Their religious observances, it seems,
came before all else. On this day, Legionary Sabinus would have asked the
Syrian sun god to watch over him, as he did every day. No doubt now, as
admiring 3rd Augusta friends helped him strap on his armor and handed
him his shield, Sabinus offered another silent prayer to the heavens—a
prayer for success in his mission, for the chance to greet great Baal again
the next morning.

Perhaps a worried Syrian friend, less influenced by the heady excite-
ment of the moment, might have voiced the age-old disdain that soldiers
have for volunteering. To volunteer at any time was foolish, he might
have said, but to volunteer for a mission like this was lunacy. He may
have reminded Sabinus of the old Latin proverb "Wise men learn by other
men's mistakes, fools by their own." And this mistake could well be fatal.
But the little legionary of the 3rd Augusta had set his mind to the task,
and he was not going to be diverted from his chosen course.

A little before noon, as the men of the Roman army watched from
their lines, Legionary Sabinus led the group of volunteers in a sudden rush
at the new wall, shield raised, sword drawn. From the top of the wall
above, defenders opened up with a barrage of missiles. While companions
all around him were hit and tumbled back under a hail of javelins, arrows,
and stones, Sabinus scrambled up the rubble unscathed. Josephus says that
as the lone legionary kept coming, climbing the rubble like a veritable
monkey and without a scratch, Jewish defenders thought the diminutive
Syrian must be some kind of superman and fled, leaving him free to climb
up onto the top of the wall.

From the uneven summit, turning back to his watching army, Legionary Sabinus, grinning, raised his shield and sword victoriously. The cheers
of thousands of his comrades would have reached his ears. For this deed,
for being the first to mount the wall of the enemy city, he could expect to
be presented with the Corona Muralis, the Mural Crown, one of the most
prestigious bravery awards available to a Roman soldier, equivalent to the
U.S. Congressional Medal of Honor, or Britain's Victoria Cross.

The solid gold crown, crenellated in imitation of the walls of a city,
singled out the holder as an exceptional soldier. Polybius tells us that the

holders of golden crowns—there also were crowns awarded for storming an entrenchment and for conspicuous gallantry in a sea battle, the Corona Vallaris and the Corona Navalis, respectively—were given place of precedence in religious parades when they went home after leaving the military, and they hung their crowns in a prominent place in their houses for all to see. He says that Romans of all classes had an almost obsessive concern with military rewards, attaching immense importance to them. So it wasn't surprising, Polybius said, that Romans emerged "with brilliant success from every war in which they engage."

This quest for glory had driven Legionary Sabinus to climb the Antonia wall. As he stood there, he would have pictured himself called to the front of an assembly of the entire army. General Titus Flavius Vespasianus, the emperor's son, would read his citation, then personally place the heavy crown of gold on his head. Tens of thousands of Sabinus's comrades would cheer and applaud. And how he would be received when he went home once his current enlistment expired in another ten years. Perhaps to Beirut, hometown of many men of the 3rd Augusta, so we gather from Josephus. Sabinus's fame would precede him, of course. He would write home, perhaps paying a literate comrade to pen a note to his family, and sending the letter with a traveler plying the coastal road north, or slipping it, along with a bribe, into the hands of a bronze-badged rider of the *Cursus Publicus* courier service. How proud they would be in Beirut of their son, brother, cousin, and uncle Sabinus, winner of the Mural Crown.

But then, in that instant of success, the brave, daydreaming soldier lost his balance. To the horror of the watching Romans, Legionary Sabinus fell, landing with a crash of his segmented metal armor inside the wall. The noise alerted the fleeing partisans. They turned to see Sabinus, injured by the fall, raising himself up onto one knee. They swarmed back and surrounded him. Sabinus raised his shield to defend himself, but his arms were soon a mass of wounds. The shield dropped, and Sabinus was cut to pieces.

The Roman army didn't make a habit of bestowing bravery awards posthumously. One of the rare instances on record was when Caesar buried Chief Centurion Crastinus of the 10th Legion after the Battle of Pharsalus. So it seems that Sabinus's death robbed him of the glory that precipitated it.

Of Sabinus's fellow volunteers, three were killed and eight wounded before they could even reach the top of the wall. As Jewish defenders reoccupied the wall, other legionaries dashed forward and brought the wounded men out and carried them away to the nearest field hospital behind the lines.

Two nights later, another party of volunteers—twenty legionaries and the eagle-bearer from the 5th Legion, plus two cavalrymen and a trumpeter—quietly climbed the rubble in the darkness and overpowered the Jewish sentries on duty. The legion trumpeter then blew his instrument. This signal sent panic through the other Jewish guards, who thought the entire Roman army had broken into the Antonia in the darkness, and they ran for it. In fact, the trumpet was merely the signal to summon more Roman troops waiting in the night. Titus and his officers were among those who flooded, unopposed, over the wall. The Jewish defenders withdrew to the Temple via a tunnel connecting it with the Antonia and dug by John of Gischala, presumably filling in the tunnel behind them.

The Roman army had secured the Antonia. In the end it was achieved much more easily than either side would have imagined weeks or even days earlier. The Roman success signaled the beginning of the end for the Jewish defenders. But a lot of blood was yet to be spilled. Legionaries surged through the Antonia and into the Sanctuary of the Temple. Here, warring Jewish factions combined to stand shoulder to shoulder against the invaders in the desperate hand-to-hand fighting that followed in the tight confines of the Sanctuary courtyard. From the moment the first Roman mounted the wall, the struggle lasted from the middle of the night until the afternoon of the next day.

Julianus, a centurion from Bithynia, in the north of present-day Turkey, tried to exhort the exhausted Roman troops as more and more Jews pressed forward. Single-handedly he drove the partisans back across the Temple forecourt. Then his feet went from under him, slipping on blood on the paving stones. He fell on his back with a crash of his armor. Jewish fighters sprang forward and surrounded him. Somehow, Centurion Julianus killed seven of his assailants before he was hacked to pieces. Inspired by this Pyrrhic success, the Jews rallied and drove the Romans back into the Antonia. Its walls became the new front line.

Titus ordered the fortress destroyed to create a broad entrance into the Temple from outside the First Wall. During the week that this demolition work was being carried out, Titus again sent Josephus to offer surrender terms. In tears, Josephus implored his fellow Jews to save themselves and the city. Again the resistance leaders refused.

Leading Jews, especially priests, who managed to escape the Temple and surrender were sent by Titus twelve miles north to the town of Gophna. Garrisoned by Vespasian early in the campaign, it now served as a POW camp for Jewish prisoners, with the inexperienced men of the four cohorts of the 18th Legion almost certainly acting as their guards. When partisan leader John of Gischala spread the rumor around Jerusalem that these senior prisoners had been executed by their Roman guards, hoping to dissuade others from attempting to emulate their escape, Titus got wind of it and brought the prisoners back, parading them outside the walls for all to see that they were safe and well.

Once a path had been cleared through the Antonia, Titus gave Colonel Sextus Vettulenus the task of leading a surprise night attack in force, with the goal of penetrating as far as the forecourt of the Temple. But this time the Jewish sentries weren't taken by surprise, and they summoned support as the Romans launched their assault. A bitter fight took place in the forecourt. Colonel Vettulenus and his troops charged in their maniples of up to 160 men at a time, closed up and with their shields locked together. They held the courtyard until daylight, then withdrew to the Antonia again when it was obvious they couldn't proceed any farther forward against determined and concentrated opposition.

Amid the ruins of the Antonia, Titus had his legions start constructing four more embankments so he could launch his troops into the Temple from four different assault points at once. His main target was the Sanctuary, which lay on the other side of the Court of the Gentiles, the courtyard that was as far as non-Jews had been permitted to venture in peacetime. With timber trundling up from the coast, work proceeded slowly.

Jewish raiding parties continued to slip out from behind the First Wall to create a nuisance behind the front line. One day, an hour before sunset, a large party surged up the Mount of Olives to attack the 10th Legion's camp. Taught a rude lesson by the two Jewish raids earlier in the operation, the 10th was ready this time. There was a fierce battle along the length of their fortifications, until the guard cohort of the 10th drove the attackers back down into the ravine at the foot of the mountain.

The men of the 10th were joined in the pursuit by cavalrymen. One trooper, named Pedanius, galloped after the fleeing Jews and, leaning from the saddle, grabbed a sturdy Jewish youth by the ankle as he ran, then pulled him from his feet and dragged him off, kicking and screaming. The teenage prisoner was presented to Titus. Unimpressed by his tender years, he had him executed.

After the Jews tried to burn the eastern porticos linking the Temple with the Antonia, unsuccessfully, on August 15 they tried another of their many ruses. Up to that point resistance fighters had occupied the roof of the western portico. Now they made an obvious withdrawal. Roman troops climbed up and victoriously claimed the rooftop, running along its length above the Jews in the courtyards below. Once the roof was crammed with Romans, the Jews set fire to pitch and bitumen that they'd previously packed between the rafters at one end. Some soldiers at the Antonia end managed to jump back down to their anxious comrades. Others had to jump into Jewish-held sections of the Temple to escape the flames, and were immediately killed by waiting partisans. Rather than jump, some legionaries were burned to death on the roof, or took their own lives.

On August 16, the Romans burned down the northern portico. Five days later the rams were at work again, battering the massive white marble blocks of the Sanctuary walls, trying to force a breach. On August 27, frustrated by lack of progress, Titus sent a storming party armed with scaling ladders and grappling hooks against the porticos surrounding the Sanctuary. Although they sustained heavy casualties, the Jews repelled this attack.

Next, Titus had the massive gates to the Sanctuary set alight. The silver decoration on the woodwork melted in the flames, but the huge doors remained intact. The flames spread to the adjacent porticos. They burned until the following day.

Titus now called a council of war with his senior officers: Colonel Alexander his chief of staff, General Lepidus of the 10th; General Cerialis of the 5th; General Titus Phrygius of the 15th; Colonel Fronto of the 18th/3rd Augusta detachment; and Colonel Antonius Julianus, the acting Procurator of Judea. Josephus gives no commander for the 12th Legion, so apparently it was led by its senior tribune. Later, the colonels of the legions and colonels who had been appointed procurators for the Galilee and Idumaea regions also were brought in and asked for their views. There was lengthy, perhaps heated debate about whether the massive white marble Temple, said to be one of the most handsome buildings in the ancient world, should be left standing in the final assault.

Two differing accounts of the meeting remain. Josephus says that Titus wanted to preserve the Temple and brought his officers around to his way of thinking. Josephus apparently was present at the meeting, but subsequently he would have wanted to paint Titus, now his patron, in a good light. The fourth-century Christian writer Sulpicius Severus, thought to have been quoting a now lost reference from Tacitus, wrote that Titus was all for destroying the Temple, the symbol of Jewish resistance. On one hand Titus had a reputation for being a kindly and fair man, and was well liked, but he also didn't hesitate to execute POWs, so he wasn't all sweetness and light. The Tacitus version, if accurately reported, is more likely to be correct.

Titus gave orders for the burned gate to be stormed. It gave way to ram and axes and swords before legionaries surged into the Sanctuary. The fight that followed was a stalemate, and Titus withdrew his troops beyond the Sanctuary and retired to his bed. In the night, Jews made a raid out against the Roman lines. Legionaries on guard drove their assailants back, into the Sanctuary. According to Josephus, one Roman soldier tossed a burning brand through a golden gate, which quickly started a raging fire in the Sanctuary.

Titus was summoned in time to see the Sanctuary ablaze. Josephus says that Titus issued orders for Roman troops to put out the fire, but in the noise and confusion the orders either didn't get through or, as is more likely, many legionaries actively stoked the fire, determined to see the place that had caused them so much grief for so long go up in flames. While Jews tried to fight the fire, Roman troops swept into the Sanctuary.

Titus and his bodyguard of lanky auxiliary spearmen made their way to the inner sanctum—through the Outer or Women's Court and then the Court of Israel, up a circular flight of fifteen steps to the Court of Priests and the Altar of Burned Sacrifice, through a massive arch, and up another twelve broad steps to a door of solid gold. Men of the general's bodyguard, using wooden clubs, forced the golden door.

Titus walked into the so-called Holy Place, where only the Jewish high priest had been allowed to tread. A flat ceiling soared 150 feet above. In front of him stood the Altar of Incense, the Table of Shewbread, and the symbol of Judaism, the golden Seven-Branched Candlestick, the branches representing the sun, the moon, Mercury, Venus, Mars, Jupiter, and Saturn. He walked a little farther on, through a curtained opening, into the Holy of Holies, God's abode, where even the high priest could venture only on the Day of Atonement. On the day the Temple fell, Titus found God's room to be empty.

Once before, a great Roman general had succeeded in storming the Jewish Temple of Jerusalem and stood in this place—Pompey the Great, back in 63 B.C., during his conquest of the East with legions including the 1st and the 2nd. Pompey, too, had personally entered the Temple's inner sanctum. But he had left it intact.

Now, with flames engulfing many parts of the Temple, Roman legionaries were putting any Jew who stood in their way to the sword as they removed the obvious treasures—gold, silver, and brass doors, and the implements of the Jewish religion, such as the golden candelabra—and the massive hoard of treasure hidden here by the Jews. The treasury was plundered and every nook and cranny of the massive Temple complex scoured for more loot.

With their eyes only for booty, many plundering legionaries let some refugees flee past them, unless they were carrying valuables. Other legionaries went on a killing frenzy, climbing over piles of the dead to kill more.

Blood flowed across the Temple flagstones like water. The tumult of the spreading inferno, the smoke, the heat, the crashing timbers, the yelling of excited Roman troops and their centurions barking orders, the screams of the victims, the wailing of the dying and those who feared for their lives, would have been deafening.

In the confusion, a number of resistance leaders mixed with the refugees and escaped the city, some using water viaducts to reach the Upper City. Meanwhile, the Zealots looked to the heavens, certain that the prophecies of old would be fulfilled and God would smite the heathen violators of the Temple and save the Jews. But their prayers went unanswered, their expectations were unfulfilled.

The fires didn't spread quickly enough for some legionaries, who went about lighting new blazes. On an undamaged portico clustered six thousand men, women, and children, Jewish refugees. Legionaries who still had vivid memories of comrades who'd been burned to death on one such portico as a result of Jewish duplicity torched the portico, and all six thousand perished. At the same time, priests who tried to surrender were put to death.

The Temple had finally been taken. It was August 30. But even in succeeding days, as the flames died down and the legions assembled in the ruins to sacrifice to their gods, the siege of Jerusalem was not yet over. Partisans still held Herod's Palace, and the surrounding Upper City, in western Jerusalem.

Now two resistance leaders, John of Gischala and Simon the Idumaean, asked for a peace conference. When they met Titus, on the wall of the Temple platform, Titus offered them their lives if they surrendered now, the same offer he'd made numerous times over the previous weeks and months. In turn, they offered to end their resistance if permitted to pass unmolested through the Roman lines and depart into the desert with their families. Titus was furious. "The vanquished do not dictate the terms of their own surrender," Josephus reports him saying. He abruptly terminated the talks.

As the rest of the city was put to the torch, Titus concentrated on the sector remaining in the hands of the resistance, the Upper City. The lay of the land made an assault from the west, from near the Camp of the Assyrians, the most practical. On September 8, the legions began work raising embankments against the massive white marble blocks of the eastern wall of Herod's Palace. Seventeen days later the embankments were completed.

Many partisans lost heart and slipped away, hiding in underground passageways. The remaining rebels retired to one of the three tall towers of the palace, the 135-foot Phaseal Tower, whose base still stands today, and which was Simon's headquarters. The four rams began their work on the western wall. It quickly gave way, and legionary assault troops went surging over the ruined barrier. John and Simon and their last remaining supporters planned to burn down the palace, then cut their way through the legionaries and escape. But the fire didn't spread, and the escapees were repulsed. They, too, then fled into the subterranean passageways.

The glittering standards of the legions appeared on the top of the tower. A mighty cheer rang around the valley as the Roman troops realized that the siege was over. Jerusalem was theirs. Much of what was left of the city was burned, and ninety-seven thousand prisoners were accounted for. Those identified as resistance leaders were executed. The seven hundred most handsome prisoners would adorn Titus's and Vespasian's joint triumphal procession in Rome the following year. Other able-bodied young men were sent to the mines of Egypt. The children were sold into slavery. Adults were dispatched to many provinces of the empire, to fight wild animals in the arena. A million people were said to have died in Jerusalem, from wounds inflicted by the Romans, or at the hands of their own people, or from starvation. Roman losses in the siege were never put on paper, but the dead and wounded would have run into the thousands.

The legions now assembled in a formal parade outside the ruined city, and Titus addressed them, praising them for their victory. He then presented the customary bravery awards to men of the legions who had shown outstanding courage during the campaign. Civic Crowns and golden Mural Crowns and Crowns of Valor, golden torques, miniature golden spears, and silver standards were presented, with citations for each recipient read aloud to the legions. Many legionaries received promotion as well as an additional portion of the massive booty that was to be shared by every soldier who had lived through the assault. The legions' rules of plunder were clear: Jerusalem had been taken by storm, and while some major items were reserved for the imperial treasury, most of the plunder was shared among the legionaries.

From the tribunal, Titus then announced the new assignments for the legions. The 5th and 15th were to accompany him on a triumphant progress through the region, which would lead them back to Egypt in the new year. The 5th would eventually be posted to Moesia after its A.D. 80 reenlistment, which would take place in Macedonia. The 15th was to go straight to a new station in Cappadocia. Undergoing its latest twenty-year discharge and reenlistment in the new year, the 15th Legion would leave eight hundred of its retiring veterans in Judea to settle on land grants at

Emmaus. The 12th was going north, to be based at Melitene, also in Cappadocia, not far from the Euphrates River. And the 10th was staying in Judea—from now on it was to be the resident legion in the province.

Days later, John of Gischala was discovered in his underground hiding place beneath the city. Titus spared him, sentencing him to life imprisonment. Simon ben Gioras was captured by soldiers of the 10th some days later and sent in chains to Titus, who had returned to Caesarea by this stage. Titus paraded both John and Simon at Rome in the Triumph of A.D. 71, at the end of which Simon was customarily lashed, then strangled. The commander of the third Jewish faction, Eleazar, had died while defending the Temple.

After spending several months parading his prisoners around the region and pitting them against wild beasts and each other in provincial arenas, in the new year Titus set sail from Alexandria for Rome, with Titus's father, the new emperor Vespasian, to join Titus's fractious younger brother Domitian, who was already in Rome with Field Marshal Mucianus. The former Governor of Syria had marched the 6th Victrix and the rest of his task force to Italy to join legions from Balkan bases loyal to Vespasian in overthrowing Vitellius's army and occupying Rome. Subsequently Vespasian was to appoint Titus commander of the Praetorian Guard, a post he would hold until his father's death in 79. Titus would then ascend the throne, reigning for only a little over two years before his premature death brought Domitian to power. Titus would be greatly mourned throughout the empire. But not by the Jews.

In September A.D. 70, as Titus marched away, he left a newly appointed Procurator of Judea, Colonel Terentius Rufus, in command at Jerusalem. Rufus had orders to destroy any evidence that a city had ever stood there, although Titus did spare the surviving towers of Herod's Palace. Cohorts of the 10th Legion were to occupy a base on the site of Jerusalem in addition to the existing legion base at Caesarea. As they destroyed much of the Jewish city, stone by stone, the men of the 10th recycled the building materials and used them to build a legionary fortress.

All the time they labored on construction work, the men of the 10th were on the lookout for treasure hordes hidden by the Jews during the siege. Early in A.D. 71, as Titus returned from his triumphal progress through Syria, which had taken him as far as the 6th Victrix's base at Zeugma on the Euphrates, where Parthian envoys had come to present him with golden crowns to commemorate his victory, he came back through Jerusalem on his way to Alexandria. And in Jerusalem he was amused to see the men of the 10th highly delighted with themselves. Jewish prisoners had just revealed the hiding place of a vast cache of gold, which the legion retained.

Such quantities of gold were taken from Jerusalem that when it was sold, with so much on the market, the price of gold in Syria halved overnight. Not that the surviving legionaries of the 10th would have minded. They still emerged from the siege of Jerusalem comparatively wealthy men.

But the 10th hadn't finished with fighting Jewish partisans just yet. There was a little nut to crack down by the Dead Sea that would demand their attention before long. A nut called Masada.

XXIV

MASADA

T he civil war in Europe was over. On December 21, A.D. 69, a day after the murder of Emperor Vitellius, the Senate at Rome had declared Vespasian the new emperor. Vespasian wouldn't set off for Rome from his headquarters in Alexandria until the summer of A.D. 70, but his deputy, Field Marshal Mucianus, formerly the Governor of Syria, was firmly in charge of affairs at the capital. A tight-fisted new Palatium was soon controlling the administration of the Roman army and navy, a task made difficult—and more importantly, expensive—by the fact that thirteen new legions had been raised by Nero, Galba, Otho, and Vitellius during the two years of civil war. Faced by a huge war debt racked up by his four predecessors—estimated by Vespasian himself at three times the revenue of the empire—he had to reduce the army to a manageable and affordable size. An old Latin proverb says that economy is too late at the bottom of the purse, but in this case Vespasian had no choice.

Taxation was his first remedy—taxes were as much as doubled throughout the empire. But in restoring Rome's finances to an even keel, Vespasian also was to implement a major shake-up of the army, the first since Augustus's remodeling of the Roman military a hundred years earlier. Vespasian was able to promptly merge four new legions, but apart from two units made up of seamen, noncitizens, Vespasian couldn't just abolish legions overnight—legally, legionaries were entitled to their retirement bonuses on discharge, and the funds for this simply did not exist. But, just as it been little touched by the civil war, the 10th Legion escaped the drastic measures that would see the abolition over the next decade or so of a number of long-established legions such as the 1st, 17th, and 18th as their normal reenlistments fell due.

General Lepidus left the 10th Legion following the wrapping up of the Judean offensive at the end of A.D. 70, and for a time the legion would have been commanded by its senior tribune once more. But by the spring of A.D. 71 the Palatium had sent the 10th a new commander, Brigadier

General Lucillus Bassus. Once he'd taken up his post at Jerusalem, General Bassus took the 10th campaigning in southern Judea to mop up the last isolated Jewish resistance.

After securing Hebron, the ruins of which had been occupied by refugees from Jerusalem following its fall, General Bassus's first objective was the hill fortress of Machaerus, to the east of the Dead Sea. Built one hundred and fifty years before by Alexander Janneus and remodeled by King Herod Antipas, the palace, atop a cone-shaped hill, was surrounded by a wall forty feet high into which were built four towers. It was at this palace that John the Baptist had been beheaded some forty-five years earlier to satisfy the whim of Herod's stepdaughter Salome.

In A.D. 66 a cohort of the 3rd Augusta Legion on garrison duty here had been surrounded by rebels, who agreed to let the Roman troops depart unharmed and retaining their arms if they abandoned the fortress, and the Syrian legionaries of the 3rd Augusta had marched out behind their standards and made it back to Caesarea. The Machaerus fortress had been occupied by rebels ever since, and in the wake of the fall of Jerusalem, the small Jewish garrison had been augmented by a number of resistance fighters who'd escaped the city.

Down the northern slope from the old fortified palace on the hilltop stood the walled town of Machaerus, referred to as the Lower Town, and as the 10th Legion and its auxiliary cavalry crossed the Jordan River and marched around the head of the Dead Sea toward it in the spring of 71, the Jewish residents closed the town gates and took up defensive positions.

The 10th surrounded the hill, cutting off the town and the four-thousand-square-yard fortress above it, preparing for a lengthy siege. In their usual fashion, the Jews sent raiding parties out to harass the legionaries as they dug the trenches and threw up the walls of a two-mile circumvallation, with the raiders always returning to their hilltop refuge. But on one such raid a handsome and confident young partisan named Eleazar lingered outside the wall, chatting with his friends on the ramparts. As he did, a legionary named Rufus of the 10th crept up and grabbed him, then dragged him back to the Roman lines.

The Jewish defenders were mortified by the capture of young Eleazar, and even more so when General Bassus had him tied to a cross in front of the walls for a long, lingering death. Eleazar begged his comrades to surrender so that he didn't have to die. Amazingly, the defenders of the fortress agreed to give up the fortress to save his life, if General Bassus let them go unharmed, and marched out. Bassus kept his word and let them all go, Eleazar included.

Meanwhile, the people of the Lower Town continued to defy the Romans, and the siege continued, with the legion starting work on a ramp to the northwest of the town. Then one night the townspeople tried to creep by the 10th Legion sentries in the darkness, in a mass exodus. Perhaps they were betrayed, because apparently the legionaries were waiting for them. Seventeen hundred were intercepted and put to the sword. Little more than a hundred townspeople managed to escape in the night. The men of the 10th then surged into the town, looted it, and put it to the torch.

Leaving Machaerus a smoking ruin the next day, the 10th Legion went looking for more resistance fighters. Their search led them to the Forest of Jardes, on the western side of the Dead Sea. There, Jude ben Ari, one of the resistance leaders who'd escaped from Jerusalem via the city's underground passageways, was holed up with three thousand supporters—fellow escapees from Jerusalem and refugees from Machaerus. General Bassus surrounded the forest with his cavalry, then sent in the 10th Legion. All three thousand Jews hiding in the forest were tracked down and killed.

At this point General Bassus died, apparently from natural causes, and the 10th Legion's campaign was stalled as it waited for a new commanding general. The legion returned to its fortress at Jerusalem, and doesn't appear to have received its new commander, Brigadier General Flavius Silva, until well into A.D. 72, or even the following year.

A motion picture made in the 1970s about the siege of Masada starred British actor Peter O'Toole, portraying Silva as a man in his fifties or sixties. We know that, typically, legion commanders were men in their early thirties. There is no mention of Silva prior to this appointment in any of the histories, but he went on to become consul eight years after he took command of the 10th Legion. At about the same time, Julius Agricola, father-in-law of the historian Tacitus, was made commander of the 20th Valeria Victrix Legion in Britain at age thirty, and he would also go on to become a consul within eight years, at thirty-eight, only three or four years before Silva. So it's likely that Silva was only thirty or so when he came to the *praetorium* of the 10th, after being promoted from the position of second-in-command of another legion, the usual route to legion command. It's unlikely he'd been second-in-command of the 10th prior to this—the Palatium made a habit of bringing in new blood when legion commanders were appointed.

In the spring of A.D. 73, General Silva resumed military operations in southern Judea. Only one Jewish center of resistance remained, at Masada. In March, with General Silva at their head, the men of the 10th Legion tramped out of Jerusalem and headed south for the Dead Sea, just a day's march away.

Masada is a table-topped mountain of golden-brown rock that rises 1,700 feet above the level of the Dead Sea, 1½ miles from its western shore. On the oval-shaped summit, 650 feet by 190 feet, King Herod the Great had built a palace in the grounds of an earlier fortress. In the spring of A.D. 73, the fortress was occupied by 960 Zealots under the leadership of Eleazar ben Jair. Another of the Jewish commanders was one of the partisan officers involved in the defense of Jerusalem, the Zealot Jude. He had escaped to Masada after the capture of the city, and joined his colleagues in preparing for a long stay.

King Herod had maintained Masada as a place he could retreat to in times of emergency. There was always the possibility that his own people might rise up against him, and he had also known that Queen Cleopatra of Egypt had an eye on his kingdom. Only his firm friendship with Mark Antony had kept him on his throne. Apart from the comfortable palace Herod built at the western end of the summit, he also kept a vast arsenal at Masada. When the Zealots seized the fortress they found a stockpile of weapons, enough to equip an army of ten thousand men, as well as iron, bronze, and lead for the manufacture of weapons and ammunition. The storehouses on the eighteen-acre summit were filled with grain, oil, dates, and wine, while the fertile summit gardens could grow fresh food, and conduits hollowed out of the limestone caught and conducted rainwater to vast underground water reservoirs with a capacity of more than two hundred thousand gallons.

When General Silva and the 10th arrived opposite the giant limestone crag of Masada— its name means "mountain fastness"—the Zealots had already occupied the mountaintop redoubt for seven years since the day they'd massacred the 3rd Augusta cohort stationed there back in A.D. 66, at the start of the revolt. Silva immediately set the 10th Legion to work building camps to the west of the mountain.

Eight camps were created—traces of their walls and streets can still be seen today—with an estimated fifteen thousand legionaries, auxiliaries, camp followers, and enslaved Jewish prisoners involved. General Silva also had a wall of circumvallation built right around Masada. More than two miles long and intersected by forts and towers, it was some ten feet high. Like the camps, it's still there today, although half its height has collapsed over the centuries.

The Romans had to bring in all their food and water supplies to the site from many miles away, and General Silva used Jewish prisoners for this labor. But the construction work that lay ahead was reserved for the men of the 10th Legion. Not even auxiliaries were involved in building work where the legions were involved. Legionaries had the necessary skills, and they could be trusted. Besides, Romans had long felt that tough work made tough men.

There were only two ways to reach the summit of Masada. A path on the eastern side, called the Snake Path, ran for almost four miles up the side of the mountain, a path so narrow that anyone using it had to put one foot in front of the other. A path on the western side was guarded by a fort fifteen hundred feet from the crest.

Four hundred fifty feet below the top of Masada to the west, and separated from it by a rocky valley, was a promontory called White Cliff. From this point, Silva decided, a single ramp would be built up to the summit of the mountain. Giving his chief engineering officer instructions to undertake the massive operation, he watched the earth-moving work proceed for weeks.

Day by day, the ramp crept over the gulf between White Cliff and Masada and up the mountainside. At a gradient of 1 in 3, and 695 feet wide at its base, it eventually rose 300 feet. On top, a pier of fitted stone 75 feet high and 75 feet across was erected. A wooden siege tower 90 feet tall was built and rolled up the ramp, then lodged against the wall of the fortress. While artillerymen on several levels of the tower maintained a constant fire with Scorpions and *Ballistas*, keeping the nearby ramparts cleared of Jewish defenders, down below, a battering ram pounded away at the base of the stone wall.

In time the wall gave way, and men of the 10th Legion poured through the breach. They found that the Zealots had built a second, inner wall. When the Roman rams were brought up against this and their first blows loosened the earth covering, it was revealed that this second wall had been built using timber balks laid lengthways, alternating with layers of stone. As Julius Caesar had discovered in Gaul a century before when he and the 10th Legion were besieging Gallic fortresses, battering rams have no effect on walls built with wooden cross members. The timber absorbed the blows of the ram.

On the afternoon of May 2, General Silva called off the battering ram crews and sent in men armed with flaming torches. The wall was soon burning well. A strong wind then sprang up, at first blowing the fire into the faces of the Romans, before it changed direction and blew the other way, fanning the flames. Leaving a strong guard at the burning wall to ensure that none of the Jews on the summit escaped in the night, Silva gave orders for preparations to be made for an all-out assault through the burned wall next morning, then went to his bed.

The Zealots of Masada could see the writing on the burning wall. They knew that next day the final Roman assault would take place. That night the men agreed that rather than fall into the hands of the Romans, they would prefer to die. They went to their wives and children and cut their throats. Then they submitted their own throats to their comrades. Once the fighting men had been dispatched, ten Zealots, including Eleazar ben Jair, remained. They burned all their possessions, scrawled their names on pieces of broken pottery, and drew lots to see which of them would kill the others. In the end, one man remained. After setting fire to the palace, he fell on his sword beside his dead family.

At dawn on May 3, the Spanish legionaries of the 10th came storming through the ruined second wall, ready for anything—except, perhaps, for the desolate silence that greeted them. They shouted for the Jews to come out. In answer, an old woman emerged, followed by a younger woman, a relative of Eleazar, with five small children. While all the killing had been going on, these women and children had hidden in one of the underground water conduits.

Combing through the buildings on the summit, the legionaries found the bodies of the dead, and they praised the nobility of the Zealots' end. It was also the end of the First Jewish Revolt. After Masada, there were no more partisans left to fight.

In the second half of the twentieth century, following the creation of the modern state of Israel, new recruits into the Israeli Army were required to vow that, as long as they lived, Masada would never fall again.

The ramp built by the 10th Legion in A.D. 73 still runs from White Cliff to Masada today. An earthquake in 1927 caused it drop some 30 feet from its original height, but it otherwise remains much as the legion constructed it.

While he marched back to Jerusalem with most of the legion in mid-May of A.D. 73, General Silva delegated a detachment of the 10th to clean up Masada and repair its defenses, then set up quarters for themselves in the fortress. A detachment from the 10th, probably of cohort strength, continued to occupy Masada until A.D. 111.

The 10th Legion underwent its latest reenlistment in A.D. 104, during the early years of the reign of the Spanish-born soldier-emperor Trajan, son of the 10th's commander back in the early stages of the Jewish Revolt. It appears that for the first time in its history, the legion now took in new recruits from a recruiting ground other than Spain. Trajan was in the middle of his Dacian Wars at this time, and had recently raised four new legions, one or more of them possibly in Spain. Increasingly during the second century, reenlistments took place in the regions where legions were stationed, and it appears that the 10th's new recruits for A.D. 104 came from the provinces of Bithynia-Pontus, in northern Turkey. The second-enlistment senior cohorts would continue to be made up of Spaniards for the next twenty years, and some third-enlistment men would have stayed on in A.D. 124, But by A.D. 144 not a single Spaniard would have marched in the ranks of the 10th Legion.

XXV

LAST DAYS

I n A.D. 132, a new rebellion exploded across Judea. The Second Jewish Revolt took the Roman authorities completely by surprise. The uprising had two catalysts. Emperor Hadrian, Trajan's cousin and successor, had issued an edict declaring castration and circumcision capital crimes. At the same time, he ordered that a temple to Jupiter be built on the site of the old Jewish Temple in Jerusalem. Both acts incensed the Jews, who once more flourished in Judea.

A new Jewish leader, Simon bar Kochba, considered the Messiah by some Jews, skillfully organized his followers into guerrilla bands, and for three and a half years he ran the Roman military ragged. The men of the 10th Legion, mostly twenty-eight-year-old soldiers from northern Turkey at the outset who had seen no action in all their eight years with the legion, seem to have been surprised in their garrisons and ambushed on the march during the early stages of the revolt, sustaining heavy losses.

The 10th Legion seems fated to have suffered in Judea. The 10th had been the legion trapped at Jerusalem in 4 B.C. by the riots following the death of Herod, it had taken countless casualties in the A.D. 67–70 offensive, and now it was being stung by Jewish partisans yet again.

After the initial bloody uprising, the then Procurator of Judea, Tinnius Rufus, desperately sent to his superior at Antioch, the Governor of Syria, for reinforcements. But even the legions that came marching down into Judea in A.D. 132–133—probably the 4th Scythica, which didn't gain its title until about A.D. 179, and the 16th Flavia—struggled against the hit-and-run tactics. More reinforcements had to be brought in, including the 6th Ferrata Legion, the "Ironclads."

Issuing coins bearing his name and styling himself "Prince of Israel," Simon bar Kochba continued to send his bands darting from their secret strongholds to ravage the countryside before they melted away again. Unprotected Gentile communities such as that peopled by the descendants of the 15th Legion veterans who had settled at Emmaus in A.D. 71 were savaged mercilessly.

So serious was the situation considered by Rome that the Palatium dispatched Lieutenant General Julius Severus from Britain, where he was governor, to head the Roman forces fighting the rebels in Judea. General Severus eventually wiped out the guerrilla bands by fighting fire with fire—he broke up his legions and cavalry wings into scores of small, mobile units commanded by tribunes and centurions, rapid-reaction groups that could respond quickly whenever reports of guerrilla activities in their locality came in.

Many of the rebel strongholds had been ingeniously built underground, making them almost impossible to locate. But gradually, one by one, the legions did track them down and destroy them—50 of the most important hideouts were obliterated, according to Cassius Dio, who also writes that 985 Jewish villages were destroyed in the campaign, and 580,000 Jews killed by the sword, with many more dying from starvation. The war was brought to an end in A.D. 135 when General Severus finally cornered and captured Simon bar Kochba himself in his last stronghold, at Bether, near Jerusalem.

This Second Jewish Revolt devastated the province. And it sealed the fate of Jews in Judea. Following the termination of the revolt, Jews were banned from Jerusalem, and before long from all of Judea. It would take them eighteen hundred years to return.

The 10th Legion seems to have suffered badly during the revolt, as did many of the units involved in the forty-two-month war, which resulted in so many Roman casualties that Emperor Hadrian omitted the customary "I and the legions are well" at the commencement of his A.D. 135 letter to the Senate in which he advised that the revolt had finally been put down.

After the revolt, the Palatium increased the strength of the Judea station to two legions, based permanently in the province to police the strict laws that from that time forward prevented Jews from even clapping eyes on what used to be Jerusalem. The city was renamed Aelia Capitolina after 135, in honor of Hadrian—Aelius was his family name—and the principal Roman god, Jupiter. In another step designed to eliminate all reminders of the Jewish era, the province's name was also now changed, to Syria Palaestina—Palestinian Syria. But the name of Judea would continue to be used colloquially for Palestine and would reassert itself over time.

The Palatium had a tendency to relocate any legion that took heavy casualties in its theater of operations, and, apparently, because its strength had been so reduced by the revolt, the 10th Legion was now withdrawn to

Caesarea, the provincial capital, on the coast, and the 6th Ferrata Legion took over its quarters at Aelia Capitolina. From A.D. 89, following a decree of the emperor Domitian in the wake of the Saturninus Revolt on the Rhine, no two legions could share the same base, anywhere in the empire. As a consequence, separate bases in Judea for the 10th and the 6th Ferrata were the norm.

The 6th Ferrata, a unit raised by Galba in Spain in A.D. 68 during the early stages of the civil war that brought Vespasian to power, soon undertook a number of construction projects on orders from Rome, including the rebuilding of the legionary fortress at Jerusalem. Over the gates they installed the motif of a boar, believed to be the 6th Ferrata Legion's emblem, and a symbol considered very powerful by the Spanish legionaries' Celtic ancestors. The legionaries also built the planned temple to Jupiter on the site of the Jewish Temple, and constructed another Roman temple at Golgotha outside the city, over the site where the annoying Christian sect claimed that its founder, Jesus Christus, had been crucified in the reign of Tiberius.

The 10th Legion and the 6th Ferrata Legion were still based in Judea in A.D. 233. To the south, another legion was stationed in Egypt, one in Arabia, two in Mesopotamia. To the north, there was a single legion in Phoenicia, two in Syria, and two in Cappadocia.

By the fifth century, Syria would be divided into five provinces, of which Palestine was one, administered from Constantinople, the former Byzantium, as a part of the Byzantine Empire, the eastern remnant of the Roman Empire. In the West, Rome had by then fallen to the barbarians.

Of necessity, with their old recruiting grounds in foreign hands, recruits for the legions in the East were raised locally as a matter of course, although that process had, as was the case with 10th, already begun as early as the second century. From the third century, "Caesar's finest," the 10th Legion, like all the legions in the Syrian provinces, if it still existed in its old form, occupied the line of forts along the Euphrates, the *limes*. The concept of the legions as totally self-contained mobile forces had given way to a Byzantine strategy of defending the frontier from static fortifications, in an attempt to counter masses of heavily armored mounted raiders from the East. Fifteen centuries later, similar monuments in concrete and stone, such as the Maginot Line, would prove even less effective against mobile armor.

Five new legions, the Palatine Legions, of just fifteen hundred men each, were created in the fourth century by the Byzantine emperor Constantine the Great, as rapid reaction forces, and for a time they proved successful in that role. But before the fourth century was out one of Constantine's successors, Valens, led his Palatine legions to their destruction. His crushing defeat by the Germanic Visigoths at Adrianople in Turkey in A.D. 378, in which forty thousand of Valens's troops are said to have died, well and truly signaled the end of the golden age of the legions.

By the seventh century, Syria and the Middle East generally were in the hands of Muslim invaders. The latest invasion had begun in 633–634. Damascus fell the following year, and an attempt in 636 to regain Syria by the Byzantine emperor Heraclius ended in defeat at the Battle of the Yarmuk River in Turkey, in the vicinity of Julius Caesar's great 47 B.C. victory at Zela. Like Caesar, the Muslim invaders came, saw, and conquered. And in the process, the 10th Legion, in whatever form as a border guard unit it had survived to this point, would have been obliterated by the invaders.

Such was the fate of the legion of proud, determined Centurion Gaius Crastinus. The legion Julius Caesar trusted with his fate, and his life, more than once. The legion Pompey the Great recognized at his opponent's stoutest. The legion that rediscovered its grit under Corbulo's tough tutelage and that shed its blood under the walls of Jefat and Jerusalem for Vespasian and Titus.

Many legions were granted official titles over the years in recognition of their courage and their loyalty. The original 6th became the Conqueror, the 12th the Thunderer, the 20th the Powerful Conqueror, while, for the same reasons, others were bestowed with the names of emperors—the 2nd, 3rd, and 8th Augustans, the 7th and 11th Claudians, the 4th and 16th Flavians. Others had titles that celebrated where they had been raised, or where they achieved a great victory, such as the 5th Macedonica and the 9th Hispana. The 10th Legion didn't need an official title. Everyone knew the "world-famous" 10th, knew where it had been, what it had done, what it was capable of. With its glory days lasting perhaps 135 years from the day Julius Caesar founded it in 61 B.C., it would always be remembered as Caesar's finest. And Rome's best.

APPENDIX A

THE LEGIONS OF ROME,
30 B.C.–A.D. 233

A. The Augustan Legions

According to Cassius Dio, legions marked with an asterisk were still in existence in A.D. 233.

1st Legion: Founded by Pompey the Great in 84 B.C. Believed to have been disbanded by the emperor Vespasian in A.D. 74.

2nd Augusta Legion: Founded by Pompey the Great in 84 B.C. Granted "Augusta" title, meaning "Augustus's," by the emperor Augustus circa 25 B.C.*

3rd Augusta Legion: Founded by Pompey the Great in 65 B.C. Granted "Augusta" title by the emperor Augustus circa 25 B.C.*

4th Macedonica Legion, later *4th Scythica Legion:* Founded by Pompey the Great in 65 B.C. Took title "Macedonica" circa 33 B.C., when its recruitment was transferred from Spain to Macedonia. Believed to have been granted "Scythica" title by the emperor Marcus Aurelius in A.D. 179 for victory over a Scythian tribe, the Cotini.*

5th Legion, later *5th Macedonica Legion:* Founded by Pompey the Great in Spain in 65 B.C. Recruited in Moesia in A.D. 60. Believed to have been renamed "Macedonica" in A.D. 80, when the legion's recruitment was transferred from Moesia to Macedonia.*

6th Victrix Legion: Founded by Pompey the Great in 65 B.C. Granted "Victrix" title, meaning "Conqueror," circa 25 B.C. by the emperor Augustus.*

7th Claudia Pia Fidelis Legion: Founded by Pompey the Great in 65 B.C. Granted "Claudia Pia Fidelis" title, meaning "Claudius's Loyal and Patriotic," following the Scribonianus Revolt, by the emperor Claudius in A.D. 42. The "Pia Fidelis" soon fell into disuse.*

8th Augusta Legion: Founded by Pompey the Great in 65 B.C. Granted "Augusta" title by the emperor Augustus circa 25 B.C.*

9th Hispana Legion: Founded by Pompey the Great in 65 B.C. Granted "Hispana" title, meaning "Spain's," by the emperor Augustus circa 25 B.C. Apparently wiped out by the Dacians in A.D. 86 and never re-formed.

10th Legion: Founded by Julius Caesar in 61 B.C.*

11th Claudia Pia Fidelis Legion: Founded by Julius Caesar in 58 B.C. Granted "Claudia Pia Fidelis" title along with the 7th by the emperor Claudius in A.D. 42. The "Pia Fidelis" soon fell into disuse.*

12th Fulminata Legion: Founded by Julius Caesar in 58 B.C. Granted "Fulminata" title, meaning "Thunder," by the emperor Marcus Aurelius in A.D. 174 for a victory in a thunderstorm against Germanic tribes.*

13th Gemina Legion: Founded by Julius Caesar in 58 B.C. Granted "Gemina" title, meaning "Twin," by the emperor Augustus in 31–30 B.C., after combination with another legion—any one of twenty-eight civil war legions abolished at this time.*

14th Gemina Martia Victrix Legion: Founded by Julius Caesar in 58 B.C. Believed to have been granted "Gemina Martia" title after combination with the Martia Legion in 31–30 B.C. and granted additional "Victrix" title by Augustus circa 25 B.C. By A.D. 233 the "Martia" and "Victrix" titles had fallen into disuse.

15th Legion: Founded by Julius Caesar in 54 B.C.*

16th Flavia Legion: Founded by Julius Caesar in 54 B.C. Believed to have been granted "Flavia" title by the emperor Domitian in A.D. 89 along with the 4th Flavia as a reward following the Saturninus Revolt.*

17th Legion: Founded by Julius Caesar in 49 B.C. Believed disbanded by the emperor Domitian in A.D. 87 as part of the long-term demobilization program set in train by his father, Vespasian.

18th Legion: As for the 17th Legion.

19th Legion: Founded by Julius Caesar in 49 B.C. Wiped out by Germans under Arminius (Hermann) in Teutoburg Forest in A.D. 9; never re-formed.

20th Valeria Victrix Legion: (A.) 20th founded by Julius Caesar in 49 B.C. (B.) Valeria (meaning "Powerful"), founded by Pompey in 84 B.C., was given vacant 20th number by the the emperor Augustus in 31–30 B.C. Augustus granted the legion the "Victrix" title circa 25 B.C.*

21st Rapax Legion: (A.) 21st founded by Julius Caesar in 49 B.C. (B.) Indications are that the Rapax (meaning "Rapacious") was founded for Pompey in the same year and originally called the Indigena, the "Native" or "Home-Grown" Legion. Given vacant 21st number by the emperor Augustus in 31–30 B.C. The 21st Rapax was apparently wiped out by Dacians in A.D. 86; never re-formed.

22nd Deiotariana Legion, later *22nd Primigeneia Legion:* The 22nd Deiotariana Legion was formed by Julius Caesar in 47 B.C. from remnants of two legions of King Deiotarus of Galatia. Renamed "Primigeneia" by the emperor Claudius in A.D. 41–54, probably in relation to the goddess Fortune, a leading military deity.*

23rd Legion: Founded by Julius Caesar in 49 B.C. Apparently abolished by the emperor Titus in A.D. 80 as part of a long-term demobilization program established by his father, Vespasian.

24th Legion: As for the 23rd Legion.

25th Legion: Founded by Julius Caesar in 49 B.C. Believed to be one of three legions wiped out by Germans in Teutoburg Forest in A.D. 9; never reformed.

26th Legion: As for the 25th Legion.

27th Legion: Founded by Julius Caesar in 49 B.C. Apparently abolished by the emperor Titus in A.D. 80 as part of Vespasian's long-term demobilization program.

28th Legion: As for the 27th Legion.

B. Post-Augustan Legions

In order of creation. According to Cassius Dio, legions marked with an asterisk were still in existence in A.D. 233.

1st Italica Legion: Founded by the emperor Nero in A.D. 66–67, for his planned but never executed invasion of Parthia. Took its name as the first legion recruited in Italy south of the Po River in almost 120 years.*

1st Legion of the Fleet: Recruited by the emperor Nero from sailors of the Roman navy in A.D. 68. Saw action in A.D. 69. Abolished by the emperor Vespasian in A.D. 70.

1st Adiutrix Legion: Believed to have been raised by the province of Gallia Narbonensis for the emperor Galba in A.D. 68, as a "supporter" of, or "assistant" to, the 1st Italica Legion, then stationed nearby.*

4th Flavia Legion: Founded by Emperor Galba in A.D. 68. Believed to have been granted Flavia title, his family name, by the emperor Domitian in A.D. 89 along with the 16th Legion, as a reward following the Saturninus Revolt.*

Second 5th Legion: Founded by the emperor Galba in A.D. 68. Folded into Galba's 7th or the second 10th to form the 7th Gemina Legion or the 10th Gemina Legion by the emperor Vespasian in A.D. 70.

6th Ferrata Legion: Founded by the emperor Galba in A.D. 68. The origin of its title, which means "Ironclad," and when granted, is uncertain, but almost certainly related to the armor of its legionaries—with new-style segmented armor then coming into use, it may have been the first legion fully outfitted in this manner. Otherwise it probably gained its title during the Dacian Wars, although there is no historical record of this.*

7th Gemina Legion: Originally a second 7th, founded by the emperor Galba in the Spanish recruiting grounds of the original 7th in A.D. 68 and called for a time Galba's 7th. Combined with the second 5th or the second 15th Legion in A.D. 70, when it took "Gemina" title.*

10th Gemina Legion: Originally a second 10th, formed as for the 7th Gemina Legion.*

Second 15th Legion: The same history as the second 5th Legion.

2nd Adiutrix Legion: Believed to have been raised by the province of Gallia Narbonensis for the emperor Vitellius in A.D. 69 as a "supporter" of, or "assistant" to, the 2nd Augusta Legion, which was normally recruited in the province at that time.*

2nd Legion of the Fleet: Recruited by the emperor Vitellius from sailors of the Roman navy in A.D. 69. Surrendered without a fight to forces of Vespasian, who abolished it in A.D. 70.

3rd Cyrenaica Legion: Believed to have been recruited in Cyrenaica, North Africa, in A.D. 67 by the province's governor, but not commissioned until A.D. 69 by the emperor Vitellius.*

3rd Gallica Legion: Believed to have been recruited in Gaul in A.D. 69 by the emperor Vitellius and commissioned by the emperor Vespasian the following year.*

1st Minervia Legion: Founded by the emperor Domitian, circa A.D. 86. Named after his patron deity, the war goddess Minerva.*

1st Traiana Legion: Raised by the emperor Trajan, apparently in A.D. 100 for his Dacian Wars, and named after him. Believed abolished by the emperor Hadrian in A.D. 120.

2nd Traiana Legion: Raised by the emperor Trajan, apparently in A.D. 100 for his Dacian Wars, and named after him.*

29th Ulpia Legion: Raised by the emperor Trajan, apparently in A.D. 100 for his Dacian Wars, and given his family name. Believed abolished by the emperor Hadrian in A.D. 120.

30th Ulpia Legion: Raised by the emperor Trajan, apparently in A.D. 100 for his Dacian Wars, and given his family name.*

2nd Italica Legion: Raised in Italy by the emperor Marcus Aurelius between A.D. 161 and 180, for his Germanic Wars.*

3rd Italica Legion: Same history as the 2nd Italica Legion.*

1st Parthicae Legion: Founded by the emperor Severus Alexander in A.D. 231–232, for his invasion of Parthia.*

2nd Parthicae Legion: As for the 1st Parthicae Legion.*

3rd Parthicae Legion: As for the 1st Parthicae Legion.*

APPENDIX B

THE REENLISTMENT FACTOR

Unlike present-day armies, which have intakes of recruits on an ongoing basis, from republican times the men of the Roman legions were all recruited into their units at the same time, in mass intakes. It was exceptionally rare for replacements to be brought into a legion during the course of an enlistment, unless, as in the case of the 14th Legion in 54 B.C., it was to replace an enlistment that had been completely wiped out in battle. Sometimes, by the end of an enlistment period, particularly if the legion had suffered heavy casualties during its sixteen- or twenty-year enlistment, a legion could be significantly understrength.

The recruiting of auxiliary units was much more haphazard, as auxiliaries were not Roman citizens and did not have the protection of Roman contract law like legion recruits, who signed a binding contract with the state on enrolling with their legion. New auxiliary units were frequently recruited as and when required, with the new units put at the disposal of the legions, particularly those legions that were understrength, to serve alongside them in particular conflicts as support units.

The Augustan legions were all originally founded by Pompey and Caesar, but not at the same time—their foundation went back to 84 B.C. for the 1st Legion and the 2nd Augusta Legion, through to 49 B.C. for the last of the original twenty-eight legions. As a result, reenlistment years varied, legion by legion. Down through the ages there were years when no legions underwent reenlistment, and years when several reenlisted at the same time because they had been founded in the same year. For example, the 6th, 7th, 8th, and 9th Legions were all founded in Spain in 65 B.C., and subsequently would have always reenlisted in the same year down through the centuries.

Until the time of Augustus, legionaries served for sixteen years. During his reign, the legions moved to twenty-year enlistments. By knowing the year in which each legion discharged its veterans and enrolled a new enlistment of legionaries, it is possible to garner a great deal of information about each unit.

It is not difficult to determine the establishment and reenlistment dates of just about every legion and of the Praetorian Guard, from data in historical texts. This information allows us to pinpoint legion movements and locations. For example, by using the reenlistment factor, it becomes clear that legions were frequently transferred to new assignments at the end of their enlistment periods, so that new recruits started fresh at the new post.

On discharge, legionaries were often set up in military colonies in the province where they were serving. These military colonies frequently grew into major cities, such as Cologne in Germany, Colchester in Britain, and Beirut in Lebanon. By correlating the date a colony was established with the date of legion discharges and reenlistments, we can identify the legion that provided the veterans for each settlement. This allows us to know for example, that the first legionary settlers of Cologne were from Switzerland, that the settlement at Colchester was made by ex-soldiers from northeastern Italy, and that Spaniards from the Córdoba area originally settled Beirut. By reversing this process, we can confirm that a particular legion was serving in a particular province at a particular time.

By correlating the reenlistment factor with changes of provincial governors, we can see that new gubernatorial appointments frequently took place at the time of the reenlistment of legions based in their provinces. This may have been coincidental, or deliberate policy of the Palatium.

It also seems that new intakes were usually recruited several months in advance of the discharge date of the veterans they were replacing, to allow time for the recruits to march from the recruitment ground to the legion's station and undergo basic training before the veterans retired from the legion. Sometimes legions were left understrength when veterans were discharged on the due date, ahead of the arrival of the new intake of recruits. For example, the latest enlistment of the 20th Valeria Victrix Legion apparently hadn't arrived in Britain after its veterans had been discharged in A.D. 60, and this may have led to the Boudicca Revolt taking place when it did. Boudicca also would have known that the 9th Hispana Legion had only just received a new intake of green recruits from Spain, youngsters who were soon annihilated.

A study of the reenlistment dates of the legions also tells us that the changeover from sixteen-year enlistments to twenty-year enlistments was phased in by Augustus between 6 B.C. and A.D. 11, as each individual legion's latest reenlistment fell due.

By knowing that a particular legion reenlisted in a particular year, we open a whole new door to our understanding of the legions. When the 12th Legion performed so badly against the Jewish partisans in Judea in A.D. 66, losing its eagle and taking heavy casualties, it had much to do with the fact that the legion was due for reenlistment in the new year and its youngest legionaries were thirty-nine years of age while its senior cohorts were manned by men no younger than fifty-nine, all thinking about their looming retirement and neither mentally nor physically equipped for the serious fighting they would encounter—the last men an astute commander would choose as the main element of his combat force.

By using the reenlistment factor, we can determine that the recruits snared by Piso at Celenderis in A.D. 19 after the assassination of Germanicus Caesar were

Greek or Spanish youths bound for the 4th Macedonica or 6th Victrix Legions in Syria, which were both due for reenlistment in the new year.

The reenlistment factor even allows us to calculate the ages of many legionaries in any given year, because all new recruits were a minimum of twenty years of age on entry into the imperial legions. If a legion underwent its latest reenlistment three years ago, say, then this year many of its legionaries would be twenty-three, some would be forty-three, and one or two would even be sixty-three. The ages of centurions are less easy to calculate, because they moved around among the legions as they were promoted, and the legion they started with might well have a different reenlistment date to that of their current legion.

The reenlistment factor allows us to determine that the four 12th Legion legionaries who carried out the crucifixion of Jesus Christ were quite possibly forty-one-year-olds who'd recently commenced a second enlistment with their legion—the senior 2nd or 3rd Cohorts would have been posted to troublesome Jerusalem; besides, second-enlistment men would have earned the perks that went with carrying out executions—and that the men of the 3rd Augusta Legion who escorted St. Paul to Rome in A.D. 60–61 were probably raw recruits who'd just joined the legion.

Thanks to Roman efficiency and consistency, we are able to use the reenlistment factor in furthering our knowledge and understanding of the Roman Empire and its legions.

APPENDIX C

THE UNIQUENESS OF THE LEGION COMMANDS IN EGYPT AND JUDEA

During his reign, and following the example set by Julius Caesar, Augustus appointed officials of Equestrian Order rank to govern Egypt and decreed that no Roman of senatorial rank could even enter the province of Egypt, at any time, for any reason, without the emperor's specific permission. This was because Egypt was at the time considered the breadbasket of the empire. Between them, Egypt and the province of Africa produced almost all Rome's grain. He who controlled the grain supply could control Rome, and to ensure that no senator ever even thought about challenging the emperor by taking the revolutionary road via Egypt, it was off-limits.

Germanicus Caesar, heir to Tiberius's throne, caused uproar when he went to Egypt as a tourist in A.D. 19. If a senator trod the sands of Egypt, as Vespasian did in A.D. 69, it was seen as a deliberate contravention of the law, the first step on the quest to empire. For this reason, at least until the third century—Cassius Dio refers to Egypt still being governed by a prefect in A.D. 218—and probably much later, the governor of Egypt was always a prefect, an officer of Equestrian rank, never of consular rank, as in other important provinces. He was also paid as much as a top proconsul, to maintain his loyalty and his incorruptibility.

Yet there were always legions in Egypt—three during the early part of the reign of Augustus, two throughout the first century, one by the third century. Imperial legions were ordinarily commanded by legates, officers of senatorial rank. If legates had commanded legions in Egypt, their presence would have contravened the law of Augustus.

We know that the Prefect of Egypt issued orders to the legions in the province, just as Tiberius Alexander called the legions in Egypt together on July 1, A.D. 69, and required them to swear allegiance to Vespasian as their new emperor. Vespasian sent his son Titus, then only a prefect, a colonel, to Egypt to bring the 15th Legion to Caesarea so it could take part in the A.D. 67 Judean offensive, and in doing so didn't contravene the law.

Tacitus confirms that from the time of Augustus, Rome's armed forces in Egypt were always commanded by knights of the Equestrian Order—colonels. So

277

a unique but simple solution was arrived at to solve the Egyptian dilemma. As the emperor Claudius was to tell the Senate on one occasion, all things are precedents at one time. A precedent was set regarding the command of the legions in Egypt. In deference to the Augustan law, legions stationed in Egypt were commanded by their second-in-command, a senior tribune, an officer of Equestrian rank, and these officers were subordinate to the Prefect of Egypt, who outranked them in terms of Equestrian Order seniority.

Once a legion left Egypt, a legate took command again. When a legion passed through Egypt, marching to an adjoining province, the legate commanding it would have traveled by sea to join it, never setting foot in Egypt.

A similar situation existed regarding the garrison in Judea. One or two writers have in the past put forward the theory that no legion could have been stationed in Judea prior to A.D. 70, and the province could only have been garrisoned by auxiliaries, because the governor of the province was merely a procurator, and the general, or legate, commanding a legion in his province would have outranked him, an unacceptable situation.

As it happens, the administrator of Judea until the reign of Claudius was not a procurator at all, but a prefect. Pontius Pilatus, celebrated famously in countless books, films, and television programs as Pilate, the Procurator of Judea, similarly held the appointment as *Prefect* of Judea, not Procurator, a fact confirmed by an inscription relating to Pilate found at Caesarea in 1961. And in the same way that the Prefect of Egypt could command legions stationed in his province because they were led by their senior tribunes, so the Prefect of Judea, and later the Procurator, once the status of the administrator changed after A.D. 44, could command legionary forces in his province.

There is ample evidence that legions were stationed in Judea during this period. Varus, Governor of Syria, stationed a legion, the 10th, in Jerusalem in 4 B.C. The Jewish historian Josephus several times writes of the "legionaries" of the Judea garrison in the years leading up to the First Jewish Revolt of A.D. 66–70, and provides plenty of clues about the identity of the legion stationed in the province between A.D. 48 and 66—"the Augustans," "the Syrians," "the men from Beirut"—for us to know that it was the 3rd Augusta, a Syrian legion with a major recruitment station at Beirut, a military colony founded by veterans of the 10th Legion. The fact that elements of the 3rd Augusta Legion were stationed at Jerusalem and Caesarea is confirmed by the Christian Bible, which talks of men of the "Augustan" legion saving and escorting St. Paul the Apostle in A.D. 58–61—there were three "Augustan" legions, and the 2nd Augusta and the 8th Augusta were never stationed in the East, but the 3rd Augusta was. Indications are that the legion stationed in Judea between A.D. 6 and 48 was the 12th.

There is never a mention of a general commanding the legion stationed in Judea prior to A.D. 70. Interestingly, Josephus tells us that after serious trouble in the province in A.D. 51–52, Claudius sent for the Procurator of Judea, Cumanus, and a subordinate, "the tribune Celer." Civil tribunes—Tribunes of the Plebs—did not serve outside Rome. Military tribunes only officered legions. Had there only been auxiliary units stationed in Judea, the most senior Roman military officers in the province would have been prefects, not tribunes. And Josephus had more than enough exposure to the Roman military to know the difference. If he said Celer was a tribune, not a prefect, then a tribune he was.

Josephus went on to say that Tribune Celer was subsequently tried at Rome for his rapacious conduct in the province, then returned to Judea, where he was executed by his own troops, and Cumanus was replaced as procurator. Cumanus and Celer were obviously the two most senior Roman officials in Judea at the time. Junior tribunes were merely officer cadets, without responsibility or power. Even so, they, too, only served with legions.

There was only one senior tribune with each legion, its second-in-command. Celer was obviously a senior tribune, second-in-command of the 3rd Augusta Legion, the legion stationed in Judea at the time, and as such was the only senior tribune stationed in Judea and the province's military commander in the same way that senior tribunes commanded legions in Egypt.

There are several other examples of imperial legions outside Egypt being commanded by their senior tribunes, for years at a time—the 6th Victrix and 12th Legions in Syria during the Jewish Revolt of A.D. 66–70, for instance, when brigadier generals were scarce on the ground—so it appears to have been an accepted practice.

The conclusion that can be drawn is that until A.D. 70 Judea was treated in the same way as Egypt—the officer commanding the legion based in the province was its senior tribune, normally the legion's second-in-command, who would have been outranked by the prefect/procurator and could therefore take orders from him. As with the legions in Egypt, when the Judea legion left the province, a legate could be appointed to command it.

As further evidence of this, when Corbulo brought six cohorts—three thousand men—of the 3rd Augusta Legion up from Judea to take part in his A.D. 58 campaign in Armenia, they were apparently commanded by their camp prefect, Capito, the legion's third-in-command. This would have permitted their senior tribune to remain in Judea with the other four cohorts, as the province's military commander.

The situation in Egypt continued because of the Augustan law, but the situation in Judea could be changed at the discretion of the emperor. Vespasian did just that in late 70. When he permanently stationed the 10th Legion in Judea that year, he left it under the command of a legate, a general, even though there was also a procurator stationed in the province. The procurators who had commanded the Judea garrison in the past had, almost without exception, done a poor job with the troops at their disposal, so now the Judea legion would be autonomous. To ensure that there was no conflict between the procurator and the general of the legion, Vespasian duplicated his orders to them—both received the same directives, and both were expected to carry them out, one via his civil officers, the other through his soldiers. And both would have reported to the Syrian governor, the regional commander in chief.

APPENDIX D

THE NAMING AND NUMBERING SYSTEM OF THE ROMAN LEGIONS

Until 31 B.C., legions had numbers or names, but apparently not both. In 84 B.C., Pompey the Great began the habit of always numbering his new legions, a habit subsequently adopted by Julius Caesar. In his major reform of the Roman army, begun in 31 B.C., Augustus reduced the legions to twenty-eight in all, giving each a number between 1 and 28. It was an admirably practical system. For less practical, more nostalgic reasons, he also allowed several existing legions to combine their old names with their new numbers. For the next hundred years, it was sufficient to know a legion's number to be able to identify it. But in the civil war that followed the demise of Nero, in A.D. 68–69, things changed dramatically.

Considerable confusion has been caused over the years by the fact that from about A.D. 67 the numbers of the legions of Rome began to be duplicated so that by the end of the war of succession—late A.D. 69—there were four 1st Legions, three 3rd Legions, and two of each of the 2nd, 4th, 5th, 6th, 7th, 10th, and 15th Legions.

New legions continued to be added and others abolished as the years passed. By A.D. 233 there had been seven different 1st Legions, and there were still four 2nd Legions. To identify a Roman legion after A.D. 68, it's necessary to also look at its title—was it the 6th Victrix or the 6th Ferrata, for example, the 10th or the 10th Gemina?—two quite different legions.

It had all begun very methodically. The four original legions annually levied in Rome in republican times were numbered 1 through 4. Other legions supplied to Rome by the Italian allies carried the names of their tribes rather than numbers—the Martia Legion, famous in its day, would have been supplied by the Marsi tribe southeast of Rome, for example, the tribe and the legion being named for the war god Mars.

The numbering system that developed in the first century B.C. carried through the subsequent history of imperial Rome. It was begun by Pompey the Great when he personally raised and financed several legions in the Picenum region of eastern

281

Italy in 84 B.C., naming two of them the 1st and 2nd Legions. Pompey subsequently raised the 3rd, 4th, 5th, 6th, 7th, 8th, and 9th Legions. When Julius Caesar arrived in Farther Spain in 61 B.C. to take up his appointment as governor of the province, he raised a new legion locally and, following Pompey's system, he called it the 10th. Over the next few years, Caesar raised six more legions for his campaigns in Gaul and Britain—the 11th through the 16th. Shortly after, the triumvir Crassus raised a number of legions to take to war against the Parthians, managing to have himself killed and most of his legions wiped out at the Battle of Carrhae. It appears that these legions may have had names rather than numbers.

A few years later, Cicero took two new Italian-raised legions to Cilicia when he became governor there in 51 B.C. They, too, may have had names, but none that is recorded. When Pompey the Great took them over in 49 B.C., these two units were simply known as the Cilician Legions, because they were based in Cilicia. Pompey's father-in-law, Metellus Scipio, commanded two Italian-raised legions based in Syria at this time, survivors of Carrhae, and in the same way they were known as the Syrian Legions.

Between 49 and 48 B.C. Caesar created nineteen new legions for use in the civil war against Pompey, numbering them 17 through 35. After he defeated Pompey at the Battle of Pharsalus, he took two cohorts of one of Pompey's surrendered legions, the 6th, into his army, and had his officers seek volunteers from Pompey's other legions, giving the resulting two new legions created from POWs the numbers 36 and 37.

By 31 B.C., after Caesar's assassination on the Ides of March, 44 B.C., and the new civil wars that followed, at least fifty-nine legions were in the field—some accounts suggest as many as sixty-two—most with their Pompeian and Caesarean numbers.

Once Octavian had defeated Antony and Cleopatra in 31 B.C. he inherited all fifty-nine legions, most of them well understrength after years of fighting. Augustus reduced these to twenty-eight, abolishing some of the old legions, or sometimes combining two legions into one.

When Pompey the Great combined men from two so-called Cilician legions in 49 B.C., he named the resulting single legion the Gemina, meaning "twin." Several legions folded into each other by Augustus in 31–30 B.C. also took the name Gemina. Two Augustan Gemina legions were still in existence in A.D. 233—the 13th Gemina and the 14th Gemina Martia Victrix. The Gemina tradition was to be continued by later emperors—a legion created in A.D. 68, the second 10th, became the 10th Gemina two years later via combination with another. In the same way, Galba's 7th, also founded in A.D. 68, was likewise combined with another legion in A.D. 70, to become the 7th Gemina.

Four legions created in the changes of 31–30 B.C.—the 14th Gemina, the 20th Valeria, the 21st Rapax, and the 22nd Deiotariana—bore titles as well numbers from that time. This was because Augustus gave the old Martia Legion, one of the most celebrated of its day, the number 20 when he discharged the Italian legionaries of the 20th in 31 B.C. and allowed the legion to keep its famous old name in addition to its new number. Likewise, the equally famous Valeria Legion, raised by Pompey, took the number 20. That legion's second title, Victrix, was added a few years later. And when the Galatian legion called the Deiotariana was given the number 22, it also retained its title, until the reign of Claudius, in deference to the memory of King Deiotarus of Galatia, the legion's founder. The 21st Rapax also seems to have taken a pre-30 B.C. title with it.

Early in his reign, Augustus bestowed titles on legions as a reward, or to celebrate their land of origin, no doubt an honor and a reward to the province concerned. Later emperors granted titles to legions for varying reasons. Some, like the 15th, were never granted a title, despite having played important roles in major campaigns. And the 12th Legion wasn't granted its title of Fulminata until A.D. 174.

There was one blip in the Augustan numbering system. After three legions were wiped out in Germany in A.D. 9, Augustus retired their numbers. One, we know, was the 19th. There are good reasons to believe that the others were the 25th and the 26th. Augustus never replaced the annihilated legions and never used their numbers again, a step respected by every subsequent Roman emperor, none of whom used the numbers retired by Augustus, even though many of them raised new legions. For the next twenty-five years the Roman army consisted of twenty-five legions, still bearing the numbers 1 through 28 but minus 19, 25, and 26.

Nero raised a new legion in Italy, the 1st Italica, in A.D. 66–67, setting the scene for the overuse of the number 1 in coming years. In A.D. 68, Nero created the 1st Legion of the Fleet as one of his last, desperate acts as emperor. That same year, Servius Galba, Governor of Farther Spain, built an army to challenge Nero. Galba levied new legions in the traditional recruiting grounds of established Spanish legions. Within a few months he had created second the 4th, 5th, 6th, 7th, and 10th Legions in Spain.

There was a logic of a kind to his system, but the numbering of some subsequent new legions applied a logic all their own. For example, in A.D. 68, the city of Vienne in southern France created a 1st Adiutrix Legion to "support" the 1st Italica Legion, which was stationed nearby, to prove the town's loyalty and to discourage the 1st Italica from sacking their city. When the 1st Adiutrix subsequently fought on the losing side, the people of Vienne hurriedly raised a 2nd Adiutrix to prove their loyalty to the new emperor—the original 2nd, the Augusta, was also raised in their province, hence the duplication of its number, as a "supporter" to the original 2nd.

The 3rd Gallica Legion takes its name and number from the fact that it was the third new legion raised in Gaul at that time, after the 1st Adiutrix and the 2nd Adiutrix. There are in fact explanations for the numbering of all but one of the many legions created in 68–69. The exception is the 3rd Cyrenaica. There is no obvious reason for the new legion raised in Cyrenaica to be yet another 3rd Legion. It is possible that Syrian veterans of the 3rd Augusta Legion discharged eight years before had settled in Cyrenaica and formed the basis of the new legion hurriedly recruited in A.D. 68, but there is no proof of this.

Vespasian consolidated the army once he came to power at the end of A.D. 69, abolishing some of these new legions created during the civil war and merging others, in the first major reorganization of the Roman army since the time of Augustus. Occasionally Vespasian's successors raised new legions, and almost always they chose to keep the numbers they allocated these new units within the bottom end of the existing number range, so that we find several new legions taking the numerals 1, 2, or 3 over the next 150 years.

The reasoning behind the numbering of these later legions varies. Domitian raised one legion and called it his 1st—the 1st Minervia, named after his patron deity. Severus Alexander founded the 1st, 2nd, and 3rd Parthicae Legions for operations against the Parthians. Marcus Aurelius raised two new legions in Italy, so they naturally became the 2nd and 3rd Italica, since Nero had raised the 1st Italica.

Yet Trajan complicated matters with the numbers he gave the four new legions he raised in A.D. 100 for his campaigns in Dacia. Only two of the these lasted into the third century—the 2nd Traiana and the 30th Ulpia, both named after Trajan. Their numeration means there were also at one time a 1st Traiana and a 29th Ulpia Legion.

A full listing of the legions of the late first century B.C. to the early second century A.D. is given in Appendix A.

APPENDIX E

THE TITLE "FRETENSIS"

It has been suggested that the 10th Legion carried the title "Fretensis" while serving in Judea. No classical author confirms this. The 10th Legion, famous in its heyday, is the most referred-to legion in all the classical histories, yet never once does the meticulous first-century historian Tacitus or any other writer of the classical period give the legion a title of any kind. Tacitus in particular is cited because he made a habit of giving both the titles and the numbers of legions, unlike some classical writers. And when Cassius Dio listed all the legions in existence in his day, in about A.D. 233, he made a point of giving the official titles, present and past, of every legion. Although the 10th Gemina, a different legion, is mentioned, no title is ascribed to the 10th.

This does not necessarily mean that the 10th did not perhaps carry the name Fretensis as a sort of unofficial nickname, used by its own men but not by officialdom. Official or unofficial, does the Fretensis title stand up to examination?

The word Fretensis is said to come from *fretum Siciliense* and means "of the Straits of Sicily"—the modern Strait of Messina. For a legion to carry such a title is, to say the least, odd. The titles that other legions bore—and not all imperial legions carried titles as well as numbers—came via four routes. It was the title the legion carried with it in 30 B.C. from the civil war and was retained by Octavian; or it took the Gemina title because of combination with another; or it was granted a title in imperial times either in recognition of its valor or loyalty or both; or, less often, it took its title in recognition of its place of origin.

In terms of both its origin and its ongoing recruiting, the 10th Legion had no known connection with the Strait of Messina. The 10th Legion originated in Spain, and all evidence points to it being recruited there continuously until its recruiting ground was changed to northern Turkey in the second century. The 10th Legion is believed to have served in the Middle East throughout the imperial era, going nowhere near the Strait of Messina.

Yet, a possible explanation can be conjured for the Fretensis title, suggested by a tile found in Palestine in the twentieth century that bore the inscription "LEG X F." A galley was depicted above the inscription, a boar below. The 10th Legion's symbol is thought to have been the bull, and that of the 6th Ferrata,

285

which joined it in Judea in the second century, the boar. But assuming for a moment that the 10th's symbol was the boar, consider the following scenario.

In 38 B.C. Octavian, ruling the western part of the empire from Rome, was locked in conflict with Sextus Pompey, Pompey the Great's youngest son, who had occupied Sicily with substantial land and naval forces. At this time, all evidence points to the 10th Legion being based in the East, serving Mark Antony, who ruled Rome's eastern possessions. Octavian launched a series of campaigns against young Pompey, suffering several naval defeats, one in the Strait of Messina from which Octavian only just escaped with his life. Two years later, Octavian's admiral Marcus Agrippa would finally defeat Pompey in a naval battle off Mylae, on the northeastern coast of Sicily but some distance from the Strait of Messina.

It is possible that the 10th Legion was embarked on vessels of Octavian's several fleets in 38 B.C., playing a particularly valorous part in this ship-to-ship fighting, and was granted the right to carry the galley symbol in the same way Julius Caesar granted the 5th Legion the elephant symbol after Thapsus. Following this defeat, Octavian swapped twenty thousand of his legionaries for 120 of Antony's warships to cover his own naval losses, and perhaps in this way the 10th found its way back into Antony's army, having served him a decade earlier, and where it remained until Actium.

Going against this theory is the following. First, while legions were in later times occasionally granted titles in celebration of their parts in one battle or another, it was in celebration of a victory, not a defeat. Further, before about 25 B.C. no titles were granted to legions that were already identified by a number, that we know of. After Octavian was himself granted the title Augustus by the Senate in 27 B.C., it appears he began the habit of entitling legions by soon giving titles to the seven legions that eventually won the Cantabrian War of 29–19 B.C. for him. As for the 38 B.C. sea battles in the Straits of Messina, Appian, who gives a very detailed account of these campaigns and names several legions involved, including the 1st and the 13th, makes absolutely no reference to the 10th in any context, let alone describes a performance that would earn the legion distinctions. Yet it is Appian who tells us of the 5th Legion's distinctions as a result of its part in the victory at Thapsus in 46 B.C.

For all this, the 10th Legion may have been known colloquially as the Fretensis. There is simply no evidence to support a suggestion that this was an official title.

APPENDIX F

IMPERIAL ROMAN MILITARY RANKS AND THEIR MODERN-DAY EQUIVALENTS
(IN ORDER OF PRECEDENCE)

Rank	Description	Equivalent
Miles classicus	A soldier in the Roman navy's marine corps.	Marine
Miles gregarius	Literally, a "common soldier" of the legion.	Private
Signifer	Standard-bearer for legion cohort and maniple. No real authority. Unit banker.	Corporal
Aquilifer	Eagle-bearer of the legion. Most prestigious post for a standard-bearer.	Corporal
Tesserarius	Orderly sergeant; sergeant of the guard.	Sergeant
Optio	Second-in-command of a century and of a cavalry squadron. Unit training, administration, and records officer.	Sergeant major
Decurio	Decurion. Cavalry officer, commanding a squadron of legion cavalry. Several grades, based on length of service.	Second lieutenant
Centurio	Centurion. Officer commanding a century, maniple, and cohort. Sixty to a legion (including six *primi ordines*). Eleven grades, including *primi ordines* and *primus pilus*. Seniority usually determined by length of service.	First lieutenant
Primi ordines	Six most senior centurions of a legion, all serving in the first, double cohort.	Captain
Primus pilus	Literally the "first spear," the most senior centurion of the legion, one of the *primi ordines*.	Captain

Praefectus castrorium	Camp prefect. A former centurion, the third-in-command of a legion, quartermaster, and officer in charge of major detachments separated from the legion.	Major
Tribunus angusticlavius	Tribune of the thin stripe, a staff officer, serving a six-month officer cadetship.	Lieutenant colonel
Navarchus	Commander of a warship in the Roman navy.	Captain (naval)
Praefectus	Commander of an auxiliary cohort or wing.	Colonel
Tribunus laticlavius	Tribune of the broad stripe, second-in-command of a legion.	Colonel
Praefectus praetoria	One of two commanders of the Praetorian Guard, of equal rank. While, nominally, Prefects of the Guard held the rank of colonel, some rose through the ranks and were former centurions, while others were ex-generals, and on several occasions they commanded field armies.	Colonel
Praefectus classis	Commander of a squadron or a fleet in the Roman navy. Frequently a former or serving general, occasionally a freedman with no military experience.	Admiral
Legatus legionis	Legate of the legion. Legion commander.	Brigadier general
Praetor/ propraetor	A praetor was a senior magistrate in Rome. Former praetors—propraetors—could hold the governorship of minor provinces and command a legion and armies in the field.	Major general
Consul/ proconsul	A consul was the highest official in Rome after the emperor. The two consuls for the year shared the presidency of the Senate and gave their names to the year. Former consuls, proconsuls, could receive the most senior provincial governorships, commanding all military forces in their province. Roman field armies were normally commanded by men of consular rank.	Lieutenant general

The Roman Field Marshal or Five-Star General

Occasionally, emperors endowed generals of consular rank with special powers usually reserved for the emperor alone, on a temporary basis, for particular military operations. These powers made the generals involved senior to all other generals and officials in their sphere of operations, no matter what their seniority otherwise, and allowed them to lead troops across provincial boundaries. We would equate this special rank with a modern-day field marshal or five-star general. Agrippa, Tiberius, and Drusus would have been granted these powers by Augustus, Germanicus was under Augustus and then under Tiberius, Corbulo and Vespasian were under Nero, and Mucianus and Titus were under Vespasian.

APPENDIX G

SOURCES

Primary Sources

Historians and historical writers are detectives. They seek evidence, they follow clues, they put 2 and 2 together, and hopefully they come up with a reasonably accurate picture of the people we have been and the events that have shaped the people we are.

Those dealing with Rome from the first century B.C. are fortunate to have a wealth of source material to refer to. That material takes two forms. There are inscriptions, most on monuments, slabs of stone that have lasted two thousand years of weather and war, some on slivers of bronze often unearthed in farmers' fields in recent times. And, more numerous, the surviving writings of men who lived in the period and chronicled it—surely never imagining that two millennia later, people like ourselves would be reading their words.

The inscriptions tell us about the careers of men such as Gaius Mannius, legionary of the 20th Valeria Victrix Legion, from a village just outside Turin. And Tiberius Maximus, the cavalry officer from Philippi who tracked down Decebalus, the fleeing king of Dacia in A.D. 106 just as the Dacian put a knife to his own throat. And Gaius Minicius, the twenty-seven-year-old colonel from Aquileia thrust into the civil war in A.D. 69 in the service of Vespasian and soon to earn Rome's highest bravery award.

The historical writings available to us are many and varied. Different classical authors writing of the same events often give different and sometimes differing information, so that Plutarch, Suetonius, and Dio, for example, each report the bloody demise of Emperor Vitellius a little differently. None was an eyewitness; each relied on other accounts to create his own. In the same way, no two reporters today will cover the same current event in exactly the same way. Each may choose to use different sources; each approaches the event from his or her own perspective.

Imagine an historian in a future time with the task of writing about a major news event that took place today. He or she will pull together all the different present-day reports and will then write a single account based on those reports. If they are fair-minded, they will endeavor to present the most balanced yet most informative view they can. So it goes for today's historical writer.

The 10th Legion was probably the most written-about Roman legion of its day. It was certainly the most famous legion in the first centuries B.C. and A.D. In the twenty-eight years of research preceding the two years of writing that went into this book, many contemporary and classical sources were consulted, and they are listed under "Additional Sources." Some, such as Roman writers Seneca and Livy, provided valuable snippets. But, overall, this book is based on the works of the following, listed in order of relevance.

Julius Caesar. *Commentary on the Gallic War* and *Commentary on the Civil War.* Caesar wrote his memoirs, with the first book, dealing with his conquest of Gaul and covering the period 58–51 B.C., being published in his lifetime. He was still working on his account of the civil war, which leaves off after the Battle of Pharsalus, when he was murdered in 44 B.C. At the urging of Caesar's private secretary, his former chief of staff Lucius Cornelius Balbus, these published and unpublished works were collated by Caesar's loyal staff officer Aulus Hirtius shortly after the dictator's death. Hirtius, promoted to general, would himself be dead within another year. Hirtius combined them with additional material, some which he wrote himself, the rest apparently penned by officers who had been on the scene for the last battles of the civil war, before they were published by Balbus.

Caesar's own writings are in the third person, as if produced by an independent observer, and strive to paint him in the best light possible while denigrating his opponents. Despite the propagandist overtones, they still provide a fascinating insight into one of history's greatest generals—and engineers—and his campaigns. Most importantly to historians seeking data on the legions of Rome, Caesar regularly identifies the legions involved in his various campaigns and battles.

In the associated material, Hirtius strove to both emulate and praise his master, sometimes distorting the facts to paint Caesar's adversary Pompey the Great in a bad light. Other authors, such as Plutarch, occasionally give us a truer picture, such as when Pompey loaned Caesar a legion in 52 B.C., without the approval of the Senate, when Caesar was in deep trouble in Gaul. Plutarch tells us Pompey was greatly criticized by the likes of Cato the Younger for helping Caesar like this, but you wouldn't know it from Hirtius's narrative.

Often, where there were passages in Caesar's original text that depicted an error by Caesar, Hirtius—or possibly Balbus—simply cut it out. We know this because there are several instances where Caesar says "as mentioned before" or the like, and the before-mentioned material is missing. Fortunately, sufficient references were overlooked by the editors in their hasty edit for the truth to emerge.

In their haste, too, the editors missed passages in the additional material that don't exactly flatter Caesar, with a picture of an impatient and sometimes petty man emerging.

Another of Caesar's loyal staff officers, Gaius Asinius Pollio, is quoted by Suetonius as writing that he felt Caesar's memoirs showed signs of carelessness and inaccuracy. Pollio said that in his experience Caesar didn't always check the truth of reports that came in and had been either disingenuous or forgetful in describing his own actions. But Cicero, also quoted by Suetonius, said that Caesar wrote admirably, composing his memoirs cleanly, directly, and gracefully. Cicero added that Caesar's sole intention had been to supply historians with factual material, and that subsequently "several fools have been pleased to primp up his narrative for their own glorification."

The fools in question would appear to be Hirtius and Balbus, and perhaps, like Cicero, we should be blaming them, not Caesar, for any distortions. As for myself, I have taken the middle view. The editors must certainly come in for criticism, but I suspect that, in addition, Caesar's ego prevented him from being entirely honest in his writings, with himself as well as with his readers.

For all this, Caesar's memoirs are still a lively and informative resource.

Among best of many translations: *The Commentaries of Caesar*, transl. W. Duncan, Dodsley: London (1779); *Caesar: Commentaries on the Gallic and Civil Wars*, transl. W. A. M'Devitte & W. S. Bohm, Bell: London (1890); *Caesar: The Gallic War & The Civil War*, transl. T. Rice Holmes, Loeb series: London (1914–1955); also, *Caesar: The Conquest of Gaul*, transl. S. A. Handford (1951), rev. J. F. Gardner (1967), Penguin: London; *Caesar: The Civil War*, transl. J. F. Gardner, Penguin: London (1967).

Plutarch (A.D. 46–c.120). Plutarch was a Greek scholar who wrote in the reigns of Roman emperors Nerva, Trajan, and Hadrian. Shakespeare used his *Parallel Lives* as the basis for his plays *Julius Caesar* and *Antony and Cleopatra*. This, Plutarch's great work, gives short comparative biographies of numerous historical figures and provides background material on key players in the history of the legions—Sulla, Marius, Lucullus, Sertorius, Cato the Younger, Crassus, Pompey the Great, Julius Caesar, Mark Antony, Brutus, Cassius, and emperors Galba and Otho.

Plutarch, who considered himself more biographer than historian, occasionally makes reference to his sources, most of which have not come down to us, such as Emphylus, a rhetorician and colleague of Caesar's assassin Brutus, who, in Plutarch's words, produced "a short but well-written history of the death of Caesar" entitled *Brutus*, an account that may have come from Brutus himself.

The author of hundreds of books and essays, Plutarch was well respected in his own day. Occasionally biased but only once in a while making a demonstrable error, he remains a valuable resource on people and events related to the legions.

Recommended English translations: John Dryden's *The Lives of the Noble Grecians and Romans*, publ. London, 1683–86, republ. 1952, *Encylopaedia Britannica*, Chicago; also J. & W. Lanhome's 1875 transl., *Plutarch's Lives of Illustrious Men*, Chatto & Windus: London; B. Perrin's Loeb series transl., *Plutarch's Lives*, London (1914–26).

Appian. Born in about A.D. 95 at Alexandria, of Greek stock, Appian worked as an advocate in the courts at Rome and later served as a financial administrator in the provinces. In the middle of the second century he wrote a number of books on Roman history, of which his *Civil Wars* is the most helpful to writers interested in the legions. He is the least well regarded of the Greek historians of the Roman Empire, but for the historical events that took place between 133 and 70 B.C. he is considered the only continuous source of any quality. For the period from the foundation of the 10th Legion in 61 B.C. he is one of several sources. His work is at times disjointed, at others error-strewn. He sometimes also lapsed into what have been described as rhetorical flourishes, or just plain fiction. Despite this, Appian used many well-placed sources and provides a useful basis of comparison, particularly when his account can be considered alongside those of Plutarch, Suetonius, and Cassius Dio.

Recommended English translations: *Appian: Roman History*, transl. H. White (1889), rev. for Loeb series, I. Robinson: London (1913); *Appian: The Civil Wars*, transl. J. Carter, Penguin: London (1996).

Suetonius. Biographer Gaius Suetonius Tranquillus was born in about A.D. 69, in the middle of the civil war that followed the demise of Nero. At the time, his father was serving in the army of the short-lived emperor Otho as a tribune, and probably second-in-command, with the 13th Gemina Legion. Suetonius went on to join the Roman civil service, rising to be briefly in charge of the government archives at Rome, which were closed to the public. For a year or two he worked at the Palatium as a correspondence secretary to the emperor Hadrian, but was fired for disrespect to the empress Sabina while Hadrian was away.

Suetonius was subsequently denied access to the official records, but it is clear from his collection of pocket biographies, *Lives of the Caesars*, that he had begun researching a book on Roman leaders while he was running the archives. His biographies of Julius Caesar, Augustus, and Tiberius are filled with detail that could only come from official sources—excerpts from emperors' private letters, for example—while his later biographies rely on gossip, hearsay, myth, exaggeration, and sensational anecdote in place of hard fact, suggesting that his researches had only reached Tiberius at the time of his dismissal and fall from favor.

Even in territory where he had good material to work with, Suetonius managed some obvious errors, mostly, it seems, from sloppiness. For example, where Caesar describes 30,000 arrows found in the Dyrrhachium fort of the 9th Legion after Pompey's surprise attack in 48 B.C., Suetonius ups it to 130,000. And he puts the 6th Legion on Caesar's side, when its surviving cohorts were actually in Pompey's army at that time—some 900 men of the legion would go over to Caesar after the Battle of Pharsalus several months later.

Suetonius was to write a number of books, including those aimed at capturing a broad market, such as *The Lives of Famous Whores, The Physical Defects of Mankind,* and *Greek Terms of Abuse.* But it is his *Lives of the Caesars* that has proven of most interest down through the ages, despite its errors and imperfections, and in terms of the legions from Caesar up until the end of the first century, his access to official records makes him a source that cannot be ignored.

Recommended among many English translations: *Lives of the Twelve Caesars,* 1606 transl. P. Holland, republ. New York Limited Editions Club: NY (1963); rev. transl., F. Etchells & H. Macdonald, Haselwood: London (1931); a 1796 transl. by A. Thompson, Robinson: London, republ. Corner House: Williamstown, MA (1978); Loeb series edition, transl. J. C. Rolfe: London (1914); *The Twelve Caesars,* transl. R. Graves (1957), rev. M. Grant, Penguin: London (1979).

Tacitus. Publius Cornelius Tacitus was the king of Roman historians. His *Annals* and *Histories* and, to a lesser extent, his *Agricola* and *Germania* are treasure troves of information about Rome and her empire in the first century. Living between about A.D. 55 and 117, Tacitus was a consul in 97 and governor of the province of Asia in 112. With apparently unlimited access to the official archives, his hugely detailed books abound with facts and figures taken directly from the records of the proceedings of the Senate and other sources as varied as back issues of the *Acta Diurna.* He acknowledges liberal use of the work of other writers, much since lost, men such as Pliny the Elder, whose writings on Germany after serving with the legions on the Rhine undoubtedly helped shape Tacitus's attitude to Germany, Germanicus, and Arminius, as well as serving soldiers such as Vipstanus Messalla, second-in-command of the 7th Claudia Legion during the crucial civil war battles of A.D. 69, who went on to write his memoirs.

For the period A.D. 14–70, Tacitus can be read as the unrivaled authority on the legions of the first century. He also makes several telling remarks about earlier eras. He identifies the legions taking part in the wars, campaigns, and battles of the time, inclusive of their names, commanders, and frequently the names of individual officers and enlisted men. Almost always resisting gossipy anecdote in favor of documented fact, and making only very occasional errors, it is Tacitus who renders any history of the legions possible, and this particular work is in his great debt.

Recommended English translations: A. J. Church & W. J. Brodribb transl., *Annals & Histories*, London 1869–72; Republ. Chicago (1952), *Encyclopaedia Britannica*. Also a Franklin Library edition, Franklin, PA (1982); Loeb series, transl. W. Peterson: London (1914–37); *Annals*, transl. M. Grant, Penguin: London (1966); *Annals*, transl. D. R. Dudley, Mentor: New York (1966); *History*, transl. A. Murphy, Dent: London (1900); *The Agricola & The Germania*, transl. A. J. Church & W. J. Brodribb: London (1869–72); also, transl. of H. Mattingly & S. A. Handford, Penguin: London (1948); a combined works of Tacitus, including all of the above, transl. C. H. Morre & J. Jackson, Heinemann/Putnam: London (1931).

Cassius Dio. Also referred to as Dio Cassius and Dion Cassius (his father was also a Cassius, his grandfather a Dio), Cassius Dio Cocceianus was a Greek historian born in the Roman province of Bithynia in about A.D. 150. Going to Rome, he joined the Senate under the emperor Commodus. Twice consul, and governor of several provinces during his long career, Dio had considerable military experience and was well versed in the ways of the legions. He wrote a history of the Roman Empire in eighty books in the years leading up to his death in 235. These histories took the form of a year-by-year synopsis of major events, with occasional diversions into anecdote.

Dio worked from existing sources, and clearly based much of his first-century narrative on Tacitus. With the A.D. 37–47 chapters of Tacitus's *Annals* lost to us, it is from Dio that we glean the little we know about Claudius's invasion of Britain. We can also see where Dio borrowed from Suetonius in his books on the first centuries B.C. and A.D., although some of his errors and exaggerations are glaringly original—he has Titus save his father, Vespasian, on a British battlefield in A.D. 47, when the boy was only seven. Dio also assumed that some customs prevalent in his day had been current in earlier times.

Unlike Tacitus, Dio rarely makes reference to individual legions, and when he does, he is sometimes in error—he puts the 3rd Gallica Legion in an A.D. 69 civil war battle, when from Tacitus we ascertain it was the 3rd Augusta. The 3rd Gallica, a new legion, had not even taken the field by that time. But he does tell us how the 12th Legion gained its Fulminata title from Marcus Aurelius in A.D. 174. More importantly, Dio provides a list of all the legions in existence in his day, with brief background information on each, which, although not entirely accurate, provides a proverbial bookend to any history of the legions of the early imperial era.

Most valuable English translations include: Loeb series, *Dio's Roman History*: London (1914–27), transl. E. Cary; and *Cassius Dio. The Roman History: The Reign of Augustus*, transl. I. Scott-Kilvert, Penguin: London (1987).

Josephus. Born in about A.D. 37, Josephus Flavius was a Jew who commanded Jefat during the town's siege by Vespasian's army in A.D. 67, where he was captured. He claims he won his freedom and the favor of Vespasian by predicting that both he and his son Titus would become emperor of Rome. Collaborating with the Romans, Josephus several times tried to talk the Jewish partisans holding Jerusalem into surrendering, ultimately witnessing and documenting the city's destruction. He later wrote extensively about the Jewish peoples, providing a detailed background on Herod the Great. But it is his coverage of the A.D. 67–70 Judean offensives of Vespasian and Titus that is of most use to anyone interested in the legions.

Tacitus wrote of the early stages of these campaigns, identifying units such as the 3rd Augusta and 18th Legion detachments involved, but most of his account of this episode has been lost, so that Josephus is the only continuous source of the events in Judea of A.D. 67–71. Identifying the five main legions involved in the campaigns, including the 10th, Josephus reports the Judean operations in impressive detail, right down to the legions' order of march. He is not without error, and while he praises individual Jewish fighters, he was at pains to paint the Jewish leaders in a bad light and depict their cause as folly. His intent was to ingratiate himself with the Roman leadership, and he succeeded. Granted his freedom, citizenship, property, and wealth by the Flavian emperors, he wrote for a Roman readership, and his stance is far from objective. But as an eyewitness to one of Rome's most bitter wars and one of history's most pivotal events, he is a rare source.

Recommended English translations among many: *The Jewish War*, transl. H. St. John Thackery, R. Marcus, & L. H. Feldman, Loeb: London (1926); also, transl. of G. A. Williamson, Penguin: London (1959, rev. 1970). A nineteenth-century *Complete Works of Josephus*, transl. W. Whiston, Winston: PA, republ. by Kregel in United States in twentieth century.

Polybius. This Greek statesman and historian lived between 200 and 118 B.C. At Rome, initially as a hostage, he became a friend of and adviser to Scipio Aemillianus, the Roman consul and general who conquered Carthage. Traveling widely, Polybius wrote his *Histories* in forty books after returning to Greece in 150 B.C. Having broad experience of Roman political and military matters, he wrote with intelligence and authority about the Roman army of the mid-second century B.C. Some chapters are so detailed they read like a legion owner's manual. It is from Polybius that we know so much about legion practices and procedures, many of which seem to have remained unchanged for centuries after, from camp layout to bravery decorations, sentry details to punishments.

Recommended English translations: *The Histories of Polybius*, transl. E. Shuckburgh, Macmillan: London (1889). *Polybius. Histories*, transl. W. R. Paton, Loeb: London (1922–27). *Polybius. The Rise of the Roman Empire*, transl. I. Scott-Kilvert, Penguin: London (1979).

Pliny the Younger. His full name was Gaius Plinius Caecilius Secundus. He was a consul in A.D. 100 and governed Bithynia-Pontus between A.D. 111 and 113. His correspondence, in particular his exchange of letters with the emperor Trajan at Rome on matters that came before him for judgment, give a fascinating insight into Roman life of the time. They are especially enlightening about the wisdom of Trajan and the workings of Roman imperial government, from the operations of the *Cursus Publicus* to how Christians were then tolerated, and how slaves who illegally enrolled for legion service were dealt with.

Recommended English translations: *The Letters of Pliny the Consul*, transl. W. Melmoth, London (1746), rev. W. M. Hutchinson, Loeb: London (1915). *Pliny's Letters*, transl. A. J. Church & W. A. Brodribb, Blackwood: Edinburgh (1872). *The Letters of the Younger Pliny*, transl. B. Radice, Penguin: London (1963).

Acts of the Apostles. From the Bible, these provide insights into several aspects of legion activity in Judea during the first century. One deals with a centurion who retired from his legion to live in Caesarea and who was converted to Christianity by St. Peter. Indications are that the centurion was of Greek heritage, that he retired from the 1st Legion, then based on the Rhine—confused by the *Acts* author with the 1st Italica, which had in effect replaced the demobilized 1st Legion by the time *Acts* was written—and probably entered the army by enrolling with the 3rd Augusta Legion at its Beirut recruiting station.

The other episode of interest, almost certainly written by St. Luke, tells of St. Paul's arrest in Jerusalem, his trial and detention in Caesarea, and then his conveyance under escort to Rome to have his appeal heard by the emperor, Nero, as was his right as a Roman citizen. From *Acts* we ascertain that Paul's escort was made up of a centurion and legionaries from the 3rd Augusta Legion based in Caesarea, and the story Luke tells of the journey he and Paul took to Rome in A.D. 60–61, inclusive of a shipwreck on Malta with their legionary escort, is the only detailed eyewitness account we have of a first-century sea journey, making this a treasure trove for historians.

Additional Sources

Abbott, F. F. and Johnson, A. C. *Municipal Administration in the Roman Empire*. Princeton, NJ: University Press, 1926.

Allegro, J. M. *The Dead Sea Scrolls*. Harmondsworth, U.K.: Penguin, 1956.

Arrian. *History of Alexander, and Indica*. Trans. P. Brunt. London: Loeb-Harvard University Press, 1976.

Aurelius, M. *Meditations*. Trans. G. Long. Chicago: Encyclopaedia Britannica, 1952.

Azzaroli, A. *An Early History of Horsemanship*. London: E. J. Brill, 1985.

Birley, A. *Marcus Aurelius*. London: Eyre & Spottiswoode, 1966.

Birley, E. *Roman Britain and the Roman Army*. Kendal, U.K.: Titus Wilson, 1953.

Boardman, J.; Griffin, J.; and Murray, O. *The Oxford History of the Classical World*. Oxford: Oxford University Press, 1986.

Bouchier, E. S. *Spain under the Roman Empire*. Oxford: B. H. Blackwell, 1914.

Brogen. *Roman Gaul*. London: Bell, 1953.

Broughton, T. R. S. *The Romanization of Africa Proconsularis*. NY: Greenwood Press, 1968.

Bryant, A. *The Age of Elegance*. London: William Collins, 1954.

Buchan, J. *Augustus*. London: Hodder & Stoughton, 1937.

Carcopino, J. *Daily Life in Ancient Rome*. London: Pelican, 1956.

Casson, L. *Ancient Egypt*. Alexandria, VA: Time-Life, 1965.

Cave, W. *Lives, Acts, and Martyrdoms of the Holy Apostles*. London: John Hatchard & Son, 1836.

Chevalier, R. *Roman Roads*. Trans. N. H. Field. London: Batsford, 1976.

Church, A. J. *Roman Life in the Days of Cicero*. London: Seeley, Service & Co., 1923.

Clausewitz, C. P. G. von. *On War*. Trans. J. J. Graham. NY: Penguin, 1968.

Colledge, M. A. R. *The Parthians* Leiden: E. J. Brill, 1986.

Cottrell, L. *Enemy of Rome*. London: Pan, 1962.

Cottrell, L. *The Great Invasion*. London: Evans Bros., 1958.

Cowell, F. R. *Cicero and the Roman Republic*. Harmondsworth, U.K.: Penguin, 1956.

Croft, P. *Roman Mythology*. London: Octopus, 1974.

Cunliffe, B. *Rome and Her Empire*. Maidenhead, U.K.: McGraw-Hill, 1978.

Cunliffe, B. *The Roman Baths at Bath*. Bath: Bath Archeological Trust, 1993.

De La Billiere, General Sir P. *Looking for Trouble*. London: HarperCollins, 1994.

Department of the Army. *U.S. Army Survival Manual; FM 21-76*. NY: Dorset Press, 1991.

Depuy, R. E. and T. N. *The Encyclopedia of Military History: From 3500 B.C. to the Present*. London: Military Book Society, 1970.

Divine, A. *Secrets and Stories of the War: Miracle at Dunkirk*. London: Reader's Digest Association, 1963.

Duff, J. D. *Lucan*. Cambridge: Harvard University Press, 1977.

Emile, T. *Roman Life under the Caesars*. NY: Putnam, 1908.

Forestier, A. *The Roman Soldier*. London: A. & C. Black, 1928.

Frank, T., ed. *An Economic Survey of Ancient Rome*. New Jersey: Pageant, 1959.

Frere, S. S. *Britannia: A History of Roman Britain*. London: Routledge & Kegan Paul, 1987.

Frontinus. *Stratagems & Aqueducts*. Trans. C. E. Bennet and M. B. McElwain. London: Loeb, 1925.

Furneaux, R. *The Roman Siege of Jerusalem*. London: Rupert Hart-Davis, 1973.

Gardner, J. F. *Family & Familia in Roman Law & Life*. Oxford: Oxford University Press, 1998.

Gibbon, E. *The Decline and Fall of the Roman Empire*. Chicago: Encyclopaedia Britannica, 1932.

Grant, M. *Cleopatra*. Harmondsworth, U.K.: Penguin, 1972.

Grant, M. *Gladiators*. Harmondsworth, U.K.: Penguin, 1967.

Grant, M. *History of Rome*. Harmondsworth, U.K.: Penguin, 1978.

Grant, M. *Julius Caesar*. Harmondsworth, U.K.: Penguin, 1969.

Grant, M. *Saint Paul*. Harmondsworth, U.K.: Penguin, 1976.

Grant, M. *The Army of the Caesars*. Harmondsworth, U.K.: Penguin, 1974.

Grant, M. *The Jews of the Roman World*. Harmondsworth, U.K.: Penguin, 1973.

Grant, M. *The Roman Emperors*. Harmondsworth, U.K.: Penguin, 1985.

Graves, R. *I, Claudius*. London: Arthur Barker, 1934.

Haywood, R. M. *Ancient Greece and the Near East*. London: Vision, 1964.

Haywood, R. M. *Ancient Rome*. London: Vision, 1967.

Highet, G. *Juvenal the Satirist*. Oxford: Clarendon, 1954.

Horrocks, Lieutenant General Sir B. *Secrets and Stories of the War*. London: Reader's Digest Association, 1963.

Jones, A. H. M. *Augustus*. New York: W. W. Norton, 1972.

Kenyon, K. *Jerusalem: Excavating 3,000 Years of History*. London: Thames & Hudson, 1967.

Ker, W. C. A. *Martial*. London: Loeb, 1919–20.

Laking, G. F. *A Record of European Armour & Arms through Seven Centuries*. NY: A. M. S., 1934.

Leach, J. *Pompey the Great*. NY: Croom Helm, 1978.

Livy. *The War with Hannibal*. Trans. E. de Selincourt. Harmondsworth, U.K.: Penguin, 1965.

Lytton, (Lord) E. G. E. B. *The Last Days of Pompeii*. London: Alexander, 1834.

MacArthur, B., ed. *The Penguin Book of Twentieth Century Speeches*. London: Penguin, 1992.

MacMullen, R. *Soldier and Civilian in the Later Roman Empire*. Cambridge, MA: Harvard University Press, 1967.

Mannix, D. P. *Those About to Die*. London: Mayflower, 1960.

Marsden, E. W. *Greek and Roman Artillery*. Oxford: Oxford University Press, 1969.

Mommsen, T. *The Provinces of the Roman Empire*, ed. T. R. S. Broughton. Chicago: University of Chicago/Phoenix, 1968.

Morton, H. V. *In the Steps of the Master*. London: Rich & Cowan, 1934.

Napthali, L. *Life in Egypt under Roman Rule*. Oxford: Clarendon, 1983.

National Geographic Society. *Jerusalem*. Washington: National Geographic Society, 1996.

Parker, H. D. M. *The Roman Legions*. NY: Barnes & Noble, 1958.

Payne-Gallwey, Sir R. *The Crossbow, Mediaeval and Modern: With a Treatise on the Ballista and Catapults of the Ancients.* London: The Holland Press, 1995; reprint, 1903.

Peterson, D. *The Roman Legions Recreated in Color.* London: Windrow & Greene, 1992.

Petronius Arbiter, G. *The Satyricon.* Trans. M. Heseltine. London: Loeb, 1913.

Pliny the Elder. *Natural History,* ed. and trans. H. Rackman. London: Loeb, 1938–1963.

Powell, C. L. *A Soldier's Way.* London: Hutchinson, 1995.

Raven, S. *Rome in Africa.* London: Longman, 1969.

Robertson, D. S. *Greek and Roman Architecture.* Cambridge, U.K.: Cambridge University Press, 1943.

Robinson, H. R. *The Armour of Imperial Rome.* Oxford: Oxford University Press, 1975.

Romer, J. *Testament: The Bible and History.* London: Michael O'Mara, 1988.

Rossi, L. *Trajan's Column and the Dacian Wars.* London: Thames & Hudson, 1974.

Rostovtzeff, M. I. *The Social and Economic History of the Roman Empire.* NY: Biblio & Tannen, 1957.

Ryan, C. *The Longest Day.* London: Victor Gollancz, 1959.

Salway, P. *Roman Britain.* Oxford: Oxford University Press, 1981.

Schwarzkopf, General H. N. *It Doesn't Take a Hero.* NY: Bantam, 1992.

Seager, R. *Tiberius.* London: Eyre Methuen, 1972.

Seneca. *Letters from a Stoic.* Trans. R. Campbell. Harmondsworth, U.K.: Penguin, 1969.

Sherwin-White, A. N. *The Roman Citizenship.* Oxford: Oxford University Press, 1939.

Simkins, M. *Warriors of Rome.* London: Blandford, 1988.

Smith, F. E. *Waterloo.* London: Pan, 1970.

Strabo. *The Geography of Strabo.* Trans. H. L. Jones. London: Loeb, 1924.

Sulimirski, T. *The Sarmatians.* NY: Praeger, 1970.

Syme, R. *History in Ovid.* Oxford: Oxford University Press, 1979.

Theiring, B. *Jesus the Man.* Sydney: Doubleday, 1992.

Times (London) Concise Atlas of World History. London: *Times,* 1982.

Todd, M. *The Early Germans.* Oxford: Blackwell, 1992.

Todd, M. *The Northern Barbarians, 1000 B.C.–A.D. 300.* NY: Blackwell, 1987.

Trench, C. C. *A History of Horsemanship.* NY: Doubleday, 1970.

U.K. War Office, General Staff. *Field Service Regulations.* London: H. M. Stationery Office, 1914.

Utley, R. M. *The Lance and the Shield.* NY: Henry Holt, 1993.

Vernam, G. R. *Man on Horseback.* NY: Doubleday, 1964.

Waldeck, C. *Secrets and Stories of the War.* London: Reader's Digest Association, 1963.

Ward, G. C., with Burns, R. and K. *The Civil War.* NY: Alfred A. Knopf, 1991.

Warmington, E. H. *Nero*. Harmondsworth, U.K.: Penguin, 1969.

Warry, J. *Warfare in the Classical World*. London: Salamander, 1989.

Watson, G. R. *The Roman Soldier*. Ithaca, NY: Cornell University Press, 1969.

Webster, G., and Dudley, D. R. *The Roman Conquest of Britain*. London: Pan, 1965.

Webster's New Twentieth Century Dictionary of the English Language. Cleveland: World Publ., 1953.

Weigall, A. *Nero: Emperor of Rome*. London: Butterworth, 1930.

Wheeler, R. M. *Rome Beyond the Imperial Frontiers*. London: Bell, 1954.

White, K. D. *Greek & Roman Technology*. Ithaca, NY: Cornell University Press, 1983.

Wightman, E. M. *Roman Trier and the Treveri*. NY: Praeger, 1970.

Wilkinson, L. P. *Letters of Cicero*. London: Hutchinson, 1969.

Wilson, E. *The Scrolls from the Dead Sea*. London: W. H. Allen, 1956.

Wilson, I. *Jesus: The Evidence*. London: Pan, 1984.

Wiseman, F. J. *Roman Spain*. NY: Bell, 1956.

Yadin, Y. *Masada: Herod's Fortress and the Zealot's Last Stand*. NY: Grosset & Dunlap, 1966.

GLOSSARY

ACTA DIURNA Rome's *Daily News;* world's first daily newspaper. Handwritten daily by the Palatium at Rome and sent around the empire. Founded by Julius Caesar in 59 B.C.

AQUILIFER The standard-bearer who carried the *aquila,* the legion's eagle.

AUXILIARY Noncitizen serving in Roman army. Light infantry and cavalry. Recruited throughout empire. In imperial times served 25 years. Paid less than legionary. From first century, granted Roman citizenship on discharge. Commanded by prefects.

BALLISTA Artillery piece firing round stones weighing 60 to 100 pounds.

BATTLESHIP Roman warship of Deceres class, 145 feet long with a beam of 28 feet, crewed by 572 oarsmen, 30 sailors, and up to 250 marines.

CAMP PREFECT *Praefectus castrorium.* Imperial legion officer, third-in-command after commanding officer and senior tribune. Promoted from centurion. Quartermaster, commander of major legion detachments.

CAMPAIGNING SEASON Traditionally, early March to October 19, when legions conducted military campaigns, after which they went into winter quarters.

CENTURION Legion and Praetorian Guard officer, sixty to a legion, in eleven grades, equivalent to lieutenant and captain. Usually an enlisted man promoted from ranks—there were some Equestrian centurions in late republican and early imperial times.

CENTURY Legion subunit. In republican times, of a hundred men. In imperial times, of eighty men in ten squads. Commanded by a centurion.

CHIEF CENTURION *Primus pilus,* "first spear." Legion's most senior centurion.

CIVIC CROWN Crown of oak leaves, Roman military bravery award for saving the life of a Roman citizen in battle. Highly prized.

COHORT Battalion. Ten to a legion. In Caesar's time, of 600 men. In imperial times, cohorts 10 through 2 had 480 men; the senior first cohort, 960. Second-enlistment veterans served in senior cohorts.

COLONEL   See TRIBUNE.

CONSUL   Highest official at Rome, president of Senate. Two held office annually. Also commanded Roman armies—equivalent rank of lieutenant general. Former consuls first to speak in Senate debates and were eligible for most important provincial governorships.

CONTUBERNIUM   Legion subunit, the squad. In imperial times, of eight men.

CRUISER   Midsize warship, including Trireme and Quinquereme classes. The latter were 120 feet long, had a beam of 17 feet, a crew of 270 oarsmen, 3 banks of oars, 30 sailors, and 160 marines.

CURSUS PUBLICUS   Imperial Rome's courier service. Wheeled vehicles and mounted couriers sped documents across the empire. Horses changed at way stations checked by inspectors every six to ten miles. It was a capital offense to interfere with Cursus Publicus couriers or their loads.

DECIMATION   Literally, to reduce by one-tenth. Legions punished for mutiny or cowardice by one man in ten being clubbed to death by their comrades after drawing lots. The 9th Legion, later the 9th Hispana, is the only legion on record to be decimated twice.

DECUMAN GATE   The main gate of a legion camp, it faced away from the enemy.

DECURION   Legion cavalry officer, a junior lieutenant. Four to each legion cavalry unit. Also, an elected civil official of a Roman town.

DUPLICARIUS   A legionary whose pay was doubled as a reward for service.

EAGLE   The aquila, sacred standard of a legion; originally silver, later gold.

EQUESTRIAN   Member of Roman order of knighthood. Qualified for posts as prefect, and for Senate membership. Had to have a net worth of 400,000 sesterces. Imperial Equestrians undertook mandatory six-month military cadetships as junior tribunes at ages eighteen to nineteen.

EVOCATI   In the imperial era, militia of retired legion veterans, serving behind their old standards in emergencies, most likely for a total of four years service, as in republican times.

FASCES   Symbol of Roman magistrate's power to punish and execute, an ax head protruding from a bundle of wooden rods. Carried by lictors. Denoted rank—legates had five fasces; praetors, six; consuls and most emperors, twelve; dictator and some emperors, twenty-four.

FIRST-RANK CENTURIONS   Primi ordines, legion's six most senior centurions.

FREEDMAN   Former slave, officially granted freedom.

FRIGATE   Liburna, light, fast class of warship. Length, 108 feet; beam, 12 feet. Crew—144 rowers; 10 to 15 sailors; and 40 marines.

FURLOUGH FEES In camp, one legionary in four could take leave by paying a set fee to his centurion. In A.D. 69 the state took over the responsibility for paying centurions these fees.

GEMINA LEGION "Twin" legion formed by merger of two existing legions.

GLADIUS Roman legionary sword twenty inches long, double-edged, with a pointed end.

GOLDEN SPEAR Military bravery award, inferior to Civic Crown and torque.

IMPERATOR Title. Literally, chief or master. Highest honor for a general. Became reserved for emperors after their armies' victories. The title "emperor" grew from *imperator*.

IMPERIAL Relating to the period of Roman history from 27 B.C. to the fall of the empire.

LEGION Regiment. Main operational unit of the Roman army. From *legio* (levy, or draft). Republican legion nominal strength, 6,000 men; imperial, 5,345 enlisted men, 72 officers. Ten cohorts, plus, in imperial times, own cavalry unit of 124 men. At the beginning of the first century there were 28 legions, numbered 1 to 28. By A.D. 100 there were 30 legions, but in the intervening period 5 had been wiped out, 11 abolished, and 18 new legions formed.

LEGIONARY Soldier of a legion. Mostly a draftee, always a Roman citizen. Most recruited outside Italy in imperial times. Republican recruits were aged seventeen to twenty and served sixteen years. Imperial recruits were twenty, and from late in the reign of Augustus served twenty years.

LICTORS Attendants of senior Roman officials, carrying their fasces.

LUSTRATION The *Lustratio exercitatio*, or Purification Exercise, a religious ceremony performed by legions in March. Standards were purified with perfumes and garlands prior to new campaigns.

MANIPLE Company. Legion subunit, of 160 men in imperial times. Three to a cohort.

MANTLET Wooden shed, on wheels, used in siege works.

MARCHING CAMP Fortified camp built by legions at the end of a day's march.

MARINE A soldier with the navy. Freedman. Served twenty-six years; paid less than an auxiliary.

MURAL CROWN Crown of gold awarded to the first Roman soldier over an enemy city wall.

ONAGER The "wild ass," a heavy *Ballista* invented by Greeks in the third century B.C.

OPTIO   Sergeant major. Deputy to centurion and decurion. Unit records and training officer. One to a century, four to legion cavalry units.

ORBIS   The Ring; the Roman legion's circular formation of last resort.

PALATIUM   Residence and military headquarters of the emperor at Rome. The first Palatium complex was established by Augustus on the Palatine Hill, from which the name derived. All emperors' headquarters were thereafter called the Palatium, no matter where they were located. It is from Palatium that the word "palace" originated.

PALUDAMENTUM   General's cloak. Scarlet in republican times. In imperial times, legion commanders wore a scarlet cloak; commanders in chief, a purple cloak.

PRAETOR   Senior magistrate and major general. Commanded legions and armies.

PRAETORIAN GATE   Gate of a legion camp facing the enemy.

PRAETORIAN GUARD   Founded by the Republic to guard Rome. Imperial military police force. Only unit usually based in Italy south of the Po River. Recruited in Italy, better paid and with a shorter enlistment period than legionaries—sixteen years in imperial times. From A.D. 23 based at *castra praetoria* at Rome. Varied between seven and fourteen cohorts of a thousand men, plus Praetorian Cavalry, strength unknown. Accompanied the emperor when he left Rome and took part in military campaigns he personally led.

PRAETORIUM   Headquarters in a legion camp.

PREFECT   Commander of auxiliary units, Praetorian Guard, and City Guard; a citizen of Equestrian status. Prefects also governed Egypt and, between A.D. 6 and 41, Judea.

PROCURATOR   Roman official superior to prefect; deputy of a provincial governor.

QUADRIGA   Roman chariot drawn by four horses. Golden *quadriga* used in Triumphs.

QUAESTOR   "Investigator." Lowest-ranking Roman magistrate. Responsible for treasury matters. Minimum age thirty from 82 B.C. Served consuls and provincial governors—chief tax collector and quartermaster; forty in Caesar's time, reduced to twenty by Augustus.

SCORPION   *Scorpio*, quick-firing artillery piece using metal-tipped spears, or "bolts."

SECOND-ENLISTMENT MEN   Legionaries who voluntarily served another sixteen- or twenty-year enlistment with their legion when their first enlistment expired.

SENATE   Rome's most powerful elected body. Members needed a net worth of one million sesterces and qualified for legion commands and consulships. Minimum age thirty in imperial times.

SIGNIFER   Literally a signaler, the standard-bearer of legion subunits.

TESSERA   Small wax sheet on which was inscribed the legion or army watchword for the day.

TESSERARIUS   Legion guard/orderly sergeant. Distributed the tessera to his men.

TESTUDO   The "tortoise." Legionaries locked shields over their heads and at their sides.

THIRD-ENLISTMENT MEN   Legionaries voluntarily serving a third enlistment.

TIRO   A legion recruit.

TOGA VIRILIS   Toga worn by young Roman men after coming of age in their fifteenth year.

TORQUE   A neckchain of gold, one of the Roman military's highest bravery awards.

TRIBUNAL   Reviewing stand in a legion camp; built in front of tribunes' quarters.

TRIBUNE   Legion and Praetorian Guard officer. Six of equal rank in republican legions shared command. In imperial legion, a junior tribune, tribunus angusticlavius, was an officer cadet serving a mandatory six months; five to a legion. One senior tribune, tribunus laticlavius, was a full colonel and second-in-command of his legion. Praetorian tribune numbers are unknown. Tribunes of the Plebs were elected officials at Rome; their republican powers were absorbed by the emperor.

TRIUMPH   Prestigious parade through Rome in a golden quadriga by a victorious general, followed by his soldiers, prisoners, and spoils. Officially granted by a vote of the Senate.

TRIUMPHAL DECORATIONS   Crimson cloak, crown of bay leaves, and laurel branch awarded senior generals celebrating a Triumph. Later given in lieu of a Triumph.

WATCH   Time in Roman military camps was divided into watches of three hours, at the end of which sentries changed, on a trumpet call. The officer of the watch was a tribune.

WATCHWORD   Password in a Roman military camp. Changed daily, at sunset.

WINTER CAMP   Permanent base where a legion usually spent October to March.

INDEX